221.6
D34a

LUCY A. PHILLIPS LIBRARY
SNOW COLLEGE
EPHRAIM, UT 84627

SO-ATA-556

WITHDRAWN

THE ACHIEVEMENTS OF BIBLICAL RELIGION

A Prolegomenon to Old Testament Theology

Simon J. De Vries

UNIVERSITY
PRESS OF
AMERICA

LANHAM • NEW YORK • LONDON

Copyright © 1983 by

University Press of America,™ Inc.

4720 Boston Way
Lanham, MD 20706

3 Henrietta Street
London, WC2E 8LU England

All rights reserved

Printed in the United States of America

ISBN (Perfect): 0-8191-3141-5
ISBN   (Cloth): 0-8191-3140-7

221.6
D34a

Acknowledgements

We gratefully acknowledge the generosity of the following copyright owners to make quotations from their publications, as follows:

Sections cited as from ANET and ANES, from James B. Pritchard, ed., Ancient Near Eastern Texts Relating to the Old Testament, 3rd edn. with Supplement. Copyright (c) 1969 by Princeton University Press. Selections reprinted by permission of Princeton University Press.

Sections of pp. 15-16 and 19-20 from H. and H. A. Frankfort, John A. Wilson, Thorkild Jacobsen, and William A. Irwin, The Intellectual Adventure of Ancient Man. Copyright (c) 1946 by The University of Chicago. Selections reprinted by permission of The University of Chicago Press.

Sections of pp. 44-46, 282, 341, 342-343, 346, and 349-50 from Simon J. De Vries, Yesterday, Today and Tomorrow. Copyright (c) 1975 by William B. Eerdmans Publishing Co. Selections reprinted by permission of William B. Eerdmans Publishing Co.

Sections of Simon J. De Vries, art. "THE FALL" and art. "SIN, SINNERS" from The Interpreter's Dictionary of the Bible, vols. II, IV. Copyright (c) 1962 by Abingdon Press. Used by permission.

In memory of Ronald Leigh Williams

1942-1981

In The Achievements of Biblical Religion, Professor De Vries approaches biblical understanding from a
strictly historical and exegetical methodology, placing
special emphasis on the emergence of distinctive insights at the points where Israelite religiosity di-
verged from its cultural rivals within the ancient
civilizations of the Near East. Sharing much with the
ideology and practice of its neighbors, it nevertheless
differed drastically from them in a number of crucial
areas, specifically in its view of God, of man, of society, of history, and of finite existence. In each
of these, a commitment to a transcendental monotheism
produced a seriously developed personalism which came
to be applied to God and to man equally, defining every
aspect of their mutual interaction, together with the
apprehension of total reality.

It is the claim of Professor De Vries that Israel's
distinctive stance accounts for its survivability and
for its contemporary relevance. In his book, he under-
takes the responsibility of elucidating and illustrating
from concrete textual data the process by which this
took shape. The validity of his argument will be
judged first of all by exegetical specialists and ex-
perts in biblical criticism. It has not been his intent, however, to speak only to fellow specialists, but
rather to prepare a synopsis that can inform the edu-
cated public generally in the essentials of biblical
truth. Thus his book makes recurring reference to rival philosophies of religion, contemporary as well as
ancient, for he aspires to make his interpretation com-
municable in this language of universal human thought.
It is with this in mind that he has turned to me with
the very congenial request to provide his book with an
introductory essay, couched in the professional language of philosophical and psychological discourse, out-
lining the way in which a personalistic epistemology
underlies both his and my perception of Old Testament
faith. This I gladly do, and I do it with the understanding that my function is to initiate with him a dialogue, a dialogue on the same subject but carried on in
two distinct kinds of language. I shall speak in the
language of philosophy; he speaks in the language of
theological exegesis. We do not believe that the two
contradict each other, but say the same thing in two
different ways. It is our intent that as the reader
proceeds with Professor De Vries's book, he will bear

in mind the observations that I shall present in the words that follow.

Old Testament faith and personalistic epistemology

The question to be answered here is, "How did a personalistic epistemology contribute to and shape the achievements of biblical faith reflected in the Old Testament?"

There is a possible misunderstanding that such a question can raise. I am not raising this question with the presupposition that the writers of the Old Testament had a well thought-out, fully articulated epistemological position. I agree with Gerhard von Rad's claim that the Old Testament traditions "do not develop or define the contents of faith 'systematically'."[1] It should be pointed out, however, that an epistemology can be presupposed without being articulated. Furthermore, and this will be an underlying thesis of this essay, the reason why the Old Testament writers did not fully articulate an epistemology could be, itself, a manifestation of an underlying epistemological orientation. If Old Testament writers wrote within the framework of beliefs which can roughly be called a personalistic epistemology, they would be disinclined to systematize their orientation.

Personalistic epistemology

I shall present five major distinctions reflected in epistemological positions. The distinctions arise from fundamental questions about the nature of knowledge.

1. Basic versus inferential

One fundamental question to be answered is, "What type of knowledge is basic, direct, immediate or non-inferential, and what type of knowledge is derivative, indirect, mediate or inferential?" Empiricists have treated sense-data propositions as basic. Logical empiricists, in the tradition of David Hume, have attempted to reconstruct the entire edifice of knowledge on a sensory foundation. Rationalists have treated some knowledge about the world as derived from basic postulates of reason--knowledge which is prior to sensory experience. From this basic knowledge other knowledge can be inferred by logical deducation.

Personalistic epistemology treats knowledge of other persons as basic, noninferential knowledge. It is not derived from more direct knowledge.

2. Social versus solitary

Basic knowledge for the epistemological personalist is, contrary to the empiricist and the rationalist, a social phenomenon; it is not characterized in the basic propositions of either a sensory or innate variety, the context of the solitary ego. Basic knowledge presupposes a community of persons.

There is, for the personalist, no epistemological problem of other minds. This problem is the predicament of those who treat basic knowledge as a product of the solitary ego. This is a predicament for those who treat the knowledge of other persons as inductively inferred from one's own case. For the personalist, knowledge of the self and its ideas is not the beginning point, not the foundation of our edifice of knowledge. Rather, self knowledge is itself a by-product of social interaction. The personalist shares this notion of self knowledge with those in the pragmatic tradition: William James, John Dewey, George Mead and the later Wittgenstein.

3. Holistic versus atomistic

At the heart of British empiricism is the belief that knowledge is a product of sensory atoms. For Locke, these are simply ideas, for Hume they are ideas and impressions, and for recent empiricists, with a phenomenalistic orientation, the atoms are sense date (e.g., Bertrand Russell and A. J. Ayer).[2] Greek philosophy featuring Platonic forms and Aristotelian universals, roots the edifice of knowledge in the building blocks--discrete units of knowledge. The units of knowledge are mortared together by various means of association. Knowledge reflected in sentences is a product of this association, and sentential meaning is a function of a relationship of word and discrete unit of reference. An atomistic theory of meaning often accompanies an atomistic theory of basic knowledge. The empiricist and the rationalist may disagree about the ontological status of the discrete referents; they may disagree about the principles of association, the mortar that binds the atoms. For the rationalist the basic building blocks of knowledge may be whole propositions acting as axioms.

The epistemological personalist, by contrast, will want to point out the holistic and contextual nature of basic knowledge. The atoms of knowledge seen as basic by both empiricists and rationalists turn out to be secondary by-products of analysis and abstraction from a holistic perception. Instead of the wholes being constructions of cognitive atoms of direct knowledge, the atoms are a product of analyzing direct and immediate holistic cognitions--undifferentiated experience which may be given an analysis later. These cognitive wholes are not experienced as a series of discrete units of Humean data. This holistic orientation is not restricted to a personalistic terrain. There is in Hegelian idealism and pragmatism an appreciation for basic knowledge characterized in holistic terms. This is reflected in John Dewey's claim that "in actual experience, there is never any such isolated singular object or event; an object or event is always a special part, phase of aspect of an environing experienced world--a situation."3

4. Supra-propositional versus propositional

There is a temptation for both rationalists and empiricists to limit knowledge to what can be said. The epistemological personalist need not deny that a great deal of our knowledge is propositional; it can be expressed in propositions, but he points to what Michael Polanyi calls the tacit dimension.4 This belief that we can know more than we can tell follows, in part, from the holistic orientation cited above. Our concepts (and therefore the propositions made up of concepts) are themselves by-products of more basic, holistic experience.

The epistemological personalist with a theistic orientation has the option of viewing revelation as something which extends beyond a body of proposition about God. The content of revelation is an historical encounter with God. Knowing is supra-propositional, reflecting a personal relationship that cannot be fully characterized in propositions (without remainder). To say that knowledge of God is supra-propositional is not to claim that there is no truth in propositions about God. Theological propositions have their value, but they do not, as propositions, fully reflect the encounter of a personal God acting in human history. Theological propositions do not constitute basic knowledge of the divine encounter. The linguistic unit of inquiry into the divine encounter is not the isolated proposition presenting God's attributes or his essence; it is not an argument form instantiated with propositions; it is, rather, the historical narrative reflecting the engaging dialogue with God. The pragmatics of language reflected in the prayerful response, the apprehensive dialogue and the emotive interest of the perceiver are as indicative of the personal encounter as one can hope to find in the content of declarative theological propositions about God. A free display of the pragmatics of language can only be found in narratives, the wider context of activity, the forms of life. It is here that one finds the rich variety of language games embedded in the _Lebensform_ of personal encounter.[5]

To summarize, supra-propositional knowledge does not replace propositional knowledge; the former is basic in the sense that it is presupposed in propositional discourse; the tacit dimension surrounds discourse; furthermore, insofar as language can be used to express a personal encounter, the best that can be done is "expression" through the pragmatics of language: propositions-in-use, the story.

In Anglo-American philosophy rooted in British empiricism, the fundamental unit of cognition in expressed in a proposition or its component concepts. The edifice of knowledge is built on basic propositions and protocol statements.[6] The epistemological personalist points to the wider situation within which discourse takes place, the knowing that surrounds and conditions the "knowing thats".

5. Interested-active versus disinterested-passive

There is a watershed in epistemology which separates those who see knowledge as the object of disinterested, passive implantations on the _tabula rasa_ and those, on the other hand, who see knowledge as the product of personal activity. The epistemological personalist will fall on the interested, active side of the dichotomy. Successful cognition makes demands upon the knower. In the words of Bergson, "The normal work of the intellect is far from being disinterested."[7] Marxists have taken this one step further noting that "the philosophers have interpreted the world in various ways; the point, however, is to change it."[8] Not only is cognitive interested in the sense of active interpretation; the ultimate goal is action. Given the pragmatist's understanding of belief and knowledge, the cognition of the world cannot be separated from praxis. "Only that which has been organized into our dispositions so as to enable us to adapt our aims and desires to the situation in which we live is really knowledge."9

The epistemological personalist, in characterizing
the cognition of God in the divine encounter, will
stress the demands in action that are so intimately tied
to that encounter. If action and personal response did
not follow on the heels of cognition, the cognition
would be suspect.

Epistemological personalism and Hebrew thought

If Old Testament writing presupposes epistemological personalism, (a) the writing must reflect the
noninferential, basic status of cognitions of the divine
encounter; (b) the basic knowledge will be social, not
solitary; (c) it will be holistic, not atomistic; (d)
it will be supra-propositional, not propositional; and
(e) it will be interested-active, not disinterested-
passive. These are the demands of the divine encounter
insofar as it is a personal encounter. If the Old
Testament writers presupposed epistemological personalism one would expect to find:

1. little inference proving the existence of the
   Thou in the encounter;
2. emphasis on the social and intrapersonal nature
   of divine revelation;
3. little theological analysis of the tacit dimension;
4. a reliance on story and historical narrative to
   point to what cannot be said;
5. interested-active participants in the knowing
   process - a knower whose knowledge makes demands on his behavior.

Are these elements present in the biblical writings? Let us examine each point.

1. There is wide acceptance among biblical scholars that God's existence is not, in the Bible, a matter
of inferred knowledge. God's existence is viewed as
basic knowledge. No attempt is made in the Old Testament to establish God's existence by means of an argument from more basic premises. The praises of Israel
are a response to a divine datum which is epistemologically basic. The Hebrew verb, yādāh, generally translated "to praise," properly means "to confess," "to accept," and "always refers to a preceding divine
datum."10

2. The divine encounter is social and intra-

xii

personal given the personal character of the <u>relata</u> in knowing relationship. Biblical scholars have pointed to the connotations of yāda', "to know," reflecting a close personal relationship. The concept is flexible enough to range from "to understand" to "to sleep" with a woman.[11] Knowledge is not the activity of a solitary ego caught in the epistemological predicament of having to infer the world of others on the basis of one's solitary data. Furthermore, knowledge is not an asymmetrical, one-way relationship between mental act and object; it is, in fundamental usage, a symmetrical relationship between persons. In the Hebrew ontology of the knowing situation relative to the divine encounter, the <u>relata</u> in the knowing relationship are persons--not isolated egos and their subjective, mind-dependent objects of knowledge.

> There is no special faculty of the intellect of reason in Hebrew psychology. The word most commonly used for "mind" in Hebrew is simply the common word for heart (R. Dentan).[12]

The consequences of this are wide ranging. If knowing is, in its basic usage, a relationship engaged in by persons <u>qua</u> persons (not <u>qua</u> solitary egos), Hebrew epistemology is not compatible with much of western epistemology. In the mainstream of western epistemology, the ontology of the knowing situation is a relationship between mental act and object. Idealists and realists simply disagree on the ontological status of the object. Phenomenology is grounded in Husserl's ontology of the knowing situation in which an ego "intends" its objects. What I want to suggest is that whereas much western philosophy treats mentalistic acts such as knowing, believing, hoping, yearning, and desiring as subjective acts of the solitary ego, the Hebrew treats such concepts as intrapersonal. It is one of the great ironies of philosophical inquiry that very recent analyses of mentalistic concepts are closer to the Hebrew orientation in their intrapersonal treatment. Philosophy of mind since Ryle, Wittgenstein and Strawson reflects more of a tendency (a) to reject the act-object analysis of knowing and (b) to resist the reduction of personal concepts to sub-personal categories. By sub-personal categories I mean para-mechanical events taking place in solitary egos or mechanical events taking place in the central nervous system.[13]

Robert Dentan suggests that the Hebrew concept of mind "is a result of the Hebrew inability to think in analytical terms."[14] What I want to suggest is that the Hebrew orientation does not reflect an inability at analysis, but rather a refusal to be reductionist, a refusal to replace the language of personal dialogue with a sub-personal technical language. Post-positivistic linguistic analysis does not equate analysis with reductionism, and a more perceptive view of the Hebrews might be that they refused reductive analysis because of their apprehension of knowing (and other like concepts) as part of the personal (rather than, a sub-personal) language. Although there may be no explicit concept of personhood in the Old Testament, the Hebrews did not reduce the family of person-related concepts to the sub-personal, technical language of Cartesian egos, disembodiable spirits or the psysicalistic language of bodily characteristics and functions. In so doing they were treating person-language as irreducible.

3. Just as the Hebrews refused to reduce the _relata_ in the knowing relation to sub-personal categories, they refused to abstract the knowing relation from the historical situations of encounter. The divine encounter reflects holistic knowledge which no series of propositions can fully express.

4. The characterization of the divine encounter falls, therefore, upon propositions embedded in stories and historical narratives of events. No attempt is made to give a fully propositional account of Yahweh, but rather, to show the situation in which Yahweh manifests himself. The manifestation itself is supra-propositional.

5. Both knowledge and wisdom in Hebrew thought are behaviorally demanding. Both parties in the knowing situation are responsive and active. The beginning of wisdom is not a private act of cognition but a response: the "fear of Yahweh." The Hebrew enters the historical event of a knowing relationship with a sense of awe and leaves it with a sense of obligation. Yahweh's chosen are not the passive objects of his will, but free moral agents who relate to Yahweh with obligations resulting from the moral responsibility that comes with freedom. But obligation is mutual, and Yahweh in his sovereignty chooses to take on obligations to his chosen.

The contribution of epistemological personalism to Old Testament theology

In what precedes I have presented the major dis-

tinctions within which epistemological personalism may
be understood. An attempt was made to correlate this
epistemological orientation with Hebrew thought. I now
wish to show how such a position relates to the major
theological themes of the Old Testament as Professor
De Vries presents them.

1. The transcendence and immanence of God

     The transcendence of God bespeaks his lordship, but
there is an epistemological dimension to transcend as
well. The transcendence of God is reflected in the
supra-propositional nature of the knowing situation.
God cannot be captured in propositions. The most that
can be done is to use historical narrative to point to
the wider situation, the tacit dimension, in which Yahweh reveals himself. This epistemological transcendence
of God does not imply that God cannot be approached, but
that God cannot be adequately captured by propositions.
The epistemological dimension of the immanence of God is
reflected in the availability of the Other to related in
a personal encounter.

     Although we generally tend to think of transcen-
dence as an attribute of God alone, it is interesting
to note that in the epistemological sense, all parties
in a knowing situation are transcendent. Persons qua
persons cannot be fully described by a string of propositions without remainder. Whether the person is
God or one's spouse or loved one, there is always an
element that transcends the verbal, yet is presupposed
in a personal relationship: the tacit dimension. Persons qua persons escape the laws of prediction and con-
trol--the prediction and control possible in the natural
sciences but not the social sciences. No person,
divine or human, is, qua free person, subject to prediction and control. It is this recognition of the
epistemological transcendence of the other that existential and humanistic counselling psychologists have attempted to restore to psychology.

2. The divine image mirrored in human personhood

     In the knowing relationship person meets person;
this is not the relationship of mental act and object,
the solitary Cartesian ego and the objects it "intends".
To reduce person-talk to the technical language of pure
body-talk or Cartesian ego-talk is to give up the primitive status of the concept of person. Such reduction
presupposes abstractions and a conceptual framework of
mind-body dualism such that personhood must be identi-

fied with one half of the dualism or the concatenation of the two elements thus abstracted. The concept of God as Pure Subject must be guarded against the dualism which forces personhood into either physicalistic or spiritualistic categories. The notion of a pure subject abstracted from person-language is not found in Hebrew theology. Ruach, the Hebrew word translated as "spirit", has its etymological roots in the physical world of breath and wind; if it were forced to one side of the dualism it would be the physicalistic side. To coerce Hebrew thought into such dualism is a temptation of translators who may be taking sidelong glances at their own conceptual system and its Cartesian heritage. Such dualism goes back even further than Descartes; the claim of John 4:24 that God is spirit has a hellenized cast to it.

3. A life of fulfilling integrity within a covenant community

Once the knowing relationship in the divine encounter is seen as intrapersonal rather than as a subpersonal relationship among solitary egos, personal knowledge is "out of doors" and communal. In the covenant community, basic knowledge of the Other and others is possible. There is here no epistemological problem of other minds; this problem presupposes an ontology of the knowing situation that the Hebrews did not have. The problem arises when the solitary Cartesian ego must make inferences about the other on the basis of self-knowledge. The personalistic epistemology of the Hebrews (a) relocates basic or immediate knowledge, (b) treats the relata of the knowing situation as persons, not sub-persons and (c) refuses to reduce persons to Cartesian egos or their bodies. The problem of other minds dissolves within this framework.

The political analogue of the Hittite suzerainty treaty should not overshadow the personalistic dimension reflected in covenant knowing. (I have already commented on this intimate relationship.) There are ethical responsibilities which are directly proportional to the intimacy of the knowing relationship. There are active demands placed on the knower. This is expressed very well in the following passage from Amos:

> You only have I known of all the families
> of the earth. Therefore I will punish
> you for all your iniquities. (3:2)

4. History as responsible dialogue with God

Reference to historical events has a more elevated role for the epistemological personalist than might be found in other epistemological orientations. There are several reasons why history is important:

1. God is made manifest to persons in historical events (not to Cartesian egos in the solitude of closet contemplation).
2. The supra-propositional status of God-knowing follows from the assumption that there is an historical personal encounter.
3. Historical narrative and the pragmatics of language are, for personalism, as important as the more descriptive statements about God. Both point to divine revelation but neither constitute it.

Having already discussed (1) and (2), I shall concentrate on (3). It is tempting to view religious language as a series of descriptive propositions about God, but in covenant knowing there is a wide variety of language games to be played other than description of the personal encounter. In fact, given the supra-propositional nature of the encounter, such descriptions fail the knower anyway.

Speech acts are historical events in an historical context. The search for meaning without context reflects a bias for propositional knowledge divorced from the tacit dimension. The semantics of a language cannot be divorced from its pragmatics, the language at work in contexts of praise, admonition, threat, moral judgment, and devotional cooing. To focus on the semantic, lexical content of a static language-at-rest, without seeing the speech act in its telic and pragmatic context, is to retain but a shadow of its full meaning. A speech act without its pragmatic context is a mere mouth movement or a string of phonemes. An action qua action is a telic event, an event with a background of purpose. (This is the difference between my raising my arm and my arm's moving upward; signalling for a cab or merely moving my arm; performing a speech act or merely making noises.) It follows that if an historian studies human actions, the subject matter of history is, to a great extent, teleological.[15]

5. A meaning and purpose in the evils of finite existence

Epistemology cannot be separated from ontology, the ontology of the knower and the known. If Hebrew religious epistemology treats the knower as a person (as opposed to knower qua solitary ego or tabula rasa), one can get a view of a Hebrew personalistic ontology through the lenses of the personalistic epistemology. The knower has an ontological status such that, qua person, the knower cannot be reduced to some more basic entity (e.g., spirit, mind, matter) without loss. Persons are ontologically basic types of entities; to analyze them in terms of more basic types of entities is to lose them.

The consequences of the ontological basicness of persons are far-reaching. The proper subject of cognitive predication is the person qua person, but ascriptions of cognition are only part of that whole collection of characteristics which are most appropriately ascribed to persons. Person-death, for example, is a concept which cannot be reduced to body-death nor the separation of body and spirit. Personhood is communal and relational, and the meaning of personhood cannot be captured in solitary, nonrelational ascriptions any more than the concept of chess-king can be captured in descriptions of plastic or onyx. Person-death is a role disagreement, walking off stage, as it were, leaving Yahweh and the Telic Play. Offstage there is only silence, the silence of Sheol. Person-life (like person-knowing) is, on the other hand, a role engagement in a script filled with praise for Yahweh.[16]

> The dead do not praise Yahweh nor do any that go down in silence. (Ps. 115:17)

It is the Telic Play, the script of Yahweh's purposes, that gives meaning to the historical set; it is the play that gives purpose to the cast.

In the Telic Play there is always room for improvisation. Indeed, that is what one would expect from interested and active knowers. Knowing is not the passive, mechanical absorption of data by the tabula rasa. In the personalistic orientation the very process of knowing presupposes an active agent, an agent who contributes to what he experiences through an interpretation of events. In this activity lies both the freedom and the fallibility of the knower.

Evils and tragedies gain significance in the Telic Play; there are different scripts which carry the cast toward various conclusions. The necessity of the consequences which follow the choice of scripts is a moral necessity, not a mechanistic and fatalistic necessity. God's purposes transcend nature's mechanisms, and teleological explanations of events supersede mechanical explanations.[17]

Personalistic epistemology versus apocalyptic epistemology

In presenting the presonalistic epistemology reflected in the Old Testament, I do not wish to give the impression that this is the only epistemological orientation represented therein. I have set out the categories which I think will be an aid to further research into Old Testament epistemology. Second, I have presented the poles of emphasis defining personalistic epistemology, the orientation which I consider to be the dominant orientation of the Old Testament. Let us look at an epistemological orientation which represents the greatest deviance from the personalistic orientation.

The greatest deviance from the personalistic model is found in apocalyptic. First, apocalyptic locates knowledge of Yahweh in the solitary individual, the fantastic visions of the seer. There is no need for communal corroboration; there is a "gnostic" elite having direct access to the visions. The criterion for truth and understanding comes within the vision itself if it comes at all. Second, the content given in the apocalyptic vision is stated in propositional terms by the figures appearing in the visions. What is not always given is the interpreter's guide to the utterances of those appearing in the visions. (See Dan. 4:13, 8:15, 9:24-27, 12:7.) Third, the seer is passive in the uninterpretive sense. By the device of pseudonymity,[18] the seer presents the claims of angels and other characters in his visions. The passive receiver is relieved of the burden of his infallibility since only the active knower is fallible. With active interpertation comes fallibility, but the apocalyptic seer passively receives both sign and significance. (This is not to say that the significance is always given. See Dan. 12:9.)

Visionary seeing is to be contrasted with the teleological seeing of the personalistic orientation. What one sees in teleological seeing is determined, in part, by the telic categories (the categories of Yahweh's purposes) brought to the event by the perceiver. The categories used in the interpretation are a product of the perceiver's faith. The categories are not given as pure data of experience; they belong to the faithful.

Teleological seeing is compatible with a scepticism, an epistemological humility involving the realization (a) that experience is mediated by a conceptual structure and (b) that the conceptual structure does not capture Yahweh.

The apocalyptic vision is an immediate awareness of a futuristic Yahweh event, whereas the personalistic awareness of God, though mediated by teleological categories, is an awareness with a more immediate referent: God at work in the present event. The irony of this is that in the epistemological immediacy of the apocalyptic vision, Yahweh, as a referent, is more distant; in the personalistic orientation God is "seen" in the current event, a perception mediated by the categories held by faith.

In understanding various epistemological orientations, it is sometimes helpful to understand the various points at which scepticism may arise. An epistemology reflects not only the nature of knowing, but also, the nature of the failure of knowledge. Personalistic epistemology can be contrasted with apocalyptic epistemology in the accounts of the limitations of knowledge. Insofar as Yahweh-knowing in the personalistic orientation is supra-propositional, this orientation is compatible with a scepticism about the possibility of full and comprehensive propositional knowledge of Yahweh. Insofar as propositional knowledge of Yahweh involves an investment of the categories of faith, it is possible that the faithless do not see the work of the Lord. (Isa. 5:12, 5:19) Insofar as the claims of faith bridge the gap between a mere chronological event and the cognition of divine purpose in it, the Hebrew perceiver is making a teleological investment. If one accepts the standard definition of knowledge as justified, true belief, Yahweh is not known. Faith does not justify belief; faith provides the categories for teleological seeing, and the perceiver is fallible.

By contrast, the visionary seer of apocalyptic, since he does not recognize any active investment in what he sees, can attribute his lack of understanding to information withheld. The words are shut up and sealed until the time of the end (Dan. 12:7). The visionary seer receives self-justified atoms of experience; his limitations are a result of information withheld rather than a result of interpretations invested. A passive receiver, after all, is not fallible in interpretations if he is not the author of any. The episte-

mological atomism of apocalyptic cannot be separated
from the qualitative orientation to time designations
found in apocalyptic.19 Given the dominant epistemological orientation of apocalyptic, an orientation which
supplanted teleological seeing with visionary seeing,
one would expect a more mechanistic, less teleological
view of time.20

In summary, apocalyptic epistemology emphasizes
the solitary, atomistic, propositional and passive poles
of our epistemological polarities; the personalistic
orientation emphasizes the social, holistic, supra-propositional and active poles. Although, in apocalyptic,
the seer passively receives both sign and signification,
this epistemological immediacy comes at the cost of a
temporal "distance" from the reality of Yahweh. In the
personalistic orientation, on the other hand, epistemological mediacy and fallibility allow for a healthy
scepticism21 and an active, fideistic, teleological
seeing of an historically intimate Yahweh. Yahweh is
close at hand for those with the eyes of faith.

I think there is good reason to believe that if
ancient Israel had a dominant epistemology at all, it
was a consistently personalistic epistemology. I have
attempted to outline the nature of such an orientation
and to show how this orientation fits within (a) the
wider range of epistemological positions and (b) the
central theological themes of the Old Testament that are
to be dealt with in this book.

With the rise of modern existential philosophy the
personalistic elements featured in existential epistemology have been rediscovered in Hebrew thought. But
personalistic epistemology as I have defined it is an
ideal type and is not actually represented in any particular current philosopher's position, although a full
explication of Martin Buber's epistemology would reveal
some essential similarities. There are a number of major differences that will be found between personalistic
epistemology, as I have presented it, and current existentialist epistemology. First, I have charted a position more intimately tied to an epistemology (although
not necessarily the metaphysics) rooted in the pragmatic
tradition. Such a position stands over against a narrow
empiricism and a rigid rationalism. Second, the basic
status of persons, not reducible to minds and bodies,
seems to be the major concern of recent language-philo-
sophers more than among Husserl's followers. Third, a
major theme in current existentialist philosophy, the
act-object ontology of the knowing situation, is now

replaced by the person-person ontology of the knowing situation; the intentionality of consciousness is itself an abstraction from more primary person-person knowing experiences. Fourth, no wholesale attempt has been made to contrast Hebrew and Greek thought on the dubious basis of Greek proclivities toward logic, abstraction and analysis.[23]

With these observations before the reader I extend the invitation to all who will take this book in hand to ponder the deeper philosophical issues that arise for the reflective mind as one comes face to face with The Achievements of Biblical Religion.

David C. Mellick
Adjunct Professor of
  Philosophy
The Ohio State University

---

1. Gerhard von Rad, Old Testament Theology, I (New York: Harper, 1962), 116

2. For an excellent development of this theme see J. O. Urmson's Philosophical Analysis (London: Oxford University Press, 1956). This book shows the influence of Russell's logical atomism on positivistic notions of analysis.

3. John Dewey, Logic: The Theory of Inquiry, Ch. IV, reprinted in John Dewey's Philosophy, Joseph Ratner, ed. (New York: Random House, 1939) p. 892

4. Michael Polanyi, The Tacit Dimension (Garden City, New York: Doubleday, 1967)

5. For a development of the technical notion of Lebensform see Ludwig Wittgenstein's Philosophical Investigations (New York: Macmillan, 1953).

6. I am referring to the atomic propositions of the early Wittgenstein and Bertrand Russell; the logical empiricists (e.g. Hempel and Neurath) carried on the notion with their concept of Protokollsatze.

7. See Henri Bergson, _Introduction to Metaphysics_, translated by T. E. Hulme (New York: Putnam's, 1912), pp. 40-43.

8. Friedrich Engels, _Ludwig Feuerbach_ (International Publishers, New York, 1941). See pp. 82-84.

9. John Dewey, _Democracy and Education_ (New York: Macmillan, 1916) p. 400

10. cf. von Rad, _op cit_, p. 357. Further support for this position can be found in John Baillie's _Our Knowledge of God_ (New York: Charles Scribner's Sons, 1959). Chapter III, "Is Our Knowledge of God's Existence Inferential?" is relevant to the present discussion.

11. Denis Baly, _God and History in the Old Testament_ (New York: Harper, 1976), p. 73. See also Delbert R. Hiller's _Covenant: The History of a Biblical Idea_ (Baltimore: John Hopkins, 1969), pp. 120ff.

12. Robert Dentan, _The Knowledge of God in Ancient Israel_ (New York: Seabury, 1968), p. 37

13. D. C. Dennett, _Content and Consciousness_ (London: Routledge & Kegan Paul, 1969), pp. 90-96, 189-190. Following Ryle and the later Wittgenstein, Dennett refuses a reductionistic analysis of the personal language.

14. Dentan, _op. cit._, p. 37

15. I have dealt with the metaphysical issues concerning human actions in my doctoral dissertation, _The Metaphysics of Behavior_, Ohio State University, 1973. I chart the vast range of possible metaphysical positions characterizing the relation between bodily movements and actions. I develop a non-reductionistic but monistic position. The logical consequences are further developed relative to persons and personhood in "Locating Personhood: A Metaphysical Study" published in _Research in Mental Health and Religious Behavior_, ed. William J. Donaldson Jr. (Atlanta: The Psychological Studies Institute, Inc., 1976) pp. 18-24, with reaction papers, pp. 25-32.

16. Von Rad alludes to what I am calling "person-death" in Vol. I of his _Old Testament Theology_, p. 389.

See Psalm 88 and Isa. 38:18.

17. The logic of the Covenant relationship can be stated in terms of what logicians call Constructive Dilemma:

> If p then q
> If r then s
> p or r
> Therefore, q or s

The conditionals involve a moral necessity; the consequents set out blessings or curses, and the choice of antecedents is left to the Hebrew nation. Yahweh does not predetermine a particular disjunct in the third premiss or in the conclusion. See Exodus 19 and Leviticus 26 for example conditionals.

18. Pseudonymity, whereby words are placed in the mouths of others, allows for the passivity of the receiver of the vision. Both symbol and interpretive significance, when given, come from the vision itself.

19. Professor De Vries describes the apocalyptic orientation toward time in his "Observations on Quantitative and Qualitative Time in Wisdom and Apocalyptic" printed in Israelite Wisdom: Samuel Terrien Festschrift, (J. Gammie et al, edd., Philadelphia: Fortress, 1979), pp. 263-276, and in his Yesterday, Today and Tomorrow (Grand Rapids: Eerdmans, 1975) pp. 342ff.

20. Epistemologically speaking, apocalyptic is ateleological, although divine purposes await a future manifestation. See De Vries in Gammie, ed., Israelite Wisdom, p. 270.

21. See von Rad, Vol. I, pp. 453 ff. (especially p. 453, n. 1), for a discussion of scepticism in the Old Testament.

22. This is true of Sartre, who is more Cartesian in his analysis of cognition.

23. The Hebrew-Greek contrast is overstated in existentialist circles, but the development of this theme lies outside my goals in this present essay. I defer to James Barr on this point. See his Old and New in Interpretation (London: SCM Press, 1966), especially Chapter 2: "Athens or Jerusalem?--The Question of Distinctiveness."

PREFACE

Some prospective readers may not look further than
the title of this book because they suspect it of a
humanistic bias. Is biblical religion a cultural
achievement--the achievement of man? Should we not
rather be pointing to God's achievements, the blessings
he has obtained for mankind and which he offers them
as the gift of free grace? Unless such a demand is
made in support of an absolutistic theocentricity, denying any role for man, this writer would affirm it,
but would hasten to explain that the title uses "religion," the genitive modifier of "achievements," in a
semi-metaphorical sense. Neither "religion" as such
nor religious people have achieved anything by setting
out to create something new, yet biblical religion did
surely come to certain insights concerning God and the
world that were distinctive and that were able to prepare the way for a whole new approach to God and a new
understanding of the world.

The term "biblical religion" refers not to sacrifices or rituals or holy places, but to a distinctive
stance on the part of biblical man over against God,
determining a radically different approach to a whole
array of religious beliefs and practices. Monotheistic
personalism, unique to biblical faith, demanded a distinctive theology, a distinctive anthropology, a distinctive hamartiology and soteriology. It determined
man's place in society, his role in history, and his
attitude toward life and death.

It is with sad regrets that I dedicate this book to
my dear departed colleague, Professor Ronald Williams,
prematurely removed from a ministry of fruitful service
in the teaching of theology at The Methodist Theological School in Ohio. Professor Williams saw the manuscript for this book at an early stage and helped shape
my own comprehension of central points at issue. I
cherish the notion that he might approve of it now as
it goes to the press. Alongside Professor Williams, I
am indebted to Professor Robert Tannehill of "Methesco"
and to Professor Samuel Terrien, emeritus teacher at
Union Theological Seminary in New York, for reading the
manuscript and offering numerous helpful suggestions.
I am particularly appreciative toward my former student,
Professor David C. Mellick, for graciously providing
this book with a Foreword, in which each of the Bible's

great achievements, as I see them, has been briefly
set within a framework of philosophical understanding.
I mention also the graciousness of Dean C. M. Kempton
Hewitt of "Methesco" in expediting the means for preparing a camera-ready manuscript to be presented to the
publisher. These have all been a special help and inspiration; yet I recall as most special of all what
numerous students in my course on "The Achievements of
Biblical Faith" have offered through the years by way
of dialogue, reflection, and response.

CONTENTS

ABBREVIATIONS

1. Books, monographs, journals, series

AnBib	Analecta Biblica, Rome
ANEP	The Ancient Near East in Pictures Relating to the Old Testment, ed. J.B. Pritchard, 2nd ed., Princeton 1969
ANES	The Ancient Near East, Supplementary Texts and Pictures Relating to the Old Testament, ed. J. B. Pritchard, Princeton 1969
ANET	Ancient Near Eastern Texts Relating to the Old Testament, ed. J. B. Pritchard, 3rd ed., Princeton, 1969
AOT	H. W. Wolff, Anthropology of the Old Testament, ET, Philadelphia 1974
BA	Biblical Archaeologist, New Haven, Missoula
BHT	Beiträge zur historischen Theologie, Tübingen
BKW	Bible Key Words, trans. J. R. Coates from G. Kittel, ed., TWZNT, New York, 1961-65
BO	Biblotheca Orientalis, Leiden
BWANT	Beiträge zur Wissenschaft vom Alten und Neuen Testament, Leipzig, Stuttgart
BZAW	Beihefte zur Zeitschrift für die alttestamentliche Wissenschaft, Giessen, Berlin
EJ	Encyclopaedia Judaica, Jerusalem 1971-72
EP	S. L. Terrien, The Elusive Presence, New York 1978

FRLANT	Forschungen zur Religion und Literature des Alten und Neuen Testaments, Göttingen
HAT	Handbuch zum Alten Testament, Tübingen
IB	The Interpreter's Bible, Nashville 1951-57
ICC	The International Critical Commentary, Edinburgh, New York
IDB	The Interpreter's Dictionary of the Bible, Nashville 1962
IDBS	idem, Supplementary Volume, Nashville 1976
JBL	Journal of Biblical Literature, Philadelphia, Missoula
JSJ	Journal for the Study of Judaism in the Persian, Hellenistic and Roman Periods, Leiden
NEB	The New English Bible Oxford, Cambridge 1970
NSHE	The New Schaff-Herzog Encyclopaedia, Grand Rapids 1949 [1907-]
NTT	Nederlands Theologisch Tijdschrift, Wageningen
OOTT	T. C. Vriezen, An Outline of Old Testament Theology ET, Oxford 1958
OTS	Oudtestamentische Studien, Leiden
OTT	G. von Rad, Old Testament Theology, ET, 2 vols., New York 1962-65
OTTO	W. Zimmerli, Old Testament Theology in Outline, ET, Atlanta 1978
RHPhR	Revue d'histoire et de philosophie religieuses, Strasbourg
RS	The Ras Shamra inscriptions, as listed in Ch. Virolleaud, Les inscriptions

	cuneiforms de Ras Shamra, Syria, 10 (1929), and later articles.
RSV	The Revised Standard Version of the Bible, London, New York 1952
SJT	Scottish Journal of Theology, Edinburgh, Cambridge
SNTSMS	Society for New Testament Studies Monograph Series
StUNT	Studien zur Umwelt des Neuen Testaments
SVT	Supplements to Vetus Testamentum, Leiden
TDNT	Theological Dictionary of the New Testament, ET, Grand Rapids 1964-76
TDOT	Theological Dictionary of the Old Testament, ET, Grand Rapids 1974--
THAT	Theologisches Handbuch zum Alten Testament, 2 vols., ed. E. Jenni, C. Westermann, Basel, 1971-76
TOT	W. Eichrodt, Theology of the Old Testament, ET, 2 vols., Philadelphia 1961-67
TS	Theological Studies, Washington
TWZNT	Theologische Wörterbuch zum Neuen Testament, ed. R. Kittel and G. Friedrich, Stuttgart, 1932--
TZ	Theologische Zeitschrift, Basel
VT	Vetus Testamentum, Leiden
WMANT	Wissenschaftliche Monographien zum Alten und Neuen Testament, Neukirchen-Vluyn
YTT	S. J. De Vries, Yesterday, Today and Tomorrow, Grand Rapids, London, 1975
ZAW	Zeitschrift für die alttestamentliche Wissenschaft, Giesen, Berlin

2. General

art.	article
E	The Elohist
Grk.	Greek
Heb.	Hebrew
J	The Yahwist
LXX	Septuagint
MT	Massoretic Text
NT	New Testament
P	The Priestly document
par	biblical parallel(s)
p.b.	paperback edition

3. Apocryphal and intertestamental books

Ass. Mos.	Assumption of Moses
CDC	Damascus Code from the Cairo Genizeh
Ecclus.	Ecclesiasticus (= Jesus ben Sira)
1 En.	First (Ethiopic) Enoch
1QH	Hodayoth (or Thanksgiving Hymns) from Qumran Cave 1
1QM	Milhamoth (or War Manual) from Qumran Cave 1
1QS	Serek (or Manual of Discipline) from Qumran Cave 1

TRANSLITERATIONS

Greek

α = a	ε = e	ι = i	ν = n	ρ = r	φ = ph
β = b	ζ = z	κ = k	ξ = x	σ(ς) = s	χ = ch
γ = g	η = ē	λ = l	ο = o	τ = t	ψ = ps
δ = d	θ = th	μ = m	π = p	υ = u, y	ω = ō

Hebrew

1. Consonants: א ', ב b, ג g, ד d, ה h, ו w, ז z, ח ḥ, ט ṭ, י y, כ ך k,
   ל l, מ ם m, נ ן n, ס s, ע ', פ ף p, צ ץ ṣ, ק q, ר r, שׂ ś, שׁ š, ת t
2. Pointed vowels: ָ (long qāmes) ā, ַ (pathaḥ) a, ֶ (seghol) e, .. (ṣērē)
   ē, ִ (ḥireq) i (short) ī (long), ֹ (ḥōlem) ō, ָ (qāmeṣ ḥatuph) o, ֻ
   (qibbuṣ) u
3. Vowels represented by points and vowel letters: ה ָ â, א ָ ā', י ֵ ê,
   א ֵ ē', ה ֵ ēh, י ִ î, ֹ ô, ה ֹ ōh, ו û
4. Diphthongs: ו ַ āw, י ַ āy, יֵ êw, יִ îw
5. Shᵉwas: ְ (silent) = nothing, ְ (mobile) ᵉ, ֳ ᵒ, ֲ ᵃ, ֱ ᵉ

The

Achievements

of

Biblical

Religion

Introduction

1. The perspective of vision

This is a book that will endeavor to be all that both the main title and the subtitle imply. It is about "biblical" religion; it is also about "Old Testament theology." Even though this does not intend to say that the Old Testament exhausts the full meaning of what biblical religion implies, it does suggest that the Old Testament is definitively biblical. The further implication is that the New Testament, as part of the Bible, expands and enriches, but does not distort or radically modify, the Old Testament's representation. Reaching still further, it is our claim that New Testament Christianity is in no way a new religion, but the religion of the Bible. It does not weaken or abandon the great achievements of biblical faith, as crystallized in the Old Testament witness, but cherishes and preserves them, liberating them for the challenges of a new day and age.

The reader will discover that, as we take up each of the five great achievements of biblical religion, the discussion will terminate in a brief but pointed identification of specific New Testament concepts bearing on the particular question under discussion. This is not intended merely as a bridge over the gap of centuries separating the old and the new, but to show a logical and coherent line of development, as dictated by adherence to the biblical principle in question and the stimulus of the new age out of which Christianity emerged.[1] This book does not directly aspire to be an introduction to New Testament theology; therefore it stops short of extensive discussion, leaving further treatment in the hand of specialists. Its only aim is to show significant continuity in the midst of significant discontinuity.

Numerous efforts to explain the principle of continuity from the Old to the New Testament have been disappointing because they have failed to perceive how deeply and truly Hebraic the New Testament actually is. This is true in spite of its marked Hellenistic shading, and in spite of early Christianity's anxious concern to mark off the delimitations of a solid new religious principle over against first-century Judaism. In this day of going back to one's roots, how important it is that Christians should trace their roots back to the remote beginnings, finding their spiritual model not only in a Jesus, but in an Isaiah and a Moses and an Abraham! It seems a shame that when contemporary Christians wish to have someone tell them of their Hebraic heritage, they often call upon a rabbi. Surely, a visit from the rabbi would be extremely helpful to Christians needing to learn more about their Jewish brethren--but why should Christians have to ask Jews about their own Christian heritage?[2] Perhaps this book will help Christians find their own way back to whence they have come.

A sabbatical leave spent by the writer at The Ecumenical Institute for Advanced Theological Studies in Jerusalem was an eye-opener for him. Established in Israel, but in an area where Christian and Muslim Arabs live, near Bethlehem, this unique institute brings together Jews and Muslims, but especially Christians from all the major branches, Orthodox, Catholic, Protestant, and "Third World." Many discussions concern inter-Christian problems, but it was especially interesting to observe how Christians from the various communions responded to the varied field-trip experiences sponsored by the institute. Scholars and clergymen quickly identified themselves with one of the three groups that visit the Holy Land: historians, tourists, and pilgrims. There were no "tourists" among us--mere curiosity seekers, coming to gawk. Everyone fell into the first group or the third. Many of the Catholics and almost all the Protestants belong to the first group, but the Eastern Orthodox clearly belonged to the third. They were pilgrims, coming to worship more than to learn.

Ere long it became evident that Eastern Christians are especially prone to view the Holy Land, and all things Hebraic, strictly from the perspective of Christological mysticism.[3] One particular Polish Father opted to visit St. Stephen's Church while the rest were visiting Hebron or Beer-Sheba; his reason was that the Old Testament history was, for him, no more than the record of remote historical origins, whereas the New Testament sites represented the locale of divine incarnation. Of course, this same clergyman insisted on kissing the supposed foot-marks of Jesus at the Mosque of the Ascension, in spite of the archaeologist-guide's clear explanation that the present soil level had been found to be twelve feet higher than in Jesus' time. It was also he who chided some of our group for turning their backs to the altar while standing in a circle around Jacob's Well in the chapel at Shechem/Sychar. Where precisely is the holy? For this eastern Father it was definitely not where once the Hebrews trod.[4]

For the present writer it was a thrill to walk

6

where Jesus walked. But he felt even more inspired
when he camped out, like the early Israelites, at
Kadesh-Barnea--where some scholars think they first
made their bond with Yahweh; also when I walked at
Shechem between Ebal and Gerizim, thinking of Joshua
making the covenant "this day" (Josh. 24).

Just what is faith all about? Just where is the
holy to be found? It all depends on one's perspective
of vision--and that is where we must begin our discussion.

a. The Old Testament as viewed from the vantage-
point of contemporary religion

(1) Refractory lenses in our line of sight

When modern Jews or Christians look upon the Old
Testament (the Jews call it "Tenach"), they inevitably
see it from their present perspective, unless they
deliberately condition themselves to do otherwise.
This produces blurring and distortion, because they are
actually looking through the wrong end of the telescope
of history. True enough, no one can jump out of his
own skin; what we are must color what we see. But the
vast advances of historical science over the past four
or five centuries have offered us the means of recap-
turing ancient history from its own perspective. There
is no reason, say, to depict the Hebrews in medieval
European garb, surrounded by castles, as in the art of
the Middle Ages, or even of Rembrandt. Archaeology has
been a tremendous help. Scholars have deciphered a
vast horde of ancient documents. The Old Testament is,
in itself, an unparalleled literary phenomenon--a veritable library of documents from the first millenium before the Christian era, accurately testifying to the
times in which it was produced. To hear this testimony
is, of course, possible only for those who are willing
and able to make effective use of the tools available.

When we speak of tools, we are thinking of hermeneutical (=interpretive) methods that are commensurate
with the spiritual intent of Scripture, not just of
research into cultural and physical externalities. To
take up only the latter produces startling distortions.
One example is a current comic-book and record combin-

ation being offered on television, luridly depicting
Joshua before the wall of Jericho as though he were
Buck Rogers. Another example is what Hollywood generally does when it produces a "Bible" film. Sensitive
biblical scholars usually wince with pain when they
view such a film. Why? Because the externalities may
be faithfully reproduced while the spiritual intent is
grossly abused. A notorious example was Cecil B. de
Mille's blockbuster, The Ten Commandments. The producers spent part of their vast budget in interviewing
biblical scholars and in doing archaeological research,
yet in a "white-paper" that they sent out along with
release of the film, they made it perfectly clear that
they were using all this for the sole purpose of local
color. Not even the external facts had to be correct.
For instance, after stating the scholarly conclusion
that camels had probably not been domesticated in the
time of Moses, the book announced the producers' decision that they would be introduced in the film anyway, simply for visual effect. This might be excused
as "poetic license" in a work of art (?)--but even
where visual and dramatic accuracy was maintained in
this film it reproduced only an extremely literalistic
version of the exodus-Sinai event, not that which comes
to light in terms of modern critical understanding.[5]

No doubt, the total effect on popular thinking of
this commercial exploitation of Bible themes is considerable. Aware of its deficiencies, many churches
and synagogues attempt to counteract its effect through
the preparation of more theologically responsible materials, but literaristic church-school literature
continues to attract popular preference even in the
main-line churches. The church and synagogue today are
in the position of having to re-educate their own membership, trying to correct and compensate for an erroneous method that they themselves developed.

Judaism sees the Bible history through the sympathetic but distorting lens of rabbinic tradition and
Jewish experience. Many Jews, even today, continue to
resist a genuinely historical understanding of their
own Scripture. Thus even they need to turn the telescope around, and to see themselves from the Hebraic,
biblical perspective, rather than to see the biblical
Hebrews from the perspective of ethnic Jewishness.

Nevertheless, a modern Jew is related to Abraham
at least as closely as a modern Italian is to Romulus
and Remus, or a modern Englishman to Beowulf. That is

to say, there is a distinct, unbroken line of tradition. The mark in his flesh that comes with circumcision dynamically incorporates him into the fellowship of Abraham. The matzos of his seder meal connect him with the first passover meal of the exodus. It is much more difficult for the modern Christian to make this kind of link with the Old Testament. He enters into a bond with Jesus in the Eucharistic meal, but to reach back to remoter origins exceeds the boundaries of his spiritual awareness. To be truthful, if the church confessions did not explicitly declare the Old Testament to be part of his Holy Scripture, he would be inclined to leave it entirely to the Jews--which is, in fact, precisely what theologians of a marcionizing disposition have been advising us to do.[6]

The light originating in the achievements of ancient Hebraic faith has to pass through a series of distorting lenses before it reaches the spiritual retina of the modern-day Christian. Nearest to his eye is a vast and conflicting mass of church dogma and ecclesiastical tradition, shaped over the nineteen hundred years that have passed since the apostolic period. To the Eastern Orthodox, the Nestorian, the Coptic, the Roman Catholic, the Calvinist, the Lutheran, the Anabaptist, and each of several hundred distinct sects and subgroups in modern Christendom, this mass is significantly different. Behind this prism, and affecting the vision of virtually every oriental and occidental Christian subgroup, is the heavy gauze of Hellenistic thought and culture; this has radically reshaped the message of the first kerygma about Jesus. Still further back, from our present standpoint, is the Christ-event itself--the radical reshaping of Hebraic eschatology through the presence of one who Christians believed had fulfilled it. And even beyond the radical new perspective that had come with the appearance of Jesus as Messiah, another lens distorting the original light is that of postbiblical Judaism, which made a number of drastic alterations--especially apocalypticism and Torah rigorism--in the original vision. Thus the modern-day Christian sees the Hebraic achievement in reduced scale, blurred and distorted by intervening panels of new interpretation. He has difficulty perceiving the concerns of the early church except through the lens of modernity; or the original Christian kerygma except through the lens of the hellenizing creeds; or pre-Christian Judaism except through the lens of the New Testament polemic; or original Hebraism except through the lens of its postbiblical reshaping.

(2) The Old Testament in Christian and Jewish hermeneutical tradition[7]

The distortion of distance that we have been describing can be readily illustrated from within each distinct group and period of religious development since the time when Christianity emerged out of Judaism.

The earliest Christians thought of themselves as the true and faithful heirs of authentic biblical tradition. They never had the slightest doubt that what we call "the Old Testament" was their Bible. Thus they interpreted themselves by the Old Testament, and the Old Testament by themselves. They were simply "the latter-day saints" of whom the prophets spoke!

What came to be known as rabbinic Judaism saw the Old Testament differently. The Jews who rejected the Christian claim were as much influenced by apocalypticism as the early Christians were, but to them two particular features of Old Testament religion were so important that they could not view the mild Galilean teacher--and still less his radically innovative proselytizer, Paul--as fulfillers of God's design.[8] These features were covenantal law and nationalistic messianism, now reshaped by the pressures of an age far different than the age that had given them birth.

Certain early Christian groups, particularly in Asia and Africa, retained much of the gospel's original Hebraic flavoring. This was a marked characteristic of a Christian Palestinian group known as the Ebionites.[9] But Christianity's destiny was in Europe, civilized by Greek culture and ruled by Roman might. Perhaps already in the first century, the message of Jesus' original disciples and Paul began to undergo modification at the hands of those whose minds could not escape the habits of Hellenistic thought. Paul was apparently struggling with incipient Gnosticism in his Corinthian correspondence.[10] The Johannine literature, while insisting on the veritable humanity of Christ, was already introducing significant alterations in a hellenizing, non-Hebraic direction.[11] In the subapostolic era, Marcion's proposal to reject the entire Hebraic tradition was countered by orthodoxy's earliest decision concerning the Canon, explicitly retaining the Old Testament as Scripture;[12] nevertheless, the Christological and Trinitarian formulations of the early church councils--all held in the Hellenistic area--made significant compromises in the direction of non-Hebraic

10

conceptuality.[13] From the apostolic age onward, the
Old Testament heritage was destined to undergo distortion, reduction, and obfuscation. Now it was ransacked
mainly for predictions of Christ's coming, needed especially in controversy with the Jews, who quite rightly
rejected most of the strained and contrived argumentation of an apologist like the famous Justin.[14] Old
Testament historiography--which we see as lying at the
very core of Hebraic faith--became irrelevant for Christian piety except by way of allegorical symbolism. (The
Jews themselves were responsible for developing this
method of interpretation; it became prevalent wherever
Jews lived in close community with Hellenistic gentiles,
as in the writings of Philo of Alexandria,[15] and became
an essential element in rabbinic midrash.)[16] All in all,
the early and medieval church viewed the Old Testament
as a tentative guidebook for piety and morals, now abstracted from the irrelevant history of an ancient people, from whom the Christians had separated themselves.
The Old Testament was the most esteemed where it pointed, either by direct prediction or by allegorical allusion, to Christ.[17]

    The Renaissance and the Reformation brought a re-
vived interest in the Hebraic Scriptures. After a long
period of darkness, the Crusades had made European Christians aware of the ancient homeland of their faith.
Emerging humanism began to produce new interest in the
classical world; it also brought new standards of literary criticism. Luther and the other Reformers discovered that the Hebrew Old Testament omitted those "apocryphal" books of the Greek Septuagint and Latin Vulgate that offered proof-texts for controverted Catholic
dogmas, such as purgatory and intercession for the
saints. Now that sola Scriptura had been raised to the
level of absolute religious authority, supplanting
church tradition, Protestantism began to cultivate the
study of the Hebrew language and the Old Testament
writings. Unfortunately, what Protestants were seeking
in the Old Testament was doctrine--a body of religious
truth that would combine with New Testament doctrine in
defining "the whole counsel of God" for a new age. The
Calvinistic wing took more from the Old Testament (as
in Calvin's Institutes),[18] the Lutherans took relatively
little from it;[19] but to both it was a body of propositional truth, and little else. And what was done with
uncongenial elements? In practice, the Lutherans depended mainly on the rule of Christological allusion;
what pertains to, alludes to, or points to Christ is
valid, and the rest is worthless. The Calvinists deve-

loped more consistently a rule accepted in theory by both wings of the Reformation, that of interpreting Scripture by Scripture; yet the New Testament remained as the norm by which the Old Testament should be interpreted. The Roman Catholics, meanwhile, responded by reaffirming the Old Testament, but according to the Vulgate text and literary content. It, too, needed this body of Scripture for proof-texting, even though the ecclesiastical magisterium retained status as the final arbitor. Anxious at the prospect of admitting any historical principle of interpretation, the inquisitional machinery suppressed the writings of Richard Simon (ca. 1680), who endeavored to explain certain discrepancies in the Bible on the basis of developing tradition within it.[20] Ironically, the development of tradition was precisely the principle on which Catholicism had been relying so heavily in its controversy with the Reformation: Scripture plus tradition; i.e., Scripture as modified by tradition.[21] But a tradition antedating that of the Christian church itself was felt to be too unmanageable to be tolerated by a Catholicism in dispute with Protestantism. It is only in the present century that the Roman church has felt free to accept a historical principle of biblical interpretation.[22]

The Renaissance went beyond the Reformation and the Counter-Reformation. It produced modernity, with its radical rejection of ecclesiastical authority. As the Enlightenment made headway, especially in eighteenth and nineteenth century Germany, it stimulated a rationalistic criticism of both the Old and New Testaments that was long held in suspicion in the churches.[23] Gradually, church scholars came to accept a historical criticism, but much of this went hand in hand with deistic theologies far removed from the naive belief of the ancient Hebrews and Christians. When Hegelianism had become a dominant philosophy in Europe, biblical scholars were wont to regard the Old Testament faith, and that of the New Testament as well, as infantile expressions of emergent humanism--no more. Now the Old Testament seemed very remote; the Jews were scorned, along with traditionalistic Christians, for modeling their faith and practice too much upon it. The rise of Romanticism, especially under the influence of Herder, modified this somewhat, for the Romanticistic scholars were able to admire a David and an Abraham as much as a Socrates. The nineteenth century ended, and the twentieth century began, praising the psalmists and prophets, but despising Israel's bloody heroes and dreary law-givers. Modernity had reshaped the Old Testament to its taste; its ancient, sovereign word could no longer be heard in its ears. If this had not been so, perhaps the European, and especially German, church might have retained sufficient prophetic zeal to have withstood the monstrous claims of National Socialism. But it was so; because the Old Testament was dead, the Jews had to die![24]

Although many modern-day Jews and Christians find themselves locked into one of the levels of distortion that we have been describing, the patient and diligent study of Scripture on its own terms, and in the light of all that modern historical investigation has revealed, offers the tools for at last rediscovering the real achievements of Hebraic faith and appropriating them for contemporary benefit. Literary and historical criticism have been useful; even more helpful has been the study of form and tradition, as reflected in the individual texts of Scripture. The critical approach need no longer be seen as irreverent or destructive; it is usable as a highly effective theological tool, capable of extracting the biblical witness on its own terms, and as seen in its own time but with lasting validity for all times. It invites modern Christians and Jews to step into the past and appropriate the biblical achievement directly for themselves. Those who are able to accomplish this discover that the Bible, including the Old Testament, can speak authoritatively to our times. What is distinctive about Scripture is relevant for today.

b. New Testament Christianity and Rabbinic Judaism as viewed from the vantage-point of the ancient Hebraic achievement

It is well to turn the telescope of history around, and to judge what has emerged out of the Hebraic tradition from the criterion of that tradition itself. From this perspective, we will be able to discern why certain features have been sacrificed along the road of historical progress, and why certain features may now rightly be abandoned in the contemporary light of a better day. We will also be able to see what is normative and worth preserving, in the face of all distortions produced by ancient and modern history. In the final analysis, only those biblical insights that authentically enlighten the mysteries of human existence will survive as models for modern self-understanding. The amazing thing is that, in the midst of all its histori-

13

cal relativity, biblical faith represents an achievement that not only challenged the ancient world of darkness, but challenges the darkness of today. Ours may truly be "the post-Christian age"; is this the same as to say that it is also the "post-Biblical age?" Perhaps so: but let us ponder the survivability of biblical people-hood and biblical tradition. These reach from the ancient past to now; their prognosis for the future may not be as dismal as some say it is.

(1) Biblical faith in its classical formation

The Hebrews who gave us the Old Testament were a Semitic people, living and thinking much as their neighbors did. One thing gave them an absolute distinctiveness: their emergent monotheistic faith, opening up the possibility of richer insights into the meaning of both human and divine personhood. This did not come all at once, but through a gradual historical process. All the same, the commitment the Israelites made at the very beginning of their corporate life dominated the entire course of their spiritual development, gradually weeding out inimical elements. Along the historical pathway of this people, a number of unresolved conflicts remained as elements of tension. We think especially of a nationalistic ideology, cherishing the prospect of eventual political restoration; also the notion of being a special people belonging to the one god who was also God of the whole world. These were destined to produce subbiblical elements in a new age when Israel's relative isolation from world conflict would be broken. During the classical Hebraic period--the time when the tribes joined in their alliance and later adopted the political structure of kingship--they were still fortunate to be left unmolested by any foreign power.[25] This was the time of nurturing, then, for biblical faith. Its great achievements were sown, sprouted, and grew to fruitful ripeness. It may be added that the political crises that appeared toward the end of this period, when the Assyrian and Babylonian empires began to threaten Israel's and Judah's independence, forced the flower of full-grown monotheism to reveal its richest color. This was the time of the great prophets; also the time of classic historiography. It was the age that established the noblest patterns of psalmody and brought Israel's epic literature to its fullest form. It was the time of the great biblical parenesis, Deuteronomy.[26] This was the time also when the transcendental and immanentistic dimensions of divine holiness had been fully defined; when the promise and problem of man had been

14

clearly expressed, and the way of restoration had been pointed out; when election and covenant and the law had been firmly established; when God's and man's work in history had been charted out; when God's concern for suffering and dying man had begun to penetrate the veil of mystery and misunderstanding. A coming age would enrich and clarify man of these achievements, though in some cases it would impoverish and confuse them; but history's dark pathways could never obscure them altogether.

(2) Biblical faith under the pressures of imperialistic deprivation

(a) The emergency of Judiasm

Those who are not well versed in biblical studies sometimes make the mistake of applying the term "Judaism" to the entire Old Testament phenomenon. Without denying that the roots of Judaism are indeed to be found in classical Hebraism, it is important to restrict this term to the postexilic and postbiblical extension of original Israelite peoplehood. The term "Jew" is the anglicization of Hebrew yehudî, yehudîth, which mean a person belonging to the tribe, nation, or province of Judah--and only by extension a person adhering to the faith and religion of the people originally associated with this territory.[27] Since the tribe and nation of Judah also looked upon itself as part of Israel, even during the period when there was a separate kingdom of Israel in the northern part of Palestine, the Jews took over this name as an alternative, exclusive appellation once the northern kingdom had ceased to exist.[28] Although numerous "Jews" in the diaspora traced their tribal origins to one of the northern tribes (Tobit to Naphtali, Saul of Tarsus to Benjamin, etc.), it was in fact only remnants from the territory of Judah that were able to return to Palestine at the end of the Babylonian exile, ca. 520 B.C., and restore what they could of the original national and religious structure. Here commences the actual history of the "Jews" in the accepted meaning of that word.

We have mentioned that the Assyrian and Babylonian empires swallowed up the ancient Israelite kingdoms, ending their respective nationalistic structures. Both these empires followed the policy of massive depor-

15

tation. In both territories, numerous individuals were allowed to remain behind, but they were forced to accept the presence of deportees from various foreign lands, brought to live among them (II Kings 17:24ff.). In any event, the leading classes were taken away (II Kings 24:15-16, 25:11, Jer. 40:1), the intent being to keep them in exile permanently. Were it not for the abrogation of the policy of deportation, put into effect by the Persians, allowing significant elements of strongly ideological leadership to restore Yahwistic leadership in Jerusalem, this might have brought Israel's grand spiritual achievement to final extinction.[29] Upon what a slender thread was suspended the destiny of western and world culture!

Despite the high hopes that accompanied the Jews' return to Palestine, their expectation of restoring covenantal society as it once existed were doomed to disappointment. Never for the next five hundred or a thousand years was the grip of imperialism to be relaxed. Each foreign power exercising political control in Palestine would exceed its predecessor in effecting the policy of stifling nationalistic independence and religious distinctiveness. The deliberate program of the Greeks who supplanted the Persians, and after them the Romans, was to discourage, or even suppress, the most distinctive practices of ancient Hebraism. Throughout the Mediterranean world, this was an age of religious eclecticism and cultural homogenization.[30]

Certain notable modifications of classical Hebraic religion emerged as a response to this situation of deprivation. Reacting against the apostacy of Jews who could not resist adopting Greek and Roman ways as their ticket to worldly success, a faithful core drew tight their circle of ethnic distinctiveness, relying ever more heavily on a rigoristic observance of the Torah to give themselves the indelible self-identification that would be needed for survival. In times of intolerable pressure, as under Antiochus Epiphanes, ca. 167 B.C. and under the last Roman procurators, the Palestinian Jews were driven to armed revolt--in the second instance with disastrous results. This was in A.D. 66-70. This happened once again, in A.D. 135, under Bar Kochba, and this time the Jews were banned from Jerusalem permanently. The Romans enslaved many Jews. The temple was destroyed, their last hold on the Holy Land was ended. From now onward, the Jews were destined to exist in cultural isolation, a harried and deprived people, held together by the unrelenting hostility of gentile society.

Viewing this cultural change from the vantage point
of classical Hebraism, we observe a distinct loss of
biblical personalism. Yahweh was no longer Yahweh, a
God elusive yet intimately close. Now it was the Torah
that revealed his presence and his holiness. Israel's
consciousness of sin and unworthiness had intensified
in the face of manifold ostensible signs of God's continuing wrath. Relief from guilt, no longer obtainable
for Israel as a people, was sought through an ever more-
diligent devotion to the requirements of Torah. Election and covenant were interpreted in terms of ethnic
distinctiveness and Torah rigorism. The mystery of
death, suffering, and injustice lay hidden more deeply
than ever behind the curtain of divine inscrutability.
Worst of all, the Jews had now all but lost all sense of
Gods' role in history. The aeon in which they were now
living belonged not to him and to them, but to the
hostile forces pitted against them.

(b)   The emergence of Christianity

What was an obstacle for Judaism was an opportunity
for Christianity. That is, the eclecticism and homogenization demanded by the Mediterranean imperial system opened the way for Christianity's universal appeal
to be heard and have an impact.31 A disheartened world
was ripe for the clear spiritual call of his new faith,
even when its adherents were suppressed and persecuted.
Christianity did what Judaism could not do: capitalize
upon the leveling-out policy of imperialistic culture,
eventually adopting much of its magisterial structure
for the consolidation of its gains.32

But what were the sacrifices that were made? Features that the first Christians inherited from Judaism's
late modifications to Hebraic faith, but which later
Christians relinquished, were its ethnicity, its nationalistic aspirations, and its increasingly legalistic
definition of morality. Features that it compromised--
original and authentic elements of Hebraic faith that
Christianity relinquished--were the sense of biblical
peoplehood and Judaism's devotion to covenantal morality. Meanwhile, Christianity embraced two non-biblical
and subbiblical concepts that were destined to become

17

the root of endless controversy and fruitless speculation in the centuries to come. From Greek philosophy
the developing church adopted essential aspects of a
monistic concept of reality, assigning an ontic divinity
to Christ while encouraging the attitude that the experiential world is unreal. From late Jewish apocalyp-
ticism--meanwhile firmly repudiated within rabbinic
Judaism--Christianity took over a belief in a world
following this present world, again encouraging the attitude that the present experiential world is meaningless and ultimately unreal.

The one very large plus in Christianity's restoration and reinvigoration of the ancient Hebraic faith
was its new sense of the meaning of Heilsgeschichte--
something Judaism had utterly lost. It was Christianity
that now had a clear sense of God's purpose in history.
This was despite the fact that its earliest eschatological expectation had fallen short of realization. Perhaps the kingdom of God had not fully come in Jesus'
lifetime, nor in the lifetime of Paul. Nevertheless,
Christ was now the ruler of history.33 Death had not
crushed him; he was alive, sitting at the right hand of
the Father, preparing to come again! Unmistakeably,
Christianity regained a renewed sense of God's intimate
nearness. Jesus' earthly ministry had made God close
and accessible to men once more.

(3) Biblical faith in the setting of world culture

(a) Major directions in post-imperial Christian
     theology and religion

A second radical shift from the original situation
out of which biblical faith came into existence occurred
when neither Judaism nor Christendom found it possible
any longer to regard Jerusalem and the Holy Land as the
cultural center of their religious inspiration. This
began to happen, for Christendom, when the Emperor
Constantine made Christianity the official religion of
the Roman empire. For the followers of Jesus, neither
of the original promises to Abraham, that of land and
that of peoplehood, any longer had direct relevance.
Christianity was a religion for all the world, and all

the world (i.e., as centered in the European west) had
been claimed for the Christian religion. We can best
judge the degree of departure from the Bible's great
achievements by sketching Christendom's course of progress through two diametrically opposite situations,
from the imperial age until the present.

1) The age of Christian theocracy

European culture became Christian culture--if need
be, by the sword. Popes struggled with emperors, and
bishops with kings, to assert paramount authority, but
the European church claimed all European persons in its
membership. Those outside the church, the Jews, the
Gypsies, the heretics, and the like, were regarded as
non-citizens. The state was charged with enforcing the
church's decrees. The church, especially its western
branch, came to be structured like an empire, tolera-
ting no appeal to a divine authority outside itself.
Toward the end of this theocratic age, even those re-
ligionists who appealed directly to the Bible as the
ultimate authority found it virtually unthinkable that
deviating doctrinal and ecclesiastical systems should
be tolerated within one and the same secular community
(so Calvin's Geneva, Anabaptistic Münster, Puritan New
England, and the like).

Although in some measure each of the main achievements of original Hebraism came to reappearance in
Catholic and Protestant Europe, they were no longer held
together by any recognizable dynamic principle. Perhaps
the most noticeable loss was that of the original experience of divine personalism. Greek modes of thought
thoroughly dominated Christian dogma. The Bible had
been reduced to a collage of moral and theological
principles--revered, but no longer alive.

2) The age of secular autonomy

The western world after the Renaissance has under-
gone a process of drastic secularization--not suddenly,
but irresistably and irreversably. With the rise of
the European states and the settlement of the new lands
beyond the seas, the Catholic and Protestant churches
have gradually broken down into a myriad of rival splin-
ter groups, each endeavoring to bring in the kingdom of

19

of God in its own special way. America has witnessed
the logical extreme of this process, the complete separation of state and church. Meanwhile, the imposing
edifice of classical Christian dogma has been eroded
from within and from without. In the age of rationalism (which still dominates the minds of "free thinkers"
toward the end of this twentieth century!), the adherents of the Biblical tradition found themselves driven
into cultural isolation, while those who embraced modern culture either forsook the church or sought to
reconstitute it without the original supernatural and
personalistic basis of biblical faith. Now, today,
however, the church sees a new opportunity to choose
between life and death, good and evil. A new door of
understanding has been opened up for those Christians
who dare, and care, to follow the arduous pathway to a
rediscovery of the Bible's achievements.

(b) The pathway of post-imperial Judaism

1) "The wandering Jew"--estrangement and oppres-
    sion

For the Jew living in the post-classical age,
religion has been mainly a matter of devotion to the
past and fidelity to the norms of ethnicity. It would
be beside the point to trace this history in detail, for
it is well known. Since the first and second century,
Judaism has had no homeland--only a peoplehood. The
Jewish people have been mainly strangers in a grudging
and often hostile social environment. They have felt
that they have had no voice in the course of world history. So it has been, at any rate, until the European
age of revolution, when many Jews enthusiastically
accepted the full rights and responsibilities of secular
citizenship. This progress has not been without severe
setbacks, as we know. So violent has been the clash
between modern Slavic (in Poland and Russia) and Teutonic (in Germany) ethnicity on the one hand, and Jewish
ethnicity on the other, that the very extinction of the
Jewish people was in prospect. Ironically, even liberated Jews, those who forsook the marks of Jewish ethnicity and adopted western ways, came to be threatened by
the Nazi fury.[34]

20

Here, very markedly, the ancient Hebraic achievement has seemed remote. In the holocaust experience
particularly, God has seemed to care less for his ancient people's suffering, and their righteous cause,
than he had seemed to care for wretched Job. The one
transcendant reality remaining very near and dear has
been Torah. It is the tangible symbol that the biblical
God will at last return to recompense his beleagured
people.[35]

2) The new restorationism

Even though many present-day Jews insist that God
does not intend that they should return to the Holy Land
until the end of history, an enthusiastic majority sees
the State of Israel as the Eschaton within history. It
is ironic, but hardly surprising, that numerous Jews,
particularly in Palestine, are eager to embrace state
and nation while forsaking ethnicity, and even religion.
Suddenly, history has become relevant once more--but for
many citizens of Israel this history remains purely
secular. Those who find the goal of their ancient faith
fulfilled in the restoration of Zion do well to embrace
their duties of nationhood in the light of ancient Israel's election and covenantal calling, remembering that
the God who saves is also the God who judges.

This then, is the perspective of vision from which
we are invited to consider the achievements of biblical
religion. These achievements are still relevant for today. They are still the norm by which human culture is
to be judged. If we cherish human culture without them,
we deserve to wander in the darkness that we ourselves
have made.

2. The problem of essentiality

When one confesses that the Scripture, is, or contains, the word of God, one is groping with the problem of essentiality. Is all of it essential? Is all of it on an equal plane? Think of the fundamentalist who flips his Bible open, snatching a text to inspire him at the moment. This would be appropriate if each and every passage of Scripture were absolutely equal in truth, worth, and authority. But it is utterly ahistorical, neglects to let Scripture be the test of Scripture, and accepts biblical continuity while ignoring biblical discontinuity.[36]

a. Continuity *versus* discontinuity within scripture

Both continuity and discontinuity must be recognized, whether between the two Testaments, Old and New, or between the various parts of the respective books.

The fact that the Bible is a book (the ongoing world's best-seller) and can be purchased in a bookstore impresses us with the continuity of Scripture. It expresses the solidarity of a single religious tradition. Among the world's sacred writings, the Bible is distinctive, with a very specific stance and special concept in comparison with books like the Bhagavad Gita or the Quran. Moreover, Christians affirm that the whole Bible, Old Testament and New Testament, testifies to faith in the one same God. The God of the Hebrews is the God of the Christians, who see the eschatological predictions of the Old Testament as finding fulfillment in Christ and the events of the New Testament era. Certain essential qualities are clearly identifiable in both Testaments. The church resists the Marcionistic heresy of reducing Scripture by discarding the Hebraic element.

Within the New Testament there appears to be a greater continuity than within the Old Testament, with its wider range of materials. The Old Testament is the literary crystalization of the spiritual experience of an ancient people over a vast period of time, ranging

from <u>ca</u>. 1250 to <u>ca</u>. 150 B.C.[37]   Over so long a period,
amid drastically changing conditions, there had to be
considerable discontinuity. This was in fact much greater originally than the biblical text presently reveals,
for it is the product of enormous harmonization, normal-
ization, and translational elimination, standardizing
almost all to the norm of rabbinic piety.[38]

b. Options in contemporary research

(1) A thematic principle of unity

   Some Old Testament scholars have endeavored to identify a thematic principle of unity. Such is the work
of the Swiss scholar, Walther Eichrodt (<u>Theology of the
Old Testament</u>).[39] Eichrodt identifies the covenant as
the central, formative concept of Old Testament faith,
and in his influential two-volume work attempts to relate every religious idea of the Old Testament to it.
The results are often arbitrary and artificial. The arrangement of this work is systematic, like the classical
works on dogmatics. Somewhat similar is the treatment
of the Dutch scholar, Theodor Vriezen (<u>An Outline of the
Theology of the Old Testament</u>),[40] which identifies the
concept of the holiness of God as central to everything
else. Both these works are stimulating, informative,
and eminently worthwhile. Yet certain materials get
left dangling. Too many biblical witnesses were unconcerned with these central ideas. We have to look for
what it was among them all that accounts for their getting included in the Canon of Holy Scripture.

(2) A process of religious growth

   Another way of approaching the challenge of isola-
ting the principle of unity amid discontinuity is to
identify a process with a certain dynamic or cohesion;
or at least, a process with a significant element of
historical logic and necessity. To look for this kind
of process requires a greater degree of historical ori-

23

entation than the method just described, where common
ideas from various times and situations can be compared
and arranged. Within the last half-century we have seen
several works with this approach, each of them arranging
the materials from the various Old Testament books according to the principle of religious development or
spiritual growth. The evolutionary scheme often lies at
the basis of this approach, placing the more simple
materials at the beginning and tracing a process of internal development from one form of religion to another.
Millar Burrows, Ludwig Koehler, and Otto Procksch have
followed this method.[41] Their common tendency is to
overemphasize the simplicity and primitivity of the
early materials--such as the Genesis legends--and to assign a late date to the materials that differ from them
the most widely. According to this method, Psalm passages praising animal sacrifice are automatically dated
early, while Psalms with wisdom sayings and prayers are
dated late.

(b)   A process of theological tradition

1)   Gerhard von Rad

Valuable as some of the books mentioned have been,
they are becoming superseded by a better and more valid
approach--one that sees the biblical writings as theological testimonia within an ongoing process of witnessing to the experience of God's working. To look for
essentiality in terms of theological tradition is quite
different from looking for it in terms of relative religious sophistication. It is one thing to analyze
religious phenomenology; this is, properly speaking,
Religionsgeschichte (Ger. for "History of Religion"). It
is quite another thing to analyze the dynamic growth of
a people's testimony about their life with God. It is
only the latter that can be properly called Biblical
Theology. This holds true even in contemporary life,
where churches with different theologies may have similar liturgies, or vice versa. Or in any event, liturgy
often has little to do with a church's theological
stance. Cultic practice and theology do influence each
other, but are not identical to each other. The Israelites carried out the same burnt offerings as did the
Canaanites, but on the basis of an entirely different

24

conception of Deity.

We are especially indebted to the German scholar, Gerhard von Rad, for bringing us to this insight. Among his many important writings, the most influential is his two-volume <u>Old Testament Theology</u>.[42] Here he treats individual groups of writings, scattered among a variety of biblical books, as witnesses to what the God of Israel had done for his people in their history. Von Rad laid great stress upon <u>Heilsgeschichte</u> (saving history) as the theological tradition of God's saving acts on behalf of his people, beginning with the exodus from Egypt and continuing throughout their historical existence, on toward an eschatological fulfillment in the future. According to von Rad, those biblical writings which testify the most clearly to the experience of God's saving deeds lie at the heart of Scripture. Those that reflect it only weakly--or in traditionalistic lip-service, like Qoheleth and Proverbs--are only tangentially contained within the Canon of the Holy Word. Whether or not this is the best way of defining the principle of continuity amid discontinuity, von Rad's great contribution to our thinking is his emphasis that Yahweh, the God of Israel, revealed himself effectively in the history of his people; and secondly, that the sacred writings of the Old Testament are to be heard as testimonies to the experience of, and participation in, the divine action. God acts; the people testify. Revelation is not some private mystical experience. It is not a set of religious propositions. It is not a holy book dictated by an angel, like the Quran. It is God's action in human life, as witnessed by and to his own people. The task of Biblical Theology is not to systematize a set of religious ideas. It is to trace, critically but sympathetically, the development of the tradition about the experience of God's presence in the history of his people.

Gerhard von Rad was an Old Testament scholar who found it impossible to remain with some narrow specialization in the area of criticism or linguistic study. Although devoted to painstaking literary labors, he was driven by his insights into the broad relevance of ancient Israel's theological traditions to seek encounters within the whole range of systematic and philosophical enquiry, challenging all theologians to take more seriously the Bible's claim that God acts in and through history, and is present in every aspect of human experience.

In a biographical reminiscence of his teacher, H.
W. Wolff raises up three aspects of von Rad's life work
that were, in Wolff's estimation, definitive: (1) von
Rad's apprehension of the Old Testament documents as
elements in an ongoing, ever-growing tradition, emerging
out of the life of the ancient Israelites and witnessing
to their faith; (2) his emphasis on Israel's special
kind of realism with respect to God's presence in historical event, forbidding any abstraction of God as a
theological idea, remote from the struggling of humankind; and (3) his urgent concern to use the situation
illumined by exegesis as the model for authoritative
preaching in our time.[43]

The concept of a kerygmatic situation into which,
or out of which, a revelatory word was spoken is one of
von Rad's most stimulating insights. Through enscrip-
turation, redaction, and preservation, this is what has
become the normative body of holy Scripture. Here we
have a potent model for any who would hope to encounter
revelatory meaning in the reality they experience. Because it developed dynamically, Scripture must not be
used as a concatenation of fixed, propositional truth,
theoretically definitive for every place and age. For
modern man it may do something less, but also far better: illumine the universal dimensions of his stress-
ful situation, showing the presence of transcendental
concern. If modern man will take seriously the Bible's
claim that its God is a living God, he may expect that
the God who revealed himself in Israel's need may reveal himself in his need too. This is a valid alternative to atheistic secularism on the one side and to
pietistic dualism on the other.

2) Samuel Terrien

Von Rad has been criticized by Vriezen, Eichrodt,
and others of subjecting the whole Old Testament to his
special value-judgment in identifying the materials
within the Heilsgeschichte mainstream as primary, and
those outside as secondary witnesses. This criticism
is well taken because von Rad has not always succeeded
in establishing an organic connection between these two
groups of documents.[44]

Perhaps the impasse will be overcome by the thesis
of Samuel Terrien in his latest book, The Elusive Presence: Toward a New Biblical Theology.[45] Terrien in

26

effect bridges the gap between the method of Koehler (religious growth) and the method of von Rad (theological tradition), bringing together the insights of Religionsgeschichte and Biblical Theology. His book does more with Religionsgeschichte than analyze cultic practice and religious belief; it does more with Israel's theological tradition than trace the origin and development of the dominant motifs. It concentrates its discussion on the entire range of theological traditions which have to do with an awareness of the elusive presence of Yahweh, from the epiphanic visitations to the patriarchs, to the Sinai theophanies, to concepts of the divine presence in the temple, to the prophetic visions, to psalmody, wisdom, and cultic celebration. It goes on from there to establish, perhaps for the first time, a clear development to the New Testament's testimony to an awareness of God's presence in Jesus Christ—mainly in the annunciation, the transfiguration, and the resurrection traditions—going on to elucidate his presence in Holy Spirit, Church, and Eucharist.

c. Finding the true center of gravity

Each of the previously discussed methods has its measure of validity, yet the search for the true center of gravity within the Old Testament, and within Scripture as a whole, goes on.

One firm axiom is that the Scriptures are to be read, not as a book of dogmatic proof-texts or pious sentiments, but as the crystallization of testimony from the community of faith respecting its variegated experience of the presence and power of a living God, appearing in diverse ways and diverse places to the prophets and the apostles, but most clearly in Jesus Christ. Another clear commitment on our part is to do full justice both to continuity and to discontinuity, discerning the commonness of all the witnesses while viewing their disparity and disagreement as evidence of dynamic growth and vitality.

But is the commonness of all scriptural witnesses the only vantage-point from which to interpret and evaluate the measure of divergence? Certainly not, for this is precisely the method of fossilized orthodoxy in its rejection of so-called heresy. No, the diversity actually enriches the texture and quality of spiritual understanding. What then is the norm? Is all diversity

27

equally valid and fruitful? Is there no distinction
between degeneration and creativity?

Like finding the epicenter of an earthquake by drawing seismic arcs from two or more observatories, it may
be suggested that we seek the true center of gravity
in Scripture by finding the point of convergence between two lines or axes, those that bind it together
while keeping it distinctively apart.

Two rules may guide us:

(1) In examining all the biblical witnesses, it is
significant and essential continuity among them, illumined and put into perspective by relevant elements of
discontinuity, that will be the most revealing of what
is the most central and essential.

(2) In examining the cultural context of the Bible,
it will be the Bible's divergence and distinctiveness,
illumined and put in perspective by elements of commonality, that will be the most revealing of what is
most central and essential.

We follow first the pathway of what is common, basic
essential among all the biblical witnesses, in the
midst of their variety and discontinuity. We add the
adjectives "basic" and "essential" to "common" because
Scripture's commonness, to be significant, must be not
accidental, but constitutional--not just something that
happened through historical growth and grew into a predetermined shape because of common rootage. We must
see that there is a certain tenacity or virtual inevitability in the growth of Scripture--that in a sense
Christ and the church and the Holy Spirit are logical
and necessary outgrowths, and fulfillments of vital
seed planted long ago in the promises to the patriarchs
and the experience of deliverance from Egyptian bondage.
From Genesis to Revelation there is a witness to one
and the same God, working onward age by age, bringing
his works to ever greater perfection. This is the line
of commonality, bringing together the diverse elements
within the great flowing stream of holy Scripture.

Defining what is distinctive of biblical faith in
differentiation from its cultural context is the second
plane or line, intersecting the first at many points to
show Scripture's authentic heritage. We need to look
at the Bible, not only as the church's (and synagogue's)
holy book, but as a prize of human literature. Its

timeless quality is not only for Jews and Christians, but for all men.[46] By all means we must see the Bible within the context of its time and the civilization in which it was produced. Here again we will discover discontinuity amidst continuity, and each will prove to be equally significant. The beginner is surprised to find a great measure of continuity between the biblical world and the non-biblical world-- that is to say, between the Hebrew people, with their religion and faith in one God, and their contemporaries in the ancient Near East, the Egyptians and the Babylonians and others. One may be surprised to discover how many similar ideas they share. One should also be prepared to encounter a great measure of commonality within the thought-world of the New Testament, conditioning the religious attitudes of Jews as well as Christians. We readily acknowledge the early hellenization of the church, but it is important to know that Judaism was strongly influenced by Greek thought long before (and long after) the emergence of Christianity.

But what is common from one culture to another is not as significant, in the final analysis, as what is distinctive, and it is this by which a culture of religion or faith must finally be judged. What we need to know about the Hebrew religion is what made it different from the religions of its neighbors. So too Christianity, in opposition to Judaism as well as in opposition to paganism. Why did biblical faith, Old Testament and New Testament, hold fast to only one God? Why did the Hebrews see themselves as chosen and covenanted unto God out of all humanity? Why did they, with Christians after them, hold fast to belief in God's effective action in their historical existence?

If we are willing to ponder why Judaism and Christianity have not only survived, but grown and expanded over the world, in the face of opposition and persecution, we must recognize that they had something dear to hold on to, something that made their lives different from those of their pagan neighbors, something worth dying for and transcending death.

There are five areas in which this distinctiveness of biblical faith comes to clear expression, and this provides the structure of our book:

    1)   the transcendence and immanence of the biblical God;

2) the concept of a divine image mirrored in human personhood;
3) commitment to a life of fulfilling integrity within a covenant community;
4) an understanding of history as responsible dialogue with God;
5) a sense of meaning and purpose in the evils of finite existence.

These are the major achievements of biblical religion, defining the Scripture's distinctiveness in the midst of common human culture.

3. Methodology
   a. Theoretical basis

What is the norm of biblical faith? How do we find it? Not in the words of Scripture, or in the ideas or doctrines which it expresses or presupposes. Normativeness is not in the _ipsissima verba_ of Scripture, as biblicism affirms. It can be fairly stated that biblicists revere the words of Scripture in and for themselves, often in resistance to the charismatic presence of a higher authority. Jesus challenged the Jews of his time for doing this, for resisting him with their piddling legalisms while he was busy saving human lives. Biblicism reveres the very words of the biblical text, but without criticism and discernment, superstitiously endowing them with magical power and supernatural authority. True, for the biblicist some words do have greater potency than others, especially Jesus' words when printed in red and in the language of the King James Version! Popular as this naive and simplistic view may be in many religious circles, offering all that many superficial seekers want and expect, it cannot stand up to the kind of scrutiny that serious theological scholarship feels duty bound to apply. While posing as ultrapious, it actually involves a form of gross impiety, imposing a preconceived dogmatic stricture on the sovereign word of God, refusing to let it be seen for what it is, subjecting it to the tyranny of adolescent misunderstanding.

Those who hold to a biblicistic prejudgment are confronted by immense methodological problems, simply because the text of Scripture is actually embarrassingly fluid, hazy and unclear-- as every student quickly discovers when he begins to dig into the Greek or Hebrew original. This is very upsetting to the naive beginner, who becomes nervous without the pacifier of an inerrent and eternally comforting Bible.[47]

It is also a serious mistake to define the religious ideas and theological doctrines contained in the Bible as normative, for the Bible offers no comprehensive system of truth, no perfectly consistent pattern of religious thought. Which ideas and which doctrines are we to choose? This pietistic, yet very liberal, attitude falls readily into the trap of subjectivism. As important as the ideas of the Bible are, to affirm them as the principle of authority within the Bible is a gross misunderstanding because the Bible was never composed as a theological treatise. It contains no effective theoretical statement of a single theological proposition. The intent of the men who wrote it was something quite different than to offer dogmas and doctrines and pious ideas. This is also the point of essential weakness in the so-called proof-texting method, listing Bible texts that purport to prove a set of doctrines, as in the classical books of Catholic and Protestant dogmatics.

What is normative about the Bible is its participation in, and interpretation of, revelatory event; i.e., the whole tradition about revelatory event, witnessing to the experience of God's self-revelation--not in words, not in ideas, not in doctrines, but in face-to-face encounter. The correct methodology in biblical study is to find a principle of normativeness in terms of a revelatory event which took place not just in some person's mind but in the arena of history.

What is history? It is more than bodies bumping together on the football field. It involves the convergence of meanings in human and divine encounter. The experience of God's revealing presence in historical event needs therefore to come to expression in human words, which, preserved, cherished, and expanded under the impact of fresh occurrences of revelatory event, develop into the organism of Holy Scripture.

b. Exegesis and theology

We are now in a position to make a concluding statement about the relationship between exegesis (the scientific, critical interpretation of the biblical text)

31

and theology. The bond between them can be succinctly
stated in two principles, as follows.

(1) The only normative theology is situational and
and experiential. It is possible to abstract a theological system. This is the proper, and necessary, task
of systematic theology. We can also apply the principles of the philosophy of religion in order to develop
a system for understanding a wide variety of theoretical
subjects related to theology. But let us remember that
theology itself remains the task and responsibility of
the church. Therefore the only really effective theology is one that is drawn from the biblical tradition
of theological experience.[48] It is one that relates
directly to life--to my life and your life and the lives
of the people around us. However sophisticated, refined,
and philosophically undergirded one's theology may be,
if it does not bear directly on one's own life and the
lives of other real people, it is no valid theology at
all. If our theoretical discussions produce only an
idea of God, this cannot be valid because it does not
relate to us as persons. The God of Scripture is real
and living, no idea or doctrine. He is a God who can
help sufferers in the sickroom and comfort mourners in
the cemetery. One should feel sorrow for the clergyman
who must minister to people in need when he has nothing
in his own heart and mind beyond a set of theoretical
ideas!

(2) Only contextual exegesis has theological validity. Inasmuch as real theology is situational and
experiential, it makes sense that the kind of exegesis
that has theological validity is that which penetrates
beyond mere ideas and words to an awareness of revel-
ational experience. One cannot get at the vital experience of the writers of Scripture without a deep
and sympathetic appreciation of the literary, historical,
and cultural context of their words. The texts of Scripture require to be intensively researched, for the
writer of each individual text was himself a real, living, breathing, needing, craving, sinning, yearning
human person. He was giving witness to an experience
of God's presence in his own life and the life of his
community. It is, frankly and forthrightly stated, the
task of exegesis to recover as well as possible the
massive detail about the writer's spiritual condition,
and the existential situation out of which, and to
which, he spoke. The serious Bible student is chal-

lenged to come to any particular passage of Scripture with the expectation, hope and desire of uncovering what these particular words meant to the person who wrote them, and what they were designed to convey in the minds and souls of those who first listened to or read them.

J. Barr, Old and New in Interpretation, New York, 1966.

W. Eichrodt, Theology of the Old Testament (hereinafter
TOT), I, 25ff., 512ff.

   Old Testament theology:

      The problem and the method
      The problem of Old Testament theology

G. von Rad, Old Testament Theology (hereinafter OTT), I,
3ff.

   A history of Yahwism and of the sacral institutions
   in Israel in outline

      Origins
      The crisis due to the conquest
      The crisis due to the formation of the state
      Endeavours to restore the past
      The constituting of the post-exilic cultic
         community

idem, I, 105ff.

   The theology of Israel's historical traditions:
   Methodological presuppositions

      The subject-matter of a Theology of the Old
         Testament
      The unfolding
      The oldest pictures of the saving history

idem, II, 319ff.

   The Old Testament and the New

      The actualization of the Old Testament in the
         New
      The Old Testament's understanding of world and
         man, and Christianity
      The Old Testament saving event in the light of
         the New Testament fulfilment

S. Terrien, The Elusive Presence (hereinafter EP), pp.
9ff.

   Cultus and faith in biblical research

T. C. Vriezen, An Outline of Old Testament Theology
(hereinafter OOTT), 11ff., 91ff., 143ff.

   The Christian Church and the Old Testament

The Old Testament as the word of God, and its use
in the church
Basis, task and method of Old Testament theology

W. Zimmerli, Old Testament Theology in Outline, Philadelphia: Fortress, 1978 (hereinafter OTTO), pp.
238ff.

The openness of the Old Testament message

NOTES

1. Cf. J. Barr, Old and New in Interpretation, New
York, 1966.

2. Our generation is seeing various attempts to place
a positive Christian interpretation on the Old Testament without resorting to unwarranted allegorical
and Christological procedures; e.g., A. A. van Ruler,
Die christliche Kirche und das Alte Testament, Munich, 1955; G. A. F. Knight, A Christian Theology of
the Old Testament (Richmond, 1959). On the special
problems of validating the Old Testament from the
vantage-point of New Testament authority, see two
symposia: C. Westermann, Essays on Old Testament
Hermeneutics, Richmond, 1963; and B. W. Anderson,
The Old Testament and Christian Faith. New York,
1963; also S. J. De Vries, "Basic Issues in Old
Testament Hermeneutics," Journal of The Methodist
Theological School in Ohio, 5/1, (1966), 3-19.

3. Of various indigenous groups in the Holy Land today,
those of Greek Orthodox persuasion seem less in
sympathy with Zionistic nationalism than any other.
This unquestionably has much to do with such out-
breaks of sharp animosity on public issues as controversy in the Israel government's expropriation
of parklands adjacent to the ancient Church of the
Holy Cross in Jerusalem, which was itself desecrated
by Israeli soldiers during the War of Independence.

4. See my remarks on the significance of holy place
over against that of holy time in Yesterday, Today
and Tomorrow: Time and History in the Old Testament (Grand Rapids and London, 1975), p. 348, n. 11.
This title will hereinafter be abbreviated as YTT.

5. See G. von Rad, Old Testament Theology I, 175-187;
   M. Noth, Exodus, Philadelphia: 1962; also A History
   of Pentateuchal Traditions, trans. B. W. Anderson,
   Englewood Cliffs 1972; B. W. Childs, The Book of
   Exodus, A Critical, Theological Commentary, Phila-
   delphia: Westminster, 1974; J. Plastaras, The God
   of Exodus: The Theology of the Exodus Narratives,
   Milwaukee 1966; E. W. Nicholson, Exodus and Sinai in
   History and Tradition, Richmond: John Knox, 1973;
   S. Herrmann, Israel in Egypt, Naperville 1970.

6. So especially A. Harnack and the antisemitic
   "Deutsche Christen" movement. R. Bultmann, though
   he denies being marcionistic, relegates the Old
   Testament to pre- and subChristian "Vorverstandnis"
   in his articles, "The Significance of the Old Testament for the Christian Faith," Anderson, op. cit.,
   pp. 8-35, and "Prophecy and Fulfillment," Westermann,
   op. cit., pp. 50-75 (both translated from German
   originals); so also the articles of F. Baumgärtel,
   F. Hesse, C. Michalson, and J. Dillenberger in these
   two volumes. To assess the significance of the
   strong opposition to this position among all the
   remaining contributors to this volume, see De Vries,
   "Basic Issues," pp. 17-19; also S. J. De Vries "The
   Early Years of Barth and Bultmann," Journal of The
   Methodist Theological School, 5/2 (1967), 22-29.

7. For what follows, see R. Grant, The Bible in The
   Church, A Short History of Interpretation, New York,
   1954; P. R. Ackroyd, et al., edd., The Cambridge
   History of the Bible, 3 vols., Cambridge 1963-1970.

8. See S. Sandmel, We Jews and Jesus, New York 1965.

9. See art. "Ebionites," (G. Uhlhorn), NSHE, IV, 57.

10. Cf. W. Schmithals, Die Gnosis in Korinth, eine Unter-
    suchung zu den Korintherbriefen, 2nd. ed. Gottingen,
    1965; R. Bultmann, Theology of the New Tesament, I
    (New York 1954), pp. 164-183.

11. Cf. Bultmann, ibid., II (1955), pp. 15ff.; R. E.
    Brown, "'Other Sheep not of This Fold': The Johan-
    nine Perspective on Christian Diversity in the Late
    First Century," JBL 97 (1978), 5-22.

12. See art. "Canon of the NT" (F. W. Beare), IDB; I,
    52ff.; J. Knox, Marcion and the New Testament,
    Chicago 1942; H. Lietzmann, The Beginnings of the

Christian Church (New York 1937), pp. 333-353.

13. Cf. A. C. McGiffert, A History of Christian Thought, I (New York-London, 1932), 246ff.; J. L. Gonzalez, A History of Christian Thought, I (Nashville-New York, 1970), 268ff.; J. Pelikan, The Christian Tradition, A History of the Development of Doctrine, I (Chicago 1971).

14. See art. "Justin Martyr"(N. Bonwetsch), NSHE, VI, 282ff.

15. See art. "Philo of Alexandria" (O. Zöckler), NSHE, IX; 38ff.

16. See G. Vermes, "Bible and Midrash: Early Old Testament Exegesis," Cambridge History of the Bible, I, 199-231; H. L. Strack, Introduction to the Talmud and Midrash (Philadelphia 1945), pp. 201ff.; A. G. Wright, The Literary Genre Midrash, New York 1967.

17. Cf. B. Smalley, The Study of the Bible in the Middle Ages, Oxford:1952.

18. Cf. J. T. McNeill, The History and Character of Calvinism, Oxford: 1954, pp. 212-214.

19. See H. Bornkamm, Luther and the Old Testament, trans. E. W. and R. C. Gritsch, ed. V. I. Gruhn, Philadelphia 1969.

20. See J. Steinmann, Richard Simon et les origins de l'exégèse biblique, Bruges, 1960; Cf. H. J. Kraus, Geschichte der historischkritischen Erforschung des Alten Testaments (2nd ed., Neukirchen-Vluyn, 1969), pp. 65-70.

21. Cf. G. H. Tavard, "Tradition in Theology," J. F. Kelly, ed., Perspectives on Scripture and Tradition (Notre Dame: Fides Publishers, 1976), pp. 84ff.

22. Cf. O. Cullmann, Vatican Council II; The New Direction. Essays selected and arranged by J. D. Hester, New York 1968.

23. See Kraus, op. cit., 80ff.; S. J. De Vries, Bible and Theology in The Netherlands (Wageningen 1968), pp. 7ff., 22ff., 45-87.

24. Cf. Kraus, op. cit., pp. 425-433; J. Smart, "A Mat-

ter of Life or Death," The Divided Mind of Modern Theology (Philadelphia 1967), pp. 206ff.

25. Egyptian dominance over Palestine ended ca. 1200 B.C., and, apart from occasional raids like that of Pharaoh Sheshonq (= Shishak, I Kings 14:25f.), was never restored until, very briefly, in the time of Necho I (609-604 B.C.). Once David subdued the Transjordanian kingdoms (II Samuel 10, 12), Israel remained safe on its eastern border until the Aramean raids of the ninth century and the Assyrian and Babylonian conquests of the eighth centuries, respectively. That is to say, once inimical groups like the Philistines and Edomites had been either assimilated or brought under vassalage, David's kingdom was able to enter a period of relative security and international peace lasting for two or three centuries.

26. For details concerning the growth of the various Old Testament documents one should consult the major works on Introduction. See now particularly the innovative, comprehensive treatment offered in B. S. Childs, An Introduction to the Old Testament as Scripture (Philadelphia: Fortress, 1979), where a complete list of similar works is given.

27. See art. "Jew" (R. Posner), EJ, X, 22ff: "Jewish Identity" (A. Hertzberg), EJ, X, 53ff.; art. "Jew, Jews, Jewess" (J. A. Sanders) IDB, II, 897ff.

28. Cf. art. "Israel, Names and Associations of" (A. Haldar), IDB, II, 765f.

29. For details, cf. P. R. Ackroyd, Exile and Restoration, Philadelphia 1968.

30. See E. Mary Smallwood, Jews Under Roman Rule, Leiden: Brill, 1976; cf. also E. Schürer, A History of the Jewish People in the Time of Jesus, N. N. Glatzer, ed., New York 1961; S. Safrai and M. Stern, edd., The Jewish People in the First Century, 2 vols. Assen: van Gorcum, 1974-.

31. Cf. the classic study of W. M. Ramsay, St. Paul the Traveller and the Roman Citizen, New York and London, 1896; also S. V. McCasland, "New Testament Times: The Graeco-Roman World," IB, 7, 75ff.

32. Christianity changed from a persecuted sect to a

privileged state-religion after the time of the
emperor Constantine, A.D. 313 (Edict of Milan).
Subsequently the church developed a centralized
hierarchy, with the See of Rome taking over elements of imperial authority at the collapse of
the city in the mid-fifth century.

33. Cf. O. Cullmann, Christ and Time; The Primitive
Christian Conception of Time and History, Rev. ed.,
London 1962; C. H. Dodd, The Apostolic Preaching
and its Development, Chicago 1937.

34. Cf. Richard Gutteridge, The German Evangelical
Church and the Jews 1879-1950, Oxford: Blackwell,
1976; especially Chap. V, "The Nüremberg Laws and
their Effect upon the Evangelical Church, 1935-
1938" (pp. 152ff). The Evangelical Church was
paralyzed when facing the duty of witnessing
against the immorality of Nazi antisemitism by
a traditionalistic maintenance of the two-realms
doctrine, leading it to the pretension that political matters were none of her concern. It was
not until the Nazis interfered with the internal
church matter of enforcing the so-called "Aryan
Clause" against pastors of Jewish descent that
formidable opposition arose within the church.
The church was always concerned to protect Jewish
church-members, and especially pastors, but had
little to say about the plight of the Jewish people as a whole. The Nazis were very effective in
playing off the latter against the former, enti-
cing the church authorities into leaving the non-
Christian Jews in their hands at the price of laying off the non-Aryan church members.

35. See the burgeoning literature on the Holocaust
experience, especially as interpreted by Elie
Wiesel; cf. H. J. Cargas, Harry J. Cargas in Con-
versation with Elie Wiesel, New York: Paulist
Press, 1976; J. K. Roth, A Consuming Fire: En-
counters with Elie Wiesel and the Holocaust, At-
lanta: John Knox, 1979; E. L. Fackenheim, God's
Presence in History: Jewish Affirmations and
Philosophical Reflections, New York: New York
University Press, 1970.

36. Cf. J. Barr, Fundamentalism (Philadelphia: Fortress, 1978) pp. 36ff.

37. The song of Deborah in Judges 5 is likely the

earliest (<u>ca.</u> 1250 B.C.), additions to Daniel the latest (164 B.C.), literary materials contained within the canonical Old Testament. However, the bulk of this was composed between <u>ca.</u> 950 B.C. (J) and 350 B.C. (completion of the Pentateuch, the Prophets collection, most of the Writings).

38. The story of the transmission of the biblical text is long and involved; cf. S. Talmon, "The Old Testament Text," P. R. Ackroyd, ed., <u>The Cambridge History of the Bible</u>, I, 159ff., E. Würthwein, <u>The Text of the Old Testament</u>, Oxford 1957.

39. Two vols., trans. J. A. Baker, Philadelphia 1961-1967

40 Tr. S. Neuijen, Wageningen, 1958; 2nd. ed. 1969

41. M. Burrows, <u>An Outline of Biblical Theology</u>, Philadelphia 1946; L. H. Koehler, <u>Old Testament Theology</u>, Philadelphia 1957; O. Procksch, <u>Theologie des Alten Testaments</u>, Gütersloh 1950.

42. New York, 1962-65, tr. D. M. Stalker

43. Wolff, "Gerhard von Rad als Exeget," pp. 9-20 in H. W. Wolff, ed., <u>Gerhard von Rad, Seine Bedeutung für die Theologie, Drei Reden von H. W. Wolff</u>, R. Rendtorff, W. Pannenberg, Munich 1973

44. Cf. G. F. Hasel, <u>Old Testament Theology: Basic Issues in the Current Debate</u>, Grand Rapids: Eerdmans, 1972; W. Eichrodt, <u>Theology of the Old Testament</u>, I (Philadelphia 1961), 512-520 ("The Problem of Old Testament Theology")

45. New York: Harper, 1978

46. Literary studies concerning the Old Testament were stimulated by the writings of Robert Lowth (d. 1787) and especially scholars of the German Romanticistic movement such as Johann Gottfried Herder (d. 1803). Throughout the nineteenth century it was much the vogue to approach the Bible, and especially the Old Testament, in terms of its aesthetic appeal. This approach continues to inspire such books as P. C. Sands, <u>The Literary Genius of the Old Testament</u>, Oxford 1926, and C. A. Dinsmore, <u>The English Bible as Literature</u>, Boston 1931. Although the Romanticistic bias that the Bible is

nothing more than admirable human literature must now be set aside, its beauty as literature needs to continue to be studied and admired, as in the recent writings of Luis Alonso-Schökel and James Muilenburg (see particularly the latter's Commentary on Second Isaiah in _IB_).

47. Cf. J. Barr, _Fundamentalism_, pp. 310ff. ("Objectivity").

48. See the impressive argumentation of W. Zimmerli in his article, "Promise and Fulfillment," C. Westermann, ed., _Essays on Old Testament Hermeneutics_, pp. 89-122. A number of present-day systematicians are responsive to this call (notably H. Diem in Germany, H. Berkof in Holland), but they are still very much in the minority.

Chapter I

The Transcendence and Immanence of God

"THE HOLY GOD"

Yahweh, the god of the Israelites (see Ex. 3:14f.), who is also the God and Father of our Lord Jesus Christ, is unique in his holiness, transcendently distinctive while intimately near in his immanence.

Ontologically, he is absolutely different from all created being, sharing nothing of the metaphysical substance of the world.

Personalistically, we know him as the absolutely Other, who nonetheless shares our lives by ruling and healing them. It is in a relational sense that we speak of him as "the HOLY God."

Introduction: The concept of holiness

   a. Otto: The Holy as mysterium tremendum

   Rudolf Otto's book, The Idea of the Holy, first
published in German in 1917, began a new phase in the
discussion of transcendantal realities.[1] Otto coins a
special term, "the numinous." The Latin word numen
means divine will and power, hence a god or goddess, also
a spirit or apparition. In Otto's view the Latin numen
is equivalent to Heb. qādôš, Grk. hagios and Lat. sacer.

   He goes on to analyze the contents of the numinous
and then describes mankind's subjective response to it.
He gives this the name "mysterium tremendum," another
Latin expression with two distinct elements, viz., the
tremendum, which is man's trembling before the aweful
and majestic numen; and the mysterium, which includes
the element of fascination in the presence of the Great
Unknown. According to Otto the trembling or shuddering
(tremendum) is more than natural, ordinary fear, implying that a mysterious reality is beginning to loom before the mind and touch the feelings. It may be manifested as demonic dread--a horror in the presence of a
dangerous unknown force--or as worshipful awe in the
presence of a deity who is known, loved and trusted. It
is the uncanny feeling that we all experience when we
listen to ghost stories and when our flesh shudders with
a sense of horror too irrational to be called fear. It
is also the marvelous experience of ecstatic awe that
causes one to cry "Holy, holy, holy!" as the God of
heaven and earth draws near. The feeling of tremendum
overpowers us and takes complete possession of our will.

   The opposite reaction to the numinous presence--
ever an inseparable element in man's total subjective
emotion--is what Otto calls mysterium. Being confronted by the Wholly Other, feeble man is struck dumb with
blank wonder, amazement, and astonishment. He succumbs
to a state of stupor and numbness, unable to flee in
terror.

   The qualitative content of the numinous experience
is the element of fascination. As Otto says, "The numinous is something that allures with a potent charm, and
the creature, who trembles before it, utterly cowed and
cast down, has always at the same time the impulse to

turn to it; nay, even to make it something of his own.
The 'mystery' is for him not merely something to be
wondered at but something that entrances him ...a
strange ravishment, rising often enough to the pitch of
dizzy intoxication." (p. 31)

Such are the elements that Otto has analyzed in the
numinous experience. One may experience them--shudder-
ing, stupification, fascination--in various situations.
They hold a vital position in all religions, however
high or low, that are more than pure abstraction. In
religious forms such as Hinduism, the numinous may be
expressed in the fearful, horrible, or even disgusting.
There are traces of demonic dread in isolated biblical
stories as well; but as a whole, the Old Testament and
New Testament lie on a much higher plane, in which the
character of the divine Being is rationalized, being
worthy of trust and love because he is both rational and
moral. The Old Testament/New Testament God is more than
numen; he is a personal and loving Father.

b. The sacred and the profane

The Bible, expecially the Old Testament, knows
nothing of our distinction between secular and religious
orders (church and state). It does, however, sharply
distinguish between the sacred/sacral (qādōš) and the
profane (Heb. tāmēʾ, "unclean"). Although God is everywhere and in all things, he is effectively and actively
present only in the qādōš. This need not be, but usually is, institutionalized. The essence of biblical
religion, in distinction from other ancient religions,
is that its God, Yahweh, is elusively present; i.e.,
present where he freely and sovereignly chooses to be
present and reveal himself. A completely different
religious impulse interacts with this in the biblical
tradition (especially in the Solomonic temple with its
cultic apparatus) to tie this God to one place, one land,
one people, one religion. It is especially in the service of this kind of religious domestication that the
Israelites built up an elaborate system for offering
the qōdeš (holiness) of God to the needs of a worshiping people in the form of priesthood, shrine, ritual,
and liturgy. Eventually a special day (the Sabbath),
a special book (the Torah) and a special people became
the prime bearers of the divine holiness.

c. The fear of God

Among a variety of Hebrew words expressing humankind's reverential response to the presence of Deity,
the most widely used is the verb yārē' and noun yir'â,
"fear." True to the basic epiphanic tradition, the
"fear of God" refers in many early passages to the spon-
taneous emotion that comes with an immediate awareness
of the divine transcendance. This is the mysterium
tremendum described by Otto. We read of Jacob in Gen.
28:17: "And he was afraid (wayyîrā') and said, 'How
awesome (nôrā') is this place!'" Of the Israelites
gathered before Mount Sinai, Ex. 20:18 tells us this:
"Now when all the people perceived the thunderings and
the lightnings and the sound of the trumpet and the
mountain smoking, the people were afraid (restoring YR'
from the ancient versions; cf. v. 20) and trembled."
II Sam. 6:6-9 tells of a certain Uzzah falling dead
because he had transgressed a taboo against touching the
ark of Yahweh, leading David to "become afraid" of Yahweh (wayyîrā' dāwîd' et YHWH, v. 9).

The competing tradition of institutional formalism,
seen especially in postexilic passages, tends to reduce
"the fear of God" to something less direct and intuitive.
Much of the spontaneity of primitive worship is lost as
the God of the Israelites becomes progressively more remote and abstract, as that "God-fearing" comes to mean
Torah-observing, religious, faithful to the pious
practices of orthodoxy.[2]

1. The Elusiveness of the divine presence

    Among the numerous images for the supernatural used
in the history of world religions, some are more fitting,
others are less fitting. The two particular images
applied to Yahweh, the God of Israel, are especially
suited to expressing the paradoxical opposites of transcendental and immanant. These are the figure of lordship, expressing the more transcendantal side of personalism, and the image of parenthood, expressing more
the immanentistic side of personalism. These two images
together, the ancient Hebrews found worthy for expressing their peculiar conception of divine holiness.

    a. In extrabiblical religion

    (1) the gods and cosmic process

    Nonbiblical religiosity associates the supernatural
with the rest of reality by way of ontic identity. All
beings share the same substance; it is only the form of
that substance that differs within experiential and non-
experiential reality (see Aristotle's sophisticated
philosophy based on this distinction). All worldly
phenomena are a part of cosmic process. Even Diety is
involved in it. The reality known as "God" is not distinguished from the phenomenal world. The animate world
is especially suffused with Deity; but inaminate reality
is a potent bearer of Deity as well. Deity is everywhere
present as the element of awesomeness, mysteriousness;
but it readily lends itself to localization and institu-
tionalization in specially numinous locales, persons,
and practices.

    The following excerpts from an outstanding inter-
preter of ancient Near-Eastern mythology, Henri Frankfort, may help us understand the nonbiblical mode of
intellectual conceptuality:

    Natural phenomena, whether or not they were personi-
    fied and became gods, confronted ancient man with
    a living presence, a significant "Thou," which . .
    exceeded the scope of conceptual definition . . .
    The mythopoeic mind, tending toward the concrete,
    expressed the irrational, not in our manner, but by

admitting the validity of several avenues of approach at one and the same time. The Babylonians, for instance, worshiped the generative force in nature in several forms: its manifestation in the beneficial rains and thunderstorms was visualized as a lion-headed bird. Seen in the fertility of the earth, it became a snake. Yet in statues, prayers, and cult acts it was represented as a god in human shape. The Egyptians in the earliest times recognized Horus, a god of heaven, as their deity. He was imagined as a gigantic falcon hovering over the earth with outstretched wings, the colored clouds of sunset and sunrise being his speckled breast and the sun and moon his eyes. Yet this god could also be viewed as a sun-god, since the sun, the most powerful thing in the sky, was naturally considered a manifestation of the god and thus confronted man with the same divine presence which he adored in the falcon spreading its wings over the earth.

Since the phenomenal world is a "Thou" confronting early man, he does not expect to find an impersonal law regulating a process. He looks for a purposeful will committing an act. If the rivers refuse to rise, it is not suggested that the lack of rainfall on distant mountains adequately explains the calamity. When the river does not rise, it has refused to rise. The river, or the gods, must be angry with the people who depend on the inundation . . . . Some action, then, is called for . . . In Egypt, where annual records of the heights of the Nile flood were kept from the earliest historical times, the pharaoh nevertheless made gifts to the Nile every year about the time when it was due to rise. To these sacrifices, which were thrown into the river, a document was added. It stated, in the form of an order or a contract, the Nile's obligations . . . . (The intellectual Adventure of Ancient Man, pp. 19f., 15f.)[3]

(2)   Supernaturalism within the immanentistic
       thought-world

As we compare biblical religion with nonbiblical religion, we find that, as far as the experience of the Holy is concerned, there is nothing phenomenologically distinctive in the one or in the other. Psychologically speaking, the Israelite worshiper shares an experience similar to that of the Hittite or the Egyptian or the Babylonian. The important distinction is ideological and philosophical, for we find that all forms of ancient oriental and classical religions grounded their conception of the supernatural in immanentistic monism.

Definitions. IMMANENTISM: the concept of the supernatural as inherently and necessarily present in experiental reality.
MONISM: a philosophical system in which all reality, divine as well as creaturely/human, shares the same ontological substance.

In nonbiblical religions, the supernatural is never couched in terms that distinguish it sharply from the natural order. Somehow, the worshiper is part of what is worshipped. The world of nature, the world of deity, and the human world are all interpreted as part of the same essential process. Thus supernatural means "bigger than," rather than "other than," the natural. The familiar gods of the Greeks and Romans, for instance, were not understood as essentially or ontologically different from humankind, but were rather larger, more powerful, more fierce and frightening than humankind. Just as ancient cultures failed to distinguish the metaphysical substance of various persons from one another, they failed to distinguish the person of the worshiper from the being of the deity.

One should not be surprised, actually, to hear of the wide-spread classical institution of emperior worship. Ontologically, there was no distinction between man and Deity. The Egyptians actually believed that the pharaohs were "sons of God," i.e., embodiments of Deity. Perhaps it was Egyptian influence on the Romans, as earlier on the Greeks, that encouraged their kings and emperors to insist on the honors and distinctions (including formal worship) belonging to the gods. Their power and achievements tempted them to forget their motality; their religion and philosophy put no obstacles in the way.[4]

On the other hand, Judaism and Christianity, with their monotheism and their conception of God's grand transcendence and universal sovereignty, were never able to compromise on this sorely disputed point, even if it meant persecution and death for their refusal. Ultimate issues of religious philosophy were at stake; for those who stood within the biblical tradition, it was no mere dogma or theory, but their life and death commitment to a living God, that was in dispute.

(3) The identification of the Holy with special places, phenomena, and institutions: readings from ancient Near-Eastern mythology

The primeval hillock (cf. holy mountain traditions in other religions)[5], ANET 31[6]

There is a city in the midst of the waters [from which] the Nile rises, named Elephantine. It is the beginning of the beginning, the beginning nome, (facing) toward Wawat. It is the joining of the land, the primeval hillock of earth, the throne of Re, when he reckons to cast life beside everybody. 'Pleasant of Life' is the name of its dwelling. 'The Two Caverns' is the name of the water; they are the two breasts which pour forth all good things. It is the couch of the Nile, in which he becomes young (again)....He fecundates (the land) by mounting as the male, the bull, to the female; he renews (his) virility, assuaging his desire. He rushes twenty-eight cubits (high at Elephantine); he hastens at Diospolis seven cubits (high)....

COMMENT: Reference is made to the island of Syene in the Nile just north of the lowest cataract. Wawat is the adjoining territory in Nubia. The myth identifies this spot as the center of creation.[7] The Egyptians reproduced it symbolically in their pyramids, representing the most elemental geometric form.

Hymn to the Nile, ANET 372-73. An extensive liturgy praising Nile as deity[8] contains the following excerpt:[9]

Worship of the Nile. Hail to thee, O Nile, that issues from the earth and comes to keep Egypt alive! Hidden in his form of appearance, a darkness by day, to whom minstrels have sung. He that waters the meadows which Re created, in order to keep every kid alive. He that makes to drink the desert and the place distant from water....The Lord of fishes, he who makes the marsh-birds to go upstream....The bringer of food, rich in provisions, creator of all good, lord of majesty,

53

sweet of fragrance....He who makes every beloved
tree to grow, without lack of them. He who brings
a ship into being by his strength, without hewing
in stone....He who was sorrowful is come forth
gay....Vomiting forth and making the field to
drink, anointing the whole land, making one man
rich and slaying another....A maker of light when
issuing from darkness, a fat for his cattle. His
limits are all that is created. There is no dis-
trict which can live without him....Entering into
the underworld and coming forth above, loving to
come forth as a mystery....He who establishes
truth in the heart of men....Men began to sing of
thee with the harp, and men sing to thee with the
hand. The generations of thy children jubilate
for thee....When thou risest in the city of the
Ruler [Thebes],[10] then men are satisfied with the
goodly produce of the meadows....When the Nile
floods, offering is made to thee, oxen are sacrificed to thee, great oblations are made to thee,
birds are fattened for thee, lions are hunted for
thee in the desert, fire is provided for thee.
And offering is made to every other god, as is done
for the Nile....O all men who uphold the Ennead
[the nine-god pantheon], fear ye the majesty which
his son, the All-Lord, has made by making verdant
the two banks. So it is "Verdant art thou!" So it
is "O Nile, verdant art thou, who makest man and
cattle to live!"

Hymn to Enlil, ANES 573-74. Representing the
tendency toward universalization, the Hymn to
Enlil celebrates Ekur/Duranki, his temple at
Nippur, as pre-eminent shrine:

Enlil, whose command is far-reaching, lofty his
          word (and) holy,
Whose promouncement is unchangeable, who decrees
          destinies unto the distant future,
Whose lifted eye scans the land,
Whose lifted beam searches the heart of all the
          land--
When Father Enlil seats himself broadly on the
          holy dais, on the lofty dais,
When Nunamnir carries out to supreme perfection
          lordship and kingship,
The earth-gods bow down willingly before him,
The Anunna humble themselves before him,

Stand by faithfully in accordance with (their)
    instructions.
The great (and) mighty lord, supreme in heaven
    (and) earth, the all-knowing one who under-
    stands the judgment,
Has set up (his) seat in Duranki -- the wise one,
Made pre-eminent in princeship the kiur, the
    "great place,"
In Nippur the lofty bellwether of the universe he
    erected (his) dwelling.
....
In Nippur, the beloved shrine of the father, the
    Great Mountain,
The shrine of plenty, the Ekur, the "lapis lazuli"
    house, he raised up out of the dust,
Planted it in a pure place like a (high) rising
    mountain,
Its prince, the Great Mountain, Father Enlil,
Set up (his) dwelling on the dais of the Ekur,
    the lofty shrine.
....
Enlil, when you marked off holy settlements on
    earth,
You built Nippur as your very own city,
The Kiur, the mountain, your pure place, whose
    water is sweet,
You founded in the Duranki, in the center of the
    four corners (of the universe),
Its ground, the life of the land, the life of all
    the lands,
Its brickwork, of red metal, its foundations of
    lapis-lazuli,
You have reared it up in Sumer like a wild ox,
All lands bow the head to it,
During its great festivals, the people spend (all)
    their time in bountifulness.

Enlil, the holy Earth that fills you with desire,
The Abzu, the holy shrine, so befitting for you,
The deep mountain, the holy cella, the place where
    you refresh yourself,
The Ekur, the "lapis-lazuli" house, your noble
    dwelling, awe-inspiring --
Its fear (and) dread reach heaven,
Its shade is spread over all the lands,
Its front stretches away to the center of heaven,
All the lords, all the princes,
Conduct thither (their) holy offerings,
Offer (their) prayers and orisons to you.

COMMENT: It is well to remember hymns like this when discussing the pious ideology that made Jerusalem the center of the universe, and Yahweh's throne.

Hymn to Aton, ANET 369-71. Representing the tendency toward consolidation:[12]

Thou appearest beautifully on the horizon of
    heaven,
Thou living Aton [sun-disk], the beginning of life!
When thou are risen on the eastern horizon,
Thou hast filled every land with thy beauty.
Thou art gracious, great, glistening, and high
    over every land;
Thy rays encompass the lands to the limit of
    all that thou hast made:
As thou art Re, thou reachest to the end of them;
(Thou) subduest them (for) thy beloved son [Akh-
    en-Aton].
Though thou art far away, thy rays are on earth;
Though thou art in their faces, no one knows
    thy going.
. . . .
At daybreak, when thou arisest on the horizon,
When thou shinest as the Aton by day,
Thou drivest away the darkness and givest thy rays.
The Two Lands [upper and lower Egypt] are in
    festivity every day....
All beasts are content with their pasturage;
Trees and plants are flourishing.
The birds which fly from their nests,
Their wings are (stretched out) in praise to
    thy ka.
All beasts spring upon (their) feet.
Whatever flies and alights,
They live when thou hast risen (for) them.
. . . .
Creator of seed in women,
Thou who makest fluid into man,
Who maintainest the son in the womb of his mother,
Who soothest him with that which stills his weeping,
Thou nurse (even) in the womb,
Who givest breath to sustain all that he has made!
When he descends from the womb to breathe
On the day when he is born,
Thou openest his mouth completely,
Thou suppliest his necessities.
When the chick in the egg speaks within the shell,
Thou givest him breath within it to maintain him.

56

When thou hast made him his fulfillment within
    the egg, to break it,
He comes forth from the egg to speak at his
    completed (time);
He walks upon his legs when he comes forth from it.

How manifold it is, that thou hast made!
They are hidden from the face (of man).
O sole god, like whom there is no other!
Thou didst create the world according to thy
    desire,
Whilst thou wert alone:
All men, cattle, and wild beasts,
Whatever is on earth, going upon (its) feet,
And what is on high, flying with its wings.

The countries of Syria and Nubia, the land of
    Egypt,
Thou settest every man in his place,
Thou suppliest their necessities:
Everyone has his food, and his time of life is
    reckoned.
Their tongues are separate in speech,
And their natures as well;
Their skins are distinguished,
As thou distinguishest the foreign peoples.
Thou makest a Nile in the underworld,
Thou bringest it forth as thou desirest
To maintain the people (of Egypt)
According as thou madest them for thyself,
The lord of all of them, wearying (himself) with
    them,
The lord of every land, rising for them,
The Aton of the day, great of majesty.

All distant foreign countries, thou makest their
    life (also),
For thou hast set a Nile in heaven,
That it may descend for them and make waves upon
    the mountains,
Like the great green sea,
To water their fields in their towns,
How effective they are, thy plans, O lord of
    eternity!
The Nile in heaven, it is for the foreign peoples
And for the beasts of every desert that go upon
    (their) feet;
(While the true) Nile comes from the underworld
    for Egypt.
....

Thou art in my heart,
And there is no other that knows thee,
Save thy son, Nefer-kheperu-Re Wa-en-Re,
For thou hast made him well-versed in thy plans
    and in thy strength.

The world came into being by thy hand,
According as thou hast made them.
When thou hast risen they live,
When thou settest they die.
Thou art lifetime thy own self,
For one lives (only) through thee.
Eyes are (fixed) on beauty until thou settest.
All work is laid aside when thou settest in the
    west.
(But) when (thou) risest (again),
[Everything is] made to flourish for the king,...
Since thou didst found the earth
And raise them up for thy son,
Who came forth from thy body:
    the king of Upper and Lower Egypt,...Akh-en-
    Aton,... and the Chief Wife of the King...
    Nefert-iti, living and youthful forever and
    ever.

COMMENT: While recognizing interesting parallels with
Psalm 104, one should note the many differences. Aton
is all; all is Aton. Though he cares specially for
Egypt (as the true Nile), he cares also for other lands,
coming as the Nile of rainfall. This hymn is not truly
monotheistic because of its patent immanentism and pantheism.

(4) On the resort to manipulation: readings in
ritual and magical texts

A classic study is W. Robertson Smith's book, The
Religion of the Semites.[14] For the ancient world, many
new texts have been published, supplementing what Smith
had to say.[15]

We need to look at ancient nonbiblical religion as
an institutional process with its priesthood, its
rituals and sacrifices, its myths. All of this was
developed by the pious mentality of the ancient world,
as an expression of the mysterium tremendum, that reaction within the creaturely mind and heart that recognizes the special presence of the supernatural at par-

ticular places and times. More and more, this all tends
to become institutionalized, making man's role in religion essentially manipulative. Man is terrified by
the presence of the numinous; he needs to control and
manipulate it to his profit -- or at the very least to
ward off its potent evil. So myth, the form of sacred
story explaining how things are what they are in deepest
reality, is developed as one way of comprehending the
mysterious, numinous reality behind all earthly phenom-
ena.16 Ritual is developed in face-to-face confrontation with the numinous reality represented in the institutional cult. By these two together, the supernatural
world is somehow brought under man's control. Or at
least, such the priestly guilds led their followers to
believe. They introduced themselves as an indispensable
go-between, gaining untold profit for themselves, and
power beyond belief, becoming in various times and
places more powerful than the king himself. (Such was
the case with Akh-en-Aton, for instance, whose downfall
was engineered by the offended priests of Thebes.)17

Few moderns have any notion of ancient ritual.
Here is a recently published example from Ugarit, a
second-millenium, B.C., city in upper Syria:

> Month of Ḫiari: On the day of the New Moon
> a bull and a ram for the Mistress of the Mansion.
> On the fourteenth: Baᶜlu two loaves of layer-bread.
> On the eighteenth the king shall wash himself clean.
> On the following day: sacrificial meat in the pit
>   of Ṣapānu;
> ingots of silver and gold, an offering of two rams
>   for Bittu-bēti;
> a bull and a ram as a burnt-offering, a bull as a
>   peace-offering for Baᶜlu;
> a bird for Ṣapānu; a throat and a ram for Rišpu
>   of [Babātu]; two birds for Inšu-Ilīma;...
> In the pit of Rišpu human semen as a burnt-
>   offering and a dainty bit from the basin.
> On the following day: in the pit of Ḫiari
> thirty-eight head of small cattle, seven bulls;
> the house of Baᶜlu of Ugarit two rams.
> On the following day: for Rišpu-Māliku a bull
>   and a ram;
> for the Mistress of the Mansion a ram that has
>   been pierced and a ram;
> the Brackish Fountain a ram; the Vineyard of
>   Milku a ram.
> On the following day: for Koṯaru two (rams).

> On the following day the well-being of the people
> will be the result of (the offering of) this
> sacrificial meat. (J. C. de Moor in Ugaritica
> V, p. 318, RS 24.249)

COMMENT: For us this is boring and sterile, but for
the ancient worshiper it was full of fascination.[18]
The priest responsible for following out the prescribed
sacrificial calendar, presenting a variety of valuable
and numinous offerings to a variety of deities, or to
the same deity under different appelatives, would not
dream of departing a hair's breadth from it. Fear and
terror were present, but no doubt love and devotion as
well. Ancient ritual is predicated on the concept of
quid pro pro ("this for that"; "something for something
else"), following a certain order of doing honor to the
Deity, with the purpose of receiving proportionate benefits in return.

This also explains the psychology of magic. Inasmuch as the primitive mind could not be readily satisfied with a manageable number of dieties, there was
always the dread of unidentified powers beyond the recognized order. Within this uncontrolled world, beyond
the range of effective ritual manipulation, supernatural
power could become dangerous and hostile. In order to
secure oneself from evil in the spiritual area beyond
the reach of ritual, men sought to ward off malevolence,
and enlist beneficence, through the whole secret order
of magic and incantation. This was extra insurance.
Magic is still with us even in our scientific order of
reason; how much more in the ancient world!

Here is an incantation from ancient Egypt (ANET
328, Magical Protection for a Child):[19]

> Another charm. Mayest thou flow away, he who comes
> in the darkness and enters in furtively, with his
> nose behind him, and his face reversed, failing in
> that for which he came!

> Mayest thou flow away, she who comes in the dark-
> ness and enters in furtively, with her nose behind
> her, and her face turned backwards, failing in that
> for which she came!

> Hast thou come to kiss this child? I will not let
> thee kiss him! Hast thou come to silence (him)?
> I will not let thee set silence over him! Hast
> thou come to injure him? I will not let thee in-

jure him! Hast thou come to take him away? I will
not let thee take him away from me!

I have made this magical protection against thee
out of clover -- that which sets an obstacle --
out of onions -- which injures thee -- out of honey
-- sweet for men, (but) bitter for those who are
yonder [the dead] -- out of the roe of the abdju-
fish, out of the jawbone of the meret-fish, and
out of the backbone of the perch.

COMMENT: In the dynamistic conception underlying this
incantation, the spoken word -- recited in precise order,
style, and inflection -- was potent; yet it was accompanied by the administration of esoteric medications,
powerful in the spiritual world like healing herbs in
the physical.

Excursus on ritual in Hebrew religion.[20]

In critiquing nonbiblical religion, we are not
losing from mind how important sacrificial ritual was
throughout the Old Testament period, from the patriarchs
until the time of Christ. In earliest times it was
minimally regulated, and could occur away from established shrines. But we can clearly trace a tendency
toward regulation, centralization, and institutional-
ization, putting all under the authority of a priestly
aristocracy while eliminating all traces of pre-Yahwistic and sub-Yahwistic belief and practice. It was only
at a period of devastation and dispersion -- the exile
in Babylon -- that the sacrificial cult was entirely
interrupted; so too when the Romans captured, and later
destroyed, Jerusalem in the Christian era.

It appears that the Israelites accepted sacrificial
worship as normal and expected; no doubt they simply
inherited it from their ancestors and predecessors.
Numerous narratives mention it as part of orthodox practice. Moreover, the Pentateuch -- particularly Leviticus, Numbers, and Deuteronomy -- have sections that
are very largely given over to cultic legislation. Two
literary genres predominate: ritual (as in Lev. 1),
specifying the precise procedure for bringing an offering, of which there were several different kinds; and
torah (as in Lev. 7:19-27), instructing the people with
regard to what were, and were not, proper sacrifices.[21]
The Israelite priests were much concerned to assure that

worshipers and sacrifices met the criteria of purity,
and that the ritual proceded in proper order. This
accorded with what the laity expected of them, so much
so that when they did become slack they were severely
chastised, as in the classic words of Malachi (2:7-8):

> The lips of a priest should guard knowledge, and
> men should seek instruction (tôrāh) from his mouth
> ....But you have turned aside from the way; you
> have caused many to stumble by your instruction
> (tôrāh); you have corrupted the covenant of Levi,
> says Yahweh of hosts....

Nevertheless, the fact that biblical religion was
able to survive without the sacrificial cult during the
exile reveals that it did not really depend on it. The
prophets sometimes polemicize against it, or appear to
do so (e.g., Isa. 1:10-17). Amos 5:25 is difficult,
but may be taken to mean that the earliest writing prophet, Amos, was aware of a time in Israel's prehistory
when its religion had no place whatever for sacrificial
worship (see also 5:21-22). Most recent scholarship
agrees, however, that the prophets were condemning hypocrisy, formalism, externality, and eclecticism -- faults
of the worshiper's heart and mind. All the same, Old
Testament religion was clearly moving away from a reliance on sacrificial worship, as can be clearly seen
from several surprising declarations in the Psalms:

> Sacrifice and offering thou dost not desire;
>   but thou hast given me an open ear.
> Burnt offering and sin offering thou hast not
>   required. (40:6)
>
> If I were hungry, I would not tell you;
>   for the world and all that is in it is mine.
> Do I eat the flesh of bulls or drink the blood
>   of goats?
> Offer to God a sacrifice of thanksgiving,
>   and pay your vows to the Most High. (50:12-14)
>
> Thou hast no delight in sacrifice;
> Were I to give a burnt offering thou wouldst not
>   be pleased.
> The sacrifice acceptable to God is a broken spirit;
> A broken and contrite spirit, O God, thou wilt not
>   despise. (51:16-17)

In conclusion, we may say that sacrifice and ritual
were vehicles by which the Israelite people were able

to carry out an organized and regular worship. Mechanically, it functioned like similar practices in non-biblical religion. The Yahwists were not different in being more sincere, or more devout, in their praise and adoration. The difference was not phenomenological but theological. The fact that their God was one, not many, and presented himself to them as purely spiritual, rejecting every emblem and image, encouraged the development of a more highly personalistic interaction between deity and worshiper. Thus, ritual and liturgy remain purely instrumental wherever biblical religion is true to its higher personalistic understanding of God.

b.   The God of Israel

(1) Apprehended in terms of personalistic
     dualism

We have described, explained, and illustrated the concept of divine holiness -- and of human response to it -- within the immanentistic beliefs of the ancient peoples neighboring the Israelites. In many ways their experience and response paralleled those of their neighbors, yet a profound difference remained. What was the distinctive element in Israel's apprehension of, and response to, the world of the supernatural? It is clearly the Bible's radical transcendentalizing of the God-concept. Israel's God is not part of the cosmic process. The attribution of personhood is developed along the lines of separation and distinction. Not only does he become bigger, stronger, more powerful ("supernatural" in a literal sense), but radically other, and sovereign in his differentiation.

We may refer to this as "personalistic dualism" in the sense that it denies monism. Israel's God, Yahweh, is in no way ranked with other deities, but stands radically alone. He is in no way controllable or manipulatable through ritual or magical formulae, but operates as sovereign Lord over all, exercizing his will upon the animate and inanimate world, but also upon mankind. Martin Buber's classic, I and Thou,[22] has helped modern theologians take divine personhood more seriously. It stands at the very core of biblical religion, giving it a radical distinction over against its rivals in the

63

ancient world.

Definitions: PERSON; PERSONALISTIC. Lat. etymology, "mask," "stage character" is not in consideration. A person is an intelligent, willing, acting being, conscious of his/her feelings and rational processes. A person is the subject of action; may also be its object. We apprehend other persons first of all as objects, and continue to treat them as such because objects are manipulable, useful for the gratification of our own desires. Many people fail to grow as persons, especially in social interaction; likewise, the full personhood of others is often abused or ignored. We grow as persons as we recognize ourselves and other human beings as subjects, responsible for intelligent and moral behavior. We cannot develop our personhood in isolation (see the feral children), but only in creative interaction with other persons as subjects

God as person. Setting aside the trinitarian reference of this term, we mean that the biblical God is not just a numinous power greater than other numinous powers. His majestic Presence is analogous to the otherness that distinguishes human persons from one another, but infinitely greater. God is pure Subject over against us as acting, willing subjects -- acting upon us and interacting with us. As sovereign Subject he is Lord, not making irrational demands and threats like a blind despot, but controlling our lives, with all of reality, for a benign purpose.

On the caricaturing of divine personhood in non-biblical religion, see below. Within the parameters of biblical faith, the greatest sin is to abuse or neglect the sovereign Personhood of God.

DUALISM. Alternately: PLURALISM. The philosophy that sees more than a single ontic reality. Opposite to monism.

Excursus on God as absolute Subject

There is an essentiality in using personalistic
images in our analogical speech about the supernatural,
for in no other way can we effectively preserve a worthy
concept of divine subjecthood.

Some recent theological treatments of this topic
have been especially helpful. We think particularly
of the analytical work of the German-American theologian,
Paul Tillich, culminating in his influential Systematic
Theology.[23] We are indebted to Tillich for his stern
warnings against the all-too-common tendency to object-
ify God, treating him as an object to be analyzed and
put into logical propositions. Do we not tend to conceive of God as an entity outside ourselves, possessing
some kind of objective existence? Tillich insists that
we must think of God as pure Subject, for an object is
something that may be approached by, and perhaps manipulated by, the observing interpreter. All objects that
we know are limited entities. We cannot conceive even
of the universe as otherwise than limited -- and yet
what lies beyond its outer limits? At least every
object that we know is limited by being outside ourselves as observers, and this is equally true whether
the object in question be material or spiritual. Thus
every object has limits; but does God have limits?
Whatever exists, except God himself, is limited in scope,
size, strength, impact, and conditions of existence.
Whatever exists, except God, is qualified by other
beings. The existence of all objects is qualified,
contingent, conditioned, and dependent. But when we
talk about God, we talk about One who is beyond all
conditions and qualifications. He is himself absolutely
incontingent, yet he absolutely impinges upon all other
existences.

If God is no object, he must indeed be pure Subject.
We apply to him the analogy of subjecthood from our
human experience of subjecthood. Although we human
beings are objects, with all the contingencies and limitations of objects, we do participate in the experience
of subjecthood. We are self-conscious, rational creatures, aware of our individual existence, and in a
limited way, able to control it. Although we know that
we are contingent beings, there is something within our
being that reaches beyond contingency and conditionedness. Although each of us must act within his own

limitations and contingencies, at least in our imagination and in the exercise of our will, we can reach beyond them. It is this analogy of subjecthood that is the most appropriately applied to the concept of God. Our power of imagination, reason, and will are attributes that we necessarily ascribe to God, but in an absolute sense. We can imagine many things -- but he can imagine all. We can know more and more things, and then still more things -- but God already knows everything that we shall ever know. We can will great things -- even space flights and empires -- but God wills everything that is.

If God is indeed pure Subject, it is altogether inappropriate that one should attempt to control or manipulate him. As we become aware of him, we can do no other than respond to him. Our fitting response is the mysterium tremendum: trembling in awe, gazing in wonder.

(a)   The epiphanic tradition as normative

Biblical scholars universally recognize two competing conceptions of God in Israelite religion: (1) cultic and institutional; (2) epiphanic and charismatic. The first belongs to the temple and the Davidic establishment; the second belongs to the patriarchal and the exodus traditions -- taken over but not completely assimilated within the mainstream of classical Hebraic worship. We must look to the epiphanic tradition for the primitive roots of Yahwism. Israel began as something radically different from its neighbors, and became normalized to the ideals of international culture only when it adopted the political structures of statehood.

Definitions: EPIPHANY/EPIPHANIC. Terrien's book (see above)[24] has clarified a distinction which he insists upon -- often confused in contemporary discussion. A theophany (from Grk. theou-phaneia, "manifestation of deity") refers to spectacular displays of numinous power in a natural cataclysm, as in the Sinai revelation of Exodus 19. An epiphany (from Grk. epi-phaneia, "manifestation," "revelation") need not be spectacular or involve natural phenomena. It occurs wherever the presence

of Israel's God is mysteriously revealed, usually
through his sudden address. He is seldom perceived in visual form (Deut. 4:12, 15 deny that
God can be seen; but see Ex. 24:10-11 for a very
old and authentic contrary tradition); patriarchs
and prophets preferably apprehend God in his word
to them. As might be expected, the temple ritual
made much of visual symbols of the divine presence,
especially in a mystical cloud of glory, the
skekinah.[25]

1)   Primitive epiphanic legend

     Two spectacular examples occur in composite liter-
ary contexts, Gen. 28:10-22 and Ex. 3:1-6.[26]   The
Yahwistic and Elohistic materials interwined in each
of them emphasize distinctive conceptions of the divine
presence.

     Gen. 28:10-22: Jacob left Beer-Sheba and went
toward Haran. And he came to a certain place
(māqôm), and stayed there that night, because the
sun had set. Taking one of the stones of the place
(māqôm), he put it under his head and lay down in
that place (māqôm) to sleep. And he dreamed that
there was a ladder set up on the earth, and the
top of it reached to heaven; and behold, the angels
of God were ascending and descending on it! And
behold, Yahweh stood above it and said, "I am
Yahweh, the god of Abraham your father and the god
of Isaac; the land on which you lie I will give to
you and your descendants; and your descendants
shall be like the dust of the earth, and you shall
spread abroad to the west and to the east and to
the north and to the south; and by you and your
descendants shall all the families of the earth
bless themselves. Behold, I am with you and will
keep you wherever you go, and will bring you back
to this land; for I will not leave you until I
have done that of which I have spoken to you."
Then Jacob awoke from his sleep and said, "Surely
Yahweh is in this place (māqôm); and I did not
know it." And he was afraid, and said, "How awesome is this place (māqôm)! This is none other
than the house of God, and this is the gate of
heaven." So Jacob rose early in the morning,

and he took the stone which he had put under his
head and set it up for a pillar and poured oil on
the top of it....Then Jacob made a vow saying,
"If God will be with me, and will keep me in this
way that I go, and will give me bread to eat and
clothing to wear, so that I come again to my
father's house in peace, then Yahweh shall be my
god, and this stone, which I have set up for a
pillar, shall be God's house; and of all that thou
givest me I will give the tenth to thee.

Ex. 3:1-6: Now Moses was keeping the flock of his
father-in-law... and he led his flock to the west
side of the wilderness, and came to Horeb, the
mountain of God. And the angel of Yahweh appeared
to him in a flame of fire out of the midst of a
bush; and he looked, and lo, the bush was burning,
yet it was not consumed. And Moses said, "I will
turn aside and see this great sight, why the bush
is not burnt." When Yahweh saw that he turned
aside to see, God called to him out of the bush,
"Moses, Moses!" And he said, "Here am I." Then
he said, "Do not come near; put off your shoes from
your feet, for the place (māqôm) on which you are
standing is holy ground." And he said, "I am the
God of your father, the God of Abraham, the God
of Isaac, and the God of Jacob." And Moses hid
his face, for he was afraid to look at God.

COMMENT: Māqôm, "place," regularly has the specific
meaning, "holy site," "shrine"; so here. Bethel became
an established Israelite shrine,[27] but Sinai did not.[28]
The site of each story, in the most primitive underlying
tradition, was remote and lost to memory. The divine
act of self-revelation, not man's celebration, made
each holy.

Definitions: YAHWIST/IC and ELOHIST/IC: Historical
criticism has long established separate documentary
sources in the Pentateuch. The two earliest are
the one that refers to the patriarchal God as
"Yahweh," and is hence called the Yahwist (abbr.
J), and another that calls him "Elohim" (pl. "gods,"
but sing. for Israel's God in monotheistic faith),
and is hence called the Elohist (abbr. E). J is
probably Judaean and dates from ca. 950 B.C.,
while E is probably northern Israelite, dating
from ca. 850 B.C.[29]

In Genesis 28 and Exodus 3 the two are compositionally intertwined, as the variation of the divine names shows. J's version of Genesis 28 is an epiphany, since Yahweh speaks but is not seen; E's version moves toward theophany in that Jacob sees God's angels in a dream, even though he does not see God himself.[30] J's version of Exodus 3, on the other hand, is strikingly theophanous, for he sees the marvelous burning bush, a visible symbol of the divine presence; E's version, meanwhile, remains staunchly epiphanous, for God only speaks.[31]

The Pentateuch also has a late Priestly source (P), which was intertwined with an earlier redactional intertwining of J and E.

Both these narratives bring to clear expression the meaning divine holiness in personalistic terms. In the burning-bush story of Exodus 3, the god Yahweh first reveals himself to Moses (and through him, to Israel). The very strange phenomenon of a bush that is all ablaze, yet upon close inspection is not being consumed by the fire, expresses powerfully the elusive presence of God's supernatural power. It is especially important that the locale of divine self-revelation is no established shrine or temple, but the empty desert. In the story of Jacob at Bethel, Yahweh (E: God) mysteriously reveals himself at a place (māqôm) far from every known religious observance or distinction. In the J version, this God, previously unknown to him but now identifying himself with the gods/God of his ancestors, surprisingly promises him to be with him wherever he may go, even in a foreign country far away from the land of promise, bringing him back in his own good time.

This narrative's significance cannot be over-rated. It shows that in Israel's early epiphanic tradition, God displays his numinous power and presence not in particular shrines and rituals, but freely and sovereignly, always in terms of personal endearment and commitment. In other words, Jacob does not manipulate God, but God "manipulates" him. In terms of the narrative context this is especially important, for Jacob has just deprived Esau of the patriarchal blessing in a cynical effort to control his own destiny at the expense of all who might stand in his way.[32]

2)   Classical liturgy: Psalm 18 = II Samuel 22

Under a line of Davidic kings, ruling in an unbroken dynasty for more than four hundred years, the
people of Judah developed a strong liturgical tradition
in praise of their god Yahweh. Most of this is preserved in the Psalter, the hymnbook of the Jerusalem
temple. This contains a remarkable variety of individual compositions, differing in length from very short to
complex; in mood, from bitter lament to exulting joy.
Many psalms are for recitation by individual worshipers,
others are designed for the worshiping congregation.
In all of them we discern an intimate relationship of
trust.   One who suffers appeals to the God who has
known him from the womb (Ps. 22:9-11); one who has been
delivered from suffering or peril praises the same God,
adoring him in passionate love and devotion. The psalms
are designed, no doubt, to be used over and over again,
by clergy and by laity, in situations parallel to the
original predicaments which inspired their composition.
As such, they were able to function as worthy appeals
to the Almighty. But they did not rely on a magical
pattern of holy words; rather, on the reality of a
deeply trustful relationship which each believer experienced. For each Israelite believer, three things
were certain: (1) Yahweh was his God; (2) this God
was accessible through prayer, quick to answer; (3)
this God was all-powerful and able to help him in his
need.

The creative genius of the psalm-writer ranged far
and wide to find appropriate images for bringing this
all to worthy expression. He drew from two special
realms, nature and history, often mingling the two together.[33]

Psalm 18, which appears also in II Samuel 22,[34]
eloquently expresses the psalmist's feeling of mysterium
tremendum. It was designed for recitation by the
Davidic kings in celebration of their victories, imi-
tating the style of the individual thanksgiving psalm.
We offer extracts from its fifty one verses:

1   I love thee, O Yahweh, my strength.
2   Yahweh is my rock, and my fortress, and my
      deliverer; my god, my rock, in whom I take
      refuge; my shield, and the horn of my
      salvation, my stronghold.

COMMENT: In this hymnic ascription of praise, Yahweh
is the sole source of power and strength. Unrestrainedly, the psalmist-king makes his personal claim: "He is
my god."

4 The cords of death encompassed me,
      the torrents of perdition assailed me;
5 The cords of Sheol entangled me,
      the snares of death confronted me.

COMMENT: Death, sheol, perdition -- personified in
Canaanite myth -- hyperbolically symbolize the psalmist's
specific distress in historical experience.

6 In my distress I called upon Yahweh,
      to my god I cried for help.
   From his temple he heard my voice,
      and my cry to him reached his ears.
7 Then the earth reeled and rocked;
      the foundations also of the mountains
      trembled because he was angry.
8 Smoke went up from his nostrils and
      devouring fire from his mouth;
      glowing coals flamed forth from him.
9 He bowed the heavens and came down;
      thick darkness was under his feet.
. . . .
12 Out of the brightness before him
      there broke through his clouds
      hailstones and coals of fire.
13 Yahweh also thundered in the heavens,
      and the Most High uttered his voice,
      hailstones and coals of fire.
14 And he sent out his arrows and scattered them,
      he flashed forth lightnings and routed them.
15 Then the channels of the sea were seen,
      and the foundations of the world were laid
      bare,
      at thy rebuke, O Yahweh, at the blast of the
      breath of thy nostrils.

COMMENT: Anthropomorphic (from Grk. anthropou-morphikē,
"in human form") and anthropopathic (from Grk. anthropou-
pathikē, "with human passion") images jostle elbows with
the language of theophany, featuring upheavals in nature
(storm, hail and lightning, flood). Although Israel's
neighbors took such language realistically, in the psalm,
biblical religion is already moving toward the abstra-
tive realm of pure metaphor.

16 He reached from on high, he took me, he drew
   me out of many waters.
17 He delivered me from my strong enemy and from
   them who hated me, for they were too mighty
   for me.
18 They came upon me in the day of my calamity;
   but Yahweh was my stay.
19 He brought me forth into a broad place;
   he delivered me, because he delighted in me.

COMMENT: Cosmic imagery flows into the form of historic
allusion. One special day brought Yahweh's deliverance
from overpowering enemies. "A broad place" is a metaphor borrowed from the imagery of shepherding (cf. Psalm
23). The reference to Yahweh's "delight" occasions the
testimony of integrity in vv.22-26, concluding with the
wisdom asseveration of v. 27, "For thou dost deliver a
humble (ᶜanî) people, but the haughty eyes thou dost
bring down."

     The psalm is too long to repeat the rest in full,
but one should note two special features of the following verses: (1) in vv. 32-45, the psalmist elaborates
his previous, meagre allusion to a historical victory
over an opposing military force; though metaphor continues, the description often becomes too concrete (and
too full of vengeful glee) to function well typological-
ly for worshipers in situations of need that are not
directly analogous to that of military conflict; (2) the
theme of a grateful, adoring praise continues to the
end, appearing with special stylistic finesse in vv.30,
32, and 47, where hāᵓēl is probably a vocative, producing the following translations:

30 O God -- his way is perfect, the promise of
   Yahweh proves true;
   he is a shield for all those who take
   refuge in him!
32 O God -- the one who girded me with strength
   and made my way safe!
47 O God -- who gave me vengeance and subdued
   people under me!

  (b) Its universalistic and particularistic
       dimensions

72

As we study the wide range of literature within the Old Testament, dating from a period of more than a thousand years, we discern a theological development in which Yahweh becomes more than the god of a particular individual, clan, tribe, or nation. The Israelites came more and more to the conviction that their god, committed to them as his special nation, was also the sovereign Lord of all the nations -- even of the whole world. Their exclusive loyalty to him led in logical and psychological inevitability to the claim of his exclusive divinity. Yet throughout this development, even to the point where Yahweh becomes the God of heaven and earth, they believed that he retained his special commitment and concern for them. A problem arose: did he govern the whole world for them, or had he chosen for them, or had he chosen them in order to govern the whole world? They struggled with various answers to this question. Nevertheless, Yahweh's sovereign and universal lordship became axiomatic, and it was especially this lordship image that was employed as a suitable vehicle for bringing to expression their conception of divine holiness. Yahweh was worshiped and honored as Lord of all that was dependent upon him. This lordship was expressed in terms of personal will, understood as eminently beneficent and unrestrainedly committed to the well-being of those under Yahweh's care.[35]

The mythic image which Israel chose to apply to itself as an expression of its pecular relationship to the Lord Yahweh was a saving event within history, referred to as the exodus. This was Israel's normative and constitutional, numinous confrontation with Deity. They remembered it in an ancient hymn known as the song of Miriam (Ex. 15:21):

Sing to Yahweh, for he has triumphed gloriously; the horse and his rider he has thrown into the sea.

They remembered it also in a narrative of holy celebration (Ex. 14:24, 27, 30):

In the morning watch Yahweh in the pillar of fire and of cloud looked down upon the host of the Egyptians and discomfited the host of the Egyptians ....And the sea returned to its wonted flow when the morning appeared, and the Egyptians fled into it; so Yahweh routed the Egyptians in the midst of the sea....Thus Yahweh saved Israel that day from the hand of the Egyptians; and Israel saw the Egyptians dead upon the seashore.

It is crucially significant that the people whom
Yahweh chooses for himself become his people in historical event. They are not as the Egyptians, the
Babylonians, or the Greeks, who identified themselves
as a people in terms of mythological identification
with divine substance, tracing their origins to a generative process within the cosmic order of reality. Of
all earthly peoples, Israel is singular in celebrating
the fact that they were once slaves.[36]

(2) Worshiped as uniquely spiritual

In nonbiblical religion, no ontological distinction
was made between the being of the gods and that of other
entities; hence there was no barrier to the cultic domestication of the gods in the form of visual images or
idols. It can be said that the idol represented the
god; but in a real sense the idol also was the god --
that is, a concrete manifestation of the god.[37] This
brought the god near to the worshiper, near to the
priest. The god was constantly subjected to the adu-
lation of ritual praise, and was expected to respond
effectively to the worshiper's need. Together, his
honorific name and his cultic image brought him into
the orbit of human control. Not so in Israel. In spite
of numerous clear instances of shortcoming and apostacy
-- whether on an individual or community scale -- official Yahwism forbade both the visual representation and
the idle, man-centered invocation of this god, both of
which would tend to intrude upon the elusiveness and
dignity of his sovereign holiness. Hence the second
and the third commandments of the decalogue occupy a
crucial position in the establishment of biblical religion. Each deserves careful attention.

(a) The second commandment, protecting Yahweh's
     sovereign spirituality[38]

"Thou shalt not make unto thyself a graven image,
or any likeness of anything in heaven above or in the
earth beneath or the water under the earth." So reads
the second "word," or commandment, of the Decalogue
(Ex. 20:4, Deut. 5:8).

The second commandment specifically excludes the various forms in which this prohibition might be breached, thereby guaranteeing Yahweh's sovereign spirituality. The other religions of the ancient world were constantly making all kinds of images and emblems of their deities, and offering homage to them. Why? The mythopoeic mentality behind these forms of worship is unable to recognize an essential distinction between the image or emblem, and the god which they represented. But because a particular god could be recognized with differing qualities and attributes, many images might be needed to express his full presence. Thus, for instance, the god Horus, the Egyptian falcon god. Graphic images recovered from ancient Egypt represent Horus as a falcon. To the Egyptian, the image is Horus; but the falcon soaring in the sky is also Horus. Or the bright clouds of the sunset are Horus; or the sun burning in the heavens; or Pharoah sitting on his throne. Each of these many images endeavors to express a single reality. Each image concretizes the meaning of divine presence, bringing this reality under intellectual and cultic control. Yahwism, however, forbids every effort to reduce the Deity to a managable, manipulable concept, whether represented in graphic figures or in mental imagination. All are equally invalid and equally pretentious. The biblical God is no object, subject to our control, but a sovereign Subject, ever evading our grasp while holding us under his command and control.

The second commandment is an absolute prohibition. There must be no "graven image" (pesel), i.e., no representation in glyptic art; there must also be no "likeness" (te mûnâ) -- a broader term covering every possibility of graphic or symbolic representation. Creatures in heaven, on earth, and in the underworld ocean are excluded as models. Israel is forbidden either to "bow down" or to "serve" such idols or images; i.e., show outward gestures of honor and veneration, or engage in the public and private cult of them. Even if such idols or images purport to represent Yahweh, Israel's god (think of the golden calf in Bethel and Dan, I Kings 12:28-29!), they are taboo. The worship of Yahweh cannot tolerate them, because they give a wrong and misleading notion of who and what sort of god Yahweh is. Yahweh cannot be symbolized by a concrete image because such an image tends to reduce him to a single, isolated quality or power, and Yahweh is beyond all reduction. He cannot be present in an idol because he is sovereignly present everywhere in the world. He comes to Moses out in the desert, in a bush that burns

75

but is not reduced to ashes. He comes to Jacob in the open field at night, on his way to Paddan-Aram. He is everywhere present with his power and personal concern, but he cannot be grasped or captured. The second commandment guards against a prevalent evil in the cultural world of ancient Israel: domesticating God, depriving him of his sovereign lordship. Yahweh can be no falcon soaring in the sky, or the sun shining in the heavens. He is no sacred tree growing by a spring. He is purely spiritual -- spiritual in an eminently sovereign and personalistic way. This is what is meant also in John's Gospel (4:24), "God is spirit, and those who worship him must worship in spirit and truth."

(b) The third commandment, forbidding cultic and magical manipulation[39]

"Thou shalt not take (nāśā', "lift up," "mention") the name of Yahweh in vain (leśāw', "for no good purpose," "idly.")." So reads the third commandment of the Decalogue (Ex. 20:7, Deut. 5:11).

To raise up a name means invoking it for cultic or quasi-cultic (as in swearing an oath) purposes. Here we fringe on the area of magic and dynamism. The ancients understood well the importance of knowing and using a person's name in order to get his or her attention. Without knowing a person's name, one cannot enter into effective communication or personal interaction. Hence ancient cult and magic are made effective by naming the god or demon in question. The name is an effective handle, which if accompanied by an appropriate ritual, brings the supernatural power under control. Like the bridle for a horse, the name of a god grasps hold of him and puts his power in the service of man. This is what Yahwism prohibits in the third commandment. Israel is forbidden to invoke Yahweh's name for selfish purposes or idle ends, but only for the purposes that this God himself has intended and authorized. He has given his name to man to be celebrated in praise and gratitude and adoration.

This is my name forever, and thus am I to be memorialized thoughout all generations. (Ex. 3:15)

But the third commandment guards against all misuse of Yahweh's name because it involves misuse of his divine

personhood. To understand this, one should perhaps
think of the efforts we make to protect greedy exploit-
ers from capitalizing on the name of a celebrity for
some illicit commercial gain, as, for instance, in an
advertisement or letter of recommendation. The law
would give a person whose name was thus misused the
right to sue the offender for the illicit profits, and
for punitive damages to boot. In a real sense, this
offense would infringe on the plaintiff's personhood
as well as on his property rights. One's name is an
extension of one's person, and must be guarded jealously.
How much more, then, the name of the grandest of all
personal beings, the God of the Bible? Yahweh says to
Israel, "I have given you my name, but you are not to
use it lightly, irreverently, or to selfish gain. That
is using and abusing me, violating my personhood." If
we really respect other human persons, we do not go
around using their names as handles for controlling
them, or using them to our selfish advantage. If we
truly respect and revere God, we will not use his name
idly, superstitiously, or for selfish purpose.

2. The Anthropomorphism of God

Except in primitive notions of the supernatural as
a blind power, force, or emanation, the gods came to be
envisaged in animal or human form, and are given the
attributes, powers, and passions of these higher forms
of life. Where specifically human analogies are involved, one may properly speak of anthropomorphism or
anthropopathism. The virtues and the vices of human
life are ascribed to Deity -- which is, as we have
observed, a higher, only more powerful manifestation of
the same ontic reality in which humankind itself par-
ticipates.

Books on religious phenomenology are filled with
research about various manifestations of anthropomorphism
in the religions of the ancient and modern world, and
from all of them the student of the Bible has much to
learn.[40] The latter is more specifically interested,
however, in the ancient Near-Eastern religions. Two
recent books are useful to the English reader: Siegfried
Morenz, Egyptian Religion (Ithaca: Cornell University
Press, 1973), and Thorkild Jacobsen, The Treasures of
Darkness, a History of Mesopotamian Religion (New Haven:
Yale University Press, 1978). Jacobsen brings much
relevant material for a comparative diachronic study
by showing that in Mesopotamia, fourth-millenium B.C.
religion understood the gods as providers and fertility
forces, whereas third-millenium metaphors saw them more
as rulers and second-millenium metaphors depict them as
parents. The Bible, coming into existence in the first
millenium and on into the Christian era, flatly rejected
the fertility metaphor as part of its polemic against
Baalism, but combined the rulership and parenthood metaphors.[41] It should be clear from Jacobsen's study that
the Israelites did not invent these metaphors, but
adapted them from its cultural world.

a. In extrabiblical mythologies

Most of the developed religions employ a lesser or
greater degree of an anthropomorphic characterization
of Deity, in which the gods are described in human form,
with human emotions and human activities. In some
religions the gods closely emulate human behavior. Particularly striking is the familiar mythology of Greece

and Rome, in which most of the vices and faults of humankind were attributed to the gods. These human traits are sometimes combined with the most grizzly elements of animalistic behavior. Especially is this true of aspects of the Hindu faith: the Shiva figure and the like. The inclination toward anthropomorphism must be recognized as a more or less logical and necessary development in human religious conceptuality. Wherever the numinous was seen as alive and potent, imagery was taken from the animal, but preferably the human world, to represent it.

It is revealing to compare biblical anthropomorphism with its extrabiblical counterpart. In Egypt, in the Hittite empire, and in Mesopotamia, numerous literary materials, liturgical documents, and mythical texts were developed to give expression to an anthropomorphic representation of Deity, explaining the world of the supernatural on analogies borrowed from observation of human life, and at the same time explaining various experiences and phenomena in human life as based on design and purpose within the supernatural world. The forces from beyond human control that impinged on, and threatened, man's existence were deified and anthropomorphized: the heat of the sun, the driving power of the rain, the force of the wind, the irrepressible greening of the grass.

In Mesopotamia, the first became known as Utu, the second as Ninurta, the third as Enki, the fourth as Dumuzi. Each was personified, praised and celebrated in myth and sacred song. Though there was much crossover and eclecticism, each god or goddess had a specific realm or function and represented a particular area of life force. A good example of this would be Ea/Enki from Sumerian-Babylonian religion. He is the god of fresh water, the fluid that courses through the irrigation ditches and springs up from the earth, bringing fertility to the land. He also becomes the god of wisdom and secret knowledge because of fresh water's power to appear from hidden sources. An analogy has been drawn between two separate realms of reality because each is seen as deriving its force from the same center of power. Another example would Baal, familiar to us from the biblical polemic. Baal can be understood from the Ugaritic myths as a storm god (=Hadad), but also as a god of fertility (=Dagan); the primitive worshiper has drawn an analogy, not very obvious to us but apparent to him, between these two aspects of divinity. Sometimes exceedingly perplexing combinations have been

made, as in the case of the Inanna/Ishtar/Anata figure.
She is a goddess of love, but also of war; a ferocious
lover, but also a blood-thirsty killer. She paradoxically combines the dual aspect of the life principle:
living-dying; loving-hating.

(1)   Representative varieties

(a)   "Enuma Elish," ANET 61ff., representing
       comprehensive anthropomorphism[42]

This is one of the most familiar texts from the
ancient Near East. It is called "the Babylonian creation myth," although the Semitic Babylonians and
Assyrians only borrowed it from their non-Semitic
(fourth millenium B.C.) predecessors, the Sumerians.
The title consists of the two first words in Babylonian
and means, "When above...." The work as a whole is a
classic cosmological (having to do with the origin of
the cosmos) and theogonic (having to do with the generation of the gods) myth, but is structured as a liturgy
for the annual celebration of the enthronement of
Babylon's chief god, Marduk (taking over from Enki,
chief deity of the Sumerians). Although it is highly
lyrical and poetic, it follows a tightly woven narrative
development, in which the various deities engage in
animated conversation and dynamic interaction. The
theme is that of mortal conflict between the forces of
chaos, represented by the primordial ocean, Tiamat, and
her allies, on the one side; and Marduk/Enki, with his
allies, on the other. Tiamat appears as grotesque and
demonic, yet she speaks as a human being. So does also
Marduk, and the other gods as well. Once he is installed in a postion of supreme power, he engages
Tiamat with force and strategm, in the end splitting
her body into two separate parts, which become the earth
and the sky.

As worthwhile as a careful reading of the entire
myth would be, we choose two sections for our present
purpose. We read first of Marduk's birth (ANET 62)
from Tablet I:

In the chamber of fates, the abode of destinies,
A god was engendered, most able and wisest of gods.

In the heart of Apsu [the deep] was Marduk created,
In the heart of holy Apsu was Marduk created.
He who begot him was Ea, his father;
She who bore him was Damkina, his mother.
The breast of goddesses he did suck.
The nurse that nursed him filled him with
        awesomeness.
Alluring was his figure, sparkling the lift of
        his eyes.
Lordly was his gait, commanding from of old.
When Ea saw him, the father who begot him,
He exulted and glowed, his heart filled with
        gladness.
He rendered him perfect and endowed him
        with a double godhead.
Greatly exalted was he above them,
        exceeding throughout.
Porfect were his members beyond comprehension,
Unsuited for understanding, difficult to perceive.
Four were his eyes, four were his ears;
When he moved his lips, fire blazed forth.
Large were all four hearing organs,
And the eyes, in like number,
        surpassing was his stature;
His members were enormous, he was exceeding tall.
"My little son, my little son!
My son, the Sun! Sun of the heavens!"
Clothed with the halo of ten gods,
        he was strong to the utmost,
As their awesome flashes were heaped upon him.

COMMENT: The grotesqueries of this description express
the awe and reverence of Marduk's worshipers, confronted
by the mysterium tremendum of his presence at his royal
shrine. Otherwise his description incorporates typical
human traits. He is conceived and born; he is suckled
as a little child. His father Ea is filled with pride,
boasting of his splendor and expressing tenderness and
endearment. He has a mouth, eyes, ears, and limbs
(members), but more and bigger than any other.

We choose also, from Tablet IV, the lines that
depict the confrontation between Marduk and Tiamat. As
in the story of David's battle with Goliath in I Samuel
17, there is first a mutual exchange of taunts, then
the combat (ANET 66-67):

Tiamat emitted [a cry], without turning her neck,
Framing savage defiance in her lips;

"Too [imp]ortant art thou [for] the lord of
    the gods to rise up against thee!
Is it in their place that they have gathered,
    [or] in thy place?"
Thereupon the lord, having [raised] the flood-
    storm, his mighty weapon,
To [enraged] Tiamat he sent word as follows:
"Why art thou risen, art haughtily exalted,
Thou has charged thine own heart to stir up
    conflict,
. . . .
Thou hast appointed Kingu as thy consort,
Conferring upon him the rank of Anu,
    not rightfully his.
Against Anshar, king of the gods, thou seekest evil
[Against] the gods, my fathers,
    thou hast confirmed thy wickedness.
[Though] drawn up by thy forces,
    girded on thy weapons,
Stand thou up, that I and thou meet
    in single combat!"
When Tiamat heard this,
She was like one possessed;
    she took leave of her senses.
In fury Tiamat cried out aloud.
To the roots her legs shook both together.
She recites a charm, keeps casting her spell,
While the gods of battle sharpen their weapons.
Then joined issue Tiamat and Marduk,
    wisest of gods.
They strove in single combat, locked in battle.
The lord spread out his net to enfold her,
The Evil Wind, which followed behind,
    he let loose in her face.
When Tiamat opened her mouth to consume him,
He drove in the Evil Wind that she close not
    her lips.
As the fierce winds charged her belly,
Her body was distended and her mouth was wide open.
He released the arrow, it tore her belly,
It cut through her insides, splitting the heart.
Having thus subdued her, he extinguished her life.
He cut down her carcass to stand upon it....

COMMENT: Even the monstrous Tiamat has humanlike organs:
mouth, legs, belly, heart, intestines. Like Marduk,
she uses sarcasm and irony in her taunt. One can en-
visage the scene as similar to any violent struggle
between man and man, or man and beast, except for the
fact that mysterious forces like the Evil Wind play a

crucial role (so regularly in ancient battle narratives, especially those of the Old Testament, where mysterious forces from God turn the tide of battle, rather than mere human valor).[43]

A selective anthropomorphism in the Egyptian creation myths, ANET 3-6[44]

To articulate their concept of theogony, the Egyptians made use of a variety of dynamic processes observed in animal and human life, from sexual copulation to the effective power of authoritative speech. From our sensibilities, we would rank them on various levels of spiritual value, but in the ancient Egyptian mind they rank equally as alternative concepts of dynamic force. We offer the following extracts, in which a worshiper is speaking to a god, or a god is himself represented as speaking.

> O Atum-Kheprer, thou wast on high on the
> (primeval) hill; thou didst arise as the ben-
> bird of the ben-stone in the ben-house in
> Heliopolis; thou didst spit out what was Shu,
> thou didst sputter out what was Tefnut. Thou
> didst put thy arms about them as the arms of a
> ka, for thy ka was in them.
> The gods came into being as Ptah: --
> Ptah who is upon the Great Throne...;
> Ptah-Nun, the father who [begot] Atum;
> Ptah-Naunet, the mother who bore Atum;
> Ptah the Great; that is, the heart and tongue
>   of the Ennead;
> [Ptah]...who gave birth to the gods;...
> There came into being as the heart, and there
> came into being as the tongue, (something) in
> the form of Atum. The mighty Great One is Ptah,
> who transmitted [life to all gods], as well as
> (to) their ka's, through this heart, by which
> Horus became Ptah, and through this tongue, by
> which Thoth became Ptah.
> (Thus) it happened that the heart and tongue
> gained control over [every] (other) member of
> the body, by teaching that he [Ptah] is in
> every body and in every mouth of all gods,
> all men, [all] cattle, all creeping things,

and (everything) that lives, by thinking
and commanding everything that he wishes.

His Ennead is before him in (the form of)
teeth and lips. That is (the equivalent of)
the semen and hands of Atum. Whereas the
Ennead of Atum came into being by his semen
and his fingers, the Ennead (of Ptah), however,
is the teeth and lips in this mouth, which
pronounced the name of everything, from which
Shu and Tefnut came forth, and which is the
fashioner of Ennead....

Thus all the gods were formed and his Ennead
was completed. Indeed, all the divine order
really came into being through what the heart
thought and the tongue commanded.

[Re says]: I planned in my own heart, and there
came into being a multitude of forms of beings,
the forms of children and the forms of their
children. I was the one who copulated with my
fist, I masturbated with my hand. Then I spewed
with my own mouth: I spat out what was Shu,
and I sputtered out what was Tefnut....

    Appeal to human motivation through extended
anthropomorphism in a Hittite battle ritual, <u>ANET</u> 354-
55:45

    "See! Zithariyas is appealing to all the gods;
he brings his complaints before you. So pass
judgment on his case, all ye gods! Let it be of
great concern to the gods!"

    "In fact they [the sactuaries] have been taken
away by these people not from Zithariyas alone,
they have been taken away from all you gods, all
of you; from the Sun-goddess of Arinna, from
the Storm-god of Nerik, from the Storm-god (and)
from the Patron-god, from Telepinus (and) from
all the (other) gods. From you (also) have his
cities been taken."

    "See! Zithariyas is bringing his case before all
of you, gods. Take your own case to heart! Pass

judgment on your own case in passing judgment on the case of Zithariyas!"

"Blot out the Kashkean country, O gods! Let every single god take thought for his place of worship and win it back!"

COMMENT: The crass cynicism of this appeal is appalling to our sensibilities, yet it was normal in ancient religious practice. The king Zithariyas appeals for divine help in winning back territory. In doing so, he asks not for mercy and generosity, but for jealous self-concern on the part of the gods whose shrines lie within the territory affected. They are no better or worse than the king; that is, all too human, even though mysteriously greater and more powerful.

Illustration of the irrational: Ludlul Bel Nemeqi, ANET 435[46]

The title means, "I will praise the lord of wisdom." This is a Mesopotamian complaint song in which a worshiper appeals for divine help. He approaches the Deity as a person interested in him and willing to help. The element of the irrational that often appears in human behavior emerges in the following words:

Oh that I only knew that these things are
        well pleasing to a god!
What is good in one's own sight
        is evil for a god.
What is bad in one's own mind
        is good for his god.
Who can understand the counsel of the gods
        in the midst of heaven?
The plan of a god is keep waters,
        who can comprehend it?
Where has befuddled mankind ever learned
        what a god's conduct is?

COMMENT: This represents the dead-end of anthropomorphism. Human beings conceive of the gods as like themselves in order to control and influence them. When the gods display the human traits of erratic non-responsiveness and irrational unconcern, the numinous

becomes demonic and threatening. The human worshiper
has no reward for his devotion; his god has become too
much like himself.

(2)   Anthropomorphic personification as caricature

There is very lively action going on in these
stories. The gods and goddesses do everything -- only
on a larger scale -- that any human being could be
expected to do. All sorts of human emotions, activites,
and qualities are attributed to the various gods. They
talk excitedly among themselves, plot together, and
decide the course of events in heaven and on earth.
There is a clear order of priority among them: some
are high up in the privy council, with the chief god
(Anu/El/Re) in the highest height, while other gods
occupy a rank beneath. The course of the universe is
ordained in their administration, yet the gods are
themselves subject to decrees and fates and predetermined times. None -- not even the heaven god -- is
absolutely unlimited in power and capacity. One of the
most startling facts about them is the limitedness of
each individual god. There is no universality among
them. Rank there is, but no omnipotence. The very fact
that there are so many gods is evidence of the desire of
the human heart for a principle of universality, yet
this cannot be found in one particular divine figure.
The individual gods are understood as having will,
thoughts, and emotions -- a life at least as active as
our human life -- but each limits all others, just as
in human life.

In what sense are we justified in calling this
conception "personification?" To what extent has ancient nonbiblical religion succeeded in producing a
valid concept of divine personhood? True, there is a
reaching for personhood as transcendent otherness.
Analogies are drawn from the observation of human
persons. However, in every case the distinct element
of personification remains as a caricature, rather than
as a genuine and worthy insight into the secret of
sovereign personhood.

Cartoonists are masters of caricature, delineating
in a few bold storkes one simple, isolated, and unavoidably distorted aspect of the subject's personhood. Thus

Charles De Gaulle's nose, or Richard Nixon's jowls, or
Jimmy Carter's teeth. In the realm of human interaction
we are constantly falling into the temptation of caricaturing our fellow human persons. Think of the waitress saying, as she brings her serving tray to the
table, "Let's see, you are the ham sandwich, aren't
you?" How drastically my personhood has been reduced
when I have become a ham sandwich! True, it is just
a way of speech, yet it does represent a common tendency.
Just as, to the waitress, I have no importance to her
person beyond receiving and paying for a ham sandwich,
my significance in other persons' lives is ever in
danger in becoming the caricature of my personhood.
It is easier for us to deal with other persons by getting an easy handle on them; we are really threatened
when we are confronted with the complexity of their
real personhood, along with the unavoidable responsibility of relating to them as persons.

Essentially this caricaturing is what happens in
the anthropomorphism of nonbiblical religiosity. Utu
is righteousness, Enlil is authority, Enki is creativity.
It makes no difference that paradoxical combinations are
produced, such as the depiction of Inanna/Ishtar as
goddess of love and of war, for the apparent opposites
simply express the contradictions of human life.

(3) The breakdown of personalistic interaction

Students of ancient religion agree that the gods
fall into three distinct categories: (1) representatives of primordial forces; (2) territorial rulers;
(3) personal patrons. We are reminded of Thorkild
Jacobsen's historical analysis of the development of
Mesopotamian religion, mentioned above, showing that
the first type predominated in the fourth millenium,
the second in the third millenium, and the third in the
second millenium, B.C.[47] When Mesopotamian society was
yet living close to nature, it looked for divine force
in its most patent aspects: sun, water, earth, and the
like. As more complex and sophisticated political
structures developed in this region -- and this occurred
chiefly after ca. 3000 B.C., the end of Sumerian civilization -- these peoples showed greater homage to the
ruler-gods of the various city-states, and chiefly
Marduk of Babylon or Asshur of Nineveh. Their respec-

tive myths produced a special place for each deity;
none was left out, even when relegated to a relatively
lower position within the cosmic order. With the tribal
and territorial idea came gradually the notion of a
personal patron, and evidently the individual worshiper
felt free to choose which particular god or goddess to
serve.[48] His impulse was to worship the one who had
shown, on some specific occasion, an interest in him
-- the willingness to respond to his appeals. But what
inference was to be drawn when a worshiper's appeals
went unattended? Had his god ceased to care for him?
Was he occupied elsewhere? Had some other deity --
someone hateful and malevolent -- obtained mastery?
This is the mystery of divine inscrutability that produced anxiety and profound malaise in the hearts of
ancient worshipers, especially in times of political
upheaval and social disruption. Little wonder that by
the time of Christ so many common worshipers in Asia
and Europe had given up belief in a personal god! Where
was there evidence that the ancient deities were effective in response to human need?

b.   The god of Israel

     The Bible likewise uses anthropomorphic images as
symbols of divine personhood. If God is to be understood as sovereign Subject, acting upon us as persons
and interacting with us, human language can scarcely
avoid making use of analogies from human personhood.
Yet the personhood of the biblical God is no caricature,
no reduction of cosmic force to manageable labels. Only
Those models are applied as preserve the concept of his
sovereign otherness (lordship) and the concept of his
intimate concern and commitment to human needs (parenting, fatherhood). Transcendence and immanence, paradoxically related to each other, together express the
full orbit of divine personhood. The biblical God is
near, but cannot be grasped. He responds to our appeal,
but cannot be commanded.

     This is, to be sure, the apt model of human person-
hood. Modern studies in sociology and psychology reveal
the mystery of personhood in human beings. We are all
sovereign subjects reaching out to one another, needing
one another and wanting to be needed, grasping yet
refusing to be grasped. Can any better model be found

to symbolize the transcendently Other, the supreme
Subject?

(1) The unavoidability of "myth"

The word "myth" has a wide range of definitions.
We are already familiar with its specific, formal definition as an aetiological story of gods and men in
primordial interaction, defining cosmological realities.
Nowadays the phenomenologists of religion and the depth-
psychologists are using the word "myth" as a term for
the archetypal images appearing in various kinds of
imaginative conceptuality.[49] The German New Testament
scholar, Rudolf Bultmann, has brought the word "myth"
into the center of modern theological discussion in his
program of "demythologizing" the New Testament.[50]
Mythological language, in the broad sense employed by
Bultmann, means all non-realistic or non-logical language; that is, analogical and symbolical language.
Even Bultmann acknowledges that "myth" in this sense
in inevitable in religious language; only, modern theologians must penetrate beneath the mythological structure of first-century religious discourse to get at the
heart of the Christian proclamation. In reinterpreting
this for the twentieth-century, post-Renaissance mind,
new symbols or "myths" must be found. The question we
must all face is, Can religious thought imagery in a
theological program that remains ture to the biblical
heritage while becoming relevant to the realities of
the modern world?

We cannot avoid making analogies when attempting
to speak about the "wholly Other," simply because we do
not know its (his) own proper language. Religious language therefore must be, and remain, human language.
How are we to experience and speak about God, the wholly
Other, except by comparing our experience of him with
our experience of ourselves and other finite persons?
Thus anthropomorphic language must enter into the structuring of our "mythology." We have to choose between
completely abstractive language, talking perhaps about
an "It" out there -- some kind of force or mind --, and
carefully chosen personalistic images. The Bible insists that its God is a living God. Even the image of
life, ascribed to this God, is no doubt an anthropomorphic symbol; yet a religious discourse that would

avoid   pure abstractionism must make use of it. And if
the biblical God is living, a worthy anthropomorphism
will inevitable choose the language also of thinking,
willing, feeling, and acting to express the meaning of
his being alive. The question is whether the Bible's
choice of anthropomorphic images succeeds in bringing
to better expression the fullness of divine holiness.
We need to look carefully at the principles of biblical
anthropomorphism.

(2)   The sterility of an abstractive God-concept

We recall our previous emphasis on the radical
personalism of biblical religion. This has been eloquently expounded by two eminent Jewish scholars of our
generation, Martin Buber in I and Thou[51] and Abraham
Heschel in The Prophets.[52] Especially in the latter,
one finds an impassioned defense of the concept of a
suffering, involved God. Heschel protests against the
abstractive reductionism of Greek philosophy, which has
deeply influenced Christian dogma. Greek thought rejected the silly caricuatures of mythology, but in doing
so jettisoned all effective personalism with respect to
its notion of supreme Being. Deity is no longer a
"someone" but a "something," a "causeless cause" beyond
all phenomenal experience, the unmoveable mover of all
things, a principle beyond all other principles, a
cause behind all causes. As we suggest, Christian
thought has gone far in applying these Greek notions to
its definition of God; see the treatiese of St. Augustine
St. Thomas, and others. These categories may have
some usefulness in terms of philosophical understanding;
but, as Heschel argues, they must not substitute for
biblical images of God. Biblical language helps us see
that any God who may seriously be believed in must be
one who is somehow intimately involved in our own life,
caring for our suffering, passion and frustration.[53]
How can we be comforted and helped in our sorrow and
pain if we have a God who is not vitally concerned about
them? There is a danger that we misappropriate the
analogy of human suffering and human passion, limiting
our understanding of the biblical God on that basis.
Nevertheless, can we ever do entirely without it? Can
we entrust our life to a strange, remote Deity out in
the outer fringes of the universe, who perhaps got
everything working in primordial time but now sits by,
outside the scene of human turmoil, in abstract, im-
passionate detachment? Is that the God who can help

human beings in their struggling and striving? If one believes the answer to be "no," one must accept that he cannot entirely dispense with a worthy anthropomorphism.

(3) The sobriety of biblical anthropomorphism

The important thing is that we choose appropriate analogies, those that effectively express the depth and richness of human personhood, avoiding demeaning caricature. The Bible has no direct description of God. It very rarely speaks of "seeing" God, and even then guards against irreverence by suggesting that only a fleeting image has been conveyed: thus Ex. 24:10, "there was under his feet as it were a pavement of sapphire stone, like the very heaven for clearness"; Ex. 33:21ff, "And Yahweh said, 'Behold, there is a place by me where you shall stand upon the rock; and while my glory passes by I will put you in a cleft of the rock, and I will cover you with my hand until I have passed by; then I will take away my hand, and you shall see my back; but my face shall not be seen';" Ezek. 1:27-28, "Upward from what had the appearance of his loins I saw as it were gleaming bronze, like the appearance of fire enclosed round about; and downward from what had the appearance of his loins I saw as it were the appearance of fire, and there was brightness round about him. Like the appearance of the bow that is in the cloud on the day of rain, so was the appearance of the brightness round him."[54]

The Bible much prefers the symbol of speaking, emphasizing God's intellect, will, and emotions. That is to say, spiritual qualities, those that characterize personhood, are preferred to physiological elements, except as these may become concrete representations of the spiritual realities behind them. Thus the "eyes" of God symbolize his awareness, the "ears" of God symbolize his attentiveness, his "hand" and "arm" are the symbols of his strength, the "heart" of God betokens his concern. His "mouth" and "tongue" are organs of communication, hence of revelation. Sometimes Yahweh does very human things, like walking in the garden of Eden (Gen. 3:8). This daring image may actually go back to an underlying pre-Yahwistic myth,[55] yet it produces no scandal in its present setting, lending itself very readily to a non-literalistic interpretation. When we compare even so relatively grossly anthropomorphistic

an image with the rife imagery of the Babylonian creation myth, we become aware how modest it actually is.
Certain typical human emotions, such as jealousy,
wrath, compassion and love, are attributed to Yahweh;
but these never give the impression of selfishness or
pettiness or prideful vanity, as in numerous nonbiblical documents.

It is little wonder that Yahweh's presence is often
symbolized by non-anthropomorphic images such as fire
or light, for these are the figures of glorious bril-
liance and mysterious power. A common (mostly early)
image is that of Yahweh's mal'āk, his "messenger" (not
"angel") -- meaning simply the extension of his personal
presence.[56] Another common image is that of Yahweh's
rûaḥ, appropriately rendered "spirit," but meaning also
"wind." The analogy of the force of wind expresses the
coming and the presence of the powerful God. We feel
the wind blowing on us, cooling or heating us, while
unable to see it at all; so too God as spirit. Without
our will God comes and moves and drives us. "The spirit
(pneuma = rûaḥ) blows where it wills, and you hear the
sound of it, but you do not know whence it comes or
whither it goes." (John 3:8)[57]

In late Old Testament literature there is a marked
tendency -- intensified in postbiblical Judaism --
toward an abstractive transcendentalizing of the divine
image. In the deuteronomic literature there is preference for "the Name" (haššēm) as a surrogate for "Yahweh."
[58] Eventually the Jews refused to actually pronounce
their God's proper name, even when reading it in the
sacred text. Because the Jews would speak "ᵃdōnây"
(my lord) where they read the Tetragrammeton, YHWH, the
Massoretes inserted the vocalization for that name,
resulting in the strange hybrid that became "Jehovah"
in European religious usage. The rabbis of the Talmudic
period regularly used surrogates like "the Glory" or
"the Presence."

A somewhat different tendency was at work in the
occasional hypostatization of the term ḥokmâ, "wisdom,"
which is personified as a woman in Proverbs 8 and
Ecclus. 1, 24. It is likely that more was at work here
than a purely metaphorical play on the feminine gender
of this Hebrew word. The female deity Isis plays a
wisdom-giving and life-providing function in Egyptian
mythology, similar to the role assigned to ḥokmâ in the
above-mentioned biblical passages. Furthermore, the
(male) deity of Mesopotamian religion, Ea/Enki, was

92

both a wisdom-giver and a life provider. Hebrew creationism may have seen appropriate imagery in its semi-
personification of divine Wisdom, which performs God's
work of undergirding the structure of all reality, while
bringing all of life into a pattern of harmonious purpose.[59]

    (4) The ultimate anthropomorphism: Christological
        incarnationism

    Israel knew God as "Yahweh" -- a name first re-
vealed to Moses (Exodus 3). At first he was intimately
close, but later grew transcendently remote. Neither
Jews nor Christians continue today to call God by this
all-but-forgotten name. Generic names, like God (=El,
Allah), have been forced to serve, but these are sheer
appellatives, and as such fall short of expressing the
uniqueness of a Deity who reveals himself as infinitely
personal.

    Another personal name -- that of an ancient
Palestinian Jew, Jesus -- is often spoken in contemporary Christian devotion, serving as the virtual equivalent of "God." It was Greek influence in the late
sections of the New Testament and in the early church
that ventured to confer on a mortal man the ontological
status of Deity. In the Hebraic mode of conceptuality,
Jesus would have represented Deity in a relational, not
in an ontological sense. He manifested the divine image
in unique perfection, fulfilling a task assigned to mankind as a whole in virtue of creation (Genesis 1), thus
becoming the "second Adam." Jesus Christ was the "Son
of God" because he faithfully mirrored God, even in his
tragic dying. It was natural that the early church
gradually came to assign supernatural functions and
powers to him, identifying him firmly as the victorious,
saving Messiah and also the transcendent "Son of Man."
It was a radical step beyond this that went so far as to
identify him as God.[60]

    Not surprisingly, gnosticizing doceticism -- the
view that the earthly man, Jesus, was a mere apparition
-- became a serious challenge to early Christian orthodoxy. Although the church repudiated this heresy, its
Christological compromises have never resolved the philosophical difficulties created by calling a man God.
The contemporary challenge for Christians is to take
seriously their Christology, but with proper, genuinely

biblical limits on this potent anthropomorphic symbol.
To equate the biblical God with one of his creatures is
a stark betrayal of biblical faith. To attribute ontological godhood to the creaturely man, Jesus, may be the
ultimate idolatry, Jesus was "divine", but in the sense
that he was like God, and that God was like him. The
God who was once known as Yahweh became uniquely manifest in him; even so, Jesus Christ did not exhaust the
meaning and the fulness of God.

Excursus on the Christological titles

     The title "Lord" (Grk. kúrios, equivalent to Heb.
ᵃdōnây, a surrogate for Yahweh) came to be applied to
Christ equally with God. This is honorific and appellative. It did not directly imply Deity in an ontological sense.

     The title "Son of God" was unquestionably applied
to Jesus even among the first generation of Christians.
They were, however, all Jews, who, although to some
extent influenced by Greek modes of thought, would have
remained essentially Hebraic in their thinking about
God. Both in Hebrew and in Aramaic, "son of" means one
who is very similar to someone or something else. Thus
"son of eighty" means one who belongs to the group of
octagenarians. "Son of Belial" means a worthless
fellow. "Son of man" simply means "mortal human being."
"Son of God" means one who is very much like God -- one
who reveals him and mirrors him, one who is closely
related to God and completely under his direction.[61]
Since the Hebrews rejected the pagan notion of geneo-
logical generation among the gods, how could they have
conceived of God actually begetting man, a human being?
Though "son of God" is a name that was applied to Jesus,
this was certainly not meant in a generative sense.
Jesus of Nazareth was so God-filled, in the church's
adoring memory, that he was a true "Son of God."[62]

     Once Christianity became predominantly gentile,
Greek modes of thought drastically modified this early
conception. The Greeks, like other nonbiblical religion-

ists, had no difficulty in conceiving of men actually being generated by the gods; there were in fact men who were half divine, as there were gods who were half human. Thus the Hebraic confession of Jesus as "Son of God" was modified to mean that God had actually begotten him. The early church confessed Christ as "the only-begotten Son of God" while Mary, elevated to celestial glory, became theotokos, "the Mother of God." In trinitarian formulations, the Latin church's personae (actually, actors or roles on a stage), as applied to the Father, the Son, and the Holy Spirit, retained more of the original Hebraic conception than the Greek church's equivalent, hypostaseis, "modes of being." It is the Nicene Creed that is the most insistent in declaring that Christ shared the metaphysical substance (ousia) of the Father.[63]

(5) Sexual imagery and the divine fatherhood

As has been stated, the Bible develops the image of sovereign lordship to express its notion of divine transcendence. To represent the element of immanence, it chooses the symbol of fatherhood. The two complement each other. Fatherhood prevents lordship from becoming overpowering and remote, just as lordship prevents fatherhood from becoming sentimentalized and maudlin. The biblical God is a Lord who governs us, decreeing our existence and ruling our life, yet in a fatherly, compassionate, and infinitely caring way.

The notion of divine fatherhood has been very precious to the church. Has the church not made as the first article of its Creed the confession, "I believe in God the Father, maker of heaven and earth?" Yet the advocates of a radical feminism are demanding that we cease to speak of God as Father. How does this square with the most authentic impulses of biblical religion? Is divine fatherhood offensive to the humanistic spirit? If it is really offensive, it should no doubt be discarded, along with other outworn symbols. Or have some taken offense through misunderstanding and intolerance?

The Old Testament employs frequently, and with rich variation, the image of divine fatherhood. One should observe that in the vast preponderence of occurrences, it is Israel as a people to whom God is related as Father, not the individual Israelite. Thus Jesus

enjoyed a very unique relationship with God as his
Father (cf. John 14:2-7, etc.).[64] Appropriately, the
Old and New Testaments apply the corresponding figure
of wife (but never of mother!) to the human counterpart
of God as Father. Thus we come across passages in
which Israel is symbolized as Yahweh's wife (Hosea 2,
Jeremiah 2-3, Ezekiel 16, 23), just as the church becomes the bride of Christ in Eph. 5:21-32; cf. Rev.
21:2, 9. For the Old Testament, the symbol of Israel
as Yahweh's bride is a very daring one, yet it is carefully chosen to express the intimate personalism of a
relationship that has been threatened by Israel's intimate personalism of a relationship that has been threatened by Israel's infidelity and apostasy.

Isaiah 54:1-8 has a specially beautiful expression
of the fidelity and love of a husband, conscious of his
wife's waywardness, yet yearning for her and restoring
her to himself:

> Sing, O barren one, who did not bear;
>> break forth into singing and cry aloud,
>> you who have not been in travail!
> For the children of the desolate one will be more
>> than the children of her that is married,
>> says Yahweh.
> . . . .
> Fear not, for you will not be ashamed;
>> be not confounded, for you will not be
>> put to shame;
> For you will forget the shame of your youth,
>> and the reproach of your widowhood
>> you will remember no more.
> For your Maker is your husband,
>> Yahweh of hosts is his name;
> And the Holy One of Israel is your Redeemer,
>> the God of the whole earth he is called.
> For Yahweh has called you
>> like a wife forsaken and grieved in spirit,
>> like a wife of youth when she is cast off,
>> says your God.
> For a brief moment I forsook you,
>> but with great compassion I will gather you.
> In overflowing wrath for a moment
>> I hid my face from you,
>> but with everlasting love I will have
>> compassion on you, says Yahweh, your Redeemer.

The essential bond of husband and wife is covenantal faithfulness, in which each commits him or herself

to the other. When one or the other forsakes this vow,
estrangement comes. Because this is true in the intimate interrelationships of human husbands and wives, it
is an apt image, picked up in the Bible and used effectively for the condition of Israel's apostasy, rejection, and restoration.

As early a prophet as Hosea, and later, most effectively, the prophet Jeremiah, used the image of the
faithless wife--one who has gone the way of harlotry
and has forsaken her true love--after whom this husband
nevertheless yearns and whom he seeks in redeeming love.

So bold does the Bible become. But a question arises concerning the propriety of also employing the image
of God as wife or mother.[65] Some facile popular treatments have, in fact, been playing to the galleries on
this question, claiming that the Bible does ascribe certain feminine qualities and characteristics, such as
motherly compassion, to God. Much has been made, for
instance, of the frequent ascription to Yahweh of
rahāmâ, usually translated "compassion," but from a
more concrete noun, rehem, meaning "womb." We must be
very cautious about claiming this as implying a distinctively feminine attribute, for metaphorical license
is a more appropriate explanation than any confusion
about Yahweh's sexual identity.[66] Is this not, in fact,
entirely within the bounds of proper symbolization?
Cannot a loving father experience something akin to a
mother's uterine emotions? We may be instructed by
reading very closely another passage in which Yahweh
claims this emotion for himself. It is Isa. 49:14-15,
which comes as close an any biblical text to claiming
maternal emotions for Yahweh:

> Zion said, "Yahweh has forsaken me,
>   my Lord has forgotten me."
> Can a woman forget her sucking child,
>   that she should have no compassion on the son of
>   her womb?
> Even these may forget, yet I will not forget you.

We note that the compassionate woman in question is not
Yahweh himself. Yahweh simply has more compassion,
greater fidelity, than such a mother, for he does what
they seldom, but sometimes, forget to do.

Apart from this sort of tangential allusion, the
mother image is studiously avoided in the Bible, and the
reason is actually not hard to find. In the first

place, the choice of the parenting image is a very vital one, one that is used very effectively in the Bible for expressing the intimate relationship of God to his people. It accentuates his obligation to them as well as their obligation to him. True, the parenting image does emerge in a number of nonbiblical texts as well, but never so freely and consistently as in the Bible. The Bible speaks of the fatherhood of God as the perfect epitome of a devoted, loving, concerned, conscientious care of the part of the Deity for his needy and often wayward children. Where do we find an image so moving as that of Hos. 11:1-3?

> When Israel was a child, I love him,
>> and out of Egypt I called my son.
> The more I called them, the more they went from me;
>> they kept sacrificing to the Baals and burning
>> incense to idols.
> Yet it was I who taught Ephraim to walk, I took
>> them up in my arms;
>> but they did not know that I healed them.
> I led them with cords of compassion, with the bands
>> of love,
>> and I became to them as one who eases the yoke
>> on their jaws,
>> and I bent down to them and fed them.

Yet this God is a he, not a she. He is Father, not Mother. Since personhood is vital and parenthood is important, the Bible never refers to the Deity as an "it," for this would utterly depersonalize him. It is worthwhile taking note of the fact that the Hebrew language has no neuter pronoun, as in the Greek, and in our English language. In Hebrew, nouns, pronouns, adjectives and verbs have either the masculine or the feminine gender, so that even inaminate objects are given the one gender or the other. This is not to say that inanimate objects are personified as having sexual characteristics True, this may occur metaphorically, as in the frequent references to Jerusalem as "she." However, this is scarcely more than a linguistic convention, according with the custom of referring to all geographical entitie as feminine.

So if God is to have personhood, he must be addressed--and referred to--as feminine or masculine. It cannot be feminine for a reason that we moderns can scarcely comprehend within our own cultural background. It has more to do with Israel's struggle for religious distinctiveness than with any patriarchal social bias it may have inherited from cultural ancestors. The deepest reason for Israel's avoidance of the motherhood image in reference to its God is its tense apologetic against vegetative religious concepts.[67] The alternative to emergent biblical faith were one or another form of vegetative or fertility religion, in which the principle of procreation becomes directly deified. The numinous lay immediately in the power of generation and reproduction. We find this in the Mesopotamian religions, in the religion of Egypt, but especially in the closest rival of the Hebrew's faith--that of Canaanite religion in Palestine. It was with them that the early Hebrews came into close contact. They had to struggle from the very beginning of their settlement among the Canaanites because of the overpowering attractiveness of this religion. The mythology and ritual of the Canaanite religion (known to us now especially from a near neighbor, that of the city of Ugarit on the north-Syrian coast) were rife with images and imitations of the sexual activity among the deities. Little wonder, then, that the pantheon of such cultures had numerous female deities along with the males. Sexual identification is applied without restraint to each particular deity, but particularly to those that are directly associated with the life-forces. The Israelites early on learned about the male fertility-god, Baal, and the female fertility-goddess, Astarte. It was the copulative interaction of such gods that guaranteed the fructification of nature! Little wonder that the Canaanites were so fond of these particular gods! The earth's fertility is indeed an amazing and miraculous process, one that ought to excite the wonder and admiration of any sensitive human spirit. We ourselves observe the power of animal and human reproduction: a new born lamb, a chick hatched, a baby born to a human mother, the grass becoming green in the springtime after a long period of dryness, the flowers blooming, the corn growing. Such were literally the products of a divine force for the primitive mind, and the tendency of worship it was irresistible. Little is the wonder, then, that the Israelites found it essential, in trying to maintain monotheism as the vehicle of a very meaningful personalism in their concept of God, to resist the impulse represented by Baal and Astarte. To make concessions would have lead to polytheism and a breakdown of the unity and universality of the divine image, as in the words of Elijah's challenge to the vacillating Israelites, "How long will you go on limping on two opinions?" But the people were already so far gone that they "did not anwer him a word." (I Kings 18:21) Futhermore, the introduction of sexual identifications of the gods into Hebrew religion would have tended to produce vegetative pantheism, shattering the oneness and the lordship.[68]

Thus the ancient Hebrews had to contend so directly with the concept of divine motherhood, as objectified especially in the Asherah-figures associated with the Canaanite earth mother, that they came strenuously to repudiate the motherhood image in their god Yahweh. They wanted a parent image, but had to repudiate the mother image. The danger of introducing the mother image into their concept of Deity lay in its pointedly vegetative implications. Because the infant is attached to its mother very intimately, first by the umbical cord within the womb, then in the mother's arms and at her breast, it has a feeling of direct biological derivation from her. Gradually the infant gets to know its father-- if he remains within the family circle--as intimate companion, provider, parent, teacher, but it is only the force of educational development that teaches him that this male shared responsibility for its conception. Thus the image of mother was heavily laden with pantheistic potentialities, appropriate to a monistic, vegetative religion like that of Canaan, but was unavoidably destructive to the monotheistic faith.

This is what was at stake in the Bible's rejection of the mother symbol. As we trace the further history of our religious tradition, we observe that a pristine father symbol was in danger of falling into the opposite error. The biblical God did become rigidly patriarchal, reflecting an increasingly severe social patriarchalism as experienced by the early church as well as by rabbinical Judaism. We should not be amazed, therefore, that a counter-movement arose in catholic Christianity, seeking a feminine surrogate in the figure of the Virgin Mary, dubbed "Mother of God," but in fact fulfilling the cravings of worshippers who saw motherhood as a worthy symbol for the numinous Other in control of our precarious creaturely existence.

Now that times have changed, should we begin to call God "Mother"? Who will forbid those to whom this would be a meaningful expression of authentic biblical faith? But it is not too late to rebaptize religious symbols? And besides, have the perils of pantheism in fact been permanently sanitized?

How about "Parent" for God? This would indeed allow sexual ambiguity. But the word "parent" is a functional

rather than natural term. Parents do not, in fact,
exist; only male and female human beings who may or may
not become parents exist. To call God "Parent" is as
vapid as calling him "Mind" or "Power" or "Love" because
abstractions do not make effective symbols for Deity.

If we are to retain the Bible's peculiar combination of transcendence and immanence, we may have no
other choice than to call God "Father," and to keep on
referring to him in the masculine gender. But two
things must be said: (1) the biblical God is not bi-
sexual (as some blithe spirits have been claiming!) but
radically asexual. In what text are specifically male
attributes or activities claimed for Yahweh (apart from
the forementioned husband/Yahweh, wife/Israel passages,
where only the spiritual qualities of the marriage relationship are in view)? True, Yahweh gets angry,
punishes, even fights; but females do these things too,
depending on the circumstances. (2) The masculine
gender is little more than a linguistic convention; in
the case of its use with reference to the biblical God,
it functions to express his personhood, nothing more.[69]

Excursus: On calling God "you"

Until very recently liturgical English preserved
the singular and plural distinctions in the second-
personal pronouns. Singular "thou, thy/thine, thee"
and plural "you, your/yours, ye" were retained in
prayer to the Deity, along with the appropriate verbal
inflections. Both the RSV and NEB, official versions
for the English-speaking churches, continue this usage.
But suddenly our public worship has been swept clean of
it, and we are calling God "you."

Three things have been responsible for this change:
(1) eagerness to adopt "the language of the people" and
to jettison traditionalism; (2) relative illiteracy in
a generation of newly ordained ministers, unable to
cope with the verbal forms that accompany the "thees"
and "thous"; (3) modernization of the liturgy in the
Roman Catholic Church, which has made an abrupt change
from Latin to the common English "you."

There is nothing sacrosanct about "thou" and "thee"
for the Deity. A debate in support of this claim would
fall on its face because these are only the old familiar

forms, retained for the Deity when common speech shifted over the the plurals, as has occurred likewise in current French and German. Looking to the Bible for an example is no help because the Hebrew and the Greek use the identical pronoun forms for God as for man. Yet this point should be observed: until the recent revolution, our liturgical English did possess a special pronoun for address to the Deity, and is it not an advantage to be able to speak to the divine "Thou" as a Person not altogether like human persons? What is it that we want to emphasize when we speak to God: his transcendance or his immanence? In contemporary Protestant worship, the danger of overfamiliarizing God is far greater than the danger of making him too fearful and too remote; therefore "Thou" could help preserve that sense of mysterium tremendum that our gawking, back-slapping generation seems to miss so sorely. This may be a futile plea, but it does express a concern that is genuinely relevant to the topic of divine transcendence and divine immanence within an appropriate biblical scheme of understanding.

c. A valid God-concept for today

The Bible has chosen to speak of God in analogies from human personhood that are authentically expressive of human personhood in its deepest dimensions and in its highest nobility, avoiding the superficiality and abusiveness of every kind of caricature. Because it uses images of divine personhood that open the way to a richer understanding of God as person, it leads also to a deeper awareness of human beings as persons, opening up the pathway to the dimensions of faith.

Above all, what the Bible is anxious to secure is a radical personalism in its understanding of God and of man. Yahweh may be like the wind, but he is more than wind. He may be like the fire, but he is more than fire. These are only symbols, manifestations, revelations; and his inner being remains hidden behind the supernatural appearances. Yahweh may appear in the cult, but he may also appear in the remote desert, in a fiery bush. Wherever his presence is apprehended, his worshipers see no more than sparks from the inner light of his ineffable glory.

Where the biblical God does choose to appear the

most fondly is in human life; that is to say, in certain persons and peoples he chooses as special manifestations of his presence. This was the experience of great charismatic persons like the prophets. An awareness of being vehicles of the divine presence among his people Israel inspires their preaching and draws their entire earthly existence into the divine service. Think of an Amos or a Jeremiah or an Ezekiel. The biblical tradition of the elusive Presence produces at last the most righteous Jew of all, Jesus of Nazareth, who was so highly aware of God's will governing his life that he became the very "Son of God." Jesus Christ was, as it were, the very personification of God in human flesh. This is the deepest meaning of the incarnation. He is God's final and absolute self-revelation in the sense that his life revealed the presence of God as fully and finally as human life may ever reveal it. Jesus showed in his passion and in his triumph over death the deepest secret of the divine purpose and the divine personhood; that is, Jesus' willingness to die upon the cross revealed that God himself is with us in our suffering; Jesus' triumph over death reveals that death cannot defeat God.

Thus the Bible's anthropomorphism--and especially the ultimate anthropomorphism of the incarnation--offers us a valid God-concept for today. No science or philosophy or theology will be able to dispense with the rich insights that it has to offer.

Ultimately, biblical personalism becomes the model and basis for Hebraic humanism and humanitarianism, of which we shall have more to say later. This may be the ultimate criterion of the Bible's universal validity. The Bible can stand the test of whether it is genuinely applicable to human needs in every age and at all times because it is essentially humanistic in the best sense of the word. Already in the Old Testament, and then by inheritance in the New Testament as well, the divine pathos is altogether directed toward the salvation and well-being of humankind. The appropriate image of divine personhood, still applicable today, is that of sovereign Lord, along with that of compassionate, committed Father. The biblical God is not subject to the beck and call of his human worshipers, yet he is ever responsive to them. They are unable to control or manage him, or to use him to their selfish ends, yet he always turns to them, controlling all their life to their ultimate well-being, working for the enrichment of their authentically personal existence. This is the very heart of the biblical heritage.

In attempting to identify and elaborate a valid
God-concept for today, we need to ask very seriously
whether the concept of God that we choose answers the
real and burning questions of human existence, those
that we know are real within our experience. Can we
be satisfied with any conception of God that is devoid
of personalistic pathos? That is to day, can we do
without the awareness of a God who cares, a God who
answers, a God who acts? If we have neutered our God,
or objectified our image of him, depriving him of these
endearing qualities, we have lost the essence of biblical faith. How can a man at all believe in himself
unless he sees some meaning and purpose in his existence, and how can he find these without the image of
a God who can help him, and will?

This is the first of the great achievements of
biblical faith, one worth struggling to retain, and
worth striving to fulfill.

FOR FURTHER STUDY

On the Holy; revelation:

H. Balz, G. Wanke, Theological Dictionary of the New Testament (hereinafter TDNT), IX, 189ff., phobeō, etc.

    The word group among the Greeks
    Phobos and phobeomai in the Old Testament
    Fear in Palestinian and hellenistic Judaism
    The word group in the New Testament
    Fear in the early church and gnosticism

J. Behm, TDNT, IV, 742ff., morphē, etc.

    The form of God in the Old Testament and Judaism
    The morphē of Christ in the New Testament

W. Eichrodt, TOT, I, 206ff., 228ff.

    The nature of the covenant God
    Affirmations about the divine being
    Affirmations about the divine activity

idem, II, 15ff.

    The forms of God's self-manifestation
        Manifestation of God in the realms of
            nature and of man
        The spiritualization of the theophany

idem, II, 46ff., 69ff.

    The cosmic powers of God
    The spirit of God
    The word of God
    The wisdom of God

H. Kleinknecht, et al., TDNT, III, 65ff., theos, etc.

    The Greek concept of God
    El and Elohim in the Old Testament
    The early Christian fact of God and its conflict
        with the concept of God in Judaism

A. Oepke, TDNT, III, 556ff., kaluptō, etc.

    The idea of revelation in religious history
        generally

Revelation in the Greek world and hellenism
Revelation in the Old Testament
The attitude of Judaism to revelation
Revelation in the New Testament

O. Procksch, K. G. Kuhn, TDNT, I, 88ff., hagios, etc.

The use of the term holiness in the Old Testament
The history of the term in the Old Testament
The concept of holiness in rabbinic Judaism
Hagios in the New Testament

H. W. F. Saggs, The Encounter with the Divine in Mesopotamia and Israel (London: Athlone, 1978)

S. Terrien, EP, 63ff., 106ff., 166ff., 227ff., 410ff., 448ff.

Epiphanic visitation to the patriarchs
The Sinai theophany
The presence in the temple
The prophetic vision
Presence as the Word
The name and the glory

T. C. Vriezen, OOTT, pp. 153ff.

The nature of the knowledge of God as an intimate relationship between the holy God and man

idem, pp. 205ff.

Other ways in which God reveals himself

On myth:

G. Stahlin, TDNT, IV, 762ff., muthos

The development of the meaning
Myth in the Greek world and hellenism
Muthos and myths in the Old Testament (LXX) and Judaism
Muthos in the New Testament

S. Talmon, Theological Dictionary of the Old Testament, tr. J. T. Willis from G. J. Botterweek and H. Ringgren, Theologisch Wörterbuch zum Alten Testament, (Grand Rapids: Eerdmans, 1974--; hereinafter TDOT), III, 427ff., har, gibᶜāh

World mountain
Omphalos
World axis
Cosmological references
Israel's "mountain-god"

H. Traub, G. von Rad, TDNT, V, 497ff., ouranos, etc.

The Greek usage
The Old Testament
The Septuagint and Judaism
The New Testament

On the cultus:

G. Behm, TDNT, III, 180ff., thuō, thusia, thusiastērio
The concept of sacrifice in the New Testament

W. Eichrodt, TOT, I, 98ff.
The covenant statutes: The cultus

B. Kedar-Kopfstein, TDOT, III, 234ff., dam
Ethics and law
Magical power
Eating blood
Blood of sacrifices
Blood of the covenant
Yahweh as avenger of blood

R. Meyer, F. Hauck, TDNT, III, 413ff., katharos, etc.

Clean and unclean outside the New Testament
In primitive religion
In Greek religion
In Old Testament religion
Judaism
Clean and unclean in the New Testament

G. Schrenk, TDNT, III, 221ff., hieros, etc.

The way from Old Testament prophecy to Jewish
apocalyptic and hellenistic
Judaism
The attitude of Jesus and early Christianity
towards the temple
The priest of the Greek world
The priest in the history of Israel
Hiereus in the New Testament
The high-priest in Hebrews

R. J. Thompson, <u>Penitence and Sacrifice in Early Israel</u>
<u>Outside the Levitical Law</u>, Leiden:
Brill, 1963

R. de Vaux. O. P., <u>Studies in Old Testament Sacrifice</u>,
Cardiff: University of Wales
Press, 1964

T. C. Vriezen, <u>OOTT</u>, pp. 250ff.

    The cultus

W. Zimmerli, <u>OTTO</u>, pp. 148ff.

    Israel's sacrificial worship: praise of Yahweh
and cry for help

On idolatry:

J. de Moor, <u>TDOT</u>, I, 438ff., ^{,a}sherāh

J. de Moor, M. J. Mulder, <u>TDOT</u>, II, 181ff., baᶜal

    The Canaanite Baal outside the Old Testament
Baal in the Old Testament

H. D. Preuss, <u>TDOT</u>, III, 1ff., <u>gellulim</u>

G. von Rad, <u>TDNT</u>, II, 351ff., <u>eikōn</u>

    The prohibition of images in the Old Testament

G. von Rad, <u>OTT</u>, I, 203ff.

    The first commandment and Yahweh's holy zeal
The veto on images in the Old Testament

W. Zimmerli, <u>OTTO</u>, pp. 120ff.

    Yahweh's commandment
The first commandment
The prohibition against images and against
naming the name of God

On monotheistic personalism:

E. Barbotin, <u>The Humanity of God</u>, trans. M. J.
O'Connell, Maryknoll: Orbis, 1970

C. Colpe, <u>TDNT</u>, VIII, 400ff., <u>ho huios tou anthrōpou</u>

    The linguistic problem
Old Testament concepts

The Son of Man in the New Testament

R. Kittel, G. von Rad, H. Kleinknecht, TDNT, II, 381ff.,
            eikōn

Images of God and men in Judaism and Christianity
The Greek use of eikōn
The divine likeness in the Old Testament
The divine likeness in Judaism
The metaphorical use of image in the New Testament

H. Koster, TDNT, VIII, 572ff., hupostasis

Greek usage
Hupostasis in Judaism
The New Testament
Further early Christian usage

C. J. Labuschagne, The Incomparability of Yahweh in the
            Old Testament (Pretoria Oriental
            Series, 5), Leiden: Brill, 1966

T. W. Mann, Divine Presence and Guidance in Israelite
            Tradition: The Typology of
            Exaltation, Baltimore: John
            Hopkins, 1977

W. von Martitz et al., TDNT, VIII, 334., huios,
            huiothesia

Ben (bar) as a broader term of association
Ben (bar) as a term of relationship to God
The messiah as Son of God
The Davidic Son of God
The eschatological role of the Son of God and the
    absolute ho huios

W. Zimmerli, OTTO, pp. 17ff., 70ff.

The revealed name
Yahweh, God of Israel since Egypt
Yahweh, God of the fathers: the promise
Yahweh, creator and king

W. Zimmerli, J. Jeremias, TDNT, V, 654ff., pais theou

The ᶜebed YHWH in the Old Testament
The LXX translations
Pais theou in later Judaism in the period after
    the LXX
Pais theou in the New Testament

On divine lordship:

F. M. Cross, _TDOT_, I, 242ff., ʾēl

    ʾēl in the Semitic languages
The character and function of the god El in
                    Canaanite and related texts
El in the Old Testament

O. Eissfeldt, _TDOT_, I, 59ff., ʾādhon

W. Foerster, G. Quell, Bible Key Words from Gerhard
                    Kittel's Theologisch Worterbuch
                    zum Neuen Testament, trans. J. R.
                    Coates, 5 vols., New York: Harper,
                    1951-65 (hereinafter BKW), II/I,
                    "Lord"(=_TDNT_, III, 1034ff.)

    The meaning of the word kurios
Gods and rulers as kurioi
The Old Testament name for God
"Lord" in late Judaism
Kurios in the New Testament

H. Ringgren, _TDOT_, I, 267ff., ʾᵉlōhim

    Concepts of God in the ancient Near East
The three words for God; Definition
ʾᵉlōhim as an appellative
Assertions of incomparability
ʾᵉlōhim as a designation of Yahweh

On divine creatorship:

J. Bergman, H. Ringgren, K.H. Bernhardt, G. von
                  Boterweck, _TDOT_, II, 242ff., bārāʾ
    Theological usage: Of cosmic powers; In the
                  historical realm

W. Eichrodt, _TOT_, II, 93ff.,

    Cosmology and creation

W. Foerster, _TDNT_, III, 1000ff., ktizō, etc.

    Belief in creation in the Old Testament
The doctrine of creation in later Judaism
Creation in the New Testament

G. von Rad, _OTT_, I, 136ff.

The primeval history
    The place in the theology of the witness
                concerning creation
    The pictures of Jahweh's act of creation

On divine fatherhood:

H. Ringgren, TDOT, I, 1ff., 'ābh
    God as Father

C. Schrenk, G. Quell, TDNT, V, 945ff., patēr, etc.
    The father concept in the Indo-European world
                and Graeco-roman antiquity
    The father concept in the Old Testament
    The father concept in later Judaism
    Father in the New Testament

NOTES

1. The Idea of the Holy, tr. J. W. Harvey, London,
   1923; see also Otto, Religious Essays: a Supplement to "The Idea of the Holy," London 1931.

2. See further in S. Plath, Furcht Gottes, Der
   Begriff YR' im Alten Testament, Berlin 1963; cf.
   B. J. Oosterhoff, De Vreze des Heren in het Oude
   Testament, Utrecht 1949.

3. From Chapter I, "Myth and Reality," by H. and H.
   A. Frankfort, The Intellectual Adventure of Ancient
   Man, Chicago and London: University of Chicago
   Press, 1946.

4. See art, "Emperor-worship" (R. M. Grant), IDB, II
   98ff.; E. Stauffer, Christ and the Caesars, trans.
   K. and R. G. Smith, Philadelphia 1955.

5. E. g., Zaphon in Ugaritic mythology, Carmel and
   Jerusalem in the Bible. Cf. W. Robertson Smith,
   Lectures on the Religion of the Semites, 3rd ed.
   (London, 1927), pp. 116ff.; also R. E. Clements,
   "Sacred Mountain, Temples and the Presence of God,"

God and Temple (Oxford 1965), pp. 1ff.

6. J. A. Wilson, tr.

7. Cf. the navel of the earth tradition found in various religions; thus Jerusalem in the Old Testament (see S. L. Terrien, "The Omphalos Myth and Hebrew Religion," VT, 20 [1970], 315-38; also E. A. S. Butterworth, The Tree at the Navel of the Earth, Berlin 1970).

8. Cf. Ezek. 29:1-12

9. J. A. Wilson, tr.

10. In citations, words are enclosed in square brackets as supplied in a broken text by the translator or as supplied by myself with the purpose of furnishing an essential identification for the understanding of the reader. Words in parentheses are supplied by the translator,

11. S. N. Kramer, tr.

12. J. A. Wilson, tr.

13. See J. H. Breasted, The Dawn of Conscience (New York - London, 1933), pp. 366-70; G. Nagel. "A propos des rapports du psaume 103 avec les textes egyptiens," Festschrift für A. Bertholet, W. Baumgartner et al., edd. (Tubingen 1950), pp. 395-403.

14. See n. 5.

15. The classic treatment is Sir James G. Frazer's multi-volume Golden Bough, abridged in a 1940 one-volume edition (New York: Macmillan). Another classic is G. van der Leeuw, Religion in Essence and Manifestation, 2 vols., trans. J. E. Turner from the German (New York 1963). These treat contemporary as well as ancient cultures. The rich and varied literature on ancient Near-Eastern religion is now being assimilated in the ambitious series, "Die Religionen der Menschheit," ed. C. M. Schröder (Stuttgart: Kohlhammer), in which "Aegyptische Religion" by S. Morenz (1960 = Egyptian Religion, Ithaca, N.Y., 1963) has appeared in print, along with H. Gese, "Die Religionen

Altsyriens" (1970). Volumes are projected in this series for the Sumerian (J. J. van Dijk), Babylonian-Assyrian (R. Borger) and Asia Minor (E. von Schuler) religions, with comprehensive bibliographies. A convenient summary of Sumerian, Babylonian-Assyrian, and West-Semitic religions may be found in H. Ringgren, Religions of the Ancient Near East (Philadelphia: Westminster, 1973), where recent literature is cited.

16. Cf. van der Leeuw, op. cit., II, 413ff.; also art. "Myth" (T. H. Gaster), IDB, S. H. Hooke, ed., Myth, Ritual, and Kingship, Oxford 1958.

17. Cf. Breasted, op. cit., pp. 303ff.; Morenz, op. cit., pp. 146-49.

18. On ritual and magic, see E. Lehmann in A. Bertholet and E. Lehmann, edd., Lehrbuch der Religionsgeschichte, I (Tübingen 1925), 87ff.

19. J. A. Wilson, tr.

20. On the following, compare R. de Vaux, Ancient Israel, Its Life and Institutions, trans. J. McHugh (New York 1961), pp. 415-56; H. J. Kraus, Worship in Israel (trans. G. Buswell, Oxford 1966), pp. 112-24. The classic study is G. B. Gray, Sacrifice in the Old Testament, Its Theory and Practice, Oxford 1925.

21. These primitive genres have been described by R. Rendtorff in Die Gesetze in der Priesterschrift (FRLANT 62, Göttingen 1953); cf. W. Malcolm Clark, "Cultic Law," J. H. Hayes, ed., Old Testament Form Criticism (San Antonio: Temple University Press, 1974), pp. 124f.

22. 2nd ed., tr. R. G. Smith, New York 1958.

23. Three vols., Chicago, 1951-63. On the following see especially I, 171-74.

24. The Elusive Presence, pp. 68ff.

25. On the tradition background of this concept, see now Terrien, ibid, pp. 131ff., 197ff. See also art. "Shekinah" (D. Moody), IDB, IV, 317ff.

26. Except in special instances, we offer the RSV text

with the substitution of "Yahweh" for "the LORD."

27. With respect to the Bethel shrine-site, cf. H. J. Kraus, Worship in Israel, pp. 146ff.

28. The actual location of the original mountain(s) bearing these names is unknown; cf. art "Sinai, Mount" (G. E. Wright), IDB. It is not improbable that Horeb and Sinai derive from originally independent traditions, secondarily equated as the same.

29. For further information see the Introductions to the Old Testament and art. "Pentateuch" (D. N. Freedman), IDB, III, 711ff.; see also the "Introduction" to G. von Rad, Genesis, A Commentary (Philadelphia 1961), and M. Noth, A History of Pentateuchal Traditions (tr. B. W. Anderson; Englewood Cliffs, 1970), pp. 5-41.

30. J is vv. 10-11a (up to "place"), 13-16, 19a; E is in vv. 11b-12, 17-18, 20-22. See Terrien, The Elusive Presence, pp. 84f.

31. J is in vv. 3a (up to "wilderness"), 2-4a (up to "to see"), 5, 7-8a, 16-17; E is in vv. 2b, 4b, 6 9-13, 15; v. 14 is a secondary expansion of E. On the interpretation of the meaning of the divine name in this account, see Chapter IV, Introduction, a, 4 ("The Name of God"). On the theophany-epiphany, see Terrien, The Elusive Presence, pp. 109-19.

32. Chap. 27 (J), containing the narrative of the stealing of Esau's blessing; cf. the birthright narrative (J) in Gen. 25:27-34.

33. See "The religion and piety of the psalms" in art. "Psalms, Book of" (J. Hempel), IDB, III, 942ff.; also H. J. Kraus, "Zur Theologie der Psalmen," Psalmen, I (Biblischer Kommentar, Altes Testament XV/1; Neukirchen-Vluyn 1966), pp. LXIVff.

34. See the commentaries. This is one of the rare instances in which the identical text has been preserved (with only minor variations significant to the understanding of the processes of textual transmission) within the Old Testament (cf. also II Kings 18-20 par Isa. 36-39; II King 25 par

Jeremiah 52; parallel passages in Kings-Chronicles).
The Psalms version came naturally into the earliest
Psalter collection, while II Sam. 22:2-51 entered
as a late addition to the deuteronomistic history-
book.

35. I am particularly to my student, Dale Broadhurst,
for the reminder that "in both the biblical and
Vedic traditions, there has been an evolution in
the understanding of the nature of God. Both
traditions have as their point of departure the
ritualistic worship of a god or gods within a
henotheistic cosmology. Both produced sacred
scriptures witnessing the revelatory action of God
within human existence. Both eventually moved to
a universalistic view of God. Both gave birth to
religious movements witnessing the incarnation of
God within the world of man. Trinitarian Christianity at the folklore level is almost indistin-
guishable from the Krishna cult of Vaisnava
Hinduism." (Private communication) What then accounts for the essential difference between the
two? As I have defined it, it is largely the
matter of the seriousness with which the biblical
tradition develops the concept of both divine and
human personhood, producing in Judaism and Christianity an involvement in history and a moral responsibility for social improvement that cannot be
found within the Hindu tradition.

36. See further on this in Chapter IV, 1, b, (1), (b)
"A biblical unicum: Israel is constituted historically rather than mythically."

37. See Frankfort, op. cit., pp. 10ff., also idem,
Kingship and the Gods: A Study of Ancient Near
Eastern Religion as the Integration of Society
and Nature, Chicago 1948; M. Noth, The Old Testament World, tr. V. I. Gruhn (Philadelphia 1966),
pp. 280-87; art. "Idolatry" (J. Gray), IDB, II,
675ff.

38. See B. Childs, The Book of Exodus (Philadelphia
1974), pp.404-9; G. von Rad, Old Testament
Theology, I, 212-19.

39. Cf. Childs, ibid., pp. 409-12; W. E. Staples, "The
Third Commandment," JBL, 58 (1939), 325ff.

40. Cf. G. van der Leeuw, op. cit., pp. 65-187.

41. E. A. Speiser, tr.

43. See I. Seeligmann, "Menschliches Heldentum und gottliche Hilfe," TZ, 19 (1963), 386-411.

44. J. A. Wilson, tr.

45. A. Goetze, tr.

46. R. H. Pfeiffer, tr.

47. Op. cit., passim, summarized on pp. 223-26, "Assessment of Second Millenium Religious Achievement."

48. Cf. W. Robertson Smith, op. cit., pp. 28ff., "The Nature of the Religious Community, and the Relation of the Gods to their Worshippers."

49. Cf. M. Eliade, Myth and Reality, tr. W. R. Trask, New York 1963; also the wide-ranging discussions surrounding the theories of Jung and Levi-Strauss.

50. See Bultmann, "New Testament and Mythology," pp. 1ff. in the symposium, Kerygma and Myth, A Theological Debate, H. W. Bartsch, ed., New York 1961; cf. also Bultmann's books, History and Eschatology (1957) and Jesus Christ and Mythology (1958). For a brief summary of the debate see art. "Myth in the NT" (E. Dinkler), IDB, III, 487ff.

51. M. Buber, I and Thou, tr. R. G. Smith, 2nd ed. New York 1958.

52. New York 1962.

53. Cf. K. Barth, Die Menschlichkeit Gottes, Theologische Studien, 48; Zollikon 1956,

54. Cf. S. Terrien, The Elusive Presence, pp. 257-61

55. See Chapter IV, 1, b, (4) Miracle and Wonder in the Old Testament; Chapter V, 1, c, (2) Death as punishment; (3) The search for immortality.

56. Cf. G. von Rad's discussion on pp. 75ff. in vol. I of Kittel-Friedrich, TWZNT=TDNT.

57. See art. "Spirit" (S. V. McCasland), IDB, IV, 432ff.; cf. art. "Holy Spirit" (G. W. H. Lampe),

IDB, II, 626ff.

58. See art. "Name" (R. Abba), _IDB_, III, 500ff.; also
S. Terrien, _The Elusive Presence_, pp. 138ff.,
197ff.; G. von Rad, "Deuteronomy's 'Name' Theology
and the Priestly Document's 'Kabod' Theology,"
Studies in Deuteronomy, trans. D. Stalker (London
1953), pp. 37ff.; cf. von Rad, _Old Testament
Theology_, I, 47ff.

59. Cf. B. Mack, _Logos und Sophia_, Göttingen 1973;
Terrien, _The Elusive Presence_, pp. 350ff.

60. One of the best presentations of this theme is
U. Mauser, _Gottesbild und Menschwerdung; Eine
Untersuchung zur Einheit des Alten und Neuen
Testaments_, BHT 43, Tübingen 1971, suggesting the
possibilities of fruitful work along these lines;
cf. my review in _JBL_, 92 (1973), 124f. See also
the influential work, D. M. Baillie, _God was in
Christ_ (New York 1955).

61. Cf. P. A. H. de Boer, "The Son of God in the Old
Testament," _OTS_, 18 (1973), 189-207.

62. Cf. R. Bultmann, "Lord and Son of God," _Theology
of the New Testament_, I, 121-33.

63. Cf. B. Lonergan, _The way to Nicea; The Dialectical
Development of Trinitarian Theology_, Philadelphia
1976 (especially pp. 43-55, "Of One Subtance");
E. J. Fortman, _The Triune God, A Historical Study
of the Doctrine of the Trinity_, Philadelphia:
Westminster, 1972 (especially pp. 62-70, "The
Nicene Phase").

64. Cf. J. Jeremias, "Abba," _Abba: Studien zur
neutestamentlichen Theologie und Zeitgeschichte_
(Göttingen 1966), pp. 15-67.

65. See P. A. H. de Boer, _Fatherhood and Motherhood in
Israelite and Judean Piety_ (Leiden: Brill, 1974),
especially pp. 14-48. Amidst a large outpouring
of publications on woman's new role in religion,
few have been so responsible in scrutinizing the
Old Testament on its own term as P. Trible, _God
and the Rhetoric of Sexuality_ (Philadelphia:
Fortress, 1978). Those who have patience to
explore beyond the Bible's culture-conditioned

patriarchalism discover an authentic humanism that breaks out to unparalleled examples of positive appreciation for the worth and dignity of womanhood.

66. Although the verb RḤM is generally employed of Yahweh as subject, it is used also of male human persons, as of Nebuchadrezzar in Jer. 42:12 (cf. negative in Jer. 42:12, 50:42).

67. On the religion-phenomological significance of the God-mother concept, see G. van der Leeuw, op. cit., I, 90-100 ("The Form of the Mother"); also W. Robertson Smith, op. cit., pp. 54-60.

68. See W. Harrelson, From Fertility Cult to Worship, New York 1969.

69. For a thorough and balanced discussion of the entire problem of sexual/sexist imagery and language in theology, see G. H. Tavard, "Sexist Language in Theology" TS, 36 (1975), 700-24.

Chapter II

The Divine Image Mirrored in Human Personhood

"THE RIGHTEOUS GOD"

God's true sovereignty (his responsible freedom
in transcendence) comes to full manifestation with
man's genuine personhood (responsible freedom in finiteness).   Hence, as God is like man (anthropomorphism),
man is like God (theomorphism).

It is in his capacity of being like God in a
personalistic and relational sense (imago Dei), that
man is capable of bringing wrath and judgment on himself; but, in responsible personhood, he also lies open
to the possibility of reconciliation and resoration.
As man is free to change for the worse or the better,
God is free to change the evil in man to the better.

In man's estrangement from God and in his restoration to God, he confronts God as righteous -- a
concept that involves God's judging, but also saving
action.

Introduction: Divine and Human Righteousness in
Judgment and in Salvation

The Hebrew word ṣedeq/ṣ^{e}dāqâ, usually rendered by
dikaiosunē in Greek, covers a wide semantic range. Over
its wide range of nuancing, it adequately expresses an
essential rightness and integrity, in God as well as in
man, binding them together in dynamic interaction.
Whenever this bond is shattered, man the creature experiences the consequences of transgression as wrath;
wherever it is restored, its blessings are experienced
as divine favor and salvation.

a. "Righteousness" as a covenantal ideal

Sometimes ṣ^{e}dāqâ means "firmness" or "truth";
sometimes it means "vindication," "deliverance," or
"salvation." It is, in a word, a prime term for covenant well-being, defined as total rightness in relation
to God and in relation to one's fellow men. If it is
not the full synonym of šālôm ("wholeness," "harmony"),
it is certainly the indispensalbe relational basis for
it. As such, it is the polar opposite of rišᶜâ, "wickedness" (cf. Psalm 1).

In spite of the fact that the verbal root ṢDQ is
occasionally employed in juridical contexts (cf. Ex.
23:7, Deut. 25:1ff.), it is not essentially a legal
term. It serves rather to express the demands of a
correct interpersonal relationship. This is especially
apparent in the earliest traditions, such as are found
in the Jacob-Laban story and in the narrative about Jacob
and Tamar. In Gen. 30:33 Jacob tells his father-in-law
that his ṣ^{e}dāqâ (RSV "honesty") will show up in the
sequel of the way in which he is handling their mutual
business affairs. In Gen. 38:26 the same patriarch
admits that his wronged daughter-in-law is more in the
right than he because her prostitution has been occasioned by his own derogation of duty toward her. The
obligation in each text lies more within the range of
social obligation than of legal requirement. Wherever
human persons had a bond with each other, ṣ^{e}dāqâ was
demanded (along with its synonym, ḥesed, meaning broth-
erly loyalty"). If this was true in relationships with
non-Israelites like Laban and Tamar, it was all the more

true within Israel's unique covenant society, in which
the ideal was to live in complete harmony with one's
fellows, as well as in obedience, devotion, and perfect
fidelity toward the God who had chosen this people and
given them his covenant.

    b.   The "righteousness" of God

    Inasmuch as Yahweh's integrity guaranteed his
covenant with Israel, he was himself often spoken of as
"righteous" (Zeph. 3:5; cf. Gen. 18:25, Ps. 50:6). In
simple translation, this means that God fulfills his
obligation to rule the world as its lord and creator,
for the benefit of his chosen people. Thus "righteousness" is a salvation-word. It is not strange that some
texts speak of Yahweh's saving acts as ṣidqŏt-YHWH
(Judg. 5:11, I Sam. 12:7, Mic. 6:5, Dan. 9:16). Yahweh
governs history by his "righteousness" -- also nature
(cf. Ps. 145:17) and the nations. Over his own peculiar
nation, Israel, Yahweh appointed a king, who was charged
to execute "righteousness" in his name (Ps. 72:1; cf.
110:5-6). This was a prerogative later to be assigned
to the Messiah (cf. Isa. 9:6).[1]

    c. "Righteousness" for the individual Israelite

    Inasmuch as Yahweh's initiative alone arranged the
covenant with Israel, it was clearly Yahweh's prerogative to set up the conditions of "righteousness." One
of the priestly duties, carried out in Yahweh's name and
with his authority, was to declare whether a man were
"righteous" or "wicked" (cf. Ezek. 18:9). It is the
constant source of anguish underlying many of the psalms
of complaint that the distressed worshiper had been
waiting in vain for such a declaration, whether from the
priest directly or by revelation from God. Such a suppliant might indeed have many sins -- might confess them
freely (cf. Psalm 51, Psalm 130) -- yet express confidence that Yahweh would forgive him as one of his
"righteous."

Many are the pangs of the wicked,
 but steadfast love (ḥesed) surrounds him
 who trusts in Yahweh.
Be glad in Yahweh and rejoice, O righteous,
 and shout for joy, all you upright in heart!
(Ps. 32:10-11)

Passages in which a claim is being made to "right-eousness" (cf. Ps. 7:9, 17:1-5, 18:22-24, 26:1-6) are to be understood as referring not to sinlessness or moral perfection, but to this stance of conscious in-tegrity within the framework of covenantal living.

Yahweh's commandments, particularly such codes of apodictic law as are found in the great Decalogue of Ex. 20:2-17, came to serve as an external standard for defining "righteousness" (cf. especially Ezek. 33:14-16, which makes this connection very clear). As such, the commandments were regularly recited in the covenant assemblies (see the model ritual of Deut. 27:11ff.). Before a worshiper was allowed to present himself in temple, he was confronted with the recitation of an entrance-torah, such as is found in Psalm 15 or Ps. 24:3-5:

Who shall ascend the hill of Yahweh,
 and who shall stand in his holy place?
He who has clean hands and a pure heart,
 who does not lift up his soul to what is false,
 and does not swear deceitfully.
He will receive blessing (berākâ) from Yahweh,
 even righteousness (ṣedāqâ) from the God of
 his salvation.

If one were able conscientiously to confess that he was such a person as these lines demanded, he would be wel-come to enter the šaᶜarê-ṣedeq, "the gates of right-eousness" (Ps. 118:19-20), even to full rejoicing in the presence of his God. The ideal of complete and conscious devotion to God's law is presented in such late compositions of Psalms 1 and 119 as the basis for a paradigmatic "righteousness", after which every devout Israelite earnestly strove.

d. "Righteousness" as a spiritual problem

Misconceptions arose as to the possession of "righteousness" or the lack of it, along with some vexing problems concerning God's ways with men. One problem concerned the relation between corporate and individual guilt. It was thought by some that the "righteousness" of a few could redeem many (Gen. 18:22-23, Ezek. 14:12ff.; cf. Isa. 53:4-6); contrariwise, there were some who believed that an individual's "righteousness" would not suffice to release him from the guilt that had fallen on the many. "Righteousness" had become quantified, hence it could be passed down as an inheritance from one's fathers; and so likewise its opposite, "wickedness." The prophet Ezekiel was especially anxious to correct this latter view, which he saw as leading to an immoral fatalism. In the eighteenth and thirty-third chapters of his book he declares emphatically that every individual person is directly answerable before God for his own $\text{s}^\text{e}\text{d}\bar{\text{a}}\text{q}\hat{\text{a}}$ and its consequences. "The soul that sins, it shall die!" (18:4)

Another serious source of misgiving -- closely related to the preceding -- was the undeserved evil (or good) that the practical man observed in his daily experience. "Righteousness" was supposed to produce blessing, while "wickedness" was supposed to produce suffering and evil (so Deut. 30:15ff.). Sometimes the source of inequity lay within convenantal society, and this is the occasion of the complaint psalms. Thus Hab. 1:13:

> Thou who art of purer eyes than to behold evil,
> and cannot look on wrong,
> Why dost thou look on faithless men,
> and art silent when the wicked swallows up
> the man more righteous than he?

Sometimes the problem lay in the inexplicable agonies of a private individual; so Job, with his cry, "How can a man be just (yiṣdaq) before God?" (9:2) Sometimes it lay in the tragedies of international politics, such as led to the ruin of Israel's nationhood. As long as the Jews suffered under foreign imperialism, they were confronted with the disparity between doleful experience and blissful ideal. Was it they, the covenant people, who had ceased to be righteous; or had God himself departed from righteousness? Hard as it was to admit that the first could be true, it was impossible to believe the latter. "Shall not the Judge of all the earth do right?" (Gen. 18:25)

e. Jesus Christ as the most righteous Jew

Church doctrine has made much of the impeccability
(from Lat. peccare, "to sin") of Christ, speculating
whether this should be taken to mean an inability to
sin or a simple absence of sin. The New Testament
lacks, however, unambiguous testimony to this concept.
The strongest prooftext seems to be Heb. 4:15, "We have
not a high priest who is unable to sympathize with our
weaknesses, but one who in every respect has been tempted as we are, yet without sinning." Though this may be
taken to imply more, all it actually affirms is that
Christ remained true to God in every trial and affliction (see the context).

We fall into docetic heresy when we think of Jesus
as a human being who was incapable of any creaturely
error or misunderstanding. Did he never make a mistake
in arithmetic, or never button his coat wrong? This is
hardly the conception promoted in the earliest Christological affirmations. What the primitive church did
confess was his paradigmatic righteousness, and this
because it was an indispensable attribute of the
messiahship which it claimed for him.[2] The ideal comes
to expression in Isa. 9:7:

> Of the increase of his government and of peace
>   there will be no end,
>   upon the throne of David and over his kingdom
>   to establish it and to uphold it,
> with justice and with righteousness
>   from this time forth and forevermore.

In the intertestamental literature, the image of the
righteous Messiah is combined with the figure of the
transcendental Son of Man, of whom I En. 46:3 has the
following to declare:

> This is the Son of Man who hath righteousness,
>   with whom dwelleth righteousness,
>   and who revealeth all the treasures of
>   which is hidden,
> Because the Lord of Spirits had chosen him,
>   and whose lot hath the pre-eminence
>   before the Lord of Spirits in uprightness
>   forever.

Undoubtedly it is this tradition that St. Matthew
has in mind when he tells the story of Jesus' baptism.
Unlike his Synoptic parallels, Mattew has John the
Baptist arguing that Jesus should not be baptized (3:14),
but Jesus insists, "Let it be so now; for thus it is
fitting for us to fulfill all righteousness" (v.15).[3]
This statement would remain enigmatic for us if we were
to suppose that receiving baptism were actually required
either by Jewish law or Jewish tradition; it was not.[4]
The righteousness which Jesus sought to fulfill through
baptism was the messianic righteousness of perfect harmony and rightness with God. His baptism established
a new, creative, and redemptive relationship between a
wrathful God and a wayward humanity. It became the
effective symbol by which the Christian believer becomes one with God through faith in Christ (see Paul's
moving figure of baptism as burial in Romans 6).[5]

Excursus on further Christological statements[6]

Although the synoptic tradition refrains from
attributing any blame or wrongdoing to Jesus, it makes
no statement claiming absolute sinlessness or inerrancy
for him. In the epistles, where a more speculative
Christology is developed, sinlessness is ascribed to
him as a symbolic idealization.

The earliest is the Pauline statement in II Cor.
5:12, ton mē gnonta hamartian huper hēmōn hamartian
epoiēsen, "him who did not know sin, on our behalf he
(God) made to be sin." This expresses Paul's notion of
a vicarious interchange, Christ's innocence and blame-
lessness being substituted for humanity's guilt.

Heb. 7:26 identifies Christ as a high priest
possessing the following qualities: he is hosios (sanc-
tified), akakos (blameless), amiantos (unspotted),
kechōrismenos apo tōn hamartolōn,(separated from sinners). All these were attributes of the ideal priest;
Jesus had them to perfection. But the important contrast in this context is between the temporality and
creaturely weakness of the Levitical priesthood, on the
one hand, and Christ's eternal unfailingness on the
other. The emphasis is on his office rather than on
the events of his private life, about which the writer
has nothing to say.

I Pet. 1:19 speaks of Christ as "a lamb without

blemish and without spot" -- i.e., a perfect sacrifice to atone for his people's sin.

I Pet. 2:22: hos hamartian ouk epoiēsen oude heurethē dolos en tō stomati autou, "who did not commit sin, nor was guile found in his mouth." The context is an exhortation to submissiveness under wrongful persecution, using Christ as an example (hupogrammon). His perfect suffering has not only vicariously efficaciousness, but is exemplary in intent, according to v. 24.

I John 3:5 reads: kai oidate hoti ekeinos ephanerōthē hina tas hamartias arēi kai hamartia en autō ouk estin, "and you know that that one appeared in order to bear (the) sins, and sin was not present in him." The writer goes on immediately to say that "everyone who abides in him does not sin," while "all who sin have not seen or known him." This is obviously a symbolic idealization, functioning in an exordium for Christians to emulate Christ's purity, vv. 3-10. In the sequel of vv. 11-24, this receives practical interpretation in terms of living in perfect love with the Christian brethren.

John 8:46: "Which of you convicts me of sin?" In the context of Jesus' controversy with the Jews, the sin in question is that of telling a falsehood concerning his authority; this Jesus emphatically denies.

F. Justification by faith[7]

Misunderstanding arises whenever God's and man's "righteousness" becomes identified with moral perfection or an external conformity to an ethical code. Taking our cue from the meaning of Christ's righteousness (i.e., perfect identification with, and submission to, God's redemptive plan), we need to understand a Christian's righteousness in personal, rather than in moralistic, terms.

St. Paul is the great architect of Christian doctrine of righteousness. Galatians, his earliest epistle, passionately defends it against legalism. It is in Romans that he fully articulates and explains it. That epistle commences its long and involved discourse with a programmatic affirmation in 1:16-17:

> For I am not ashamed of the gospel; it is the
> power of God for salvation to every one who has
> faith, to the Jew first and also to the Greek.
> For in it the righteousness of God is revealed
> through faith for faith....

The gospel presents divine righteousness as the essence
of a saving relationship. Dikaiosunē stands for God's
sovereign freedom to receive sinful mankind, as well as
for mankind's responsible freedom to turn from sin to
salvation, through faith in God's goodness and in man's
salvability, as demonstrated paradigmatically, and most
ideally, in Christ's own embodiment of the divine righteousness.

1.   The theomorphism of man

        As has been said, God is no object, but the un-
limited Subject who is constantly addressing us at
every point of our creaturely existence. He is absolutely free in his moral responsibility (righteousness)
toward us, as well as in his lordship over us. This
comes to its richest manifestation as it confronts us
as human persons in the responsible exercise of our own
freedom within the limits of our finite existence. Although we are but finite creatures over against an infinite Creator, we are still free within the limits of
our finitude -- free to embrace righteousness and forsake wickedness, which is the idolatrous deification
of ourselves and of other contingent, finite ends.

        Unavoidably, we speak of God -- if we speak of him
at all -- as being in some ways like man.[8] This we call
anthropomorphism. But at the same time we affirm that
man is in some ways like God, and the appropriate term
for this is theomorphism (from Grk. theou-morphismos,
"God-formliness"). The two are essential correlates of
each other.

    a. The problem and potential of man

        Inasmuch as we must talk about man in order to
learn more about God, we turn next to the problem and
potential of man. We observe man's essential dignity,
arising from his self-awareness. We observe his creativity and aesthetic powers. We observe his rational
and moral faculties, bringing purpose and worth to activities that would otherwise remain on a purely animal
level. We observe also man's propensity to misuse the
powers, and abuse the freedom, that raise him above
animal nature. And in the end, man's essential being
remains a mystery. As Alexander Pope has said, man is
a paradox -- of the earth, yet not of it; reaching for
divinity, yet far removed from it:

        Know then, thyself, presume not God to scan,
        The proper study of mankind is man.
        Placed on this isthmus of a middle state,
        A being darkly wise, and rudely great:
        With too much knowledge for the skeptic side,

With too much weakness for the stoic's pride,
He hangs between, in doubt to act or rest:
In doubt to deem himself a god or beast;
In doubt his mind or body to prefer;
Born but to die, and reasoning but to err;
Alike in ignorance, his reason such,
Whether he thinks too little or too much:
Chaos of thought and passion, all confused;
Still by himself abused or disabused;
Created half to rise, and half to fall;
Great lord of all things, yet a prey to all;
Sole judge of truth, in endless error hurled;
The glory, jest and riddle of the world!
(_Easay_ _on_ _Man_)

To review the history of civilization is to survey
a vast and amazing story of man's achievements through
the ages, yet all crumbles at last into dust. Nothing
can withstand the ravages of time, not even the great
pyramids of Egypt; yet it is not so much the desert
sands that erode what man has done, as man's own rape
of civilization. What we need above all is an awareness of history, for we cannot measure man except in its
perspective. It can make optimists of us, or pessimists.
We can look back on the history of the human race with
a great deal of sorrow and alarm, or with satisfaction
and gratitude. Along the pathway of struggle, error
and waywardness, mankind has continued to ascend the
ladder of progress, and we can expect this to continue
in the future. Before we make a facile choice between
optimistic and pessimism, let us become aware that no-
one can be solidly optimistic about the prospects for
the human race without being also firmly pessimistic
regarding man's potential for wayward self-destruction.
Mankind has amazing powers, but the most amazing power
is to misuse those powers. Sin seems to be a part of
the human condition. Standing between the animal world
and the world of Deity, all man's gifts of self-awareness, acting, willing, remembering, and imagining --
those things that make him like God -- automatically
open him up to the possibility of sin.

b. Extrabiblical anthropologies

As has been our method in the previous chapter,
we look first to see the various alternatives in primi-

tive and modern thought concerning the being and nature
of man. Here we introduce the term anthropology (Grk.:
anthrōpou-logia, "discourse about humankind"), not in
the accepted university meaning: a scientific discipline concerning the biological origin and sociological
development of the human species; but in the sense employed in classical learning, which is the theological
understanding of man's religious nature. Early civilizations reflected on man's nature, but we may subsume
all the various options under forms of monism. Previously applied to concepts of Deity, the term "monism"
pertains also to concepts of human existence. Extrabiblical religion in its various forms conceives of man
as caught up in the same universal process in which
Deity is involved. God is the macrocosm, man the micro-
cosm, but all belong within the same scheme of reality.

As we look into the ways in which the phenomenon
of human existence is contemplated in the ancient world,
we discern that beneath a facile, surface judgment of
optimism (making man like God), the ultimate verdict on
man is very pessimistic. In flattering himself, ancient
man covered himself with degradation and despair. This
is because being like God was in itself not very ennobling.

(1) The heritage of Greek thought in western
civilization

We in our western society are heavily indebted to
the heritage of Greek thought, which had very much to
say about human existence. One may turn particularly
to Plato's great treatise, "The Republic," for a perceptive analysis of the human phenomenon. We identify here
an idealistic image of man, in which man is seen to be
halfway between the ephemeral forms of sensuous reality
and the mental abstractions which form the eternal model
for his existence in this physical universe.[9] Ultimately, we can trace the major developments in modern philosophies about man to this heritage. The dominant attitude toward the question of man today may be identified
as a nominalistic nihilism; and while in many ways this
philosophy rejects Plato's idealism, at the same time
it presupposes it even in denying it. That is to say,
in the one as in the other, man's responsible personhood, independent of a monistic involvement in nature,
is sacrificed. Man as God is affirmed; but man as
animal is affirmed even more emphatically. What is

forgotten is what makes man distinctively different
from both God and the animal in the midst of all similarities.

Excursus on humanistic naturalism[10]

Humanistic naturalism is a nihilism that reduces
all things human to an ultimate nothingness. A logical
or philosophical stance which reduces individual human
events to the status of arbitrary or accidental appearances, naturalism invites the conclusion that there is
nothing lastingly and truly significant in the existence
of human beings. Hence the profound cynicism and eagre
hedonism of contemporary life. If man is God, his sins
are excused; if man is a beast, his sins are necessary.

(2)   Far-Eastern anthropology

Very much in the center of attention today is
eastern thought, especially far-eastern thought. Although this has come to popularity in the last decade,
it has been an option before us ever since the Orient
was opened up by European colonialism. The various
philosophies and religions of the Far East have their
own distinctive attitude toward human existence. (Here
we pass over Islam, which forms a bridge between western
and Far-Eastern thought because it has been so profoundly influenced by the biblical heritage in its own unique
way.) Looking at Hinduism and Buddhism, the most representative forms of Asian religion, we observe a profound
pantheistic quietism. In pantheism, all existence par-
ticipates in the being of divinity. The phenomenal
world is but an outflowing of God's own essence. Unavoidably, human life as well as animal life is a peculiar manifestation of this universal reality. The pathos
the suffering, and the sorrow that accompany human existence at most levels are seen as inevitable, hence the
practical attitude of the miserable peasant and the
luxuriating landlord is the same: a quietistic acceptance of things as they are. Man is discouraged from
attempting strenuous efforts toward self- or mutual
improvement. Social reformers in Indian and other Asian
lands are frustrated by the general attitude that the

pervasive poverty and degradation around them is part
of an eternal cycle of reality, which nothing can
change. Again, an apparent optimism, flattering man as
an outpouring of divinity, is actually a profound pessimism.

(3)   Ancient Near-Eastern anthropologies

From this look westward and eastward, we glance
backward to the ancient Near-Eastern concept of humanness, for here is the closest context for biblical anthropology. What we see here is, once more, essential
monism. Like the other extrabiblical options, it brings
a shallow optimism masking a profound pessimism.

Ancient Near-Eastern anthropology can be regarded
in terms of primitive naturism. As has been previously
stated, it belongs within the orbit of prelogical
thought, yet not without some philosophical profundity.
In what we would be tempted to call a crassly realistic
mythologizing, Israel's neighbors identified man with
the gods and with nature. We will benefit from a scrutiny of some representative examples.

The creation of man, <u>ANET</u> 7-8[12]

The All-Lord [Re] says in the presence of those
stilled from tumult [the dead].... "I did four
good deeds within the portal of the horizon. I
made the four winds that every man might breathe
thereof....I made the great inundation that the
poor man might have rights therein like the great
man....I made every man like his fellow. I did
not command that they do evil, (but) it was their
hearts which violated what I had said....I made
their hearts to cease from forgetting the West
[the realm of the dead], in order that divine
offerings might be given to the gods....I brought
into being the four gods from my sweat, while men
are the tears of my eye.

COMMENT: This Egyptian cosmology is artificially constructed on the scheme of the number four. It expresses
a beneficent intent on the part of the gods, and gives
mankind blame for social evil. One of Re's good deeds

135

was putting the fear of death into the human heart as a
motivation for carrying on the sacrificial cult. With
respect to the creation of man, it is important to observe that, just as with the gods, mankind comes into
being as an exhudation of the divine substance; the
gods come from Re's sweat, mankind from the tears in
his eye.

Mankind made from clay and Kingu's blood,
"Enuma Elish," ANET 68-6913

When Marduk hears the words of the gods,
His heart prompts (him) to fashion artful works.
Opening his mouth, he addresses Ea
To impart the plan he had conceived in his heart:
"Blood I will mass and cause bones to be.
I will establish a savage, 'man' shall be his name.
Verily, savage-man I will create.
He shall be charged with the service of the gods
        That they might be at ease!
The ways of the gods I will artfully alter...."
Ea answered him, speaking a word to him,
Giving him another plan for the relief of the gods:
"Let but one of their brothers be handed over;
He alone shall perish that mankind may be fashioned.
Let the great gods be here in Assembly,
Let the guilty be handed over that they may endure."
Marduk summoned the great gods to Assembly;
Presiding graciously, he issues instructions.
To his utterance the gods pay heed.
The king addresses a word to the Anunnaki:
"If your former statement was true,
Do (now) the truth on oath by me declare!
Who was it that contrived the uprising,
And made Tiamat rebel, and joined battle?
Let him be handed over who contrived the uprising.
His guilt I will make him bear.
        You shall dwell in peace!"
The Igigi, the great gods, replied to him,
To Lugaldimmerankia, counselor of the gods,
        their lord:
"It was Kingu who contrived the uprising,
And made Tiamat rebel, and joined battle."
They bound him, holding him before Ea.
They imposed on him his guilt
        and severed his blood (vessels).
Out of his blood they fashioned mankind.

136

He [Ea] imposed the service and let free the gods.
After Ea, the wise, had created mankind,
Had imposed upon it the service of the gods...
Marduk, the king of the gods, divided
All the Anunnaki above and below.
He assigned (them) to Anu to guard the instructions.
Three hundred in the heavens
      he stationed as a guard.
In like manner the ways of the earth he defined.
In heaven and on earth six hundred
      (thus) he settled.

COMMENT: The divine purpose in creating man is simply
to make them slaves as substitutes for the gods, who
will now be relieved to stand guard over the cosmic
ordinances. The slavery of mankind is fully justified
as an effect of the imposition of guilt on the chief
rebel-god, Kingu, whose blood -- no doubt mixed with
earth -- is sufficient in quantity, so that Marduk's
original scheme of killing off many gods becomes unnecessary. The text continues with a description of
the building of Marduk's shrine at Babylon by the gods.
At the dedication ceremony, the gods make the following
petition to Marduk with respect to mankind's duty in
providing for the temple's upkeep.

"Most exalted be the Son, our avenger;
Let his sovereignty be surpassing,
      having no rival.
May he shepherd the black-headed ones,[14]
      his creatures.
To the end of days, without forgetting,
      let them acclaim his ways.
May he establish for his fathers
      the great food-offerings;
Their support they shall furnish,
      shall tend their sancturaries.
....
May he order the black-headed to re[vere him],
May the subjects ever bear in mind their god,
And may they at his word pay heed to the goddess.
May food-offerings be borne
      for their gods and goddesses.
Without fail let them support their gods!
Their lands let them improve,
      build their shrines,
Let the black-headed wait on their gods."

COMMENT: This liturgical text naturally expresses the
desire of the temple priesthood in Babylon to secure a

regular and generous outpouring of gifts, not only for
the great central shrine in Babylon, but for the vast
galaxy of lesser sacturaries throughout the territories
under its control. It is clear that mankind has no
significance or purpose except to wait on the world of
Deity, along with the elaborate cultic apparatus designed to honor it.

The creation of Enkidu, the alter-ego of
Gilgamesh, ANET 73-78[15]

The rich Gilgamesh tradition has gathered many
accretions and embellishments in its complex development.[16] Although it contains mythic elements, it is
essentially epic in conception. Once an earthly king,
Gilgamesh here becomes semideified. With the incorporation of the Enkidu motif, this epic becomes an aetiology not only for mankind's likeness to the gods, but
also of mankind's kinship with the beasts. In the beginning of the Assyrian version, Gilgamesh' affinity
with the gods has become a problem; he is so strong and
boisterous that he is disturbing the social order. The
officials complain to the god:

"Two-thirds of him is god, [one-third of him is
    human].
....
The onslaught of his weapons verily has no equal.
....
Gilgamesh leaves not the son to his father;
    Day and night [is unbridled his arrogance].
....
Gilgamesh leaves not the maid to [her mother],
The warrior's daughter, the noble's spouse!"
....
"Thou, Aruru, didst create [the man];
Create now his double; his stormy heart let him
    match.
Let them contend, that Uruk may have peace!"
When Aruru heard this,
A double of Anu she conceived within her.
Aruru washed her hands,
Pinched off clay and cast it on the steppe.
[On the step]pe she created valiant Enkidu,
    ...essence of Ninurta.
[Sha]ggy with hair is his whole body,
He is endowed with head hair like a woman.

The locks of his hair sprout like Nisaba [the]
        goddess of grain].
He knows neither people nor land;
Garbed is he like Sumuqan [the god of cattle].
With the gazelles he feeds on grass,
With the wild beast he jostles at the water-
        place,
With the teeming creatures his heart delights
        in water.

A hunter who sees him reports to Gilgamesh, who provides
a harlot to seduce him into manhood. An earthy scene
follows. As soon as Enkidu spots the harlot he lies
with her, and ere long he forsakes the wild beasts for
the company of mankind:

For six days and seven nights Enkidu comes forth,
        mating with the lass.
After he had had (his) fill of her charms,
He set his face toward the wild beasts.
On seeing him, Enkidu, the gaselles ran off.
The wild beasts of the steppe drew away from
        his body.
Startled was Enkidu, as his body became taut,
His knees were motionless -- for his wild beasts
        were gone.
Enkidu had to slacken his pace -- it was not
        as before;
But he now had [wi]sdom, [br]oader understanding.
Returning, he sits at the feet of the harlot.
He looks up at the face of the harlot,
His ears attentive, as the harlot speaks;
[The harlot] says to him, to Enkidu:
"Thou art [wi]se, Enkidu, art become like a god!
Why with the wild creatures dost thou roam over
        the steppe?
Come, let me lead thee [to] ramparted Uruk,
To the holy temple, abode of Anu and Ishtar,
Where lives Gilgamesh, accomplished in strength,
And like a wild ox lords it over the folk."
As she speaks to him, her words find favor,
His heart enlightened, he yearns for a friend.

And so Enkidu goes off to Uruk, symbol of civilization, to become Gilgamesh' friend and bosom companion.
First he fights a contest with Gilgamesh, but is subdued
by Gilgamesh' superior strength and skill. Enkidu,
after all, is half beast and half man, whereas Gilgamesh
is half human and half divine. Together, they represent
the conflicting forces within mankind's self.

Utnapishtim, or Atrahasis, was warned by Ea that the gods intended to destroy mankind, so he made a boat and survived. In the sequel, Ea is defending his be- trayal before Enlil, the cosmic constable, by arguing that the flood that he had sent was doo drastic a means of gaining control over humankind's tendency toward boisterousness, and that he was therefore justified in allowing this one man to escape. Anyway, this man had gained knowledge of the secret through his ability to interpret a dream that he had given him, proving that he was truly wise. Having proven that he was wise, he is now to be granted immortality, making him the virtual equivalent of a god. He says:

> Enlil went aboard the ship.
> Holding me by the hand, he took me aboard.
> He took my wife aboard and made (her) kneel by
>   my side.
> Standing between us, he touched our foreheads
>   to bless us:
> "Hitherto Utnapishtim has been but human,
> Henceforth Utnapishtim and his wife shall be
>   like unto us gods.
> Utnapishtim shall reside far away,
>   at the mouth of the rivers!"
> Thus they took me and made me reside far away,
> At the mouth of the rivers.

COMMENT: The story goes to tell how Gilgamesh fails to achieve immortality in spite of his heroic efforts.[18] It is not strength and prowess that bring a man to the status of godhood, but the wisdom that Utnapishtim pos- sessed. The boundaries between godhood and manhood are blurred; yet irresistibly Mesopotamian religion specu- lates about the true nature of man's being, akin to Deity in its lowliness and in its grandeur.

(e) Merikare's instructions: Mankind as cattle of the god, ANET 417[19]

Wo choose as a final example a didactic passage from early Egypt, where instruction is given regarding the function of man in service of Deity; the language and conception are characteristically Egyptian, eloquently expressing this peculiar brand of primitive monistic immanentism:

> Well directed are men, the cattle of the god.
> He made heaven and earth according to their desire,
> and he repelled the water-monster. He made the
> breath of life (for) their nostrils. They who
> have issued from his body are his images. He
> arises in heaven according to their desire. He
> made for them plants, animals, fowl, and fish to
> feed them. He slew his enemies and injured
> (even) his (own) children because they thought
> of making rebellion. He makes the light of day
> according to their desire, and he sails by in
> order to see them. He has created a shrine
> around about them, and when they weep he hears.
> He made for them rulers (even) in the egg, a
> supporter to support the back of the disabled.
> He made for them magic as weapons to ward off
> what might happen, or dreams by night as well as
> day. He has slain the treacherous of heart among
> them, as a man beats his son for his brother's
> sake. For the god knows every name.

COMMENT: The image of mankind as cattle epitomizes this entire expostion. Men are utterly dependent on Deity, who begot them as his own perfect image.[20] At times they become troublesome to the gods, requiring chastisement. Through the cult, they can always appeal to Deity as shephered[21] and provider.

c. Biblical anthropology

(1) A personalistic Wholism

Commensurate with the biblical affirmations respecting the being of God, the Bible's anthropology identifies man as a discrete, independent subject, related to other subjects not by ontological derivation but in personalistic interaction. As an authentic person, God is not part of the world-process but is sovereign Lord over it. Man is involved in the world-process, yet in such a way that he is not altogether under control of it. He may actually stand apart from it in working creatively to master and modify it. Thus there is a transcendence in man's own stance over against the cosmic order, just as there is a transcendence in God's stance toward man and toward the world. Because man's existence finds a center in his own being, his self is unified. Not only does the Bible depict man as separate and distinct from other created entities; it depicts him also as integrated within himself as an effective center of thought, will, and action. There is nothing of Greek dualism in the Bible -- that system of philosophical thought that sees man as a comingling of the world of sense and the world of ideal reality. None of that: man is a whole, with no dichotomy between his body and his spirit, representing different stages or forms of reality within him. A personalistic Wholism prevails. There is, indeed, a spiritual aspect to man's being, yet this is not conceived as something essentially different and distinct from his physical existence. The Hebrew word used most frequently for the "soul" of man (nephesh) means also his vital self, the dynamic center of his existence.[22]

This antique biblical insight is, amazingly, now being abundantly confirmed by modern psychology. Within man's vital existence, everything is now seen as part of a single process. We are discerning more and more clearly that our mental life is deeply rooted in our physical existence, making any separation between them impossible.

(2) The essential affirmations

Over against monistic anthropologies, with their ineluctible pessimism, we may characterize biblical anthropology as realistically optimistic, even laudatory. In spite of a popular misconception that the Bible emphasizes human depravity, it is not really "down" on man. To be sure, it is in dead seriousness about sin. It does not gloss over the dreadfulness of human depravity. Yet the Bible does not depict sin as part of man's essential nature. It has no myth like Enuma Elish, preaching that man has bad blood, that he inherits his titanic rebelliousness directly from the supernatural world. It does have a fall story, and about that we shall presently have more to say; in it, man becomes sinful through his own free choice, and not through some flaw in his created nature.

142

Thus the essential biblical affimations about man are the following: (1) Man is one in his being -- not a compromise, not a duality. There is a unity in man's individual personhood, just as there is a solidarity within the human family and in society, and harmony in man's relationship to the natural world. (2) Man is essentially free, which means responsibly free. Irresponsible freedom is no freedom because it has no parameters, no perspective, no context. A person who is responsible for his actions is free, for herein lies purpose and direction. This is what man is in his created self: no flotsam on the surf, or a rudderless ship drifting on the surge of the sea, but a self-conscious chooser and actor, working creatively to change his environment for the better. Alas, nature or accident or sickness or human cruelty sometimes deprive us of the full measure of this freedom! When that happens, and it happens all too often, a severe handicap has been placed on our efforts to bring to full realization our measure of genuine personhood as human selves.[23] (3) Man is essentially good -- and hence potentially good. Because man is created good, he has the potentiality of achieving positive goodness -- perfection within the perspective of his own creaturely limitations. The fact that he can go astray, or go completely into ruin, lends even greater significance to the goodness of his real achievements. On the contrary, the possibility of great goodness for any man, and for every man, measures the depth of his failure when he fails to achieve it -- or worse still, when he fails to strive to achieve it. It is the achievements of a Beethoven and Shakespeare and a Rembrandt -- not the mumblings of the masses of mankind -- that tell the true measure of man's potential goodness.

(3) The imago dei: Man as created creator

Christian theology has made much of the concept of the divine image in man. It is mentioned twice in the first chapter of Genesis. In v. 26 God says, "Let us make man in our image (b^{e}ṣalmēnû), after our likeness (kidmutēnû), and let them have dominion...." In v. 27 we have the narrative report of what God does: "So God created man in his own image (b^{e}ṣalmô), in the image of God (b^{e}ṣelem ,^{e}lōhîm) he created him; male and female he created them."

Before the rise of modern biblical criticism, it was excusable that discussions of the creation narrative in Genesis 2 should interject the concept of the imago dei. Now that the separate origin of Genesis 1 and Genesis 2 has been firmly established (they belong to the P and J strands, respectively), we should use only chap. 1 as an immediate contextual framework for understanding what was meant by this striking terminology.

Genesis 2 (J) has an entirely different structure and ideology. Man is made first, before plants and herbs exist on the ground; forming his substance from the dust, Yahweh breathes into his nostrils the breath of life (nišmat ḥayyim) so that he becomes a living being (nepeš ḥayyâ). After this, Yahweh prepares a fertile garden, forms the animals and creates the woman, then puts man to the test of obedience. More will be said of this narrative later. In it the creation motif is subordinate and instrumental to the major theme of mankind's fall. Thus its intent is strikingly different from that of the P story in Gen. 1:1-2:4a, which is strictly an aetiology for the created order in God's good universe.[24]

Just what the divine image is, has been the subject of many lively debates and heated controversies. We shall avoid some serious misconceptions by sticking closely to the P story as a context for interpreting it. First of all, let us note that mankind is created by God. Not too much should be made of the verb bārā', "create,"[25] for it appears here as the poetic parallel for ʿāśāh, "make." The important thing is that man's existence is strictly at God's pleasure and by his power. This is made emphatic by the discourse in v. 26, in which God communes with himself (the reason for the plural remains a mystery)[26] about what he is ready to do. This structural feature is lacking in the narrative of the preceding acts of creation, where God simply commands and it is done. The creation of man comes, as a matter of fact, as a seemingly superfluous act on the sixth day of creation, for the living creatures have already been created and identified as good (v.25).[27] But God has one more thing to do before he can rejoice in his perfect work: make man. So it is evident that man has a very special purpose in God's design.

God's decision is that he will make man in his own image (ṣelem, used four times in vv. 26-27; dᵉmût, used once in parallelism, is explicative). We saw in the

Merikare text that the Egyptian mind could readily confuse appearance and reality. It read, "They who have issued from his body are his image." Man as divine progeny and man as divine image are identical, for no distinction is made between two things that are, and that only look alike. We may be sure that there is no such confusion in Genesis. To the Hebrew mind, an image is not equivalent to the reality which it images, it simply reflects that reality. Hebrew şelem means a carved object representing some other reality. Thus, in being similar to God, man is not necessarily equal to God. Yet the P writer is using a daring expression. He is saying that, just as the idols of the heathen gods were carved out to represent them, man is now appointed to image God. Man is going to serve as the visual representative of God on earth. We must keep in mind the second commandment, forbidding the making of any image or likeness of Yahweh as the object of Israel's worship. P does not in any way violate this prohibition; he only says that, what idols may not do, man has been appointed by his Creator to do in the very beginning. Man is the divine surrogate; there is no other. We must, of course, see this in the total context of the P creation story. To be God's image is to be God's representative and to do God's work. This is why v. 27 places in parallelism the striking line, "Male and female he created them." This is needed because directly God blesses them to make them fruitful, charging them with the responsibility of exercising dominion over the creatures that he had already made. Surely this passage teaches that the propagation of human life is a special manifestation of the divine purpose in creating man. What it is also affirming is that in propagating its kind, and in subduing the earth, man as divine image-bearer is carrying out two divine works. Ensuring fertility and exercising responsible care are two distinctive divine actions. In ancient Near-Eastern mythology, these are assigned to the various gods. In the Bible, they are assigned by God to man. This is the meaning of the imago dei.

Man's having dominion has been seriously misinterpreted. This text offers no sanction for the commercial exploitation, or rapacious ravaging, of the earth's resources. Against this, modern-day ecologists rightly protest. The text of Genesis 1 is simply saying that human lordship over nature is a manifestation of divinity, and by lordship is meant creatorship. The earlier verses of this chapter set forth the whole work of divine creation in a series of six days, leading to the seventh, the sabbath. God's creative activity in these days was not making something new out of nothing (the highly misleading and speculative Christian doctrine of creatio ex nihilo), but arranging the material substance of the world. God ordered the chaotic existence that was already there, separating entities from each other, putting each into its proper category and giving each an identification, a function, and a purpose. This is lordship; this is creatorship. God does this, and so now must man as well. Man is assigned the task of bearing the divine image bestowed on him in order to carry forward God's own creative, lordly task in the world. Having dominion in the world means, then, carrying forward the creative work of separating, identifying, and enabling. This is far from offering an excuse for wanton destructiveness. Man is to continue creation by giving purpose and function to the vast array of earthly phenomena which the wise God has already made. The world is full of potential good, but man must be busy bringing it to its highest fulfillment. When God looks at his creatures, he says "It is good;" when he makes man, he says, "It is very good." (v.31) Man is the crown of God's creation, without whom all else would fail to reach the highest level of potential.

Psalm 8 is the only canonical passage that directly reflects on the marvel of human greatness in the context of human smallness.[28] First the poet compares puny man with the stars:

> When I look at thy heavens, the work of thy fingers
> the moon and the stars which thou hast
> established;
> What is man that thou art mindful of him,
> and the son of man that thou dost care for him?

Immediately the psalmist uses this as an argument for man's greatness; if man is so small, how wondrous that he does so much!

> Yet thou hast made him little less than God,
> and dost crown him with glory and honor.
> Thou hast given him dominion over the works of
> thy hands;
> thou hast put all things under his feet,
> All sheep and oxen, and also the beasts
> of the field,
> the birds of the air, and the fish of the sea,
> whatever passes along the paths of the sea.

But this is not recited to glorify man; rather, to glorify God. If one so puny can perform so much, how marvelously great is the God who made him thus! Hence Psalm 8 ends as it begins (vv. 1, 8): "O Yahweh our lord, how majestic is thy name in all the earth!" The optimistic anthropology of the Bible is ultimately an acknowledgement of the divine wisdom and greatness in creation.

The New Testament is quite justified in speaking of Jesus Christ as the new or second Adam (Rom. 5:12-21; cf. I Cor. 15:20-23).[29] As the most righteous Jew, he came closer than any man to doing what Adam was charged to do; he alone fulfills the commission of the imago dei, perfectly imaging God in the world (John 14: 9, "He who has seen me has seen the Father"). The letter to the Hebrews unreservedly applies Gen. 1:26ff. and Psalm 8 to Christ:[30]

> But we see Jesus, who for a little while was made lower than the angels, crowned with glory and honor because of the suffering of death, so that by the grace of God he might taste death for every one (2:9).

We are grateful for this hint that it is only in vicarious suffering that man fully realizes the lordship and creatorship that are inherent in the imago dei. Does this suggest that God himself brings his own lordship and creatorship to effect in suffering?

(4) The aetiology of womanhood

Genesis is a book of origins, as its name implies. Although the Bible has been almost completely sanitized of pagan myth, it does offer, especially in the opening chapters of Genesis, imaginative narrative that functions like myth to provide aetiological explanations of why things are as they are. Inasmuch as maleness and femaleness are an essential and ontological aspect of human existence, we would be surprised if these chapters did not provide us with definitive declarations of their meaning. We human beings are destined to exist either as male or as female, and at the same to exist as male and female together.

There are three striking statements in Genesis 1-3 that function as aetiologies of womanhood. The first, 1:27, belongs to the late narrative source, P, while the next two, 2:18-3:7 and 3:16, belong to J.

As we have seen, Gen. 1:27 is the passage that articulates the concept of <u>imago</u> <u>dei</u>. What the untrained reader is likely to miss is the fact that this is a line of parallelistic poetry in the midst of prose:

wayyibrā' 'e̅lōhîm 'et-hā'ādām be̅ṣalmô

be̅ṣelem 'e̅lōhîm bārā' 'ōtô

zākār ûne̅qēbā bārā' 'ōtām

> So God created man in his image,
> in God's image created he him,
> male and female created he them.

Two observations are in order: (1) Even though there is progression from the second to the third stich within this parallelistic tristich, the patent synonymity between the first and the second guarantees that synonymity is also intended between the second and the third; this means that maleness and femaleness is an explication of ṣelem 'e̅lōhîm, "the image of God." (2) The reason why this verse is poetic is almost certainly that it was a popular saying prior to its incorporation in P's prose narrative. Thus it takes traditional priority over its context, particularly v. 26, which, omitting to mention male and female, has a retrospective intentionality with respect to the creative acts that precede the creation of man. We do note the shift within v. 26 from the singular to the plural styling in reference to man, in anticipation of v. 27; this is continued in vv. 28-29, where hā'ādām (generic man) is given a task which only male and female together can fulfill, viz., that of providing life and lordship in God's entire creation.

The J view of womanhood as expressed in Gen. 2:18-3:7 is more matter-of-fact and less ideological, yet it too has the intent of defining woman's place in creation. We must take this entire passage in hand, not just 2:21-25. Deep irony lies in woman's paradoxical role over against man. As in the P account, he is still hā'ādām (generic man) -- not the "Adam" of chapter 4.31 Woman is viewed as part of generic man, rather than a rival, independent existence. Throughout, there is an interplay between nepeš ḥayyâ "living crea-

148

tures" (v. 19) and the woman ('iššâ), who alone may
function as the ʿēzer keneḡdô "a helper suited for
him" (v. 18) because she has been built from one of
man's ribs. The meaning is that other sentient creatures cannot relieve man of his isolation (v. 18,
"Yahweh God said, 'It is not good that the man should
be alone'."); only from within the resources of his
own essential being can this occur! What is required
is the "bone of my bones," "flesh of my flesh," that
the man exultantly acclaims when he awakes to see the
woman before him (v. 23).

This particular aetiology of woman does not end
here, but continues in the fall narrative of Gen. 3:1-
7. Since this will be discussed at another point in
the present chapter, we shall refrain from further comment except to mention the specific role of the woman,
who becomes the principle protagonist in these particular verses, before being completely dropped from view
in vv. 22-24 at the end of chapter 3. In 3:1 the nāḥāš,
"serpent," is abruptly announced as the most ʿārûm of
all the "wild creatures" (kol ḥayyat haśśādeh) -- one
of the subgroups of nepeš ḥayyâ according to 2:19-20.
The play on ʿarûmmîm, ʿērummîm (2:25, 3:7), traditionally translated "naked," makes it certain that the serpent, universal phallic symbol that it is, has unrivaled
powers of inducing sexual fertility. Following this
lead, we follow those interpreters who recognize here
the vestiges of an early Canaanite fertility myth, in
which the snatching of forbidden aphrodisiac fruit
would open the man's and woman's eyes, teaching them
the "good and evil" of sex, and making them "like god"
by giving them possession of the divine potency to
create life.[32] No doubt, in the present structure, this
mythical substratum has been sanitized by Yahwistic
personalism, making the integrity of the divine-human
relationship the prime issue. Yet the woman's special
susceptibility to an idolatrous desire to recreate new
life is an ineradicable aetiological element within
the fall account.[33]

A third independent aetiology of womanhood appears
in the J story of Gen. 3 as a previously existing folk-
saying, now taken up as a divine declaration in consequence of mankind's fall. In v. 16 we read the poetic
lines:

To the woman he said,
    "I will greatly multiply your pain
        in childbearing;

in pain you shall bring forth children,
Yet your desire shall be for your husband
   ('îšēk),
and he shall rule over you."

This is a text that has been much misused. It is full
of paradox. A perceptive fresh traslation would be:
"I will intensify your pain along with your fruitfulness, so that you will suffer when you have children;
likewise, you will crave for your husband even while
he has mastery over you." The word t^ešuqātēk, "your
desire, craving," should be interpreted in the light of
the J passage in 4:7, where sin is described as a lion
crouching at the door, "craving" for Cain, who is challenged to "master" it in response.

   Like the curses on the serpent (3:14-15) and on
the ground (3:17-19), this folk saying is aetiological.
As such it contains a universally valid epitome of
womankind's condition within the natural order. Nature
has assigned to woman the task and the privilege of
bearing children, which bring her joy and sorrow at the
same time. In this function, her craving and expectation are directed toward her husband. She welcomes
male aggressiveness in the sex relationship and encourages male initiative in the social-economic area, in
order that in becoming fruitful, she may be sheltered
and nurtured in her own struggle to bear and nurture
her bairns. Her strength (the power to create new life)
is the occasion of her weakness; her sorrow and pain are
the condition of her joy.

   Like the curse on the serpent and on the ground,
this saying to the woman (not a curse!) is intended as
a warning not to let the primordial rivalries of nature
get out of balance. It is as fearsome for "the seed of
the woman" to annihilate the wild beasts, symbolized by
the serpent, as for them to wipe out mankind. It is as
fearsome for mankind to wear out the soil as for the
soil to wear him out. So too, it is as fearsome for a
woman to desex and cannibalize her husband as for him
to abuse and brutalize her.

   In the present age of social equality, woman's
brain has a chance to become as potent as her womb.
But a curse may come on her and her husband wherever
her freedom, or his, turns into license. License ig-
nores the parameters of a person's existence within the
natural and social orders, rendering freedom meaningless
by annihilating the conditions that give it significance

This is not the freedom that comes through the higher oneness in Christ (Gal. 3:28); it is the venomous toxin of racial suicide. Thinking of Gen. 3:14-19, we warn of three great dangers: it is injurious to mankind's well-being to ravage the natural world from which it must draw its sustenance; it is injurious to its well-being to sabotage the social fabric which makes civillized life possible; it is equally mutilating to its well-being to stifle the natural cravings of love, gratitude, and mutual concern by flinging away the vow of responsibility to one's mate and offspring.

Excursus: Male and female in biblical worship

To come to the conclusion that the symbol of fatherhood, as applied to the biblical God,[34] is not subject to reduction or compromise does not in any way suggest the same for the exclusive male priesthood of the Old Testament. This was partly the product of the cultural substratum (ancient Near-Eastern patriarchalism) and partly a pragmatic device for dealing with the special problems that arose in confrontation with Baalism. Because the acceptance of women into the ministry and priesthood is now a pressing issue, it is important to offer comments that may be useful in a search for authentically biblical principles. Neither church tradition nor magesterial authority can settle this problem. Our point will be that there is nothing distinctively and essentially biblical in an exclusively male priesthood, and that this requires adjustment toward the better realization of a genuinely distinctive and essential biblical principle, viz., that of woman's full equality with man as bearer of the divine image (see Gen. 1:27; Gal. 3:28).

This conclusion requires the clearing away of a considerable debris of misunderstanding. We need to scrutinize carefully the notion that only males had a part in Israelite worship. This seems to be stated in an apodictic requirement found in the parallel texts, Ex. 23:17, 34:23, and Deut. 16:16: "Three times in the year shall all your males appear before Yahweh God." Exodus 34 has received numerous deuteronomistic additions, but this particular rule is likely to belong to the J substratum[35]-- and hence be very early -- because it appears in the same undigested, lapidary form in each of the three quite separate passages. It most likely reflects a fairly primitive situation, both socially and culturally. The reference is to three annual assemblies at a central shrine (not necessarily Jerusalem), requiring a hard journey on the part of male worshipers of Yahweh. It is probable that this was meant as a minimum, requiring this pilgrimage of males while leaving it optional for the females, many of whom would have been needed at home to care for their children.

This line of reasoning might seem sepeculative except for abundant evidence in other texts that woman did, in fact, attend such assemblies. In parallel legislation for the three annual festivals in Leviticus 23, no sexual specification is made; in Deut. 16:11, 14, on the other hand, women are mentioned explicitly as being present. We may add to this the explicit mention of women in a number of narratives involving the setting of formal public worship. These passages have a wide range, chronologically: from the dancing girls of Shiloh (Judg. 21:19ff.), to Elkanah's two wives in I Samuel 1-2, to the women attending the ark's entrance (II Sam. 6:19), to the women mentioned in the account of Ezra's fall festival (Neh. 8:1-3, 10:28, 12:43), to Jesus' own mother (Luke 2:41-51). Although only males are mentioned in such texts as Ex. 32:1ff., I Kings 8: 1ff., 54ff., and II Kings 23:1ff., it is possible, and perhaps probable, that women were present as well. We take note, furthermore, of the special rituals provided for women mentioned in Leviticus 12 (cf. Luke 2:22-24) and Leviticus 15.

Both the Old and New Testaments assign more than a meagre role to women engaged in paracultic sacral activities, particularly that of prophesying. Prophetesses are mentioned in narrative accounts at Ex. 15: 20, Numbers 12 (Miriam), Judges 4-5 (Deborah), and II Kings 22:14-20 (Huldah),[36] as well in the prophetic passages, Isa. 8:3 and Ezek. 13:17ff. The "singing women" were also fulfilling a prophetic role; thus Miriam in Ex. 15:20-21, Jephthah's daughter in Judg. 12:34ff., and the women who greeted David according to I Sam. 18:6-7. There were also old Anna of Luke 2:36-38 and Philip's four daughters, mentioned in Acts 21:9. Women who were engaged in spreading the gospel appear prominently throughout the New Testament; we think especially of the women who were in close ministry to Jesus and those, like Prisca, who are mentioned as companions of Paul.[37]

This is the background against which we must assess the Israelite rule of male priesthood. The evidence for its existence is clear; priests there were, but no priestesses. Thus narrative passages like Gen. 14:18ff., Ex. 18:1ff., 19:22, 24, 33:10, Numbers 16-17, 27, I Samuel 1-4, and Nehemiah 12; also the rituals of Leviticus 1-7, 16-17 and the cult legislation of Exodus 28-29, Leviticus 8-10, 21-22, Numbers 5-8, 18-19, 28-29, 31, Deuteronomy 18, Ezekiel 43-47. Nevertheless, the Old Testament has no explicit regulation demanding males and excluding females. Nor does it offer a rationale why priests should be male and not female. This means that the rule sprang up in practice, rather than from a self-conscious ideology -- which is to say that there is nothing specially holy about maleness and nothing defiling about femaleness, as seen in themselves. It is vain to look to circumcision, which would normally have been performed only on males, as a clue, because this was the token of belonging to Israel, not specifically to the priesthood.[38]

What then is the explanation? In the absence of any specific statement on this question, we must resort to the reasonable conjecture that Israelite male priesthood was the pragmatic arrangement that was best suited to the purpose of maintaining an apologetic stance over against Baalism. Just how rampant this was can be surmised from the repeated, regretful remarks about the persistence of cult prostitution in the kingdom of Judah, from Asa to Josiah (I Kings 14:24, 22:46, II Kings 23:7, Hos. 4:13, Amos 2:7-8), in spite of its explicit prohibition in Deut. 23:17: "There shall be no cult prostitute of the daughters of Israel, neither shall there be a cult prostitute of the sons of Israel" (cf. Ex. 34:16). This was an unfortunate cultural heritage from Israel's Canaanite environment, one that official Yahwism struggled to eradicate as "an abomination to Yahweh." In Canaanite-tainted worship settings ("on every high hill and under every green tree" is the classic expression),[39] both male (qādēš) and female (qᵉdēšâ) prostitutes would offer themselves -- the latter being preferred by the predominantly male clientele. We must infer that the official cult of Yahweh, purged of this insidious influence, deliberately rejected female ministrants at the shrine because they would invariably become the occasion of -- or suggest the presence of -- baalistic licentiousness (see I Sam. 2:22).[40]

In postexilic times, when Baalism had been eradicated from Israelite religion, an insistence on the sexual purity of a priest came to expression in specific legislation governing his marriage.[41] We find these rules in Lev. 21:7, 13-15 and Ezek. 44:20-23. Here Baalism is no longer mentioned, yet the priests are to observe certain arbitrary restrictions. All marriage partners except pure virgins are forbidden -- even normally marriageable widows and divorcees. This was an ideological extension of an attitude that had earlier been cultivated in conflict with Baalism -- the avoidance of sexual promiscuity as an expression of vegetative religiosity. The priests, even in their marriage, were now firmly governed by the paradigmatic rule of Ezek. 44:23, "They shall teach my people the difference between the holy and the common (ben qōdeš lebōl), and show them how to distinguish between the unclean and the clean."

Jews and Christians are now living in a firmly monotheistic, non-mythical environment. There is no longer an authentically biblical, apologetic-polemic issue in depriving women of the opportunity to serve as bearers of holiness. It all depends, to be sure, on whether the church's grasp of the meaning of "holiness" be a monistic, dionysiac, vegetative notion, or the high and pure personalism of the Bible. If it be the latter, the church will welcome the richer qualities of human personhood that woman's presence in ministry can bring. Male humanness in isolation is only half-humanness, requiring female humanness for its fulfillment. If this be true in God's good and wide creation, why should it not be true in the synagogue and church? Is religion to be any less human than our common life?

This is the course dictated for today by an authentically biblical achievement, an insight into God's full presence in human personhood. Ancient Israelite male priesthood, early and medieval church patriarchalism,[42] the exclusive male leadership of rabbinical Judaism[43] -- all these have had their day. One of the Bible's most potent principles demands that they now be set aside, making way for the long-delayed social revolution that it has been preparing.

2.   Sin and atonement, estrangement and acceptance

Man, with all his grandeur and potentiality, is
ever in peril of failure and of misusing his powers.
The great danger is that he may turn against the God
whose image he bears, in effect deifying himself (the
grossest form of idolatry), while at the same time
falling lower than the beasts whom he has been ordained
to rule.

It is misleading to use the term "animalism" for
immoral and sensuous human behavior. When we human
beings abandon ourselves to unrestrained fleshliness,
whether that be drunkenness or gluttony or fornication,
we are not behaving like animals, for we have become
lower than animals. We can never be mere animals because we have the higher qualities of self-understanding, self-consciousness, memory, imagination, and a
sense of meaning and purpose in our earthly activity.
None of these characterize animal existence. The animals drink and eat what they need and they engage in
reproductive activity -- all of which is pleasurable to
them, although often accompanied by struggle and pain.
We human beings, as animals, also need food and drink,
and we readily engage in sexual reproduction. We have
discovered that these can enrich our social life as
well as our spiritual growth, so long as we engage in
them with proper self-restraint and with concern for
other persons -- our family in the case of sharing
meals and sleeping quarters; our spouse in the case of
sex. Nature has ordained that these should all be
pleasurable activities for us, for we would not eat and
drink if these were not pleasurable, and then we would
die; we would not engage in sexual concourse if it did
not bring pleasure, and then our race would perish.
Carrying out these simple animal processes is simply
part of being alive. It is right that we should try to
arrange these activities to maximize the benefit that
may be derived from them and to minimize the pain and
harm. But our very human will, our memory, our imagination, our sense of purpose threaten to divert us into
a pattern of sub-animal behavior. We can eat and eat
and eat, drink and drink and drink -- not to satisfy
our need for normal bodily functioning and the renewal
of our energy, but sheerly for the pleasure that comes
with the activity as such. We can abandon a pattern of
harmonious sexual union for one of ungoverned self-
indulgence, harming ourselves and our partner(s), and

eventually losing the very capacity for pleasure and enjoyment.

Thus man sinks lower than the beasts. The irony lies in man's self-delusion of governing his own life. He no longer rules his flesh; his flesh rules him. He no longer governs nature; he exploits and ruins it, until its tribute is exhausted. As the saying goes, "He does not have his money; his money has him." He does not have his pleasures; his pleasures have him.

The worst aspect of human sin is the estrangement that it brings. Man in rebellion is estranged from God, estranged from the universe, estranged within human society, estranged from himself. The unity of his being is shattered and the harmony of his world is destroyed. Sin is not fun; it is tragedy.

Is there hope for fallen man? The Bible says yes -- but only if sin be seen for what it truly is. God is ready to start over again. The problem is, can fallen man start over again too? If rightness (righteousness) is to be restored, it must come as God's ever-generous gift and not as man's accomplishment.

a. Man's failure; the divine image shattered

Consistent with the personalism of biblical anthropology (Grk:hamartiou-logia, "discourse about sin") and biblical soteriology (Grk: sōtēriou-logia, "discourse about salvation") distinguish themselves from ancient and modern rivals in their marked personalism. Sin is an intensely personalistic affair; so is salvation.

Because extrabiblical hamartiologies are superficially optimistic, minimizing sin's seriousness, they are ultimately pessimistic with regard to the prospect of salvation. Just the opposite in the Bible: pessimism about sin undergirds a joyous optimism about the prospect for salvation.

(1) Extrabiblical hamartiology

156

In notions about sin outside the Bible we have to
do, once again, with various forms of monism. Evil and
sin are understood as an unavoidable part of the cosmic
process.

(a) Evil in monistic thought

It is little wonder that the Greeks, for instance,
were so much concerned with the concept of ineluctible
fate. All their great tragedies follow the same sombre
theme, that of fate driving persons to their destiny,
rendering their most heroic efforts ineffectual. Somewhat different is the Hindu concept of karma, the doctrine of reincarnation, in which every sentient being,
animal as well as human, exists only as an ephemeral
manifestation of the life-force that pervades all reality. Beyond and behind the visual world lies an order
of destiny which decrees the particular existence that
each individual living being will have to experience at
a particular time in the future, when it is reincarnat-
ed. This process will continue on unremittingly until,
hopefully, the blissful state of our non-existence is
achieved. The sorrow and pain, the injustice and wrong,
that characterize societal interaction are interpreted
as unavoidable, resistant to all amelioration. How
then can there be serious moral blame? Evil is necessary and sin is necessary. They are part of things as
they are, something one can scarcely do anything about.

(b) Evil and punishment in the ancient Near East

Within the immediate context of ancient biblical
thought, evil was interpreted partly as punishment for
sin, and partly as something unavoidable and irrational.
The punishment concept was directly based on the symbolism of human interaction, attributing to the gods the
will to dispense retribution on transgressions of their
decrees. Yet an element of dynamistic taboo remained.
The mechanism of sin and retribution was beclouded by
humankind's inability to penetrate the reason behind
any sudden or undeserved calamity.

One of the Egyptian myths tries to provide a rationale for the gods' apparent indiscretion in visiting

large-scale punishment on the human race. As in some
of the Mesopotamian myths, a vague charge of rebellious
ness justifies their destruction, yet by some strange
quirk many individuals are allowed to survive.

The Deliverance of Mankind from Destruction, ANET 11[44]

Then Re said to Nun: "O eldest god, in whom I
came into being, O ancestor gods, behold mankind,
which came into being from my Eye -- they have
plotted things against me. Tell me what ye would
do about it. Behold, I am seeking; I would not
slay them until I had heard what ye might say
about it." Then the majesty of Nun said: "My son
Re, the god greater than he who made him and might
ier than they who created him, sitting upon thy
throne, the fear of thee is great when thy Eye is
(directed) against them who scheme against thee!"
Then the majesty of Re said: "Behold, they have
fled into the desert, their hearts being afraid
because I might speak to them." Then they said
in the presence of his majesty: "May thy Eye be
sent, that it may catch for thee them who scheme
with evil things. (But) the Eye is not (sufficiently) prominent therein to smite them for thee.
It should go down as Hat-Hor." So this goddess
came and slew mankind in the desert. Then the
majesty of this god said: "Welcome, Hat-Hor, who
hast done for me the deed for which I came!" Then
this goddess said: "As thou livest for me, I have
prevailed over mankind, and it is pleasant in my
heart!" Then the majesty of Re said: "I shall
prevail over them as a king by diminishing them!"

As the narrative continues, it appears that Hat-
Hor is bent on utter annihilation, which was not Re's
intention. He only wanted to gain control over mankind
by diminishing their number. Now he has to devise a
scheme for bringing Hat-Hor under control. In the sequel he orders that a huge amount of red ochre be mixed
with seven thousand jars of beer. Lusting for human
blood, Hat-Hor will swill it all down, become intoxi-
cated from the beer, and desist:

Now when day broke for the slaying of mankind by
the goddess at their season of going upstream,

158

then the majesty of Re said: "How good it is!
I shall protect mankind with it!" Then Re said:
"Pray, carry it to the place in which she expected
to slay mankind. Then the majesty of....Re went
to work early in the depth of the night to have
this sleep-maker poured out. Then the fields were
filled with liquid for three palms, through the
power of the majesty of this god. Then this goddess went at dawn, and she found this (place)
flooded. Then her face (looked) beautiful therein.
Then she drank, and it was good in her heart. She
came (back) drunken, without having perceived mankind.

Hymn to Meresger, ANET 381[45]

We can illustrate the consciousness of sin from a
variety of penitential hymns in the Mesopotamian literature, and some of them are profoundly personalistic.
Nevertheless, they generally express some anxiety regarding the precise nature of the offense, as well as
uncertainty whether the plea will be effectual.

It can scarcely be accidental that Egyptian literature provides the most poignant expressions of irra-
tionality in the sin-punishment-forgiveness mechanism,
for Egyptian religion did not develop as sharply as
Mesopotamian religion the concept of a personal Deity
with paternal concern for his worshipers. There is an
eloquent lack of assurance in the following penitential
hymn to Meresger:

Giving praise to the Peak of the West [an epithet
of the goddess]; kissing the ground to her ka. I
give praise; hear (my) call. I was a righteous
man upon earth....I knew not good or evil. When
I did the deed of transgression against the Peak,
she punished me, and I was in her hand by night
as well as day. I sat upon the brick(s) like the
pregnant woman. I called out to the wind, (but)
it did not come to me. I was tormented by the
Peak of the West, great in strength, and by every
god and every goddess.

See, I shall say to great and small who are in
the gang: "Beware of the Peak! For a lion is in
the Peak; she smites with the smiting of a savage

lion. She pursues him who transgresses against
her."

(But) when I called to my mistress, I found her
coming to me with sweet breezes. She showed
mercy unto me, after she had let me see her hand.
She turned about to me in mercy; she made me
forget the sickness which had been (upon) me.
Lo, the Peak of the West is merciful, when one
calls to her.

What Nefer-abet, the triumphant, says. He says:
"See, and let every ear of him who lives upon
earth hearken: -- Beware of the Peak of the West!"

COMMENT: Nefer-abet had become sick, but was unaware
of any particular transgression. All he was certain of
was that Meresger was punishing him. In his suffering
he continually prayed to her -- and then in despair to
"every god and every goddess." In the end he experienced Meresger's mercy; she responded to his confession
of her power. He was restored to health. What he now
confesses to "every ear" is not her mercy and kindness
but her harshness and power. "Beware of the Peak of
the West!"

Thus the basic polarity in the ancient Near-Eastern
concept of sin and punishment is between a relatively
ordered acceptance of evil and this dread of irrational
destructiveness. Since evil derives from the will of
the gods, the thing to do is manipulate them by propitiation and intercession. Within a polytheistic system,
part of the problem for the individual sinner/worshiper
is to find the right god to propitiate. An irrational-
ity counterbalances the effect of right worship, hence
the resort to magic and demonism. There are too many
mysteries. The sinner may not know of what he should
repent, and to which god or goddess he should confess.
Only the result will reveal whether he has confessed
the right sin, appealed to the right deity, made the
right sacrifice. In a word: because the diagnosis is
so poor, the remedy is often ineffectual.

(2) Biblical hamartiology

As we scrutinize the modern options that have been developed to account for human failure, we find that not much improvement has been made over these ancient concepts of sin and atonement. Generally they did not take sin very seriously, but fell short in assurance of the remedy for it. Today we find that same superficial optimism about sin in an utopian idealism and in the moralism of materialistic evolutionism, both of which urge: Evil is part of man's essential nature, but can be eradicated through strenuous effort. The trouble is that all of man's efforts to raise himself by his bootstraps have proven ineffective; the beast remains beneath the thin veneer of civilization. Perversely pessimistic, on the other hand, is nihilistic naturalism, which identifies evil as part of man's essential nature, but invites him to succumb to it and embrace it!

Biblical hamartiology is authentically pessimistic. But, since biblical anthropology is essentially optimistic, this only prepares the way for a true and triumphant optimism in the Bible's scheme of salvation. Everything is ultimately based on an intense and authentic personalism. That is to say, the Bible interprets sin as personal and relational, preparing the way for a soteriology that is personal and relational.

Sin is seen as a fault of man in his interrelationship with other beings, particularly with the supreme Being, God. The horror of sin is, ultimately, that man is himself responsible for it. Much as mankind strives to excuse itself of sin, the Bible points the finger and declares: "Thou art the man!" Man is so guilty as a sinner because he is so free, and so essentially good.

(a) The fall of mankind

St. Paul apparently develops a literal interpretation of Adam's fall in Rom. 5:12, "Sin came into the world through one man, and death through sin." It is this concept of historical derivation that has led Christian scholarship to affirm a hereditary derivation of all men from this one first man, and with it a corporate guilt and a congenital propensity toward wickedness. It seems strange, then, that Judaism preferred to derive sin from the fall of the angels, in which they intermarried with women and begot giants (Gen. 6:

161

1-4). The Old Testament itself makes only vague and ambiguous allusions to the Adam story, despite the early origin and decisive position of J's narrative within Genesis 3-11, telling of mankind's progressive descent to spiritual ruin as a preparation for the call of Abraham. Together, these considerations place ponderous obstacles in the way of the traditional Christian doctrine of inherited sin, interpreting Adam's fall as a literal historical event.

All the same, the fall story in Genesis 3 plays a foundational role in defining the occasion and nature of mankind's failure. As has been previously noted, this chapter must not be directly connected with Genesis 1, which features man's creation as _imago dei_. We also recall that Genesis 2 is no separate creation account, but a structural preparation for climactic chapter 3.[46]

These two chapters were composed or taken over by J, who added expansive materials in chapters 4, 6 -- and so further. The protagonist is not a historical personage called "Adam" but generic man, hā'ādām in Hebrew. Although a west-semitic fertility myth was almost certainly employed in 3:1-7, 23-24, this has been reinterpreted in a radically Yahwistic fashion within the present structure of chapters 2-3. Besides man and God, the story features (1) the fertile ground from which man has been derived (called hā'ādāmâ to bring out the pun on hā'ādām); (2) the living creatures; (3) the woman. The man asserts his lordship over the ground by tilling and keeping the garden; over the wild creatures by naming (i.e., identifying) them; over the woman by receiving her as ꜥēzer kᵉnegᵉdô, "his intimate helper." This right relationship is tested by the supreme challenge of a trusting obedience toward the Creator. As 3:1-6 recount, the "intimate helper" is seduced by the wiliest (pun on "sexiest") of the wild creatures, the snake; and she gets the man to sin with her in defiance of the divine prohibition. In the ensuing encounter, Yahweh curses the snake, representative of all the wild creatures, by consigning him to a desperate, hopeless struggle against the woman's seed. Next he consigns the woman to pain and male domination in her struggle to exercise her sexual fruitfulness. Finally, he curses hā'ādāmâ because of man, identifying it as the ultimate cause of his own decay into dust. After all this, the first pair are driven from the garden of Eden -- the closing of a stage curtain at the end of a tragic drama.

The story of the fall must be appreciated for its psychological perceptiveness and its theological profundity. It is superbly simple and effective. No human being who has himself sinned can escape from discerning that Eve and Adam's sin is his own. The story has pedagogical effectiveness because every reader, however unsophisticated he may be, instinctively knows that the ambitious self-assertion, the delusion of injured prerogative, the morbid curiosity for someting undiscovered and forbidden, the reckless decision against unresisting obedience, the overpowering shame that comes over the sinners as their brazen courage leaves them, are things that he too could experience. He knows that he too would hide in the trees of the garden, would tell Yahweh half-truths to disguise his guilt, and would blame others for his sin....As generic man, hā'ādām represents human nature as created in the divine image -- i.e., as related to nature and yet rising above it through the free spirit which his Creator gave him. He also represents mankind as owing unquestioning allegiance to God, as finding the meaning of his existence in harmony with his Creator and not in an independent self-sufficiency. Further, his temptation to snatch a knowledge which as a mere creature he could never have, born of anxiety and distrust, is typical of the temptation in which every man stands at every moment of his existence. Finally, the crumbling of the rebel's bravado as he is summoned before God symbolizes the hollowness of every human pretense over against his Maker. Thus, quite apart from the theory of a hereditary transmission of the effects of Adam's fall, it should be apparent that Adam's real theological importance is his representation of all mankind in its defiance of God's will....The Paradise narrative helps us understand the real nature of sin. Sin is possible only because man has been created in God's image. He has a freedom of self-assertion which is his divine endowment. Sin comes when man uses this freedom to measure himself against God, trying to be independent of his control. Immediately man discovers his terrible mistake. He learns that his freedom is only a finite freedom, and he can never really be as God. He has obtained a practical knowledge of the possibilities of good and evil, but in a way that his Creator never intended, through a life of pain and spiritual bondage which is ever a continual frustration of the true greatness for which God has made him (S. J. DeVries, "The Fall," _IDB_ II, 263f.),[47]

(b)   The Old Testament and Jewish concept of sin

     References to sin are to be found on almost every
page of the Bible, Old and New Testament. New Testament
Greek uses a variety of terms,[48] many of which are used
in the LXX to translate the Hebrew. It is especially
Hebrew that has a striking variety of terms, representing a special sensitivity on the part of ancient Israel
with respect to human failure before God. Often the
words for sin are piled together in line upon line of
poetic parallelism, as in Isa. 59:12f.:

     Our transgressions are multiplied before thee,
          and our sins testify against us;
     for our transgressions are with us,
          and we know our iniquities:
     transgressing, and denying Yahweh,
          and turning away from following our God,
     speaking oppression and revolt,
          conceiving and uttering from the heart
          lying words.

     If we were to classify the language of sin, we
would find formal terms like ʿābar, "transgress;" relational words like māʾan, "disobey;" psychological
words like ʿāwāh, "be twisted;" qualitative words like
rāʿāh, "be bad;" words referring to the consequences,
like ʿāmal, "do mischief;" and words for the responsibility for sin such as ʾāšam, "be guilty." (Such words
occur both a nouns and as verbs.) Furthermore, there
are words for each and every particular kind of sin.

     The most common and general word for sin is a
formal one: ḥāṭāʾ "to err;" the verb means, literally,
"to go astray," "to miss the mark."[49]

     The most important social and juridical term is
rāšaʿ, "be wicked"; rešaʿ, "wicked person"; rišʿâ,
"wickedness."[50] It is the precise opposite of ṣādaq,
ṣaddîq, ṣedāqâ, and in covenantal passages refers to
the disregard of covenantal norms and practices.

     By far the most expressive theological term offered
by the Old Testament is pāšaʿ, "rebel"; with the noun
form, pišʿâ, "rebellion." It appears with striking
frequency in the prophetic books. Because it is the
privileged people, Israel, who are often accused of it,
it emphatically involves an express act of perverse

wilfulness.[51] Similar to it is šûb, "to turn away," "apostasize."[52]

Survivals of taboo-consciousness are clearly present in certain early elements in the Old Testament.... It cannot be denied, however, that generally the Old Testament conception of sin appears on a much higher moral and spiritual level. Apart from the cultic rituals, most of the laws contained in the Pentateuch and elsewhere evince a strong awareness of ethical right and wrong. This awareness needs to be understood mainly in relation to the rising understanding of Yahweh's own supremely moral being. It was as he came to understand what was wrong in relation to the will of Yahweh that the Israelite understood what was wrong in relation to his neighbors. Sins of all kinds were rightly interpreted as, first of all, sins against God (Gen. 39:9; Ps. 51:4). It was chiefly the great prophets who led Israel to see that sin is something intensely spiritual, and consequently deeply tragic. They proclaimed that sin in its awful reality involves, not the violation of a taboo or the transgression of an external ordinance, but...a man's personal standing with God.

The notion that sin arises either from creatureliness, as such, or from sexual generation does not appear in the Old Testament....According to the Hebrew writers, and particularly Jeremiah, sin comes from the corrupt heart of man...:

> This people draw near with their mouth
>   and honor me with their lips,
>   while their hearts are far from me (Isa. 29:13)

> The heart is deceitful above all things,
>   and desperately corrupt;
>   who can understand it? (Jer. 17:9)

The heart is not so much the seat of the intellect as of the will, and it is man's will that has become corrupt and perverse. God showed man the way; he made a covenant with Israel; but man refuses to obey and continually rebels against God....Thus sin's essence lies, not in isolated acts of transgression, but in the depth of man's being. As he fell into sin through an inordinate use of his will, that same will, with its organ, the heart, has become so warped through estrangement from God that it henceforth gives rise to all sorts of evil. Thus sin becomes a fateful and tragic habitus leading at last to complete destruction. Sin begets greater sin; the sin of one individual

165

involves everyone associated with him, through its evil influence; a sin of thought leads to transgression in word and act. In short, the whole life, the whole being, of man has become sinful and corrupt. It has become his very nature to sin:

> Can the Ethiopian change his skin
>   or the leopard his spots?
> Then also you can do good
>   who accustomed to do evil. (Jer. 13:23)

The Old Testament does not theorize about the process by which humanity has become corrupt, in spite of Genesis 3; all it knows -- and it knows this for sure, through painful experience -- is that all of mankind since Adam has been sinful, that the whole man is sinful that man's entire life is sinful from its beginning.

Inasmuch as man cannot escape involvement in sin, it might seem logical to conclude that he ought not to be held responsible for it. Nothing, however, is further from Old Testament thought. For one thing, since sin is rooted in the rebellious heart, the seat of the will, it is basically an act of perverted freedom, and hence man is always responsible for it, even though its effects overwhelm him and progressively enslave his will itself. For another thing, God offers grace as a remedy for sin and urges the sinner to repent and forsake his evil ways.

God holds all men to account for their wrongdoing, even the Gentiles....It stands to reason, then, that Israelites are answerable to him. Their sin is all the greater because they sin against his covenant and against better knowledge.

The corporate involvement of sin deeply impressed itself upon the people....The prophets proclaimed that it was not only a few wicked individuals, but the whole nation, that was laden with sin (Isa. 1:4). Generation after generation treasured up wrath. (Yet) there was hope for the individual if he would repent.

A true spiritual sense of guilt, which includes deep sorrow and shame, follows from the knowledge that sin is a personal affront against a holy and righteous God. Such guilt is felt as a heavy burden which oppresses the soul. It comes to vivid expression in such language as this:

For my iniquities have gone over my head;
    they weigh like a burden too heavy for me.
. . . .
I am utterly bowed down and prostrate;
    all the day I go about mourning (Ps. 38:4, 6).

When I declared not my sin, my body wasted away
    through my groaning all day long.
For day and night thy hand was heavy upon me;
    my strength was dried up as by the heat of
    summer (Ps. 32:3-4).

This brings up the sinfulness of those who are called perfect or righteous in the Old Testament. It is significant that many of the most notable exemplars of piety are said explicitly to have committed sin....To be described as "righteous," one needed to conform, at least outwardly, to the commonly accepted standard of what was right. It is not so much a question of whether one ever commits sin as of one's basic walk of life and attitude toward the standard of right....A righteous man may occasionally fall into sins, but because his basic attitude is hatred toward sin, he is not charged as being "guilty" or "wicked."

Since Yahweh holds all men accountable to him for their sins, it is also he who brings their penalty upon them. As supreme Ruler over all the world, he announces the penalty of each nation's sin (cf. Amos 1:1-2:3). But his covenant people are not exempt from this judgment....Yahweh's purpose is to use Israel's enemies as the executors of his judgment (Isa. 10:5-11; Jer. 27: 6ff.). But even these are subject to his condemnation (cf. Isa. 10:12-16). Although forensic language is employed, it is plain that the penalty which results from transgression has an internal connection with it. I.e., sin's penalty follows immediately and necessarily. For the Hebrew mind sin included, beside the act itself, the guilt attaching to it and its painful results, which might be called its judgment. Thus it is said that God judges a guilty man by bringing his conduct upon his own head (I Kings 8:32). Sin is never an isolated and easily forgotten act; it sets in motion a whole series of consequences; it begets more sin and more guilt and more pain, and then the whole series over again.... Since this necessary involvement of act and consequence belongs to the essential nature of moral creation, it is indeed the judgement of God.

Thus suffering comes to be interpreted as the

penalty of sin, and great suffering as the penalty of great wickedness (adapted from S. J. DeVries, "Sin, Sinners," IDB II, 363-67).53

1) Late modifications

Everything stated here was believed by the Jews living in the time of Jesus. As Jews, the early Christians fully believed it too. The two groups came to an eventual parting of the ways because each came to seize upon and emphasize certain features at the expense of others.

To appreciate the postbiblical Jewish outlook, one needs to be aware of the drastically different social and political conditions under which Judaism was forced to live, from the Babylonian exile in the sixth century B.C. on into the period of the Roman empire. Few of the concrete and visible symbols of divine favor were restored to them. In fact, conditions grew progressively worse, until life scarcely seemed worth living any more. We can say, in a word, that postexilic and especially postbiblical Judaism felt itself to be living under divine wrath.54 Characteristic of the religious literature of this period are elaborate outpourings of confessions and appeals for divine forgiveness (see especially Dan. 9:4-19), yet little relief came. The Jews had great difficulty understanding why God remained angry with them, or what it was in their behavior or their attitude that he was punishing them for.

Some Christians naively think that the notion of divine forgiveness is a peculiar Christian doctrine; it is not. Judaism has always believed it.55 It is clearly and eloquently confessed in some of the Psalms:

I said, "I will confess my transgressions to Yahweh; then thou didst forgive the guilt of my sin.
(32:5)

If thou, Yahweh, shouldst mark iniquities,
Lord who could stand?
But there is forgiveness with thee
that thou mayest be feared (130:3-4)

As from antiquity, the Jews could still see the law of sin/punishment, repentance/restoration at work

in the lives of individual men. It is accordingly the
principle of individual retribution that they came to
emphasize. On a collective basis, they took comfort in
developing notions of a final judgment for all mankind,
recompensing the Gentiles for their injustices to the
Jews. In order to strengthen their assurance of belonging to the righteous community, they laid increasing
emphasis on keeping the Mosaic law. Sin came to be defined, for all practical purposes, as the breaking of
this law. To assure the righteous that they could overcome sin by keeping the Law, a notion of a good and evil
impulse (yetser),[55] inside man but not part of him,
supplanted the prophetic concept of the depraved heart.
But anxiety remained. Even so enthusiastic a rigorism
as was practiced in the Qumran community failed to
quiet the troubled soul, or assure the pious that he
was fully without sin (see especially the Hodayoth, the
Thanksgiving hymns):

> But I--I belong to wicked mankind,
> to the communion of sinful flesh.
>   My transgressions, my iniquities and sins,
> and the waywardness of my heart
> condemn me to communion with the worm
> and with all that walk in darkness
>   (1QS XI 9-10, Gaster trans.).[57]

2) The theory of demonic seduction

So pernicious and persistent is sin's power that
speculation developed to the effect that sinister
supernatural forces must be seducing mankind -- devils
or demons. It is virtually absent in the canonical
Old Testament, begins to proliferate in the apocryphal
and pseudepigraphical writings, and is taken over as a
normative tradition in the New Testament. It must be
frankly stated that this is clearly subbiblical. It is
rife in certain sections of the Bible -- the later parts
-- but it is constitutionally incompatible with authentic biblical personalism.

The concept of demonic temptation appears to be
a melange of pagan dynamism and polytheism, which believed in all sorts of malevolent forces at loose in
the universe, and Persian dualism, which attributed
good and evil to metaphysically independent forces.
The core of biblical tradition is emphatically mono-

theistic, hence precludes both these lines of speculation. In classical Hebraism even evil comes from Yahwe (I Sam. 18:10, Amos 4:6), and the "satan" of the Job prologue, who can do nothing without Yahweh's consent, is the bringer of calamity rather than a seducer (but cf. I Chr. 21:1). It is a fair assessment to say that an intensifying notion of divine transcendence -- removing God far from the scene of human life -- along with the postexilic period's profound sense of human sinfulness, provided fertile ground for this aberrant speculation. It ought to be entertained by modern adherents of the biblical tradition, Christian as well as Jewish, in no other than a symbolic sense.

(c)   Sin in the New Testament

The presence and the problem of sin are just as much a part of the New Testament as of the Old Testament, and yet one who reads it is immediately struck by an astounding difference. All the old terms and concepts are here in the New Testament, but deepened and strangely transformed. The one factor which makes this great difference is the work of Jesus Christ.... The doctrine of sin in the New Testament is dominated by the assurance that Christ has come to conquer it.

Jesus showed that his understanding of the will of God was far wider, and of the darkness of sin far deeper, than the scribes and Pharisees imagined. In the Sermon on the Mount he showed that all the hidden attitudes and emotions are involved in sin, just as much as the outward actions by which legalism judged a man (Matt. 5:21-48)....It is sin in the depths of man's being that defiles him the most (Mark 7:21-23).

The apostle Paul goes completely beyond the law as a standard of sin and righteousness....He does not deny that if a person could really keep the law perfectly, in spirit as well as in letter, he would be considered righteous in God's sight. The sad truth is that no one can keep it perfectly. Thus the law points out a man's failures. It shows the depth of his sinfulness (Rom. 3:20, 5:20, 7:7-24, Gal. 3:19-24).

The Jew looked upon Gentiles as slaves of darkness and evil. Paul agrees with this judgment, but in a

17C

notable passage (Romans 1-3), where he explains how the Gentiles have perversely and rebelliously corrupted themselves in spite of the better knowledge that God had given them in his natural revelation, he includes the Jew under the same condemnation, because he sins against even greater light....Paul shows that the sin of the Jew is even more heinous than that of the Gentiles, because while teaching others he does not teach himself, while preaching to others he forgets to follow his own admonition, while boasting of the law he dishonors God by breaking the law (2:9-23).

As all men are sinners, so also the whole being of man is infected with its poison. It is in all the organs and members of the body (Rom. 6:19, 7:23), in the intellect (Rom. 1:21, Eph. 4:17-18), and even in the will, since this is held captive by the desires of the flesh (Rom. 7:15-20). One of the results of sin is physical death (Rom. 5:12ff., 6:23); but to "die in one's sins" (John 8:24) or to be "dead through trespasses and sins" (Eph. 2:1, 5) means something far more dreadful than this. It means to be dead to God, beyond hope of spiritual revovery apart from his grace (S. J. DeVries, "Sin, Sinners," _IDB_ II 372-75).[59]

The Bible's penultimate word about sin is expressed by Paul in Rom 7:24: "Wretched man that I am! Who will deliver me from this body of death?" The Bible's ultimate word about sin immediately follows: (v. 25): "Thanks be to God through Jesus Christ our Lord!" It took Jesus Christ to show what God really intended to do about the problem of sin.

b. The acceptance of God's acceptance

(1) Nonbiblical soteriologies

No more than a brief word need be said respecting nonbiblical schemes of salvation, whether of the ancient or the modern variety -- for all is implied in the respective concepts of sin.

Primitive heathenism presupposes that sin is completely or partially irrational, hence can be remedied by a mechanistic or manipulative process of salvation.

Whether the afflicted sinner has to deal with a god well known and fondly trusted, or with a frightful demon, he will seek to bring a change in the numen rather than in himself. True, he must show at least outward repentance; trouble is, he does not always know what he must repent of. The main thing is to get the numen from being angry with him. He does this by flattery, by appeal to the god's compassion or obligation, and by the offering of sacrifice. The principle is quid pro quo, something for something. He who is prudent will pay diligent service to the great gods. Where even this fails, he must try to find a medium or a magician -- the canny amateur who has powers which even the haughty priesthood lacks.

This is but silly superstition to the modern mind. As a matter of fact, the proud cosmopolitan of the Hellenistic empire had already discarded it. Yet great evils continued to plague human society, and a consciousness of sin remained. The philosophers developed sophisticated theories to deal with it, but never brought much relief because they continued to treat sin as either irrational or as necessary; i.e., something you could do nothing about or something you simply had to accept. The classical remedies for sin were: (1) stoicism, depending on moral self-improvement, treating both happiness and suffering as not ultimately real; (2) the intellectual self-improvement programs of the Platonic or Gnostic varieties, encouraging man to relegate sin to the shadow world of fleshly life and seek personal fulfillment in reason.

(2)   Subbiblical soteriologies

Our discourse has been emphasizing what is different and distinctive in biblical thought, continually contrasting this with the characteristic notions of the world outside the influence of the biblical tradition. From this, some may get the mistaken impression that we have no eye for the many things, good and harmful, that the Israelites borrowed from the religions of their neighbors. It has been said before that this is not our intent. Israel was indebted to its cultural environment. Seen diachronically, its progression to a more noble faith and life was not uniform. Numerous individuals failed to perceive or embrace the more ennobling insights achieved by the great spiritual leaders.

172.

In the end, however, we judge biblical religion at the points where it made clear and lasting improvements toward a more true and satisfying belief, and a more ethical, life-fulfilling practice.

It is important to say this here as a context for our statements about a normative biblical soteriology. We must understand that it was an achievement that did not come without struggle. The Bible gives evidence for a faltering at the wayside on the part of many who struggled for breath and light. There were what we may call subbiblical soteriological systems, imperfect or inadequate graspings at the more perfect solution which the Bible has to offer. Because these subbiblical options still offer themselves to adherents of the biblical heritage, they must be clearly identified before the authentic choice can appear in its proper light.

(a) Cultic atonement

The Old Testament offers numerous examples of the concept of atonement[60] for sin attained through cultic sacrifice.[61] Not only is this mentioned in narratives of various kinds; it is regulated in long and complex cult-legislative texts occupying a sizeable portion of the Pentateuch.[62] Cultic sacrifice for the purpose of obtaining relief from the guilt of sin was practiced at all the Israelite shrines, and when Jerusalem became the exclusive sanctuary, it was continued there as well. Even upon return from foreign exile, the Jews reinstituted atoning sacrifice. But this must have been due solely to the weight of sacrosanct tradition. In Babylon before the return; for a large number of Jews in the diaspora throughout the postexilic period; and for the entire body of Judaism since the Roman dispersal, sacrificial ritual was no longer possible. Furthermore, the Qumran community, even with its fierce zeal for the Law, did not practice it because they were banished from the Jerusalem temple.[63] All this shows that biblical faith does not have an integral place for the mechanism of atoning ritual. Its benefit lay more in the psychological relief it could offer to the worshiper, than in moving God to change his mind about punishing the sinner. Besides this, an important part of sacrifice was to celebrate communion between God and his people. It was a natural development that the Old Testament prescribes special offerings for sin, for guilt, for

thanksgiving, for communion with God. Perhaps the
private offerings produced a deeper spiritual understanding than the great public sacrifices, the numerous
slaughterings of beasts in the regular routine. The
latter were ostentatious demonstrations of the deity's
greatness, as reflected in the prosperity of the nation
and power of the king.

As has been said, Judaism eventually was forced to
abandon sacrificial worship. Although Jesus and the
apostles (Paul) participated in temple worship,[64] certain isolated New Testament traditions reject it with
considerable animosity. We think of Stephen's harsh
diatribe in Acts 6-7, exhibiting an iconoclastic sec-
tarianism that might have never surfaced in the body of
Scripture except for the need to preserve the memory of
Christendom's earliest martyr. We think also of the
long discourse in Hebrews 6-10, where Christ is identified as the fulfilment of Israel's most worthy cultic
traditions. It is less the priesthood and its sacrifices, and more the atonement obtained by it, that
occupy this book's attention. It was probably to console a group of Jewish Christians at the destruction of
the temple that this book was written. Although its
aim was to direct attention to the lasting benefits of
Jesus' earthly ministry, the strong emphasis upon his
death as an atonement for sin eventually influenced the
notion of a sacrificial Eucharist within Roman Catholicism, which gradually built up an imposing cultic establishment more grandiose than the one that once stood
in Jerusalem.

(b) Legalism

Devotion to the Law (Torah) is not in itself legalism. The concept of law developed naturally from the
concept of covenant. The Law is simply a device for
explicating the requirements of the covenant. Therefore to honor and obey the Law is to respect the covenant and obey God. There is a joy in observing the Law
(the Jews call it "simchath-Torah") when it is followed
out of love for God.

All the same, legalism did emerge in postexilic
and postbiblical Judaism. It was an undesirable by-
product of biblical religion, appearing also in various
Christian movements. Wherever a written code, or an

oral code functioning with formal authority (think of
the stern mores of the Amish!), becomes sacrosanct, we
have a form of legalism. Here is the apotheosis of a
historically conditioned formulation for public morality and ritual practice. We can see this happening to
the Jewish Torah in its progress through history.[65]
At first, Israelite covenant morality had only the
sanction of secular and religious authorities: the
elders, the king, the covenant celebrant, the priest.
As the Pentateuchal laws were codified, they were ascribed to Moses and traced back fictionally to Sinai.
In certain pseudepigraphical books of the intertestamental period, such as Jubilees and the Assumption of
Moses, Moses prepares the Torah by dictation from
heaven.[66] Probably this was a speculation that was not
shared by all the Jews of first-century Palestine, but
it does show how something historical and relative may
become absolutized. It had now become an effective
surrogate for God himself. The formula is now, very
simply: to honor God is to obey his Torah.

Judaism came only gradually to the full apotheosis
of the Torah. Historical perils such as the persecution
under Antiochus Epiphanes in the second century before
Christ played an important role in hastening this process.[67] We will not say that Jewish religion had become
pure legalism by Jesus' time; if it had, it could not
have produced a man with such intuitive awareness of
divine power as Jesus the Nazarene. Nevertheless,
legalism had come to play an important role, and it
continued to play an even more important role as Judaism moved into the separatism of Mishnaic distinctiveness. It was this misconception more than anything
else that led Paul to break with Torah piety and offer
the gospel to non-Jews[68] -- a move that led to the
irreconcilable break between the Christians and the
Jews.

The severe critique of legalism is that it allows
a symbol of divine presence to take the place of the
reality itself. What is this but another form of idolatry? When the Jewish Law, or any other law, comes to
assume a greater level of authority than a fresh and
intuitive apprehension of the divine will, we are confronted with legalism. A temporary and finite manifestation of Deity blocks out the eternal and infinite
reality behind it. Transcendent authority is radically
depersonalized. In extreme forms of legalism, the
awareness of the divine will is effectively frustrated
in deference to the external code. This is apparently

175

what happened when Jesus was condemned by the Jewish leaders. God was in their presence, but they were blinded by their superstitious attachment to the pale record of God's former presence among their fathers.

Legalism externalizes the concept of sin, but also the concept of salvation; both are depersonalized. Hypocrisy is now invited with open arms. Religious man remains as lost as he ever was!

(c) Apocalyptic dualism and futurism

Although the apocalyptic view of time and history are to be discussed in Chapter IV, apocalyptic dualism and futurism must be mentioned here as another form of subbiblical soterism. As a soteriological mechanism, it falls far short of the high personalism of the prophets and the Christian gospel. It does not appeal to the sinful Israelite to repent; it admonishes the righteous Israelite to wait, and be faithful in his devotion to God and the Law. Although it is addressed as consolation to the pious, it is also a soteriology because it tells him how God intends to deal with the problem of sin. This is seen in cosmological terms. It lies not in the heart of the faithful Israelite, but outside the circle of the righteous, among the Gentiles and the apostates. Apocalyptic has come to a fateful decision: the fault for the continuing experience of divine wrath lies neither with God nor with true Israel, but in a principle of evil which God is allowing to exist and operate until this age shall be completed. So it must remain until the "end" that God has decreed, when he will judge the wicked and abolish sin forever.[69]

This too can be idolatry. The apocalypticist sees the basic failure not in himself or the group to which he belongs -- only in others. Thus he views himself and his own as the center of the universe. He comes to imagine that, of all the races of mankind, God loves only Israel -- and, among them, only the truly pious. The world outside is utterly beyond redemption; it can only be judged. God has structured the entire course of human history in order, at last, to rescue and exalt these, his faithful ones.[70]

This narrow kind of particularism threatens to

destroy the Bible's astounding paradox of divine transcendence revealed in paternal immanence. To acknowledge electing grace with humility and gratitude is
beautiful. It can become ugly and grotesque when the
object of grace succumbs to the conceit that only his
own salvation matters. Thus apocalyptic can foster a
highly egocentric ideology, perpetuating man's sin in
the garden. Man still acts as God, peering into God's
secrets in order to know good and evil even as God
knows them!

Excursus on the development of pre-Christian
apocalypticism

We would sketch briefly the main stages through
which apocalyptic(ism) probably passed prior to the
rise of Christianity. Insights derived especially from
M. Hengel, Judaism and Hellenism,[71] and O. Plöger,
Theocracy and Eschatology,[72] may be organized as follows:

1) Restorationism. Situation: The imminent end
of the exile. Presupposed is P's model of a purely
sacral Israel. Ezekiel 38-39 and expansions to Obadiah
develop the holy-war theme; Ezekiel 40-48 (successively
expanded) and Zechariah 1-6 furnish models for the ideal
congregation; Trito-Isaiah, Malachi, and Joel 1-2
express a prophetically oriented disillusionment and
envision Yahweh's imminent return to purge worship.
Time-speculation is not yet a prominent feature.

2) Theocratic dualism. A new development under
the auspices of the eschatological wing of the theocratic party (cf. Plöger), who are the editorial
redactors of the prophetic collection. The time is the
early Hellenistic era, presupposing Ezra's reform, the
work of the Chronicler and the Samaritan schism, which
cut off deviant groups from "Israel." Alexander's
conquest has definitively removed further hope for a
national restoration or an historical solution to foreign oppression. Persian dominance is reflected in the
growth of dualism. Here we assign additions to Ezekiel
38-39, Joel 3-4, Isaiah 24-27, Zechariah 9-14. Gone
is prophetism's ethical call (Zech. 13:4), for the
antithesis is now between ideal Israel and the reprobate
gentiles. Time-ideology is prominent but not periodized
or highly schematic.

3) __Hasidism__. Against the background of the
Seleucid assimilation policy, strengthened by disillusionment with priestly venality, full-blown or
"normative" apocalyptic arises, as in Jubilees, 1 Enoch,
Testaments of the 12 Patriarchs, and early Daniel;
Epiphanian persecution produces the latest stages of
Daniel. Here are featured a sharpened particularism
and dualism, cosmic speculation, and the radical peri-
odication of time. The speculative aspects of priestly
ideology are seen in calendrical reform efforts
(Jubilees, 1 Enoch).

4) __Essenism__. Reflecting disillusionment with
Hasmonean rule and Sadducean domination in the temple,
a new apocalypticism appears in a demand for a totally
separated Israel with a "Zadokite" aristrocracy, now
opposing the apostate leadership within Judaism. An
early phase (CDC, IQH, IQS) emphasizes separation,
asceticism, and Torah rigorism, based on cosmic dualism
expressed in the two-spirits doctrine. A later phase
refocuses on the foreign enemy, activistically merging
the eschaton with the present age (IQM).73 (From S. J.
De Vries, "Observations on Quantitative and Qualitative
Time in Wisdom and Apocalyptic," __Wisdom__ __in__ __Israel__, pp.
273-74.)

(3)   Normative biblical soteriology

(a)   Terminology

The Old Testament contains a number of prominent
salvific words. These have received characteristic
Greek translations in the LXX, and as such have been
taken over into the New Testament.

The Old Testament has no abstract term to corre-
spond to Greek __sōtēria__, "salvation" (cf. its cognates
__sōtēr__, "savior," and __sōzō__, "save"), which regularly
refers to deliverance from sin.74 Because the New
Testament presents Christ's work as concerned almost
exclusively with alleviating sin, Christians readily
fall into the habit of using the word "salvation" in
this particular meaning. It is necessary to point out,
therefore, that most of the salvific words in Hebrew

refer not to deliverance from sin as such, but from the
calamities and evils of human existence. True, these
may be -- and generally are -- interpreted as a punishment for sin (see the rigid dogma of Job's friends!),
but normal Old Testament thinking always considers
other possibilities.

In Chapter V, where we discuss the problem of
suffering and evil, it will be appropriate to mention
God's saving action. It is in this context that many
salvation words appear. The important ones are nouns
and verbs derived from the following roots: YŠʿ, "save,"
"give victory"; MLṬ causative, "rescue"; PDH, "ransom";
ʿZR, "help"; RḤM, "be compassionate"; ḤNN, "be merciful"
; YṢ', "bring out." The noun yᵉšûʿâ, from which the
proper name Joshua (=Jesus) is drawn, often means
"victory."[75]

1) Yahweh's action

Strictly with reference to salvation from sin, the
Old Testament depicts three specific actions of the
Deity. It is his part:

To hear, (ŠMʿ),[76] give heed (QŠB),[77] answer
(ʿNH),[78] Yahweh regularly promises to be attentive
and responsive to the plea for deliverance. He is
not like Baal in the Mt. Carmel story, who is
away on business, concerned for his private affairs
(I Kings 18:27), and who therefore does not answer
or give heed. He is ever attentive, waiting for
the sinner's call.

To be sorry, repent (NḤM).[79] Yahweh repents
of evil, for his heart is full of compassion.

To forgive (ŠLḤ) the suppliant's transgressions.[80]

2) The sinner's action

What the sinner needs to do to be saved centers in
three essential actions, for which there are three main
Old Testament words:

To repent (ŠÛB).[81] Since the basic meaning of
this term is simply "turn around, or away," it has
been used not only of God's change of heart but of
man's apostasy. In salvific contexts it means
"turn back." Our word "repent" is a bit too weak
because it may indicate a mere change of attitude
and intent, whereas ŠÛB defines a thorough reorien-
tation of the sinner's existence, involving a
radical alteration of his life habits if they have
been at fault.

To obey (ŠMꜤ).[82] This too has multiple appli-
cations because its basic meaning is "hear." In
salvation, God hears in apperception of the sinner's plight; man hears in responding to, and
complying with, the divine will for his life.
Saving obedience is more than a formal compliance,
to be sure. It means to bring one's entire existence into harmony with the design of God.

To trust (ʾMN).[83] The Hebrew word ʾamūnâ
hardly ever refers to intellectual assent. It
means "fidelity" or "trustworthiness"; also the
act of trusting.[84] Although the Greek word _pistis_
is more ambiguous, the Pauline dictum, "We are
justified by faith,"[85] presupposes this Hebraic
concept of trusting. Again, more than attitude
and intent are involved. Saving trust means
yielding one's entire life and entire being to
divine control. Faith saves because it restores
what was lost in Adam's fall. Adam did not trust,
hence he did not obey.

3) Symbols of the saved condition

For the nation as a whole, peace, land, and prosperous peoplehood are the most commonly used figures of
restoration. These are simply the promises of ancient
tradition, once offered to Abraham and always cherished
by the people as symbols of perfection.[86]

For the individual, healing, joy, and prosperity
are familiar metaphors of restoration from sin.[87] In
profound awareness that the change has not been accomplished in the former state of unrepentance, but through
the marvelous influence of a power from God, the Bible
at times speaks of forces entirely new. These operate,

as well, to effect the restoration of the sinful nation.
Among the most striking images, the foremost is the new
heart or spirit, of which we read in Ezek. 36:26-27:[88]

> A new heart I will give you, and a new spirit
> I will put within you; and I will take out of
> your flesh the heart of stone and give you a
> heart of flesh. And I will put my spirit within
> you, and cause you to walk in my statutes and be
> careful to observe my commandments.

Secondly, we read of a new covenant or new law, as in
Jer. 31:31-34:

> Behold, the days are coming, says Yahweh, when
> I will make a new covenant with the house of
> Israel....This is the covenant which I will
> make...: I will put my law within them, and
> I will write it upon their hearts; and I will
> be their God, and they shall be my people.

It is no other than these Hebraic images that
reappear in the New Testament to express the meaning
of the saved condition. The most striking departure
from Old Testament usage is the special emphasis on
the most prominent features of the Messiah's role in
the kingdom of God.[89] It is the strong influence of
apocalyptic that has brought these images into prominence, giving them an importance that they never had
during the classic age of Hebraic religion.[90]

(b)   Salvation from sin in the Old Testament

The Old testament definition of sin prepares for,
and presupposes, the Old Testament definition of salvation. Sin in the Old Testament is viewed in the light
of the divine holiness, which confronts it as persistent
human failure. The divine will is deeply personalistic,
revealing a God who does not change. His people Israel
know his will. They are not left in the dark wondering
what he wants of them, for there is nothing arbitrary
or irrational in him. He continually reveals himself
to them, and does not withhold himself from them. Thus
their sin has little excuse, but is simply man's failure
to respect his will and respond to it. Their sin is a
fault of personal existence, the failure of persons to

respond appropriately to the supreme Person.

This tragic wrongness naturally bears many evil
consequences. What must be done to alleviate it is,
for sinners to respect the divine holiness and the
divine integrity in terms of a corresponding holiness
and integrity, which means beginning to take their
own amazing personal powers seriously, giving good use
to what has been designed as good. This brings a healing of the sinner's self and a restoration of the estranged relationship between him and his God.

Those who are dismayed by the spectacle of their
lostness as sinners need to trust that God is ready to
take them back, and will restore in them what sin has
destroyed. Here is where the symbol of his lordship
and the symbol of his parental love fuse together to
assure a sovereign freedom to forgive. There are many
passages in the Old Testament to which we could turn to
illustrate this, but no better choice could be made
than Hos. 11:8-9.91 The whole passage is full of pathos. Yahweh is speaking as an aggrieved parent, who
loved Israel as a little child (vv. 1-4). But their
persistence in sin has brought evil consequences upon
them; they are about to be taken captive by foreign
enemies:

> My people are bent on turning away from me;
>   so they are appointed to the yoke,
>   and none shall remove it. (v. 7)

Nevertheless, Yahweh refuses to surrender them to their
deserts. He will not allow their stubborn waywardness
to force him into decreeing their fate. In spite of
their unworthiness, he will love them still:

> How can I give you up, O Ephraim!
>   How can I hand you over, O Israel!
> How can I make you like Admah!
>   How can I treat you like Zeboim!
> My heart recoils within me,
>   My compassion grows warm and tender.
> I will not execute my fierce anger,
>   I will not again destroy Ephraim;
> For I am God and not man,
>   the Holy One in your midst,
>   and I will not come to destroy.

"I am God and not man!" If Yahweh were like the
heathen gods, he would most assuredly punish his people's

wickedness, for this is the function of a god. If he were an earthly king, he would surely punish them. Yahweh nevertheless refuses to destroy them. He will no doubt chasten them sorely, till they learn the folly of their self-destructive refusal.

Free in his absolute sovereignty, the biblical God refuses to be mechanically bound to the sin-punishment syndrome. Sin brings its own punishment, and to the extent that this is the law of the universe, it is the law of God. But the biblical God does not allow this to produce a permanent and irremediable estrangement and ruin. He is not such a being as can be bound by man's sinfulness, but offers his Spirit to produce a new heart within him.

Of course, a human person retains a measure of freedom even as a sinner, and God in exercising the freedom of his sovereign love continues to respect that freedom within the sinful will of man. Which is to say: in spite of what our fathers called "antecedent grace," it is the sinner who must choose to respond before the divine love can have its intended effect. True, there is never a point at which God gives up on man, yet man can and does give up on God. It is clear where the fault lies. If Israel finally must come to ruin, this is due simply to its own persistent wilfulness. A sinner can indeed drive himself into hell. Alas, it is true! But it is not his God who is driving him there. It is never the will of God to ruin him.

We can see now that the solution to sin presupposes, first of all, the sovereign divine freedom to be gracious, compassionate and forgiving. God's grace is greater than man's sin. But the solution also presupposes that man's responsible will is still operative. He can and must make a choice to repent.

Let us be very clear on this point. The history of doctrine is filled with accounts of strife between the advocates of divine sovereignty and the adherents of free will.[92] One of the early examples was the reformer, Martin Luther, writing his treatise denying the freedom of the sinful will, bringing refutation from no less a personage than king Henry VIII of England, who thereby gained for himself and his successors the honorific title, "Defender of the faith." The Calvinists and Arminians had bitter struggles over this problem. Both sides were right, both sides were wrong. To the extent that the Bible insists on the

concept of divine sovereignty, even in judging wayward
man, the Calvinists seem to be right. God is sovereign,
but his sovereignty is not exercised in such a way as
to deprive man of his freedom and responsibility. This
is where the Arminians are right. The Bible insists
that man is free to be responsible, even while suffering
under the paralysis of his sinful habitus. No matter
how depraved and fallen an individual or a group of
people may become, they are never excused of responsibility. This is a "cop-out" that sinners eagerly seek:
"I am so bad, I cannot help myself"; "This is the way
I have been preconditioned"; "It's our parents, or our
teachers, or the rotten society we live in." The one
who says, "That's the way I am, I cannot act any other
way," is in fact trying to give the blame to God. This
is judging God and taking his place -- another form of
idolatry.

The Bible simply will not "buy" this. Never once
does it intimate that man as sinner is less than free
to change.

There came a time in the history of Israel when a
prophet arose to give this clear and emphatic expression. The prophet in question was Ezekiel, and we can
read his words about this both in the 18th and the 33rd
chapters of his book. In chapter 18 he articulates
individual human responsibility in order to counteract
a fatalistic view of corporate guilt. In chapter 33
he repeats this claim in order to counteract the related
notion that nothing can be done, once a sinner has
fallen from grace. The "sinner" in question is, in
fact, the entire Israelite people, who are in despair
about the Babylonian exile.

> And you, son of man, say to the house of Israel,
> Thus have you said, "Our transgressions and our
> sins are upon us, and we waste away because of
> them; how then can we live?" Say to them, " 'As
> I live,' says Yahweh God, 'I have no pleasure in
> the death of the wicked, but that the wicked
> turn from his way and live; turn back from your
> evil ways; for why will you die, O house of
> Israel?' " (vv. 10-11)

The gospel has no appeal more eloquent than this.
The Jewish exiles of 597 B.C. had been expecting that
the Babylonians would quickly be defeated by the
Egyptians, allowing the exiles to return to Palestine.
Persistently Ezekiel, who was among the exiles, warned

his fellow Jews not to cling to this false hope. He
knew that the Jews remaining in Jerusalem were persist-
ing in an adventurous policy of making an intrique with
the Egyptians, who would not in fact be able to offer
effective help; this would simply provoke the Babylonians into destroying the last remnants of Judah's national independence, making the condition of captivity
permanent. At last, in 586, this all came to pass.
And now the old exiles gave up all hope. Instead of
recognizing that the whole people together were responsible for their condition of destitution, they began to
put the blame on what their forefathers had done. They
felt so sorry for themselves that they described themselves as spiritually dead. They said they were in a
condition of absolute estrangement from God, completely
cut off from life and given over to ruin. They could
no longer hope; no longer exert themselves. It would
not do any good to repent, for nothing could now change
things as they were.

To this Ezekiel replies in moving pathos. He
repeats the words of a divine oath, Yahweh swearing by
himself: "I have no pleasure in the death of the
wicked." "Pleasure" means enjoyment, but also will or
intent. The spiritual death that may happen because
of persistent human recklessness, but only if man wills
it and refuses the remedy that God provides. What
Yahweh truly desires, and has pleasure in, is that the
wicked turn from his evil way and live -- that is, turn
in order to live. By turning, one may find life. Life
is offered to us; but God does not force it on us. He
gave it once in his creation, but now it is up to fallen
man to decide for himself whether he will grasp the new
life that is offered. To be sure, this is not only a
wish or desire of God; God demands it. God demands it
because he is sovereign; he demands it because man,
even in his sin, is capable of responding to this demand. "Turn back, turn back from your evil ways."

Ezekiel's appeal ends with a moving plea, "Why
will you die, O house of Israel?" Is Yahweh's plan to
be thwarted? Does his long-suffering love mean nothing,
after all? Will Israel choose to die, after he has done
so much to make it live?

Man can choose to die -- to surrender to sin. It
is one way a human being has of getting even with God.
Again, a monstrous form of idolatry -- a grotesque
repetition of the sin in the Garden. By deciding to
die (physically or spiritually), we seek the psycho-

logical relief of blaming our condition on someone
else. It is man's last outcry of titanic defiance.

But God will not let us off the hook. He demands
that the sinner turn, even in his condition of complete
ruin. Even in the ruin of exile, Israel must live!
Why? Because the God who created man in the beginning
is the Creator still, and out of ruin he can create a
new being (see Ezek. 37:1ff.). If God would refuse to
forgive, there would be no hope for fallen man. But
he does forgive. Even though the sinner must deal with
the evil consequences of his sin, God's forgiveness can
create new life within and around him. But the sinner
must make his choice between titanic defiance and a
humble, grateful, believing acceptance of what God
offers. Salvation cannot come for him if he insists
on hanging on to his pathetic egocentricity.

The biblical doctrine of salvation exemplifies a
profound respect for the integrity of human personhood.
This is because the God with whom man must deal, in sin
and salvation, is himself the perfect embodiment of
personhood.

(c)   Salvation from sin in the New Testament

This is the major theme of the New Testament, and
fills its pages. Our present purpose is served by a
succinct summary of its teaching rather than a detailed
exposition of its rich and varied symbolism, which
properly belongs in a separate study of Christology.[93]

The New Testament is suffused with the joyous
awareness of salvation from sin. This may be possessed
by the individual, and is to be shared by the whole
world. It is not only for Jews but also for Gentiles,
for anyone who believes in Jesus as the Christ may have
it. This is the happy Good News that the church had to
offer to an age sunk in wretchedness and despair.

The New Testament has many images of Christ as
Savior. Its rich symbolism of salvation has given rise
to an often self-contradictory speculation about the
nature of the atonement that he had brought. Furthermore, the subbiblical mechanisms that we have previously
discussed continued to exert their influence. We must

186

look behind elements of (1) sacrificial propitiation
borrowed from cultic ideology, (2) legalistic work-
righteousness, and (3) apocalyptic dualism and futurism
-- all of which have colored, or even distorted, Christian soteriology -- in order to look squarely at what
Jesus Christ actually did to secure the salvation from
sin that the whole world had been anxiously seeking.
It is this that lies at the heart of authentic biblical
soterism.

Although the Gospels are not the earliest compositions within the New Testament corpus, it is they --
and particularly the Synoptics -- that accurately recol-
lect the earliest impact of Jesus' ministry. He could
offer righteousness to sinners because he was himself
the perfect embodiment of a right relationship with
God. He showed in all that he did that a righteous God
does not grind sinners down in his condemnation, but
welcomes them -- like the loving father in the parable
of the prodigal son -- to renew a right relationship
with him.

St. Luke has a story of sinful woman who comes to
wipe Jesus feet with ointment (7:36-50). When Jesus
does not reject her, he is criticized by his host, a
Pharisee. Jesus' reply is that the woman's love shows
greater repentance than the Pharisee's formal rightness,
and thereby gives abundant evidence of her salvation
and acceptance by God. "Therefore I tell you," says
Jesus, "her sins, which are many, are forgiven, for she
loved much; but he who is forgiven little, loves little"
(v. 47). He assures the woman, "Your sins are forgiven
....Your faith has saved you; go in peace" (vv. 49-50).
The Pharisees interpret this declaration as pretentious
arrogance: "Who is this who even forgives sins?" -- a
recurrent theme in the Gospel narratives.94 This is
not blasphemous self-deification, but authentic theomorphism. Jesus forgives as God forgives; his love
exemplifies the love of God. In his attitude and behavior, he shows the world what God is truly like.

The cross is a symbol of how far God will go in
his love.95 Historically speaking, it was a colossal
error and an indescribable tragedy. How monstrous that
the most righteous nation and the most powerful nation
of the ancient world should conspire to destroy this
most beautiful exemplar of perfect manhood, this most
eloquent image of Godhood! He was destroyed because
neither religious nor secular culture could endure the
presence of his lustrous goodness.

The cross is surely a symbol of the depth of human depravity, but it is an even more potent symbol of the triumph of God's love. Because Jesus' awareness of God's love made him the perfect embodiment of God's love, he had to die; but in his innocent death God died too (symbolically speaking -- of course -- for God cannot die except in the sorrow and dying of his beloved children).

This is the truest meaning of the resurrection. The world cannot kill love. In innocent suffering, those who are like Jesus will live even though they die.

Thus the central meaning of Jesus' life, death and resurrection is the ultimate power and extent of God's intent to save. He constantly urges sinners to repent, but they need to be shown that in sinning they injure God the most. He cares so much that he even allowed his Son, the most righeous man who ever lived, to die. To cling to sin -- knowing that -- is the grossest ingratitude of all!

Finally, we outline the mechanism of salvation according to New Testament understanding. It is the same as that of the Old Testament -- but gloriously illumined by the presence of Christ.

The sinner must first of all repent, as in Old Testament religion. John the baptist, symbolic forerunner of Christ, preaches repentance as preparation for receiving salvation in Christ.96

Secondly, the sinner must believe. Although the New Testament concept of faith has a broader ideational content than that of the Old Testament -- and this is necessarily so because of the drastically new way in which Christ represented the presence of God -- "faith" (pistis) still means, essentially, trust and commitment.97

Thirdly, the sinner must obey -- or, in a more representative New Testament symbol -- he must follow, and become a disciple. "Take up your cross and follow me."98

The unity of the Old and New Testament may be seen in the way Jesus Christ perfectly fulfilled the constitutional definition of righteousness as offered by the prophet Micah in 6:6-8. Uniquely and absolutely, Jesus dramatized the alternate choices for finding salvation:

> With what shall I come before Yahweh,
>   and bow myself before God on high?
> Shall I come before him with burnt offerings,
>   with calves a year old?
> Will Yahweh be pleased with thousands of rams,
>   with ten thousands of rivers of oil?
> Shall I give my first-born for my transgression,
>   the fruit of my body for the sin of my soul?
> He has shown you, O man, what is good;
>   and what does Yahweh require of you
> But to do justice and to love fidelity
>   (RSV:kindness),
>   and to walk humbly with your God?

FOR FURTHER STUDY

On righteousness:

G. Quell, G. Schrenk, BKW, I/IV, "Righteousness"
                (=TDNT, II, 174ff.)
    Justice in the Old Testament
    The Greek idea of justice
    Righteous
    Righteousness in the New Testament
    Justification

On man:

G. Bertram et al., TDNT, IX, 608ff., psuchē, etc.
    Psuchē in the Greek world
    The anthropology of the Old Testament
    Judaism
    The New Testament
    Gnosticism

N. P. Bratsiotis, TDOT, I, 222ff., 'ish
    Secular use
    Theological considerations

J. H. Chamberlayne, Man in Society, The Old Testament
                Doctrine, London: Epworth, 1966

W. Eichrodt, Man in the Old Testament (Studies in
                Biblical Theology), London, 1951

W. Eichrodt, TOT, II, 118ff.
    The place of man in the creation
        The peculiar value of man as compared with
            other creatures
    The components of human nature

idem, II, 231ff., 268ff.
    The individual and the community and the Old
        Testament God-man relationship
    The fundamental forms of man's relationship
        with God

A. R. Johnson, The Vitality of the Individual in the
              Thought of Ancient Israel, Cardiff:
              University of Wales Press, 1964

F. Maass, TDOT, I, 75ff., 'adhām
     Usage in the Old Testament
     Anthropological and theological consideration

H. D. Preuss, TDOT, III, 250ff., dāmāh, d^emûth

O. Schilling, TDOT, II, 317ff., bāśār
     Use in an anthropological sense
     Use in a theological sense (God and bāśār)

E. Schweizer, F. Baumgärtel, R. Meyer, TDNT, VII, 98ff.,
              sarx, etc.
     Flesh in the Old Testament
     Flesh in Judaism
     The New Testament

E. Schweizer, F. Baumgärtel, TDNT, VII, 1024ff., sōma,
              etc.
     The Greek world
     The Old Testament
     Judaism
     The New Testament

H. W. Wolff, Anthropology of the Old Testament
              (Philadelphia: Fortress, 1974
              hereinafter AOT), 7ff.
     The being of man
          nepeš -- needy man
          bāśār -- man in his infirmities
          rûaḥ -- man as he is empowered
          lēb(āb) -- reasonable man
          The life of the body
          The inner parts of the body
          The form of the body
          The nature of man

idem, pp. 93ff., 159ff.
     Creation and birth
     God's image -- the steward of the world

idem, pp. 223ff.
     The destiny of man
          To live in the world
          To love his fellow-men
          To rule over creation
          To praise God

<u>On</u> <u>sin</u> <u>and</u> <u>punishment</u>:

J. Bergman, B. Johnson, <u>TDOT</u>, I, 345ff., <u>'ānaph</u>
    Divine anger
        Linguistic analysis
        Reasons for divine anger
        Manifestations of divine anger
        Positive value of divine anger

F. Buckel, V. Herntrich, <u>TDNT</u>, III, 921ff., <u>krinō</u>, etc.
    The Old Testament term <u>mishpat</u>
    The concept of judgment in the Greek world
    The concept of judgment in Judaism
    The concept of judgment in the New Testament

W. Eichrodt, <u>TOT</u>, I, 457ff.
    Covenant-breaking and judgment
        Judgment as a guarantee and restoration of
            the covenant
        Judgment as abrogation of the covenant
        Individualist and universalist elements in
            the expectation of judgment

<u>idem</u>, II, 380ff.
    Sin and forgiveness
        The nature of sin
        The universality of sin
        The origin of sin
        The consequences of sin
        The removal of sin
        Sin and evil

W. Foerster, <u>TDNT</u>, II, 1ff., <u>daimōn</u>, etc.
    <u>Daimōn</u> in the Greek and hellenistic world
    The Old Testament and later Jewish view of demons
    The view of demons in the New Testament

W. Grundmann, <u>TDNT</u>, III, 469ff., <u>kakos</u>, etc.
    <u>Kakos</u> in the Old Testament (<u>LXX</u>)
    <u>Kakos</u> in the New Testament

V. Hamp, G. J. Botterweck, <u>TDOT</u>, III, 187ff., <u>dîn</u>
    Judging in the Old Testament
        Earthly judgment
        God judges
        Theological relevance

G. Harder, TDNT, VI, 546ff., ponēros, ponēria
    Ponēros in the Greek world
    The Old Testament and later Judaism
    Ponēros in the New Testament

D. Kellermann, TDOT, I, 429ff., 'āshām

H. Kleinknecht et al., BKW, V/II, "Wrath" (=TDNT, V,
                382ff.)
    Wrath in classical antiquity
    The wrath of man and the wrath of God in the
        Old Testament
    God's wrath in the Septuagint
    God's wrath in late Judaism
    The wrath of God in the New Testament

G. Quell et al., TDNT, I, 267ff., hamartanō, etc.
    Sin in the Old Testament
    Theological nuances of hamartia in the LXX
    The concept of sin in Judaism
    Sin in the New Testament

G. von Rad, OTT, I, 154ff., 262ff.
    The incursion and spread of sin
    The priestly document: Sin and atonement

K. Seyboldt, TDOT, III, 23ff., gāmal, etc.

On salvation:

G. Bertram, TDNT, VII, 714ff., strephō, apostrephō,
                epistrephō, etc.
    In the Old Testament
    In Judaism
    In the New Testament

R. Bultmann, A. Weiser, BKW, IV/I, "Faith" (=TDNT, VI,
             174ff.)
    The Old Testament concept
    The linguistic usage in Greek
    Faith in Judaism
    The group of concepts associated with pistis
        in the New Testament

R. Bultmann, K. H. Rengstorf, BKW, III/I, "Hope"
           (= TDNT, II, 517ff.)
    The Greek concept of hope

The concept of hope in the Old Testament
Hope in rabbinic Judaism
The hope of hellenistic Judaism
The early Christian concept of hope

H. Conzelmann, *TDNT*, IX, 310ff., phōs, phōtizō, etc.
The word group in the Old Testament
Judaism
The New Testament
The early church

H. Conzelmann, W. Zimmerli, *TDNT*, IX, 359ff., chairō,
etc.
Charis: the Old Testament; Judaism; New Testament;
Post-apostolic fathers

W. Foerster, G. Fohrer, *TDNT*, VII, 965ff., sōzō, etc.
Sōzō and sōtēria in the Greek world; in the Old
Testament; in later Judaism; in the New
Testament

W. Grundmann et al., *TDNT*, IX, 493ff., chriō, christos,
etc.
Mšḥ and mašīaḥ in the Old Testament
Messianic ideas in later Judaism
The Christ-statements of the New Testament
The Christ-statements of early Christianity
outside the New Testament

J. Herrmann, F. Buchsel, *TDNT*, III, 300ff., hileōs, etc.
Expiation and forms of expiation in the Old
Testament
Hilasmos and katharmos in the Greek world
Ideas of expiation in Judaism

A. Jepsen, *TDOT*, I, 292ff., 'āman
Niphal
Hiphil
'emeth; 'emunāh; 'āmēn

A. Jepsen, *TDOT*, II, 88ff., bātach
Security in God

G. Kittel, *TDNT*, I, 210ff., akoloutheō, etc.
Discipleship in the Old Testament and Judaism
Akolouthein in the New Testament

G. von Rad, *OTT*, I, 355ff.
Israel before Jahweh (Israel's answer)
Methodology preconsiderations

The praises of Israel
The righteousness of Jahweh and of Israel
The trials and the consolation of the
individual

O. Schilling, TDOT, II, 313ff., bŚr, be śôrāh

T. C. Vriezen, OOTT, pp. 404ff.
Man in the community of God
The kingdom of God and the expectation of the
future

S. Wagner, TDOT, II, 229ff., biqqēsh
Theological use
Seeking God
God seeks

S. Wagner, TDOT, III, 293ff., dārash
Theological use
The anthropological aspect
The specifically theological aspect
The derivative midrash

W. Zimmerli, OTTO, pp. 144ff.; 167ff.
The response of obedience
Crisis and hope
Humanity between judgment and salvation
(primal history)
The crisis of Israel in the historical
narratives
Judgment and salvation in the preaching
of the great literary prophets

NOTES

1. For details see the Biblical Theologies and P.
    Stuhlmacher, Die Gerechtigkeit Gottes bei Paulus,
    Göttingen 1966.

2. Acts 3:14, 7:52, 22:14, I Pet. 3:18, I John 2:1

3. On the significance of the Matthean idiosyncrasy,
    see A. Oepke in TDNT, I, 536; H. Ljungmann, Das

Gesetz und die Propheten, Untersuchungen zur Theologie des Evangeliums nach Matthäus (Regensburg: Pustet, 1974), pp. 198ff.

4. See O. Cullmann, Baptism in the New Testament, Philadelphia, 1950; also art. "Baptism" (W. F. Flemington), IDB. I, 348 ff. Evidence for proselyte baptism for the first Christian century is uncertain, though washing as a ritual of covenant membership was practiced among Jewish sects like that of Qumran (see A. R. C. Leaney, The Rule of Qumran and its Meaning, Philadephia 1966, pp. 141f.; L. Mowry, The Dead Sea Scrolls and the Early Church (Chicago 1968), pp. 234-38)

5. See R. Tannehill, Dying and Rising with Christ, A Study in Pauline Theology (Berlin 1967), pp. 7ff.

6. See B. Weiss, The Religion of the New Testament, New York 1905, pp. 208-12; O. Cullmann, Christology of the New Testament, Philadelphia 1959.

7, See R. Bultmann, Theology of the New Testament, I. 270ff.

8. Our usage is consistent with standard practice as defined in The Oxford English Dictionary under the entry, "Man," and resists the ideological neologisms of radical "liberation" movements. Old English had "wer" for the adult male and "wif" for the adult female, with "man" as the generic term for their mutual identity. As "woman" (from "wif-man") has acquired current semeiological function with reference to adult females, "man" alone has acquired its secondary semeiological function with reference to adult males. If this shift had been programmed for male dominance, as radical ideologists maintain, it is difficult to understand why Anglo-Saxon culture did not become more exploitative of women than the culture of Greece and Rome, with their linguistic choice between words for generic man (anthrōpos, homo) and the adult male (anēr, vīr), respectively.

9. See W. Windelband, A History of Philosophy, tr. J. H. Tufts (New York 1893), pp. 116-31.

10. This designation refers to contemporary phenomena derived from a medieval movement tracing its origins to Aristotle; cf. Windelband, op. cit., pp. 296ff.

11. On contemporary aspects of Hinduism and Buddhism in relationship to Christian thought, see H. Kraemer, The Christian Message in a Non-Christian World (New York 1946), pp. 158-81; also S. Neill, Christian Faith and Other Faiths (London 1961), pp. 70-124.

12. J. W. Wilson, tr.

13. E. A. Speiser, Tr.

14. The regular Mesopotamian idiom for humankind

15. E. A. Speiser, tr.

16. See T. Jacobsen, Treasures of Darkness, pp. 195-213, for an analysis of the Gilgamesh literary tradition.

17. E. A. Speiser, tr.

18. J. A. Wilson, tr.

19. See Chapter V, 1, b, (3), (d) "Gilgamesh fails to achieve immortality."

20. Here the "image of God" is substantive and realistic, no mere metaphor for theomorphic likeness, as in Genesis 1 (see below).

21. The symbol of shepherd is widely applied in the ancient Near Eastern literature to human kingship as well as to Deity.

22. See H. W. Wolff, Anthropology of the Old Testament (Philadelphia: Fortress, 1974), pp. 10-25 ("nepeš -- Needy Man").

23. For further elucidation of the meaning of human freedom, see Chapter IV, "Man's freedom and limitations."

24. An appropriate genre-name for Gen. 1:1-2:4a might be "mythic recital," with a probable cultic Sitz im Leben in its pre-literary status. It may actually have been a liturgy for the Sabbath; cf. P. Humbert, "La relation de Genèse 1 et du Psaume 104 avec la liturgie du Nouvel an Israelite, RHPhR,15 (1935), 1-27. Contrariwise, Gen. 2:4b-3:24 requires the genre-name, "mythic tale," with

an undefined <u>Sitz im Leben</u>. One of the clear marks of its original independence is its use of the combinational name for the Deity, "Yahweh Elohim" relinquished only in 3:1-7, where "Elohim" alone shows borrowing from a Canaanite fertility myth. All of this has been utilized as the Yahwist's introduction to his prehistory, chaps. 2-11. See the commentaries, especially now that of C. Westermann in <u>Biblischer Kommentar</u> (Neukirchen-Vluyn, 1974-).

25. Lacking cognates in primitive Semitic languages, this word has direct affinities only in non-Hebrew languages influenced by it. Virtually all biblical occurrences are in late writings such as Deuteronomy, the Psalms, and the prophetic books. It is a remarkably more highly theological word than the word used in the parallel J material of Genesis 2 (v. 7: YṢR, "shape," "form").

26. Most commentators view this as a demythified allusion to a heavenly council, borrowed by P from his tradition (cf. Ps. 82:1). There is nothing to favor the traditional Trinitarian explanation or the view that this represents a "plural of majesty."

27. For a comprehensive analysis of the form- and traditional-analysis of this pericope, see B. W. Anderson, "A Stylistic Study of the Priestly Creation Story," G. Coats and B. O. Long, edd., <u>Canon and Authority</u> (Philadelphia: Fortress 1977), pp. 148-62.

28. Cf. the encomium of man in Ecclus.10:19ff.

29. See M. Black, "The Pauline Doctrine of the Second Adam," <u>SJT</u>, 7 (1954), 170ff.; O. Cullmann, <u>Christology of the New Testament</u>, pp. 170-74

30. On the Christology of this book, see E. F. Scott, <u>The Epistle to the Hebrews</u> (Edinburgh, 1922), pp. 143ff.; on this verse, see especially S. G. Sowers, <u>The Hermeneutics of Philo and Hebrews</u> (Richmond 1965), p. 118.

31. Along with its special form for the divine name (see above), Genesis 2-3 consistently retains hā'ādām (except in 3:17, 21, where the form lā'ādām has been pointed as le'ādām, "to Adam"), rather than the personal name Adam, which,

appearing in chap. 4, signalizes the end of the special source employed by J in chaps. 2-3 (in chap. 4, LXX to Adam becomes Adam), indicating a change in the Hebrew Vorlage even in 4:1, where MT still retains hā'ādām.

32. Cf. W. H. Schmidt, Die Schöpfungsgeschichte der Priesterschrift. Anhang: Die jahwistische Schopfungs- und Paradiesgeschichte, WMANT 17, 2nd ed. 1967, pp. 194-228; J. L. McKenzie, Myths and Realities, 2nd ed. (Milwaukee 1963), pp. 146-81; C. Westermann, Genesis (Biblischer Kommentar, Altes Testament I/1; (Neukirchen-Vlayn, 1974), pp. 259ff.

33. The Old Testament furnished abundant evidence for Israelite woman's urgent concern for personal fertility, exemplified especially in the recurrent theme of the promise of a child to the barren wife (Sarah, Genesis 18; Rachel, Gen. 30:14ff.; Hannah, I Sam. 1:1-2:10; cf. Elisabeth, Luke 1). The horror of barrenness is borne out by the archeo-logical recovery of abundant fertility figurines of the Canaanite type in Israelite levels in various Palestinian sites. Yet we must understand that neither the underlying myth of Gen. 3:1-7 nor the J rewriting views woman's craving for sexual fruitfulness as something in itself evil. For the Canaanite mind this was something laudable. In J's monotheistic rewriting, it is the element of intersocial conflict -- whether directly in the husband-wife relationship or on a broader scale -- that creates the possibility of generic man departing from the simple path of harmony and obedience. The profound point of the fall story is that the complexity of human existence threatens to disrupt a perfect unity between man and God. In trying to resolve human conflicts through his own initiative, man invites greater and more damaging conflicts in his relationship with God.

34. See Chapter I, 2, b, (5) "Sexual imagery and the divine fatherhood."

35. Cf. M. Noth, History of Pentateuchal Traditions, p. 31; B. S. Childs, The Book of Exodus, p. 603

36. Also Noadiah, Neh. 6:14, here seen as a menace to God's work, reflecting a negative attitude toward prophecy intensifying in the late postexilic period.

37. Prisca (Priscilla) is mentioned in Acts 18:26, Rom. 16:3-4, I Cor. 16:19, II Tim. 4:19. Various women's names are listed in Rom 16:1-23, Col. 4:15, II Tim, 3:19-21; cf. Phil. 4:2, II John 1.

38. See art. "Circumcision" (J. P. Hyatt), IDB, I, 629ff.

39. I Kings 14:23; cf. Deut. 12:2, II Kings 16:4, 17:10, II Chron. 28:4, Isa. 57:5, Jer. 2:20, 3:6, Ezek. 6:13.

40. Even though this reference is a secondary gloss, it evidently records an accurately remembered historical fact (see the commentaries).

41. See art. "Priests and Levites" (R. Abba), IDB, III, 876ff.; R. de Vaux, Ancient Israel, pp. 345ff., 387ff.

42. See G. H. Tavard, Woman in Christian Tradition, Notre Dame 1973. The early church was influenced by the Pauline (or Deutero-Pauline) statements about the place of women, but even more by current social attitudes in the gentile world. In the light of the severe restrictions placed on women in Greek and Roman society, the Pauline dicta should be interpreted as a caution against an iconoclasm that threatened to bring emergent Christianity into severe disrepute within its social environment (see D. Balch, Let Wives Be Submissive, Missoula: Scholars Press, 1981). Unfortunately, these pragmatic deliverances, interpreted apart from their original historical setting, had a lasting effect in reinforcing ecclesiastical patriarchalism in the medieval and modern church.

43. The attitude of postbiblical Judaism is markedly more severe in its patriarchalism than the Old Testament itself; cf. already the deliverances of Sirach in Ecclus. 7:26-28, 25:24, 42:14.

44. J. A. Wilson, tr.

45. J. A. Wilson tr.

46. See n. 24.

47. Art. "Fall, The," IDB, II, 235f.

48. Hamartia, hamartanō, "sin"; hamartōlos, "sinner";
    paraptōma, "trespass"; parabasis, "transgression";
    parabainō, "transgress"; anomia, "lawlessness";
    paranomia, "wickedness"; asebeia, "ungodliness";
    kakia, ponēria, "badness"; ponēros, "bad, wicked";
    adikia, "injustice"; adikos, "unjust"; enochos,
    "guilty."

49. Judg. 20:16, Job 5:24, Prov. 8:36, 19:2

50. These are blanket terms for gentiles and their
    behavior in late Jewish texts.

51. Both the verb and noun are used of revolt against
    nations or persons in authority (e.g., I Kings
    12:19, Amos 1:3ff), but generally the Old Testament
    uses them of defiance of God's rule. A similar
    world is mārar, "to rebel."

52. See W. L. Holladay, The Root šubh in the Old
    Testament, Leiden 1958.

53. S. J. De Vries, art. "Sin, Sinners", IV, 361ff.

54. See art. "Wrath of God" (B. T. Dahlberg), IDB,
    IV, 903ff.

55. See art. "Forgiveness" (W. A. Quanbeck), IDB,
    II, 314ff.; also art, "Forgiveness" (A. Unterman),
    EJ, VI, 1434ff.

56. See art. "Inclination, good and evil"
    (S. Rosenblatt), EJ, VIII, 1315f.

57. T. H. Gaster, The Dead Sea Scriptures in English
    Translation (New York 1956), p. 120.

58. See art. "Demon, Demonology" (T. H. Gaster),
    IDB, I, 817ff.

59. Art. "Sin, Sinners" (S. J. De Vries)

60. See art. "Atonement" (C. L. Mitton), IDB, I, 309ff.

61. See Chapter I, "Excursus on ritual in Hebrew
    religion."

62. Leviticus 1-7, 11-12, 23-24, 27, Num. 3, 6-8, 15,
    18-19, 28-29; also Ezek. 45:13-46:18

63. See the definitive study by G. Klinzing, "Würde im Exil der Gemeinde ein eigener Opferkult vollzogen?," _Die Umdeutung des Kultus in der Qumrangemeinde und im Neuen Testament_ (StUNT, 7, Göttingen 1971), pp. 20ff.; also B. Gärtner, _The Temple and the Community in Qumran and the New Testament_, SNTSMS, Cambridge 1965; H. Ringgren, "The Cult," The Faith of Qumran (Philadelphia 1963) pp. 214ff.

64. Luke 2:41ff., John 2:23, 5:1, 10:22, Acts 21:26

65. Cf. M. Noth, "The Laws in the Pentateuch: Their Assumptions and Meanings," _The Laws in the Pentateuch and Other Studies_ (tr. D. R. Ap-Thomas; Edinburgh-London 1966), pp. 1-107.

66. The apocalyptic book of Jubilees begins with God's instruction to Moses on Mt. Sinai, commanding him to write what the angel dictates respecting this book's reinterpretation of the book of Genesis (chap. 1). In Ass. Mos. 1:14 Moses seems to be described as pre-existent, like the heavenly Son of Man in 1 En. 43:2 (so Charles); in 1:17 he gives to Joshua books (= the ensuing apocalyptic reinterpretation) that he has prepared in this pre-existent state, implying that the Torah is included among them or is reinterpreted by them.

67. See M. Hengel, _Judaism and Hellenism; Studies in their Encounter in Palestine During the Early Hellenistic Period_, tr. J. Bowden, I (Philadelphia: Fortress, 1974), 255-309

68. See Paul's sharp polemic in Galatians 1-2; cf. R. Bultmann, _Theology of the New Testament_, I, 340-45.

69. On the ideology of apocalyptic, see especially D. S. Russell, _The Method and Message of Jewish Apocalyptic, 200 B.C. -- A.D. 100_, Philadelphia 1964; also G. von Rad, _Old Testament Theology_, II, 301-8.

70. Thus Ass. Mos. 12:2-4: "Moses took his hand and raised him into the seat before him, and answered and said unto him: 'Joshua, do not despise thyself, but set thy mind at ease, and hearken to my words. All the nations which are in the earth God hath created and us, He hath foreseen them and us from the beginning of the creation of the earth unto the end of the age, and nothing has been neglected by Him even to the least thing, but all things He hath foreseen and caused all to come forth'..."

71. See above, n. 67.

72. Tr. S. Rudman, Richmond 1968.

73. On the eschatological programme of the Qumran
    community, see H. Ringgren, The Faith of Qumran,
    pp. 152ff.; also H. W. Kuhn, Enderwartung und
    gegenwärtiges Heil, StUNT, Göttingen 1966.

74. See art. "Salvation" (A. Richardson), IDB, IV,
    168ff.

75. Ex. 14:30, 15:2, I Sam. 14:45, etc.

76. Gen. 16:11, Josh. 10:14, Mal. 3:16, etc.;
    cf. also 'ZN hiph.

77. The hiphil is used of the Deity's saving atten-
    tiveness, chiefly in laments and prayers; cf. Ps.
    5:3, 17:1, 61:2, etc.

78. In a wider semantic application, "react" (cf. C. J.
    Labuschagne in THAT, II, 335ff. In sixty-two of
    the seventy-eight occurrences in which Yahweh is
    the subject of this verb, his response is to human
    initiative, hence the usual translation, "answer."
    See further below, at Chapter IV, 1, b, (6)
    "Prayer and divine responsiveness."

79. The niphal, often used of God (Judg. 2:18, Joel
    2:14, Ps. 106:45, etc.) in a salvific sense, may
    also refer to his refusal to give in any longer
    to Israel's backsliding, persisting in his purpose
    to punish (so. Jer. 4:28, Ezek. 24:14 etc.).

80. I Kings 8:30, Isa. 55:7, Amos 7:2, etc.

81. W. L. Holladay, The Root Šubh in the Old Testament,
    identifies one hundred sixty-four occurrences of
    the meaning "return," "be converted" to God; e.g.,
    Deut. 30:2.

82. This is especially frequent in Deuteronomy. It is
    usually followed by a specific object, e.g., the
    law, commandment, ordinance or voice of God (Ex.
    24:7, I Sam. 14:17, etc.).

83. Cf. the hiphil verb with reference to God in Gen.
    15:6, Ex. 14:31, Num. 14:11, Jon. 3:5, etc.

84. Hab. 2:4, wᵉṣaddîq be'ᵉmûnātô yiḥyeh, "but a righteous man in his fidelity shall live," includes the connotation of maintaining a trusting attitude, such that motivates faithful adherence to covenantal norms.

85. Rom 3:28, 5:1.

86. See C. Westermann, *Die Verheissungen an die Väter: Studien zur Vater-geschichte*, FRLANT 116, Göttingen: Vandenhoeck und Ruprecht, 1976.

87. E.g., "For you who fear my name the sun of righteousness shall rise, with healing in its wings," Mal. 4:2; "The ransomed of Yahweh shall return, and come to Zion with singing, with everlasting joy upon their heads; they shall obtain joy and gladness, and sorrow and sighing shall flee away," Isa. 35:10; "Peace be within your walls, and security within your towers!," Ps. 122:7; "In that day...every one of you will invite his neighbor under his vine and under his fig tree," Zech. 3:10

88. See also Ezek. 11:19-21.

89. Messianic ideology first developed in praise of the Davidic dynasty, with fervent hopes of its restoration at the end of the Babylonian exile. When these hopes were frustrated, the image of a Davidic Messiah disappeared from eschatological speculation, and is notably absent in much of the Jewish apocalyptic literature. Jesus himself apparently resisted popular speculation that he might be the Messiah -- largely because of its political-military associations -- but may have given some encouragement to those who identified him in terms of a transcendental "son of man" ideology. In any event, the early church quickly seized upon the Messiah image as the basis of its developing Christological speculation. See art. "Christology in the NT" (W. Marxsen), *IDBS*, pp 146ff.; also "Messiah, Jewish" (E. Jenni), *IDB*, III, 360ff; "Kingdom of God" (O. E. Evans), *IDB*, III, 17ff., "Son of man" (S. E. Johnson), *IDB*, IV, 413ff. Cf. also J. Klausner, *The Messianic Idea in Israel*, 3rd ed., New York 1949; S. Mowinckel, *He That Cometh*, trans. G. W. Anderson, New York 1951.

90. On the assimilation of apocalyptic ideology in New Testament Christianity, see Chapter III, 1, d, (2), (a), 1) "The influence of apocalyptic"; also Chapter IV, 1, b, (8) "Biblical historicality in the New Testament."

91. Cf. the effective analysis of this passage in H. J. Kraus, Hosea (Hermeneia; Philadelphia: Fortress, 1974), pp. 190ff.

92. See art. "Will, Freedom of the" (C.A. Beckwith), NSHE, XII, 354ff.

93. See R. Bultmann, Theology of the New Testament, I, 270-352.

94. Cf. Mark 2:1-12 par, John 8:1-11.

95. Cf. the existential interpretation of P. Tillich in his Systematic Theology (p.b., Chicago 1957), II, 153ff

96. See art. "Repentance" (W. A. Quanbeck), IDB, IV, 33f.

97. See art. "Faith, Faithfulness," (E. C. Blackman), IDB, 222ff.

98. See R. Bultmann, Theology of the New Testament, II, 203ff.; R. C. Tannehill, A Mirror for Disciples, A Study of the Gospel of Mark, Nashville 1971.

Chapter III

A life of Fulfilling Integrity within a
Covenant Community

"THE JEALOUS GOD"

"I, Yahweh thy god, am a jealous god, visiting the iniquity of the fathers upon the children to the third and the fourth generation of those who hate me, but showing steadfast love to thousands of those who love me and keep my commandments." (Ex. 20:5-6 = Deut. 5:9)

God's personhood directed in judgment and salvation to his special people, Israel, comes to manifestation in an intense pathos -- negative and positive -- that is similar both to jealousy (intolerance of rival objects of worshipful devotion) and to the jealous devotion of a lover or parent (a passionate concern for their protection and vindication). It is within the conceptual framework of the elective choice by which they came to be his people, and the covenantal arrangement by which they abide in intimate relationship to him, that "the jealous God" is experienced. It is an awesome thing to belong to this God because he takes the relationship with deadly seriousness. He acts in wrathful zeal against Israel's enemies when they have been abused (see Zech. 1:14-15, "I am exceedingly jealous for Jerusalem and for Zion. And I am very angry with the nations that are at ease; for while I was angry but a little they furthered the disaster", cf. also Isa. 9:6, Ezek. 39:25). God acts in wrathful zeal against his own people when they harden themselves against him (cf. Josh. 24:19; Nah. 1:2-3; Zeph. 1:18).[1]

The deuteronomistic addition within the second commandment is replete with the ideology of the covenant and election. "I am Yahweh your God -- a jealous God ('ēl qannā', a god of jealous passion) -- calling to accountability the guilt (pōqēd ʿăwōn) of parents passed on to all their posterity within the greater family of three to four generations -- i.e., of those who hate me (leśon'ay, 'reject, refuse me'); and performing acts of devotion (ḥesed) unto thousands (la'ălāpîm, an ideal tribal totality) -- even to those loving me (1^e, $\bar{o}h^eb\bar{a}y$, "to those desiring, choosing me') -- even to those who are keeping ($1\check{s}om^er\hat{e}$, 'to the ones observing, fulfilling') my commandments."

In election and covenant, God's part is:

Being Israel's god;
Being jealous;
Visiting iniquity on those who hate him;
Performing devotion to those who love and obey.

Israel's part is:

Loving Yahweh alone;
Keeping his commandments.

Introduction

a. Ethics grounded in theology

The whole problem of standards of proper behavior, which we call ethics, presupposes the many facts and interrelationships within the entire human family. Man exists not in isolation, but as part of a societal organism. Biblical ethics, governing man's interrelationship with his fellows, is grounded in the biblical teaching about man's own essence and about man's relationship to God. Israel as the model society was called upon to live according to the standards of harmonious behavior within their societal structure -- which from a sociological point of view was not significantly different from that of the people among whom Israel dwelt. A theological presupposition guided Israelite man in society. He lived within the frame work of a peculiar covenantal relationship with his God and with his fellowmen. Biblical ethics is, accordingly, deeply grounded in biblical theology. It must be characterized as another aspect of deeply serious personalism, put into practice.

b. Integrity (ḥesed) as the prime motivation

It must be said that the key motivation for biblical ethics is personalistic integrity, both divine and human. Integrity is being true to one's ideal self, endeavoring to be a real person according to the deepest dimensions of one's inherent potentialities, especially in response to other persons within society and to God. Integrity is even closer to the heart of biblical ethics than the much-praised quality of love. Love is, in fact, only one urgent aspect of integrity; i.e., the forthpouring of devotion and affection based on a prior loyalty and obligation. "God is love," says the New Testament (I John 4:8). But this, first of all, hyperbole; secondly, to say that God is love is not the same as

211

saying that love is God. In any event, the New
Testament is really affirming that God manifests
himself in love, and is present wherever love is
present; cf. the apostle Paul's encomium of love in
I Corinthians 13. "God so loved the world that he
gave his only son (John 3:16)" expresses the unrivaled measure of the divine integrity, God going
beyond all that stunted human expectation would
require in his personal relationship to the world
that he had created, measuring up rather to the intensity of his own sovereign personhood by coming
among men to suffer in the person of his Son, Jesus.

The word "love" is distressingly ambiguous. The
New Testament agape, used especially for God's
undeserved self-giving, comes close to an ideal expression of the divine integrity in selfless
devotion; it fits somewhat the semantic range of
Hebrew ɔāhⁱbâ, meaning "love" in a broad sense, but
especially with emphasis on the exercise of the will
in choosing (see Chapter IV).[2] A more specific Old
Testament word is hesed, which generally refers to
God's saving action on his people's behalf, as well
as to his and their mutual devotion and self-commit-
ment.[3] Along with its derivative, hāsîd, "faithful,
devoted one," it is this word above all that expresses the ideal basis for covenantal living:

> He has showed you, O man, what is good;
>   and what does Yahweh require of you
> but to do justice (mišpāṭ: fairness in social
> interaction) and to
>   love devotedness (hesed: mistranslated
>   "lovingkindness"),
> and to walk humbly with your god. (Mic. 6:8)

COMMENT: Do Christians get too sloppy and sentimental about the ideal of love? Do they really know
what love means? Perhaps they can learn from the Jew
who ironically remarked, "You Christians are always
required to love, but we Jews know how to hate when
we need to."[4]

c. The covenant presupposes election

212

The notion of election, being chosen and called by God, is the presupposition of the covenant, which expresses a pack or agreement in which the caller and the called live together. These concepts, and their ideal relationship to each other, did not come to full clarity within the Old Testament until such a time as their validity was seriously threatened by external aggression (i.e., the time of classical prophetism, the deuteronomic reform, the exile and restoration); nevertheless, they are implied in the very earliest affirmations concerning Israel's peculiar relationship with the god Yahweh. The common words, "to know (YD𝗰)" and "to choose (BḤR)," express the divine choice,[5] but also Israel's corresponding obligation toward Yahweh. As he knew and chose them, they were to know and choose him.

It is the idea of divine election that expresses the prior, vertical, relationship between Yahweh and Israel (or individual Israelites). It is the idea of the covenant, made operative in the structures of Hebraic society, that brings out the horizontal dimensions of this relationship.

1. The election of a peculiar people (the vertical
    dimension)

The notion of election involves the calling of a
people -- not just of special charismatic individuals
(like the prophets and Christ)[6] -- to belong in a
peculiar saving relationship with Yahweh. Israel developed this concept from the historical orientation of its
soteriology. All of Israel's ancient neighbors thought
of themselves as belonging from eternity to their gods,
living on their land from creation. Thus the Babylonians felt that they belonged to their gods in a proprietary sense; they were slaves of their gods, made to
do their work and run their universe.[7] Israel did not
belong to its god in a proprietary sense. For one
thing, its epic literature tells of all mankind being
created to till and keep the garden of God.[8] For another thing, it perpetuates the memory that the gods
of the patriarchs were not identical with Yahweh (though
through assimilation they did come to be identified with
Yahweh; cf. Ex. 3:15).[9] Finally this was emphatically
clear in its recollection that they had not grown up in,
or out of, their land; this had been promised to them
as sojourners,[10] and secured as their possession only
through Yahweh's special intervention upon the scene
of history. Thus in all respects they were a peculiar
people, Yahweh's special possession (s^{e}gullâ, Ex. 19:5)
among the nations of mankind. This could never have
come about except through his purposeful choice. Israel
was a people created by Yahweh's elective love.

a. Ancient Near-Eastern parallels

Only formally does there exist a parallel between
the election-covenant combination of Israel's religion
and the religions of its ancient neighbors.

Nonbiblical personalism scarcely rose higher than
gross caricature -- as we have seen.[11] An anthropomorphic personification of the gods invited the establishment of a personal interaction with them and the choice
of one or more of them as special protectors. Always
this was a pragmatic affair. Responding with quid pro
quo, the pagan worshiper offered devotion to the god or

goddess who seemed to be attentive to his prayers. The cult of national gods like Marduk (Babylon) derived entirely from the success of the Babylonian kings over their imperialist rivals. The national god would, in any case, share the people's devotion with a wide-ranging pantheon of native and foreign deities. No idea of peculiar possession, of special calling, or of contractual agreement could arise within this spiritual climate, but only where monotheism was taken seriously, being based on the memory of historical deprivation and deliverance, issuing in a societally directed pattern of mutual integrity, and based on love and responsibility.

Much has been made in recent years of formal parallels between Old Testament covenantal formulations and the political treaties of the Hittite kings with their Syrian and Egyptian counterparts (see especially the influential work of George Mendenhall).[12] The relevance of this comparison has been weakened through the observation that no biblical text actually exhibits all (or even most) of the structural elements in these treaties -- even though each of these elements show up individually in a variety of texts from the Bible. Even so, it seems assured that the idea of treaty obligation lies at the basis of covenant formulation.

As for the ideology of elective obligation underlying a treaty or covenant, we are justified in seeking Near-Eastern parallels only to the extent that a specific act of suzerain benignity is often adduced in a formal preamble in order to make explicit the basis for corresponding action.

It is important to see this structure in specific biblical formulations, particularly those that introduce a covenant or an apodictic code, the legal explication of covenantal obligation. The most important passages are Ex. 19:4, "You have seen what I did to the Egyptians, and how I bore you on eagles' wings and brought you to myself," and Ex. 20:2, "I am Yahweh your god, who brought you out of the land of Egypt, out of the house of bondage."

Something like this regularly occurs in the Near-Eastern treaties, which begin by identifying the contractual parties, and then recall the establishment of good relationships between them. As can be seen from a study of the selections in <u>ANET</u> 198ff., these tend to be strikingly similar in conception and formulation. Thus one example may suffice to represent many (Treaty between Hattusilis and Ramses II, <u>ANET</u> 202):[13]

> Now I have established good brotherhood (and)
> good peace between us forever. In order to
> establish good peace (and) good brotherhood in
> [the relationship] of the land of Egypt with
> the Hatti land forever (I speak) thus: Behold,
> as for the relationship between the land of
> Egypt and the Hatti land, since eternity the
> god does not permit the making of hostility
> between them because of a treaty (valid)
> forever....

COMMENT: Two fictions provide the ideological basis
for this particular treaty: (1) that it reflects and
perpetuates an eternal treaty, perhaps an ideal heavenly prototype; and (2) that the respective gods forbid
hostility. At any rate, both historical and theological
considerations are brought to bear in support of the
present agreement -- a meaningful parallel to the biblical references to prior acts of divine grace and saving
action.

   b. Its development in biblical thought

   (1) The epic formulation: J in Gen. 12:1-3

      The notion that Yahweh had purposefully called
Israel is represented symbolically in J's report of
Abram's call, occurring at the beginning of the patriarchal cycle in Gen. 12:1-3. This is programmatic
material, specially composed by J rather than drawn
from his sources.[14] As an eponymous ancestor, the
Abram figure of these verses is clearly intended as the
image of Israel itself -- now in J's time (the Solomonic
era) in effective possession of the land that Abram
sought.

      Although the word bāhar, "choose," does not appear
in this passage (Deuteronomy is the earliest to use it
with reference to Yahweh's election of Israel), the
notion of divine choice is thematic.[15] Abram is chosen
out of many possibilities, without volition or qualifi-
cation on his own part. All the Genesis J passages
prior to this passage are designed as preparation and

prologue, painting a dark picture of mankind's failure within its own resources. Man has lost paradisaical bliss; his civilization has become corrupted; violence and revenge threaten extinction; wickedness has so increased that all have been wiped out but one family, Noah's; humankind, in spreading out to occupy the earth, have sought to secure titanic power, but their tower of Babel has been destroyed and their speech confused. All is in chaos and despair as Genesis 11 draws to an end. It is here that the divine initiative introduces something new, hopeful, and promising.

God has not given up on humankind. He has a new design, entailing the calling of one -- hence of one people -- to live within a special new relationship with himself.

> Now Yahweh said to Abram, "Go from your country and your kindred and your father's house to the land that I will show you. And I will make of you a great nation, and I will bless you, and make your name great, so that you will be a blessing. I will bless those who bless you, and him who curses you I will curse; and by you all the families of the earth shall bless themselves (or: be blessed)."[16]

Here Abram is summoned to forsake everything he has known and loved: family, kinfolk, country, and to go completely trusting in the divine calling and the divine purpose, embracing the promise that Yahweh would make him a great people and give him the land in which this people might dwell -- all in order that his name might bring blessing to the families of mankind. From this vantage point one is expected to read the entire Pentateuchal narrative. The family grows from one to hundreds of thousands, sojourners who are to come only after many generations into possession of the promised land.[17]

(2) The concept of Israel's election in an age of crisis

The call of Israel to exclusive loyalty to Yahweh gained firm acceptance as the basis of religious ideology, even in a time when the nation had not yet refined its spiritual understanding to its highest potentiality (witness the foreign cults introduced not only by the later kings,[18] but by Solomon himself).[19]

217

It was perhaps the amazing survivability of the Davidic dynasty that secured Yahweh's growing exclusivity within the influence-sphere of the Jerusalem temple. In the northern realm, where regal and priestly institutions were in disarray, foreign cults could at times pose a serious threat to the claim of Yahweh. We witness this particularly in the narrative of Elijah's contest with the prophets of Baal in I Kings 18.

Nevertheless, the ability of the northern kingdom to survive for 200 years, and of the southern kingdom to survive for 350 years, served as a firm ideological basis for the permanence of the elective ideal. In Judah, where one single regal line remained intact from David to Zedekiah, the concept of Yahweh's special choice of the Davidic king became firmly established.[20]

All this came under serious threat from the eighth to the sixth century, B.C., as the Assyrian, and later the Neo-Babylonian, empires mounted serious threats against the territory and independence of the Hebrew kingdoms. The prophets interpreted this adversity as a divine punishment for the nation's sin against its elective distinctiveness. Israel had grown half-hearted and formalistic -- had tampered seriously with other deities -- and had accordingly incurred the divine wrath. The solution was a return to rigorous loyalty. Israel's God was still big enough to maintain his exclusive demands on the devotion of a threatened people.

(a) Deuteronomy

The book of Deuteronomy represents a solid ideological programme for Israel;s absolute loyalty in an age of crisis.[21] The parenetic passion of the following examples can neither be understood nor appreciated without the recognition that at the time Israel had begun to doubt seriously the validity of Yahweh's elective claim:

> You are a people holy to Yahweh your god; Yahweh your god has chosen you to be a people for his own possession, out of all the peoples that are on the face of the earth. It was not because you were more in number than any other people that Yahweh set his love upon you and chose you, for you were the fewest of all the peoples; but it is because Yahweh loves you, and is keeping the oath

which he swore to your fathers. (7:6-8)

> You shall remember Yahweh your god, for it is he
> who gives you power to get wealth; that he may
> confirm his covenant which he swore to your
> fathers, as at this day. And if you forget Yahweh
> your god and go after other gods and serve them
> and worship them, I solemnly warn you this day
> that you shall surely perish. (8:18-19)

(b) The prophets of judgment

The prophets do more than warn; they threaten.
Amos 3:1-2 (which may be approximately contemporary
with the earliest materials in Deuteronomy) is the
classic passage:

> Hear this word that Yahweh has spoken against you,
> O people of Israel, against the whole family which
> I brought up out of the land of Egypt: "You only
> have I known of all the families of the earth;
> therefore I will punish you for all your inquities."

Here is the strongly negative side of Yahweh's
jealousy: the privilege of election brings with it a
solemn obligation. Sinning against that obligation,
Israel can no longer rely on its special privilege as
protection against the effects of its disloyalty.

The other prophets of judgment have similar denun-
ciations.[22] Perhaps the most moving is Ezekiel's
mashal (picture story) of Israel as a helpless found-
ling, rescued by Yahweh's love, now sinning against
the covenantal loyalty that his "marriage" to her had
imposed upon her, about to be cruelly shamed and abused
by the paramours to whom she has brazenly sold her love
(chapter 16).[23]

(c) Election in the restoration literature

Once the exile was past and a remnant had returned
to the land of Judah, theological imagery could not
dispense with the concept of a revalidated choice.
This comes to moving expression in a late addition to
the book of Jeremiah (33:23-26):

The word of Yahweh came to Jeremiah: Have you not
observed what these people are saying, "Yahweh has
rejected the two families which he chose?"... Thus
says Yahweh: If I have not established my covenant
with day and night and the ordinances of heaven
and earth, then I will reject the descendants of
Jacob and David my servant and will not choose one
of his descendants to rule over the seed of Abraham,
Isaac, and Jacob. For I will restore their fortunes, and will have mercy upon them."[24]

(3) Theocracy and the covenantal congregation

During the period of the Israelite monarchy, the
promises of Gen. 12:1-3 received fulfillment in the
political and nationalistic consolidation of a self-
governing people. The Davidic king was Yahweh's specially elected representative (II Sam. 7; 23:1-7; 9:1-
7), to whom even the high priests of Jerusalem were
subservient.

Once that classical structure had been swept away
by the Babylonian invasions, it was never again to be
restored. An abortive effort to re-establish a Davidic
kingship in the person of Zerubbabel (Haggai, Zechariah
)[25] after the exile opened the door to a priestly rule.
Persian, and later Greek, administrators were in charge
of Judah's external affairs, but a line of high-priests
took over the administration of its internal affairs,
secular as well as religious. As the prophets disappeared,[26] the priests were left as exclusive repre-
sentatvies of Deity. The elective peoplehood of Israel
was no longer seen as a nation, but as a secular-
religious congregation ruled by sacral law. It is the
programme of Ezra the scribe, reported in Nehemiah 8-9
(cf. Ezra 7:1-6), that was the decisive event leading[27]
to the establishment of this theocracy (rule by God).
It called itself the qāhāl "assembly" or ʿēdāh, "congregation." It looked to the Priestly document in the
Pentateuch rather than to the ancient epics, J and E,
to provide both the mythic ideology and the pragmatic
legislation for this theocracy.[28] Correspondingly, it
produced the Chronicler's new version of Heilsgeschichte
to take the place of the deuteronomist's version in
Samuel and Kings.[29]

During the Greek period (after 333 B.C.) the Jewish theocracy was seriously threatened by apostacy and suppression. Not only Jews living abroad (the diaspora) but many who lived in Palestine came under the attraction of Greek humanism.[30] Some of these joined forces with the Seleucid Greek rulers in a drastic effort to suppress traditional piety, leading at last to the Maccabeean revolt of 167 B.C. After a long struggle, this led to the establishment of the Hasmonean state (134-64 B.C., the last period of Jewish political independence prior to the establishment of the modern state of Israel). This too was, at first, a theocracy; a priest ruled in Jerusalem.[31] But ere long the priest became a king. Towards the beginning of the Christian era, the Jews were once again ruled by foreign kings, first the Idumean Herod, then the Romans.

After the Roman war of A.D. 66-70, the Jewish theocracy was dissolved, the temple ruined and the priesthood dispersed. It was destined never to appear again. A purely ethnic peoplehood has found a way to survive with a purely non-theocratic (i.e., neither cultic nor nationalistic-political) leadership. It has been in the Christian church, rather than in Judaism, that models of theocracy have continued to raise their head.[32]

c. The First Commandment and the <u>Shema</u>

"Thou shalt have no other gods before me." (Ex. 20:3, Deut. 5:7)

"Hear, O Israel: Yahweh our god is one Yahweh; and thou shalt love Yahweh thy god with all thy heart, and with all thy soul, and with all thy might. And these words which I command thee this day shall be upon thy heart; and thou shalt teach them diligently to thy children, and shalt talk of them when thou sittest in thy house, and when thou walkest by the way, and when thou liest down, and when thou risest up. And thou shalt bind them as a sign upon thy hand, and they shall be as frontlets between thy eyes. And thou shalt write them on the doorpost of thy house and on thy gates." (Deut. 6:4-9)

All else in the Decalogue is meaningless without strict observance of the first commandment, for all of

Hebrew religion and morality presupposes it. Yahweh
takes his divine personhood so seriously that he demands
that holy transcendance be worshiped in him alone.
"Let there not be for thyself other deities in my presence (ᶜal-pᵉnāy)." Wherever Yahweh may be present, in
a cultic shrine or in the wide realm of history and
nature, no room exists for rival gods. No idols belong
in his temple because no gods belong in his universe.

The Shema is Judaism's basic creed.[33] Orthodox
ritual prescribes the literal application of the rule
for wearing the phylactery and fixing the mezuzim.[34]
A more spiritually imaginative interpretation recognizes
that the requirements of vv 8-9 may have been intended
as metaphorical expansions of vv. 6-7, where the confession of Yahweh's elective demand is to occupy
Israel's every living moment, at home and abroad, in
the daytime or at night, throughout every generation of
its existence as Yahweh's people.[35]

In any event, the Shema is less an affirmation of
monotheistic belief than of elective loyalty. The
saying is not, "Yahweh our god is one god," but "Yahweh
our god is one Yahweh," thus requiring that the
Israelite love him with all his "heart," "soul," and
"might." Yahweh is a Person, and as such claims his
people's total love. He has chosen them, that they
should pour out the strength of their own personhood
on him as Person, just as he pours out the strength of
his divine personhood on them.

d.   The contemporary meaning of election[36]

(1) Its existential validity within the framework
    of biblical religion

In our confrontation with the wholly Other, election appropriately expresses the absolute and unimpaired
prerogative of the Unconditioned over against the
conditioned, of the Infinite over against the finite,
of the Creator over against the creatures he has made.
Each one of us is only partially and imperfectly aware
of God -- as we are of one another -- yet he is at every
moment totally and perfectly aware of each one of us.

God's knowledge, will, and affection ever antedate
and precondition our own. Not our free choice of him
is primary, but his of us. Our choice is a response
to his prior choice (John 15:16, "You have not chosen
me, but I have chosen you, and have ordained you that
you should go and bring forth fruit"). God's ultimately
wise and loving concern for us outreaches our own
selfish, narrow and proximate concerns.

This is why authentic biblical religion resists
pietistic individualism, as expressed in the popular
slogan, "I found it!" If we men do find, it is only
because we have been found. We do not have to look for
God, for he is ever present to faith (cf. Paul's word
in Acts 17:28, "In him we live and move and have our
being").

Excursus on atheism

If there is a God at all, he has to be the electing
God that we have been describing. A "God" that waits
for us to discover him -- to make him in our image --
is no true God.

This is why no soul that is unresponsive to the
implicit call of God's presence can be forced to believe
in him. Logically speaking, the world may be viewed as
reasonably from an atheistic perspective as from that
of Christian theism. One can explain the world from
mechanistic causes -- to one's own satisfaction, if not
to that of others. It is just as impossible for the
Christian to prove the atheist wrong, as for the atheist
to prove the Christian wrong. Ultimately one needs to
exercise sheer faith, reaching out boldly to a reality
that constantly impinges upon us, giving perspective
and purpose to our own frail, finite existence. Our
leap of faith does not create a God who was not there
before. That God is there choosing us, calling us,
laying his obligation on us.[37]

(2) Misappropriations and misunderstandings

The best way to apply the biblical concept of
election to modern understanding is to mark off the

aberrations that have arisen within the mutually
isolated streambeds of Christianity and Judaism since
the first century of our era. For two thounsand years,
the story of their relationship to each other has been
one of estrangement, suspicion, hostility, and outright
persecution. The church became exasperated at Jewish
intransigence when early efforts at converting Jews to
Christ failed, yet their most severe Christian critics
never went so far as to deny Israel's election. Rather,
they thought that Israel had sunk to unmeasured depravity in sinning against this election (Luther).[38] St.
Paul is very explicit in Romans 9-11 with regard to
Israel's priority in divine election:

> They are Israelites, and to them belong the
> sonship, the glory, the covenants, the giving
> of the law, the worhip, and the promises; to
> them belong the patriarchs, and of their race,
> according to the flesh, is the Christ....(9:4-5)

Thus the Jews remain elect, even in Christian
polemic.[39] Nevertheless, the concept of divine election
was too precious not to be appropriated by Christians.
In the context of a refutation of Torah righteousness,
where Paul substitutes faith in the cross of Christ for
receiving circumcision and keeping the Law (Gal. 6:12-
16), the apostle implicitly gives the title of "Israel"
to the church, thereby including it among God's elect:

> Peace and mercy be upon all who walk by this
> rule, upon the Israel of God.

(a) Christian predestinarianism

1) The influence of apocalyptic

Much Christian speculation and controversy presupposes the determinism that arose with apocalyptic
dualism. As has previously been argued, this is a
subbiblical soterism, one that is out of harmony with
the mainstream of biblical religion, even while affirming something that is authentically biblical. Essentially, apocalyptic is liable to the critique that its
radical dualism and futurism distort the Old Testament's

224

authentic core. According to apocalyptic, God has chosen individual human beings from eternity with the specific purpose of consigning them to one group or the other. Each one is born -- nay, predestined before birth -- to be righteous or wicked, a "child of light" or a "child of darkness."[40] So long as this notion did not get rigidly schematized and abstracted into a fatalistic pattern, it could still express something genuinely biblical -- that is, the radical polarity between being for God or against him. The fact of the matter is that the devotees of apocalyptic thought in late Judaism were driven by the logic of their ideas into increasingly rigid forms of particularism, and hence separatism, even to the point of world-flight and ascetic renunciation, or of reckless, fantasy-driven violence.[41]

Avoiding the extremes of Essene separatism, early Christianity was clearly influenced by this apocalyptic world-view.[42] World conditions had grown very difficult for the adherents of biblical religiosity. History had become irrelevant, society had grown wicked. It was inviting for first-century Jews -- including the early Christians -- to think in dualistic and futuristic terms. In spite of all this, the historical Jesus remained essentially faithful to authentic prophetism. The Gospel accounts, products though they are of early-church reflection, remember him as one who taught and spoke for God, who healed and comforted the distressed, who interceded and intervened for God's oppressed people. They also remember that he steadfastly refused an ostensible messianic role -- even though he may have recognized that he was fulfilling some of its aspects as he saw his bitter end draw near.[43] True, the New Testament does have apocalyptic in Mark 13; this was added by the early church. It even has a special apocalyptic book, the book of Revelation. Paul, on his part, was accustomed to thinking in dualistic and futuristic categories. Nevertheless, apocalyptic remains peripheral rather than essential in the New Testament kerygma[44](contra Koch).[45] This is partly a matter of definition, for assuredly, the New Testamant is suffused with eschatological expectation, as in Jesus's proclamation of the coming "kingdom of God." Rarely, however, did it turn to full-blown apocalyptic, in spite of this. What we see in the book of Revelation is a rarity. It carried an effective witness for the assurance of Christ's ultimate victory, accounting for its ultimate acceptance in the Christian Canon, in spite of widespread and persistent misgivings in the early church.

The postapostolic church has witnessed only occasional and peripheral outgrowths of apocalyptic enthusiasm, and Judaism even more rarely. The reason why apocalyptic has always had hard going in both religions is simply that it departs so drastically from the essential norms of personalistic responsiveness. God becomes a deistic demiurge and man becomes a driven tool.

Christian dogmaticians should be as wary in constructing a theology of election on the notion of dualistic separatism as they should be of a periodizing futurism. The most serious methodological error is to subject apocalyptic imagery to a literalistic interpretation. Examples are the thousand-year rule of Christ in Revelation 20 and that symbol of ultimate perfection in the number of God's elect, the 144,000 standing before the throne in Rev. 7:4. How tragic that the Jehovah's Witnesses insist on taking the very number literally; this may give them some satisfaction in withstanding the rejection of outsiders, but it must also bring constant anxiety to those who worry whether they actually are counted in this number. Unrestrained speculation on the basis of a literal interpretation of apocalyptic imagery is an impious effort to read the mind of God -- perhaps the most blasphemous idolatry of all!

2)   St. Paul's understanding of the divine purpose

A safer guide for Christian predestinarianism is the thought of St. Paul, for whom apocalyptic modes of thoughts were suggestive, but not determinative.[46]

It can be said that Paul never forgot that he was limited to human knowledge in his grasp for the divine plan. What he now proclaimed to the world, God had already revealed. Paul exercised his vivid imagination in conceptualizing the divine purpose; this served as the motive and stimulus for his entire missionary program. He believed that the work of Christ was not something designed for the Jews alone, but was God's long-awaited plan for the redemption of all mankind. This constantly occupied his thought, filling him with wonder and awe with respect to the divine wisdom:

O the depth of the riches both of wisdom and knowledge of God! How unsearchable are his

judgments, and his ways past finding out!
(Rom. 11:33)

Paul was not offering a rigid scheme to which
God would have to conform -- just the opposite. God
was far beyond him, far beyond the world, doing something surprisingly new! God had a plan exceeding the
narrow particularism with which Paul had been brought
up as a Pharisaical Jew. Gentiles may come into God's
kingdom -- and without submitting to the ritual rules
of Judaism! Nevertheless, God's arrangement for non-
Jews needs to be interpreted in the context of a solidarity with biblical peoplehood. Surely, God has no
separate plan for saving gentiles apart from the election of God's covenant people, Israel. Gentiles are
accepted on account of their faith, not through the
righteousness that comes by keeping the law -- just as
the Jews are accepted by God. But the Jews are first;
Gentiles share with them in order to become part of
God's household of faith. Paul takes pains to argue
in Rom. 11:17ff. that Gentile converts are branches
from a wild olive tree, grafted into the good olive
tree that is Israel.[47] God had not changed his redemptive plan; he had only carried into effect what most
Jews had forgotten: that they had been called not for
their own sakes but that they might be the instrument
for saving the entire world (Gen. 12:1ff.).

3) The destiny of the individual convert is to
a _via salutis_

Individuals outside the fellowship of ancient
Judaism were given the opportunity of becoming part of
that fellowship without conforming to the ritualistic
requirements that had become normative.[48] Orthodox
Judaism would inevitably reject this view, but in the
early church, it was the doorway for opening up a vast
panorama of universalism. Such non-Torah observing
converts, called and chosen by God to belong to his
elect, would in any case need to enter into the kind of
personalistic fellowship with Israel's God that biblical
believers had always known. Paul therefore defines the
election of new adherents to biblical peoplehood as a
way of salvation (_via salutis_), involving a radical
change of life:

God has from the beginning chosen you to salvation
through sanctification of the Spirit and belief

of the truth, whereunto he called you by our
gospel, to the obtaining of the glory of our Lord
Jesus Christ. (II Thess. 2:13-14; cf. Rom. 8:28-
30, Eph. 1:4ff.).

What Paul affirms is a divine foreknowing and a
divine choice anteceding any choice of our own, opening
up a plan for the world's salvation greater, wiser,
and more wondrous than what even Israel had known.
Israel would continue to be part of this plan, but could
no longer monopolize it. Their finite, historically
limited way of worshiping him must now take second place
to the greater goal of personalistic religion, now
offered to all mankind.

What Christians must remember, in claiming divine
election for themselves, is its inseparability from the
covenant and from biblical peoplehood.

(b) Jewish particularism

Over against Christianity, Judaism has preserved
an authentic concept of peoplehood, an essential
ingredient in biblical personalism. The Jews are a
people who have remained strikingly aware of their
affinities for one another, tenaciously guarding a
peculiar set of mores and traditions designed to maintain their sense of peoplehood. It is these mores and
traditions that have produced among them the strong
marks of ethnicity -- something generally lacking in
Christendom because of its overwhelmingly Gentile
membership.

Excursus on Christian ethnicity

Ethnic coloring has arisen sporadically within
Christendom, as in strongly covenant-oriented groups
like the Scotch Presbyterians, or in separatistic
movements like the Amish. Here too, a special set of
mores and traditions may produce some features of
ethnic peculiarity while widening the gap over against
rival Christian communities. The artificiality of the
ethnic basis generally makes attrition inevitable.
Another form of ethnicity among Christians -- far more
dangerous to the integrity of the gospel -- is one that

is drawn from racial and/or national elements. This
has happened among the German people; so strong did the
sense of Teutonic peoplehood become that many German
Christians were led to a serious distortion of their
gospel heritage.[49] In candor it must be confessed that
many American Christians have similarly allowed nationalistic ideals to compromise their own religious integrity.[50]

While appreciating Judaism for maintaining what
Christendom has generally lost (and must regain if it
is to live up to the biblical ideal), certain dangers
and shortcomings must be observed. Jewish particularism
has produced three special errors in applying the concept of divine election:

1) Defining peoplehood on ethnicity

Three things have to be said: first, that as a
whole, pastbiblical Judaism has been tenaciously and
self-consciously ethnic; secondly, that Jewish
ethnicity is by no means identical with Hebraic
ethnicity -- that which characterized the self-awareness
of the people who gave us the Bible --: and thirdly,
that ethnicity is not essential to the concept of biblical peoplehood.

Excursus on ethnicity and race

Confusion is compounded when ethnicity is identified with raciality. Race is an anthropological, not
a sociological, category. As we study human groups
from an anthropological point of view, we observe that
certain biological specializations have developed in
the evolution of distinct human groupings, so that
dominant physiological characteristics tend to separate
the various branches and families from one another.
In this strict meaning, there is no Jewish race, in
spite of the tendency for blood lines to remain intact
through the prohibition of intermarriage. The fact
is that through history there has been sufficient
infusion of other anthropological stock into the blood-
stream of the Jewish people to disallow any racial
interpretation of Jewishness. (This is recognized in
a decision of the Israeli supreme court, which legally
defines a Jew as a person born of a Jewish mother --

leaving open the possibility of infusion of non-Jewish racial stock through the father.) Here lies, naturally, the extreme fallacy of Nazi antisemitism, which endeavored to eliminate the Jewish "race," killing off numerous unfortunate individuals who had but a small fraction of Jewish ancestry, or had long since converted to Christianity.[51]

It is quite certain that ethnicity does determine Jewish self-consciousness today, as in the past. Jews and Christians need to become more aware, however, that contemporary Jewish ethnicity is not identical with biblical ethnicity. The Talmudic tradition has in many cases radically reinterpreted a wide variety of biblical rules. It has raised up for peculiar emphasis certain mores and rituals which were incidental or peripheral in the Bible, and were in any event borrowed from the ancient cultural environment. Here we think especially of circumcision, practiced by the ancient Hebrews only as part of the general religiosity of their time.[52] The Sabbath was more essential to ancient Israel's distinctive ideology (it had no parallel in other religions of the ancient world), but was not the peculiar mark of ethnicity that it has become in postbiblical Judaism.[53] These observations are not directly intended as a critique upon Jewish ethnicity, but they should help clarify its status. As modern Jews and Christians learn to appreciate each other more, it is well for them both to realize that ethnic peculiarities have no more than a relative status -- not one that is essential to biblical religion as such, but one that has arisen under the special historical forces determining the existence of the Jewish people.

The earliest biblical materials referring to an entity known as Israel reveal, upon critical analysis, that the concept of physical descent from one man, Abraham, is purely schematic and symbolic.[54] Originally, Israel was no cohesive racial or ethnic community, but a conglomoration of loosely related tribes.[55] Linguistic studies have shown that ancient Hebrew is just another dialect of the Canaanite family of western Semitic, virtually identical to the language spoken in Moab and Edom as well as Palestine. Ethnically, the ancestors of the Israelites were strikingly similar to neighboring clans and tribes. They lived the same, dressed the same, thought and talked the same. The groups that joined together as Israel left similar groups outside their organization. On the other hand, once the Israelite tribes gained political consolidation, putting Palestine as a whole under their administrative control, they organized their society in such a way as to give heterogeneous groups a place in their social and religious life. Very likely certain groups (the Gibeonites,[56] cf. Joshua 9; perhaps also the Levites[57] and the Nethinim)[58] remained in an inferior status. Nevertheless, they all belonged to "Israel," sharing its religious ideology and participating in its destiny.

It is clear, then, that the most primitive Israel was primarily sociological and religious, developing strongly ethnic features only under the impact of a centralized national organization. Israel has always experienced difficulty in appropriating nationalistic modes for the expression of its peoplehood, and long ago accepted the necessity of discarding nationalism as one of the marks of its ethnicity. Furthermore, at various periods of its history, Israel has taken a stance of openness toward the rest of humankind, extending the hand of fellowship to individuals out side itself.[59] This openness was, to be sure, the invitation to adopt the biblical faith and follow the Jewish religion, but the very ideal that animated this movement was the universalism of this faith and this religion. It was the Jew' religion, but not for them alone. Ideally, it belonged to all mankind. Ethnic elements would have to remain in a status of secondary, ancillary importance.

It was a historical tragedy that the Romans destroyed Jerusalem and deported the Jewish people from Palestine just at the time when Christianity was moving out to embrace the gentile world. This final demolition of their national existence drove the Jewish survivors into an even more narrow and rigid ethnic pattern, which they felt henceforth obliged to preserve as the sole vehicle for biblical peoplehood. This widened the gap between the Jews and the Christians, who were moving away from an ethnic pattern in order to offer biblical religion to all mankind.

2) Impairing the divine choice by abstracting the promise from a fulfilment of the condition

This is the second gross error to which Judaism (but not it alone!) is susceptible. In choosing Israel to be his people, Yahweh laid a very heavy obligation on them, which could not be fulfilled in terms of mere formal adherence to an external standard. To be a people holy to the Lord is a solemn responsibility and a portentous call. Election guarantees nothing but God's love; those who sin against this love and privilege only magnify the enormity of their transgression.

It is precisely this that the deuteronomists and the prophets fulminated against. Israel was presuming upon its election. In ironic derision, Amos says for Yahweh (9:7-8):

> Are you not like the Ethiopians to me,
>   O people of Israel? says Yahweh.
>   Did I not bring up Israel from the land of Egypt
>   and the Philistines from Caphtor and
>   the Syrians from Kir?
> Behold, the eyes of Lord Yahweh are
>   upon the sinful kingdom....

A noted Jewish scholar recently remarked that Yahweh was more "antisemitic" than any human Jew-hater. He said this only to call attention to the eminently biblical theme of divine jealousy. According to the Bible, Yahweh had abundant reason to be jealous.

The question is: Is contemporary Judaism also guilty of presuming upon its privilege and election? This is a question that Jews must answer for themselves. We Christians must ask it too, but of ourselves. Whenever we assume that we are somehow worthy in ourselves, we are sinning against God's sovereign elective love.

Excursus on the sin against elective love

This is so serious because it desecrates both human and divine personhood. It is precisely analogous to a violation of personhood between closely dependent humans, particularly in the marriage relationship.

What happens within intimate interhuman relationships when those who have made a solemn agreement, as in marriage, try to take advantage of the other party's

obligation. It immediately destroys the joy of marriage.
When either or both parties of the marriage covenant
behave as though the other person is obligated to do
what he or she should do freely, it restricts the freedom and spoils the happiness of this relationship. The
purpose of the contract, viz., mutual enrichment in
dynamic interaction, is frustrated. A healthy marriage,
along with similar human relationships, involves a
recognition of the other persons's claims and needs,
and involves a deep commitment on one's own part to try
to fulfill those claims and needs, even while fulfilling
one's own claims and needs. Marriage offers the richest
possiblity for human happinesss, but paradoxically poses
the greatest imaginable threat to it as well. This is
because those who are closest to us -- to whom we commit
ourselves the most -- can hurt us the most. Similarly
the parental-filial relationship. Often we see a father
or mother injuring the personhood of their child, or the
child injuring the personhood of the parent by abusing
his or her love.

It is precisely because the Bible takes the Father/
Husband symbol so seriously in application to God that
election requires the response of perfect love and
obedience. The biblical God is no abstract idea, no
impersonal force. He is a JEALOUS God. He can be
grieved; but in grieving him we also hurt ourselves.

3)   Interpreting election as an end in itself

As we make a critical study of the biblical
materials which speak of Israel's election, we must
come to the conclusion that this people was chosen to
help other peoples. Israel's election was not the goal
of history, but God's way through history. We inevitably return to Gen. 12:1-3, the hinge between J's
prehistory and the following patriarchal cycle. Abram
is called to go to a new country and become the father
of a new people in order that all the "families" of the
land might bless themselves by Israel. Written, in all
likelihood, in the time of David's kingdom, this promise
offers high privilege and distinction to the Israel that
had come out of Abram. Two consequences follows: (1)
We as Gentile adherents to biblical faith ought never
to imagine that our relationship to God has any real
meaning apart from the primary position of Israel.
Israel's historical relationship with God serves eternally as a model and example for the rest of the world,

and Israel will always continue to enjoy this very special relationship with God. Their love-hate relationship with God is the paradox and the epitome of what election will always mean. (2) Israel can never fulfill her election in isolation. She has been called in order to bring a blessing (God's blessing) on other men. Counterbalancing the intensifying particularism of the postexilic period are noble passages in the prophets which gladly embrace this role.[60] These are remained part of Holy Scripture to stimulate the preaching of Jesus, and they remain to challenge Judaism today. Christian universalism authentically expresses the intent of Israel's call, for if there is indeed only one universal God, election must be the potential gift of all the men whom this God created.

(c) Election as an eschatological symbol

The final word that must be said about election is that it is intended as an eschatological symbol of God's lordship over all mankind. Like other eschatological symbols, it represents a goal and not an achievement.

Affirmed by the earliest historiographic records, election is always raised up as something that awaits future fulfillment.[61] Israel is called, not as a closed-off and finished entity, but as in process of becoming what it is by definition. God's peculiar people, Israel, first experienced the meaning of election, but symbolically and instrumentally, in order that all mankind might at last enter into this joyous relationship.

The sanctification of an elect people is similar to the sanctification of a special holy day, the Sabbath. The real intent of the Sabbath is to glorify God as Lord over all time. There is nothing inherently holy in one day out of seven; it is holy only because it symbolizes the potential holiness of all days.

The sanctification of a people is also similar to the sanctification of a particular piece of geographical territory, "the holy land."[62] Palestine is in itself no more sacred than other regions. The promise of this land is another eschatological symbol. Whether or not God's people actually reside in it, it serves as a

234

symbol. Whether or not God's lordship over all lands. It is folly, then, to restrict the meaning of this evocative eschatological promise to the physical possession of Palestine. Radical Zionism has forgotten what many past generations of Jews have learned all too well -- that the biblical God is Lord over all lands. Palestine is not the property of the Jews; it is the property of God.[63] It has special status only as the token of God's universal rule. If possessing it should lead to violation of God's revealed will for mankind's salvation, the symbol would be shattered and the promise made void.

2.   Covenant wholeness and the law (the horizontal
     dimension)

     Ancient Israel was not a democracy, bound together
by a "social contract" for harmonious living. It was
nonetheless a covenantal society, bound together through
mutual allegiance to Yahweh. Its covenant with him
obligated individual Israelites to one another. Their
God cared how they treated one another. The particular
societal or political arrangement of the moment could
not be allowed to disrupt Israel's allegiance to Yahweh
as king, and to one another as brothers. Israel had
been elected as a holy people, and their holiness was
designed to permeate every part of life, secular as well
as religious.

     Thus the concepts of election and covenant had a
horizontal as well as a vertical dimension. The profound personalism that produced these symbols produced
also a sense of strong obligation within covenantal
society, determining the nature of their moral system.

     a.   Nonbiblical ethical alternatives

     (1) The major options

     We have previously identified a variety of non-
biblical soteriological systems, all of which involve
a particular concept of ethical responsibility.   To
review the main options within ancient and modern
society, we would catalogue the following:[64]

     (a) Primitive dynamism. This lies at the most
elemental roots of ancient Near-Eastern society,
producing a sense of obligation that is based on an
irrational and amoral compulsion. Human persons, who
are coerced by one another, inevitably come to attribute
fear of being hurt and the hope of reward lead to a
cautious prudentialism. One does good and avoids
wickedness because this course of action generally pays.

(b) Civilized moralism. In more advanced forms
of civilized society, we find that abstract moralism
becomes important in determining the development of
codes of ethical behavior. The Greek schools of the
Stoics and Epicureans speculated on the philosophical
basis for appropriate behavior, largely discarding the
naivete of myth. Western society has borrowed heavily
from Greek culture in developing its various systems of
prudentialism, legalism, and utopianism. The basic
polarity has been that between individualism and altru-
ism, with little concern for a supernatural norm.

(c) Amoralism. Seldom developed as sophisticated
codes, amoralism has become the guide in the lives of
many peoples and individuals, especially in the modern
day. Amoralism may be frankly animalistic, yet it may
assume so highly ideological a form as that of National
Socialism in Germany.[65]

(2) Ancient Near-Eastern ethical ideals

More to the point is a presentation of ethical
alternatives within the ancient world out of which
Israel emerged. This world was characterized both by
primitive dynamism and civilized moralism -- the latter
providing a veneer of respectability upon the former.
We choose representative examples, first from Egypt and
next from Mesopotamia.

The epitome of legalistic self-righteousness: The
Protestation of Guiltlessness, ANET 34ff.[66]

One of a well-to-do person's arrangements for
burial in ancient Egypt would be the preparation of a
scroll of parchment in which he would be represented
as standing before Osiris, swearing that he had never
done any wrong. The specific wrongs mentioned ranged
from social to religious transgressions, all being
equally condemned by the gods. What is remarkable is
that according to such a text, the deceased would have
had to be utterly without blame in his earthly life.

237

One can account for this only on the supposition that
the deceased thought that the gods could be misled, or
on the supposition that the suppliant's standard of
right and wrong must have been starkly legalistic. The
following are the specific evils which he declares
himself to be free of:

I have not committed evil against men.
I have not mistreated cattle.
I have not committed sin in the place of truth.
. . . .
I have not blasphemed a god.
I have not done violence to a poor man.
I have not done that which the gods abominate.
I have not defamed a slave to his superior.
I have not made (anyone) sick.
I have not made (anyone) weep.
I have not killed.
I have given no order to a killer.
I have not caused anyone suffering.
I have not cut down on the food-(income) in the
    temples.
I have not damaged the bread of the gods.
I have not taken the loaves of the blessed (dead).
I have not had sexual relations with a boy.
I have not defiled myself.
I have neither increased or diminished the
    grain-measure.
. . . .
I have not weakened the plummet of the scales.
I have not taken milk from the mouths of children.
I have not driven cattle away from their pasturage.
I have not snared the birds of the gods.
I have not caught fish in their marshes.
I have not held up the water in its season.
I have not built a dam against running water.
I have not quenched a fire at its (proper) time.
I have not neglected the (appointed) times and
    their meat-offerings.
I have not driven away the cattle of the god's
    property.
I have not stopped a god on his procession.

Next the suppliant cries out, "I am pure, I am
pure, I am pure, I am pure." He describes his purity
in mythological lyricism, then addresses each of the
forty-two juror gods by name, denying to each some
specific transgression.

Up to this point a priest has been speaking on
behalf of the deceased, but now he requires him to say
his own appeal to the jurors and to Osiris himself:

Words to be spoken by X:

Hail to you, ye gods who are in this Broad-Hall
of the Two Justices! I know you; I know your
names. I shall not fall for dread of you. Ye
have not reported guilt of mine up to this god in
whose retinue ye are....Ye have spoken truth about
me in the presence of the All-Lord, because I
acted justly in Egypt....May ye rescue me from
Babi, who lives on the entrails of elders on that
day of the great reckoning. Behold me -- I have
come to you without sin, without guilt, without
evil.....

To Osiris himself the deceased declares:

I have effected justice for the Lord of Justice,
being pure -- my front is pure, my rear is clean, my
middle is in the flowing water of justice; there is
no part of me free of justice.

The deceased next is subjected to three examina-
tions regarding mythological allusions (something only
the priest writing this could know, and was supplying
for a fee). Having once more avowed his purity to
Thoth, the chamberlain, he is admitted into the presence of Osiris himself.

The dread anxiety that suffuses this ceremony is
testimony to a pervading element of awesome irrational-
ity in the divine-human relationship. It is evident
that the deceased suppliant is entirely in the hands of
his priestly sponsors, for unless he recites precisely
the right words, he stands no chance of passing this
ordeal. Thus the limitations of Egyptian mythicism
mar the accomplishment of this ethical affirmation.
It falls short because (1) it is cult-oriented and cult-
dominated; (2) it is available only to the powerful and
prosperous, who alone can commission such a parchment
as this for their burial; (3) inasmuch as the same text
applies to each and any paying customer, the denials of
wrong-doing must express no more than an ideal -- not
the actual behavior of individual persons; and (4) its
morality is purely negative -- a list of wrong deeds

that have ostensibly been avoided -- and says nothing of positive, voluntary good. It falls far short of biblical personalism. In the final analysis, it depends heavily on the belief that the gods -- even the all seeing and all knowing -- can be manipulated by the priestly establishment.

Pragmatic prudentialism: The Lipit-Ishtar lawcode, <u>ANET</u> 159-61[67]

The practical ethics of a given society are well illustrated in two particular genres, wisdom instructions and codes of law. The one advises, the other prescribes correct conduct, as judged by the norms of the given society. We choose our next example of ancient ethical idealism from a lawcode of the Akkadians, the earliest Mesopotamian Semites, written toward the beginning of the second millenium, B.C. It is similar in most respects to the better-known Code of Hammurabi, but shorter and less complex. It regulates the interactions of society in the realms of property, land, slaves, inheritance, family relationships, and tort for damages. This is no constitution, conceived on philosophical principles to produce the ideal society, but a putting in writing of the practices that had proven to be beneficial and therefore deserved to be confirmed by regal edict as a permanent rule. The gods are, indeed, invoked, yet the conception is strikingly atheological. We quote only from the Prologue and Eiplogue to illustrate Lipit-Ishtar's motivation of pragmatic prudentialism:

> ...I, Lipit-Ishtar, the humble shepherd of Nippur, the stalwart farmer of Ur (etc.)...[estab]lished [jus]tice in [Su]mer and Akkad in accordance with the word of Enlil...Verily...I made the father support his children (and) I made the children [support their] father; I made the father sta[nd by hi]s children (and) I made the children stand by their father; in the father's house (and) [in the brother's] house...
>
> Verily in accordance with the tr[ue word] of Utu, I caused [Su]mer and Akkad to hold to true justice. Verily in accordance with the pronouncement of Enlil, I, Lipit-Ishtar, the son of Enlil, abolished enmity and rebellion; made weeping, lamentations, outcries... taboo; caused righteousness and truth to exist; brought well-being to the

Sumerians and the Akkadians....

Sophisticated prudentialism striving toward theoretical standards: The Protests of the Eloquent
Peasant, <u>ANET</u> 408ff.[68]

This is a piece of didactic narrative from the
Middle Kingdom of ancient Egypt. As popular folk
literature, it effectively illustrates a universal
craving for just treatment, together with its precari-
ourness within the power struggles of an agrarian-
aristocratic society. It has to do with an aggrieved
peasant, Khun-Anup, a greedy landowner, Thut-Nakht, and
a corrupt Chief Steward, Rensi. Thut-Nakht siezes Khun-
Anup's donkey on a pretext, beats him, and drives him
away. When the peasant appears before the Chief Steward
for retribution, an official suggests that the matter be
set right by making the landlord give back part of what
he had stolen. The peasant will not accept this, so
appeals to the Chief Steward as the upholder of justice.
He adopts eloquence along with flattery in his appeal:

O Chief Steward, my lord, greatest of the great,
undertaker of that which is not and of that which
is! If thou embarkest on the lake of justice,
mayest thou sail on it with a fair breeze! A
squall shall not tear away they sail, thy boat
shall not lag, no misfortune shall overtake thy
mast, thy yards shall not break...because thou
art the father of the orphan, the husband of the
widow, the brother of the divorcee, and the apron
of him that is motherless. Let me make thy name
in this land according to every good law: a leader
free from covetousness, a great man free from
wrongdoing, one who destroys falsehood and brings
justice into being, and who comes at the cry of
him who gives voice. When I speak, mayest thou
hear. Do justice, thou favored one whom the
favored ones favor!

The Chief Steward is so astounded at this eloquence
that he reports to Pharaoh Neb-kau-Re of his discovery.
So rare a gift must be treasured, thus the king commands
Rensi to keep the peasant pleading for justice while
surreptitiously providing him with sustenance -- ten
loaves of bread and two jars of beer every day!

The rest of the narrative has a simple structure:

241

for eight more times Khun-Anup comes back to Rensi. His moving pleas are written down for the amusement of the king. He grows more frank and more bitter. At last, adopting the boldness of desperation, he threatens to appeal his case to a higher authority and charge Rensi with corruption. Because he has been beaten every time he has spoken, he expects now to be even more severely punished. Instead, Rensi speaks to him all the eloquent words that he has spoken. The story has a happy resolution. All the landlord's property is confiscated and turned over to the peasant.

The way the story turns out must be interpreted as an accurate reflection of how Egyptian society too often allowed justice and morality to be administered: by force and pressure. Had the peasant not been elo- quent, and had the king not wanted to be amused, the peasant might never have received retribution. All his pleas except the last (the threat of appeal), falling apparently on deaf ears, represent moral ideals that could be violated at the whim of those in power: (1) injustice upsets the social balance be- cause if the administration of justice is unjust, all is wrong; (2) the maladministration of justice pro- duces chaos; (3) it is a perversion of function; (4) evil gain will perish, and only justice is eternal; (5) injustice breeds further injustice. The Egyptian throne is depicted in literature and in pictorial representations as being founded on maat, "justice," "truth"[69] -- but this idealized the stability and order of autocratic society, rather than the practical attainment of legitimate desire among the lowest classes of society.

Thus on a practical level, Egyptian morality consisted simply of protecting one's rights as best one might, achieving an equilibrium -- if not a har- mony -- between contending forces. The man who had everything could do virtually anything; the man who had little could do little but hang on to survival.

b. Covenant morality in ancient Israel

(1) The motivation of covenant morality

"Religion is the opiate of the people," said Karl
Marx. Christian social philosophers endeavor to
refute this, but the sad truth is that church morality
has so forsaken its biblical heritage as to have given
Marx the occasion for saying this. It is irrefutably
true that the religion that he knew was strongly
allied with an oppressive economic and social system,
fostering the interests of the rich and the powerful
at the expense of the workers. Furthermore, Marx
could draw examples from many nations and many periods
to demonstrate that religion has generally been on the
side of a privileged establishment. Given their
defective religious ideologies, it is no wonder that
Egypt, Babylon, Syria, Greece, and Rome should have
made this hateful alliance. But for Christian culture
to do so was inexcusable. This is not because Jesus
and Paul were social reformers or political agitators;
they were not. It is because both Old Testament and
New Testament religion are constitutionally humanitarian. Though they do not counsel revolt, they offer
nothing to promote the "divine right of kings" or
the sacrosanctity of laissez-faire capitalism. The
truth of the matter is that the kings get a rough
going-over in the Bible.[70] If it were not for the
idealizing of David, an ideology that arose to celebrate the unparalleled longevity of his line, the
king-figure would have remained entirely in the
shadows. It is for the people -- the common people
especially -- that the Bible takes part. If Christianity had remained true to this ideal, the indus-
trial age would never have been allowed to develop
the intolerable conditions that gave birth to that
greater devil, Communistic materialism.

Every ancient record available to us confirms
that Israel had a far stronger sense of peoplehood
than any of its neighbors. It likewise had an elaborate and highly ideological code of morality.
Ultimately, the notion of being in a covenant with
Yahweh required the determined pursuit of humanitarian goals, for each Israelite was as much bound
to his fellows in this covenant as he was bound to
Yahweh.

Israel is to be holy because Yahweh is holy.
This is the highest form of theomorphism -- man
becoming like God. To be holy like Yahweh means to
be set aside from all that defiles.[71] But what is
it that Israel is to be set aside from? Naturally,
from intrusive religious cults. But that is only
part of the answer: to be holy as Yahweh is holy

243

means to honor the ethical norms and social ideals of convnantal society, loving one's neighbor as oneself.

This is forcefully stated in a chapter of the Old Testament that Christians know all too imperfectly -- the nineteenth of Leviticus. True, they know verse 18 because Jesus quoted it as the second of the two great commandments (Mark 12:31): "You shall love your neighbor as yourself." But they do not know its context, and therefore we shall do well at this point in quoting long extracts from it:

> 2 Say to all the congregation of the people of Israel, You shall be holy; for I Yahweh your god am holy. 3 Every one of you shall revere his mother and his father, and you shall keep my sabbaths: I am Yahweh your god. 4 Do not turn to idols or make for yourselves molten gods: I am Yahweh your god....9 When you reap the harvest of your land, you shall not reap your field to its very border, neither shall you gather the gleanings after your harvest. 10 And you shall not strip your vineyard bare, neither shall you gather the fallen grapes of your vineyard; you shall leave them for the poor and the sojourner: I am Yahweh your god. 11 You shall not steal, nor deal falsely, nor lie to one another. 12 And you shall not swear by my name falsely, and so profane the name of your god: I am Yahweh. 13 You shall not oppress your neighbor or rob him. The wages of a hired servant shall not remain with you all night until the morning. 14 You shall not curse the deaf or put a stumbling block before the blind, but you shall fear your god: I am Yahweh. 15 You shall do no injustice in judgment; you shall not be partial to the poor or defer to the great, but in righteousness shall you judge your neighbor. 16 You shall not go up and down as a slanderer among your people, and you shall not stand forth against the life of your neighbor: I am Yahweh. 17 You shall not hate your brother in your heart, but you shall reason with your neighbor, lest you bear sin because of him. 18 You shall not take vengeance or bear any grudge against the sons of your own people, but you shall love your neighbor as yourself: I am Yahweh. [72]

244

The passage goes on like this for fifteen more
verses, forbidding the overuse of fruit-trees,
witchcraft and superstition, selling one's daughter
as a prostitute, dishonoring the elderly, inhos-
pitality toward strangers, unjust weights and balances
(vv. 19-22 are intrusive). What is remarkable is the
heightened personalism. Only the ethics of Jesus
surpasses it!

Excursus on conflicting social ideals in the Old Testament

What superficial students of the Old Testament
do not see is that it reflects a prolonged struggle
between incompatible social ideologies. Prior to
the rise of the monarchy under Saul and David, Israel
was only a loose confederation of tribes -- bound
together, as we have seen, by a common social ideology and religious allegiance, rather than by racial
or ethnic ties. They were very much committed to an
egalitarian distribution of wealth and opportunity.
They actually believed that the land belonged to
Yahweh (Leviticus 25), hence could not be held by
private owners in perpetuity. The needs of the
unfortunate received solicitous attention. Public
affairs were conducted by tribal chiefs and village
elders.

Once David succeeded in consolidating political
power, the social and economic system began to change
(see the deuteronomistic critique placed in Samuel's
mouth, I Sam. 8:10-17). Lands newly acquired became
the property of the king and of a rising class of
nobility. City life required artisans and craftsmen.
Imperial ambitiousness demanded censuses, taxation,
and obligatory services. Slavery became institutionalized, particularly as a penalty for non-payment
of debt. Yet the old tribal attitudes persisted,
inspiring Amos and Micah, with the other prophets,
to thunder against social wrong.[73] The prohibition
against interest, inhibitive as modern economics
may know it is to be in terms of capital growth,
continued to be heard as a symbolical protest
against the monopolization of wealth and the misuse
of economic, social, and political power.[74]

(2)   Covenants and codes of law[75]

It was a gradual development that produced the
awareness that Yahweh's elective choice required a
covenantal agreement affecting every part of Israel's
moral responsibility. The following sketch will
serve to put its various ramifications into historical perspective:

> Covenants in which God binds himself uncon-
> ditionally (Ex. 24:1-2, 9-11; Gen. 15:1-12,
> 17-21; Gen. 9:8-17; Gen. 17; Num. 25:10-13)

Although the human response is implied, it is
not expressly stated. Upon source-critical and form-
critical considerations, we may judge two examples to
be very early -- perhaps antedating the establishment of the Israelite kingdom(s). Without expressly
mentioning a covenant, a promise, or an obligation,
the E document in Ex. 24:1-2, 9-11 (the narrative
climax of the Sinai pericope in this source) reports
a theophanous revelation to Moses and other representatives of Israel, gathered in a covenantal meal
before Yahweh:

> And he said to Moses, Come up to Yahweh, you
> and Aaron, Nadab and Abihu, and seventy of
> the elders of Israel....Then Moses and
> Aaron, Nadab and Abihu, and seventy of the
> elders of Israel went up, and they saw the
> god of Israel; and there was under his
> feet as it were a pavement of sapphire
> stone, like the very heaven for clearness.
> And he did not lay his hand on the chief
> men of the people of Israel; they beheld
> God, and ate and drank.

This is entirely undeveloped: Yahweh does
nothing except let himself be seen as Israel's god,
proving himself beneficent by not harming the men
worshiping before him. [76]

In another E narrative a very primitive tradition reports: "Jethro, Moses' father-in-law (ḥōtān,
"kinsman") offered a burnt offering and sacrifices
to God; and Aaron came with all the elders of Israel
to eat bread with Moses' father-in-law before God"
(Ex. 18:12). Although a covenant-type meal is

246

implied, there is no theophany, no instructions, no promise, and no obligation. In short, personal inter-action between the Deity and his worshipers does not enter into the story, as it does in Ex. 24:9-11.[77]

Another covenant narrative that is relatively early -- from J's source material -- is Gen. 15:1-12, 17-21. It has, first, a promise of vast posterity, which Abram receives by faith; then a mystic cere-mony in which Yahweh's theophanous presence passes through an arrangement of sacrificial victims; finally a promise of the land to Abram's posterity. Verse 18 epitomizes, stating the total effect in the words, "On that day Yahweh made a covenant (kārat bᵉrît), with Abram."[78]

Three other unconditional commitments appear in the latest Pentateuchal strand, P. The first states that God establishes a covenant (hēqîm/nātan bᵉrît) with Noah, his descendants, and every living creature (Gen. 9:8-17). It is actually a promise never again to destroy the world with a flood, sealed in the sign of the rainbow. This rather imaginative passage expands the original societal/cultic context of covenant making to include the world of divine ordinances, which is altogether characteristic of the priestly writer's cosmological interest. It is the same source, P, that has a narrative of God's covenant with Abram/Abraham (Genesis 17). It is essentially a promise of three things: (1) multi-plying Abraham's posterity; (2) being their special god; and (3) giving them the land of their sojourn-ings as an everlasting possession (vv. 1-8). Al-though this passage is not cosmological like Gene-sis 9, it does exhibit an expansive, universalistic claim.[79] Finally, we mention a third P passage, Num. 25:10-13, which appears to have been drawn from a special priestly tradition, legitimizing the line of Phinehas:

Behold, I give to him my covenant of peace; and it shall be to him and to his des-cendants after him, the covenant of a perpetual priesthood, because he was jealous for his god, and made atonement for the people of Israel.[80]

Covenants in which God requires Israel's acceptance of obedient peoplehood (Joshua 24;
Ex. 19:3-7; Deut. 26:16-19, 27:9-10)

Passages in which God approaches Israel with the
demand that they respond positively to his elective
love strongly exhibit the ideology of the deuteronomic movement, which does not automatically preclude
the possibility that the underlying tradition behind
each of them may have preceded the emergence of this
ideology in the fully developed form that now determines the theology of the deuteronomic literature.
It is important to see that each of these passages
involves the mediatory role of Moses (or of the new
Moses, Joshua). This is to be accounted for best on
the supposition that this tradition developed in a
ritual context, engaging the assembled people and a
sacral representative of the Deity.

Quite likely, the earliest tradition in this
group of passages is the one found in Joshua 24,
where Joshua calls the people to forsake their
foreign gods and serve Yahweh alone.[81] Language,
style, and conception show the strong influence of
Deuteronomy -- yet the underlying tradition must be
earlier than the remotest literary origins of that
book, and for two reasons: (1) in Deuteronomy (as
well as in the deuteronomistic history) the Israelites are warned against going over to idol worship,
but are not depicted as actually committed to them;
hence this reflects an early situation in which
numerous social and religious elements in Israel
were still unassimilated to normative Yahwism; (2)
although Joshua is reinterpreted in the deuteronomistic history as a new Moses (see Joshua 1), he
stands here in the foreground, without any ostensible effort to equate him with Moses. These
features have been retained in this particular
narrative simply because the deuteronomistic historian found them in his sources, for he would never
have invented them himself. Thus the tradition of
Joshua's covenantal mediatorship may have a greater
level of historical factuality than that of Moses.
The location of Shechem, which later played no
further role in Israel's cultic life, is further
evidence of an irreducable historicality behind the
story. (Deut. 27:1ff, and Josh. 8:30ff. appear to

be deuteronomistic efforts to claim the Shechem
tradition directly for Moses.)

Ex. 19:3-7 may be as early as the Joshua passage,
so far as its tradition background is concerned. It
probably does not belong to the E strand's Sinai
narrative, in spite of some scholars' opinion, because the E source makes nothing of it in terms of
structural development towards its climax in Exodus
24. Its insertion into the text is very likely due
to deuteronomic editing. It very clearly expresses
deuteronomic ideology with respect to the covenant,
laying heavy emphasis on Israel's duty to respond:[82]

> Yahweh called to [Moses] out of the mountain,
> saying, "Thus you shall say to the house of
> Jacob, and tell the people of Israel: You
> have seen what I did to the Egyptians, and
> how I bore you on eagles' wings and brought
> you to myself. Now therefore, if you will
> obey my voice and keep my covenant, you
> shall be my own possession among all peoples;
> for all the earth is mine, and you shall be to
> me a kingdom of priests and a holy nation.
> These are the words which you shall speak to
> the children of Israel.

The third passage in this category lies at the
heart of the deuteronomic corpus itself, Deut.
26:16-19, 27:9-10.[83] As elsewhere in the book,
Moses is speaking:

> This day Yahweh your god commands you to do
> these statutes and ordinances; you shall
> therefore be careful to do them with all
> your heart and with all your soul. You
> have declared this day concerning Yahweh
> that he is your god, and that you will
> walk in his ways, and keep his statutes
> and his commandments and his ordinances,
> and will obey his voice; and Yahweh has
> declared this day concerning you that you
> are a people for his own possession, as he
> has promised you, and that you are to keep
> all his commandments...and that you shall
> be a people holy to Yahweh your god, as
> he has spoken....And Moses and the
> Levitical priests said to all Israel, Keep

silence and hear, O Israel: this day you have become the people of Yahweh your god. You shall therefore obey the voice of Yahweh your god, keeping his commandments and his statutes, which I command you this day.

As Leviticus 19 shows us, to be holy to Yahweh implies the social (horizontal) dimension as well as the religious (vertical) dimension of the covenant. To keep Yahweh's commandments, ordinances (etc.) involves the carrying out of this obligation in concrete detail.

Covenants in which God binds himself on condition of a ritual response (Gen. 17:10-14, Mal. 2:4-7)

This is a very peculiar category because it reduces the covenant obligation to a single, crucial obligation -- the ritual of circumcision. The extreme lateness of this idea appears from an analysis of the literary history involved in Genesis 17, the P passage where God establishes his covenant unconditionally with Abram/Abraham. The original P narrative continued from v. 9 directly to vv. 15ff. The doublet in vv. 26ff., reporting that Abraham and his family submitted to the rite of circumcision, is a likely termination for the original narrative; the identification of circumcision as a confirmation of the covenant would not have been inconsistent with the ideology of this priestly writer.[84] However, vv. 10-14 introduce an actual torah for circumcision, specifying how and on whom the rite is to be practiced through generations to come. This is "keeping my covenant" according to v. 9. The redactor who was responsible for adding this expansion (its narrative continuation is in vv. 23-25) went beyond the original P writer, for whom the covenant was unconditional, flowing freely from God's grace and beneficence, while circumcision was only an appropriate confirmation and symbol of this covenant. For the redactor, circumcision actually was the covenant; unless one submitted to it, the promise of God was vain.

A parallel idea is found in Mal. 2:4-7, where a special "covenant with Levi" is defined in terms of faithful performance of priestly duties. To lay heavy emphasis on the seriousness of priestly commitment is not the same, however, as endeavoring to make the observance of a particular ritual the condition of acceptance into a covenant that belongs to all the people.[85]

> Covenants stipulating Israel's obligation as a legal code (Ex. 34:11-26; Ex. 20:1-17 = Deut. 5:6-11; Lev. 17-26; Ex. 20:21-23:33, 24:3-8; Deut. 12:1-26:15)

The fullest expansion of the idea of covenantal obligation is found in a number of passages where "being a people holy to Yahweh" is made explicit in terms of specific requirements. It is only here that the fullest horizontal expansion of election/covenant is to be seen.

Although this kind of structure is not necessarily late, we do not find any extremely early representatives of it. What is likely the earliest in terms of literary origins exhibits also the relatively simplest content. This is the so-called J decalogue in Exodus 34. It is early (United Kingdom period) because the apodictic code of vv. 11-26 is firmly anchored to the J narrative framework in vv. 1-9, 27-35, and because its content is entirely devoted to religious and ritualistic requirements.[86] One observes that the code of law is specifically called a covenant (berît) in vv. 10, 27, 28. It is made first with Moses, then with Israel (v. 27) -- showing that the underlying tradition may have first belonged to a separate Moses group. A gloss at the end of v. 28 identifies this as "the ten words" or commandments, but this only adds confusion to the confusion of an already highly redacted text.

From this we go to Ex. 20:1-17 (the so-called E Decalogue), which is equivalent to Deut. 5:6-21. Here a "second table of the law," commandments 5 through 10, balances the specifically ritual requirement of commandments 1-4. Unfortunately, its literary connection in Exodus is secondary; the Decalogue was not an original part of the E document, and there is no way of determining how and when it got into its present position. Nevertheless its structural position in Deuteronomy shows that the

Decalogue predates Deuteronomy, which is designed as an explication of it.[87] It is typological fiction that informs us that Moses himself spoke the Decalogue; it does not in fact reflect Moses' time, but the time of Israel's fullest cultural development during the period of the divided monarchy.[88] Its peculiar value lies in the fact that it offers a classical exposition of covenantal values.

Once the idea of articulating the covenant in terms of legal obligation had established itself, nothing could resist a tendency toward including ever-more expansive bodies of legal material. There are three notable documents of this character. All of these come from the divided-kingdom period. First we mention the Holiness Code. Leviticus 17-26, which has been simply attached to the priestly document without any effort to provide a narrative setting. Next there is the so-called Covenant Code in Ex. 20:21-23:33, with Ex. 24:3-8 as narrative conclusion. Finally there is the Deuteronomic Lawbook, Deut. 12:1-26:15.[89]

Narratives about covenant making, which simply record that the people carried out its requirements or performed certain duties implied by it, are those that involve king Josiah in II Kings 23:1-4 and Ezra in Neh. 9:1-3, 38, 10:28ff.

In the final combination, the entire Pentateuch, which the Jews call Torah, becomes the expression of Yahweh's requirement of Israel's covenant obedience.

(3) The Second Table of the Law

In Cecil B. De Mille's blockbuster movie, "The Ten Commandments," Charlton Heston appears in the classic scene of receiving the law from God. He has chiseled out two huge tablets of stone. With wind blowing his hair and beard, he stands on the holy mountain, holding aloft the tablets, that God may record his commandments upon them. Amid thunder and tempest, fingers of lightning flash down from heaven, burning blue holes in the stone, marking out in classic Hebrew script the holy words.

252

There is some disagreement in the Bible itself as
to who actually carved the words in the stone:
Ex. 34:28 (cf. v. 27) reports that Moses did it,
but Ex. 32:16 emphatically states that "the tablets
were the work of God, and the writing was the writing
of God, graven upon the tablets." In any event, the
tradition is consistent that there were two of them
(Ex. 32:15, 34:1, 4, 29). But the reason for two
tablets remains obscure. Both Jewish and Christian
traditions have become accustomed to the explanation
that one tablet held the commands for correct worship
while the second tablet held the commands for correct
social ethics. Thus the expression, "the second
tablet of the law," has come to refer to commandments
5 through 10, explicating the requirements of ethical
living.

In order to perceive the covenantal context of
these rules, it is necessary to have some knowledge
of their genre and function. The term "law" is inappropriate if one thinks of legislative promulgation
and authority. In spite of their social bearing,
they are primarily religious rules, designed as
demands direct from God. They are not like the
mišpāṭîm, "ordinances," such as those which appear
in Ex. 21:1ff. The mišpāṭîm are casuistic rules pro-
mulgated by the local authorities on the basis of
precedent, and designed to apply to specific situations arising in community life. The name modern
scholars prefer to give to the commands of the Decalogue is "apodictic commandment."[90] Spoken by or
for God, they are brief, unconditioned, and usually
negative.[91] The biblical name for them is simply
"words" (debārîm), as in Ex. 20:1, 34:27-28. Like
the prophetic "word," the apodictic "word" is a
revelation direct from God. It touches only upon the
most essential matters of covenantal living, pro-
hibiting specific actions that threaten its harmony.
Thus apodictic law "defines" covenant living, in the
etymological sense of the word (de-finere, from the
Latin, points to the marking off of boundaries). By
shutting off the most harmful possibilities, apodictic law guards the conditions under which the positive
observance of societal duties may be nurtured.[92]

Excursus on the didactic function of apodictic law

The fact that apodictic rules tend to group themselves into fives or tens reflects the simple fact that they were intended to be memorized like rules in a catechism, ticked off on the fingers. The earliest ones, which are preserved in only fragmentary form in the present biblical text, tended to deal with one single area of religious or ethical responsibility.[93] By carefully reconstructing them, we can clearly see their didactic purpose.

In recent years the German scholar Karl Elliger has hypothetically restored an original ten prohibitions in Leviticus 18, a chapter that is entirely devoted to sexual concerns.[94] The original code, as Elliger reconstructs it, has a narrowly focused point of interest: degrees of forbidden sexual liaison. Someone -- evidently a young male person -- is being instructed about which females he dare not approach:

I   Thou shalt not uncover the nakedness of thy father's wife (v. 8)

II   Thou shalt not uncover the nakedness of thy sister (v. 9)

III   Thou shalt not uncover the nakedness of thy son's daughter (v. 10)

IV   Thou shalt not uncover the nakedness of thy sister's daughter (v. 10)

V   Thou shalt not uncover the nakedness of thy father's wife's daughter (v. 11)

VI   Thou shalt not uncover the nakedness of thy father's sister (v. 12)

VII   Thou shalt not uncover the nakedness of thy mother's sister (v. 13)

VIII   Thou shalt not uncover the nakedness of thy father's brother's wife (v. 14)

IX   Thou shalt not uncover the nakedness of thy son's wife (v. 15)

X   Thou shalt not uncover the nakedness of thy brother's wife (v. 16)

One who studies this list closely will find that relations with two particular female relatives are not prohibited: mother and daughter. It is evidently taken for granted that sex with them is so utterly tabboo that it is beyond mentioning. The young male initiate knows well enough to avoid them -- but which others are off limits? The problem is made more difficult within a polygamous society, such as that of the Hebrews, where one's own mother might not be one's father's only wife, and where there were many half-brothers and half sisters. The catechism of Leviticus 18 list all the thinkable transgressions of close liaison with female relatives:

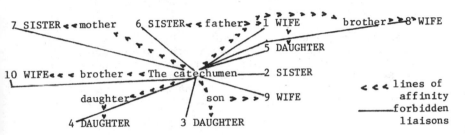

And what is the purpose of this code? Plainly, it is to guard the well-being of a closely-knit tribal structure. Let the young lad learn this lesson early, that he may observe it always! Otherwise strife, murder, incest, chaos will threaten the harmony, peace, and life of the community.

Other apodictic codes have different areas of concern, ranging as wide as in the Decalogue itself; but always their purpose is to define the limits, guarding covenant society from danger and disruption.

Commandment V: Responsibility toward one's kin[95]

"Honor thy father and thy mother, that thy days may be long in the land which Yahweh thy god giveth thee." (Ex. 20:12; cf. Deut. 5:16)

The motive clause is a deuteronomistic addition, but one that effectively states the benefit of this commandment's observance. Many days in the land that Yahweh gives is symbolic of all that life can and ought to be. This is impossible for those who

255

neglect to honor their parents, however, because the transgressor poisons every social relationship, reducing the quality, and often the quantity, of life for the transgressor, as well as for the ones transgressed against.

Here "father and mother" stand for all close kin. It is father and mother who are nearest -- also the most needy and the most deserving. No doubt this divine rule thinks especially of parents in advancing life, when the strength of youth has forsaken them and they are more dependent on their children's help and respect. It is not enough to provide a meagre subsistence for them; what they will require as long as life shall last is "honor." This is somewhat different from the "obedience" of Eph. 6:1. Honoring parents undoubtedly includes showing proper respect for their authority within the family structure, but it especially points to giving them what they need in order to maintain their role as parents, even where authority might have to be handed on to others.

This is the touchstone of covenant morality. If those closest to us, the ones from whom we have received the most and need us most, are neglected or abused, the fabric of covenant living is weakened, and every other relationship is endangered.

Commandment VI: Responsibility toward community life[96]

"Thou shalt not murder (lō' tirṣaḥ)" (Ex. 20:13, Deut. 5:17)

However noble their humanitarian aspirations, the opponents of capital punishment cannot justify using the sixth commandment as an argument against the death sentence. This commandment does not in any way impinge on the rule of Gen. 9:6, "Whoever sheds the blood of man, by man shall his blood be shed; for God made man in his own image." In that paradoxical passage, the wanton shedding of human blood is held up as especially heinous precisely because the victim is a bearer of the image of God. It deserves to be punished by "man" because, as the bearer of the divine image, man alone has the authority and responsibility of carrying out the extreme penalty that God requires.

Furthermore, pacifists will have to look elsewhere for arguments against war, which no biblical text condemns outright,[97] and in any case is not in question in the prohibition of the sixth commandment.

It may indeed be true that the acceptance of blood-vengeance and warfare in the Old Testament represents no more than a cultural residuum -- like so many of its elements -- and requires to be amended in the light of the Bible's most noble humanitarian aspirations. In any event, honest exegesis has the obligation of searching for the intent of the sixth commandment in the context of the covenantal wholeness which it endeavors to maintain. The root RṢḤ refers to the wanton and unjustified taking of human life, making a private affair of what elsewhere is carefully controlled in Israel's well-developed capital code.

In the old tribal system, the near kinsmen of the victim had the obligation of bringing a murderer to judgment, and of executing him once sentence had been passed on him.[98] There were special cities of refuge whither one might flee if the death had been accidental or unintentional, but these were required to hand over palpable murderers. In Deut. 19:11-13 we read:

> If any man hates his neighbor, and lies in
> wait for him, and attacks him, and wounds
> him mortally so that he dies, and the man
> flees into one of these cities, then the
> elders of his city shall send and fetch
> him from there, and hand him over to the
> avenger of blood, so that he may die.
> Your eye shall not pity him, but you
> shall purge the guilt of innocent blood
> from Israel, so that it may be well with
> you.

The radical individualism of our civilization is likely to cry out for protecting the "rights" of the murderer and to ignore the wrong done to the victim. This is diametrically at odds with the strongly social orientation of biblical law, designed to protect the community at all costs. Undoubtedly, this aspiration is susceptible to gross misuse, as in the statist arrogation of all powers over the individual citizen. But in itself, the sixth commandment protects something absolutely essential: the lives of a community's members against the violent and the bloodthirsty. These can never be tolerated if a community is to survive.

Commandment VII: Responsibility toward the
family circle[99]

"Thou shalt not commit adultery (lō' tin'āp)" (Ex. 20:14; cf. Deut. 5:18)

Both the Old Testament and the New Testament are severe in their condemnation of sexual transgression. In reaction against the puritanical excesses of past generations, our contemporary western culture tends to scoff at this attitude. We are encouraged to think that, except where physical violence is involved, sexual crimes have no victims, and ought therefore to be excused. "Throw off your repressions, express yourself!" the Freudians tell us. Those who treasure the biblical heritage ought to be deceived neither by the caricature of biblical sexual ethics that is involved in this attitude, nor by its grossly distorted concept of human well-being. We need to realize, first, that the ancient Hebrews were confronted with widespread lewdness within their cultural environment, officially encouraged by heathen vegetative cults. And secondly we need to realize that their rules against sexual looseness were designed for the wholeness of their community life and the well-being of individuals within it.

The seventh commandment specifically forbids having sexual intercourse with an improper partner -- the wife or husband of another person. Nothing else is so invidious to the survival of a healthy society. It threatens marriage and the family, putting in peril the happiness of the two transgressors, along with their respective spouses and their respective children. If tolerated, it leads to jealousy and reprisals. If imitated, it produces the breakdown of other families and the undermining of all the delicate social infrastructures that are dependent upon them. Thus the very circle of life is endangered wherever this rule is ignored.

Commandment VIII and Commandment X:
Responsibility toward the means of community
subsistence[100]

258

"Thou shalt not steal (lō' tignōb)" (Ex. 20:15;
cf. Deut. 5:19)

"Thou shalt not covet (lō' taḥmōd) thy neighbor's
house (etc.)" (Ex. 20:17; cf. Deut. 5:21)

These two rules are generally discussed together
because they originally referred to closely related
matters. Many scholars think the eighth commandment
has been shortened, and hence made more general, by [101]
dropping the stated object of theft, perhaps a slave.
As it now stands it forbids the wrongful appropriation
of anything belonging to another person. We call this
"property," but Hebraic notions of proprietorship were
only vaguely formed. What is meant is, whatever
results from gainful activity and adds to the further
production of "wealth" -- the means by which a human
society sustains itself. It is instinctual for human
beings to protect what is theirs, whether gained through
creative work or purchase. Hence the wrongful
appropriation of such objects or materials produces
strife and recrimination, imperiling the harmony of
covenantal society.

"Coveting" is more than merely desiring, or
wishing for, what belongs to others. It probably
refers to the unlawful appropriation of territorial
possessions -- a house to live in and a farm to till.
This original bearing of the commandment has been
rather obscured by the deuteronomistic expansions,
referring to neighbor's wife, servants, cattle, etc.,
making it forbid wrongful desires as such. But
originally it was the action more than the desire
that was in question -- the kind of crime of which
Jezebel was guilty in seizing Naboth's vineyard.[102]
What Jezebel did violated every rule of covenantal
society, oppressing the helpless and undermining the
individual's potential for feeding and housing himself and his family.

Commandment IX: Responsibility for a neighbor's
reputation[103]

"Thou shalt not testify against thy neighbor by
a false oath (lō' taᶜneh berēᶜeka ᶜed šaqer)"
(Ex. 20:16; cf. Deut. 5:20)

Some wise person has remarked that there are two
things that raise human society from the jungle:

toilet training and trust. It would indeed be difficult to conceive of civilization as we know it without
toilet training. It would be just as difficult for
civilization to exist without trust. Every element
of meaningful human interaction is based upon it.
Even though we are all continually disappointed by
the deceitfulness or incompetence of other human
beings, whether acting individually or organized
into complex groups, we continue to trust as much as
we can, because we must. The grocer, the banker, the
physician, the government official, the minister: if
we could no longer trust them, our civilization would
disintegrate into an armed chaos, with every man for
himself. Indeed, even within bandit gangs and in
prisons, persons must lend trust to others.

How important then is the good word that we all
are called upon to speak! Our modern juridicial procedures, sophisticated as they are, do not dispense
with testimony from witnesses. It is well that per-
jury, the swearing of false oaths and the giving of
misleading testimony, is severely punished. To produce gain for ourselves or to do hurt to others by
false testimony is as wicked as to go out and steal
money at gunpoint.

In the ancient world, the close social bonds of
most societies put added pressure on witnesses. There
were no clever lawyers, teaching their clients how to
tell half-truths. Thus witnesses might be expected to
tell the truth, and would be trusted when their testimony was corroborated by that of others. Yet, the
deceitfulness of the human heart often led to the
telling of damaging lies, even when the gods were
summoned as witnesses to what was being told. Since
the punishment for specific crimes was often severe,
one who was wrongly victimized by the false testimony
of others would fall into a sorry plight, with little
hope of redress. Where such gross injustice was
allowed, trust would everywhere tend to break down,
and the very fabric of society would disintegrate.

He who bears false witness against his neighbor
is therefore guilty of two dreadful wrongs against
covenantal harmony: (1) he unjustly wrongs a fellow;
(2) in his heart he scoffs against society and against
his God.

Since this sin may often go undetected for a long
period of time, and never be redressed, the ninth

commandment stands as a plug in the dike, holding against a torrent of unbridled wickedness. Yahweh threatens that, even though judges may believe false testimony, he will discern the wrong and bring the offender to account.

Excursus on the deuteronomic rule on false witnesses, Deut. 19:15-21

Inevitably, Hebrew society devised codes of juridical procedure. Two apodictic prohibitions standing outside the decalogue are in the Covenant Code at Ex. 23:1 and in the Holiness Code at Lev. 19:16. A more elaborate rule is found in Deut. 19:15ff.:

> A single witness shall not prevail against a man for any crime or for any wrong in connection with any offense that he has committed; only on the evidence of two witnesses, or of three witnesses, shall a charge be sustained. If a malicious witness rises against any man to accuse him of wrongdoing, then both parties to the dispute shall appear before Yahweh, before the priests and the judges who are in office in those days; the judges shall inquire diligently, and if the witness is a false witness and has accused his brother falsely, then you shall do to him as he had meant to do to his brother; so you shall purge the evil from the midst of you. And the rest shall hear, and fear, and shall never again commit any such evil among you. Your eye shall not pity; it shall be life for life, eye for eye, tooth for tooth, hand for hand, foot for foot.

Harsh this may seem; who can doubt that it is fair, and just, and wise? Of course, everything depends on competent judges and wise administrators. But without sound rules of moral behavior, no society can exist in happiness, harmony, and prosperity.

(4) The blessings and the curses

Probably borrowing from the structure of ancient Near-Eastern treaties, the book of Deuteronomy concludes its presentation of covenantal law with materials intended for liturgical recitation as blessings and curses.[104] The blessings are for the obedient, the curses for the disobedient:

> If you obey the voice of Yahweh your god, being careful to do all these commandments which I command you this day, Yahweh your god will set you high above all the nations of the earth. And all these blessings shall come upon you and overtake you, if you obey the voice of Yahweh your god. Blessed shall you be in the city, and blessed shall you be in the field. Blessed shall be the fruit of your body, and the fruit of your ground, and the fruit of your beasts, the increase of your cattle, and the young of your flock. Blessed shall be your basket and your kneading-trough. Blessed shall you be when you come in, and blessed shall you be when you go out. (Deut. 28:1-6)

After a lengthy expansion that comments on this recitation, the text continues with a list of curses:

> But if you will not obey the voice of Yahweh your god or be careful to do all his commandments and his statutes which I command you this day, then all these curses shall come upon you and overtake you. Cursed shall you be in the city, and cursed shall you be in the field. Cursed shall be your basket and your kneading-trough. Cursed shall be the fruit of your body, and the fruit of your ground, the increase of your cattle, and the young of your flock. Cursed shall you be when you come in, and cursed shall you be when you go out. (Deut. 28:15-19)

This is followed by an even longer expansion, elaborating in frightening detail the horrors that await those who disregard God's commandments. It is

very similar to Leviticus 26, and both passages appear
to reflect the sorry conditions of Israel/Judah's
actual historical experience under the exile and
diaspora.

Popular dogma made a rule that righteousness
brings reward, while wickedness produces retribution.
Besides the fact that experience far too often proves
this rule wrong, we must observe that the deuteronomic blessings and curses are intended as eschatological images. Certainly there was no provision
to make them automatically operative. They are not
guarantees, but evocative symbols of what it is like
to be a covenant-keeper or a covenant-breaker. The
blessings are symbols of "shalom," the perfect harmony, happiness, and peace towards which covenant
morality is striving. They are the rightful reward
of the ṣaddîq, the righteous one, whose prosperity
is celebrated in Psalm 1, in contrast to the rešaᶜ,
the wicked one, who cannot stand in the day of
judgment:

> Blessed is the man who walks not in the counsel of
> the wicked, nor stands in the way of sinners,
>   nor sits in the seat of scoffers;
> but his delight is in the law of Yahweh,
>   and on his law he meditates day and night.
>
> He is like a tree planted by streams of water,
>   that yields its fruit in its season,
>   and its leaf does not wither.
> In all that he does, he prospers.
>
> The wicked are not so, but are like the chaff
>   which the wind drives away.
> Therefore the wicked shall not stand in the judgmen
>   nor sinners in the congregation of the righteous
> for Yahweh knows the way of the righteous,
>   but the way of the wicked shall perish.

The "way" of the righteous; the "way" of the
wicked -- yes, covenant living is following a way --
walking toward the reward of perfect joy.[105] Election
and the covenant make this possible, and therefore
necessary, but they do not offer this reward except
to those whose obedience is grounded in faith. This
is why, in Yahweh's new covenant (Jer. 31:33), he
"will put [his] law within them, and ... write it
upon their hearts."

c. Wisdom and Torah

It is not only in the Pentateuchal lawcodes that
covenant morality comes to practical expression.
Aphoristic and instructional wisdom sayings, often
borrowed from Israel's cultural environment, were
intensively cultivated. Wisdom was part of folk
culture, as well as a popular pastime with the king
and his learned counsellors.[106] It fills the two
canonical books, Proverbs and Ecclesiastes (Heb.:
Qoheleth), as well as an important apocryphal book,
Sirach or Ecclesiasticus, and is scattered throughout
the Old Testament, the Apocrypha and other Jewish
books. Furthermore, it inspires more complex treatises in the wisdom vein, such as Job in the Old Testament and the Wisdom of Solomon in the Apocrypha. Not
until the beginning of the Christian era, with the
rise of Pharisaic Halaka, did the heirs of the biblical tradition begin to lose interest in its culti-
vation.

Inasmuch as biblical law is devoted to ritual
matters and to defining the boundaries of covenantal
living, wisdom fills the much needed service of
articulating the positive fulness of practical life
under the fear of God. Its stance is advisory, not
coercive. Its goal is piety expressed in wise -- that
is, suitable -- conduct. Here is the introduction of
Proverbs:

> That men may know wisdom and instruction,
>   understand words of insight,
> receive instruction in wise dealing,
>   righteousness, justice, and equity;
> that prudence may be given to the simple,
>   knowledge and discretion to the youth--
> that wise men also may hear and increase in learning,
>   and the man of understanding acquire skill,
> to understand a proverb and a figure,
>   the words of the wise and their riddles.
> The fear of Yahweh is the beginning of knowledge;
>   fools despise wisdom and instruction. (1:2-7)

We shall return to say more about wisdom in Chapter V, because it is in this genre that the pious
were best able to give expression to their hurts,
sorrows, and queries. Essentially, however, wisdom is
optimistic that by discipline, reason, and piety,

covenantal idealism, it requires to be understood in terms of the historical development that produced it.

Biblical law passed through three essentially distinct processes of development, as follows:[107]

(1) The apodictic codes, the casuistic rules, the early collections such as the Covenant Code;

(2) The ponderous Deuteronomic corpus -- itself the result of a complex process of literary crystallization -- drawing together the rules still operative in the time of Israel's and Judah's last kings, designed to unify the people's allegiance to Yahweh in an age of severe external threat and pervasive apostacy;

(3) A combinational and expansive form of the preceding, carried out by the priestly redactors of the postexilic school. This now becomes Torah -- no longer simply an ad hoc priestly instruction in correct ritual performance (its original meaning), but comprehensive instruction for Jewish piety.

This last stage began in the Babylonian exile (586-522 B.C.) and gradually gained strength in the following centuries. Though the guardians of Torah insisted on the performance of all its rules (making the text of Scripture sacrosanct), it naturally drew to itself a body of traditional interpretation and application, sometimes called "the second law."[108] This was the Halaka that eventually became the Mishna.[109] In postexilic Judaism, great emphasis came to be placed on three particular observances, kosher restrictions, circumcision, and keeping the Sabbath, not because the Bible itself gives these great prominence, but because Judaism needed them as peculiar marks of its ethnically colored peoplehood in an age when they found themselves increasingly at the mercy of their enemies. They had lost their national independence; even when tolerated by foreign rulers, they felt bereft and estranged. They were driven inward upon themselves as a people, forced to insist on the observance of Torah as their defense against absorption and disintegration, particularly during the Greek period, when assimilation to Hellenistic culture became a serious threat.[110]

In this situation, Torah became a virtual surrogate for covenant and election, to the point where it threatened to take their place altogether. The conditions that produced the Pentateuchal laws had by now been drastically modified, or had disappeared; hence the authority of these laws would seem to have been superseded by the march of human events. Not so in Torah piety. Enshrined in the biblical text, these rules required perpetual observance -- if not in literal practice, then according to the adaptations of halaka, modifying them for the increasingly ethnic particularism of Jewish culture. The Jews continued to believe in the covenant and in election, but with little of the spontaneity and intimacy of these concepts as they had originally been entertained.

If truth be told, the God of covenant and election had now become so remote, living off in high heaven. and far removed from the hard life that the Jews were daily forced to live, that they needed an apotheistic substitute. Had God (no longer "Yahweh") not abandoned the scene of history? Else, why were the Jews so long kept from the fulfillment of his promise? So Torah came to stand for "God," for "covenant," and for "election." To do Torah was to have them all; not to do it was to lose them all.

These were, then, the two forms in which covenantal idealism was being expressed at the time when Jesus was born. The following comparison shows how they complemented each other:

Wisdom

Source and authority: The intellectual leadership, articulating its observation and experience for the community; the wise in Israel correlated reality with their words of wisdom, taking account of God as the ultimate reality.

Scope: All of reality: in Israel, as interpreted within the framework of monotheistic creationism.

Torah

Source and authority: The spiritual leadership of the theocratic community, representing the divine will as continuously reinterpreted and reapplied to the conditions of intensifying cultural and religious isolation.

Scope: Moral and religious behavior as explication of the covenant (= orthopraxis, "correct practice").

266

| Form: Variegated, without genetic derivation. | Form: Displays a derivative shift from earlier to later forms. |

Wisdom played a decreasingly important role, while Torah became more and more dominant. Pirqe Aboth, the earliest tractate of the Mishna (200 B.C. to A.D. 100), shows an interesting internal shift from wisdom to halakic forms.[111] Nowhere else in the Mishna is the wisdom form or ideology in evidence.

Torah is eventually apotheosized. In the apocalyptic literature, it is no longer Moses who gives the law, or even writes it; but it is given by God's angels, written on tablets in heaven. This notion had strong influence on the development of the concept of biblical inerrancy-in Judaism, but especially in Christianity. It is another subtle form of idolatry -- substituting the product for the Producer.[112]

d. The New Testament recovery of convenantal ethics

By the time of Jesus, the concept of election and covenant had been radically subordinated to that of Torah. The transformation had produced among the Jewish people a high ethicality; they were known (but not always admired) as the most moral people on earth. The idea of a jealous God, guarding his people's love, had by now virtually lost its personalistic basis. God was still the God of the Jews -- even if it might seem that he had forgotten them. The Jews' response to the claims of God's jealousy was mainly directed to the fastidious observation of a surrogate for God -- the Torah. In the old time, election and covenant had produced an awareness of special peoplehood -- the idea of being a specially chosen and called people among other peoples, for the ultimate blessing of them all -- and convenantal law came into being as an instrument for its realization. But now, Israel had all but given up on being a model for the world's salvation, and was concentrating on simply surviving in a hostile world until God's final day of vindication.

This was the spiritual and moral environment into which Jesus was born.[113] He was remembered by his devoted followers, especially after his death, as the most righteous Jew who had ever lived -- one whose righteousness exceeded the formalistic righteousness of the scribes and Pharisees. The Gospels testify concerning his unparalleled sensitivity to the reality of interpersonal relationships, coming to expression in his sense of oneness with God first of all, and consequently in his sense of solidarity with humankind (especially those persons who were despised by the mighty, pathetically yearning for love and deliverance).

Like the topic of Christology, the topic of New Testament ethics requires its own treatise.[114] To venture upon it at all without entering into extensive discussion would lead to inevitable misrepresentation. Thus, here too, we state only those most essential points at which the New Testament carries forward an authentically biblical motif -- covenantal morality grounded in love for God and man.

One thing very briefly: St. Paul's polemic against the Law has been much misunderstood. It is entirely without warrant that antinomians (those who would discard moral law) appeal to him. He constantly insists that the new man in Christ must strive to overcome sin, and to live in perfect harmony with his fellowmen. Paul preaches the necessity of "the fruits of the Spirit" (Gal. 5:22-25, etc.), which are simply the old virtues treasured within the covenant community. How very much like Leviticus and Deuteronomy is the sound of these words from I Thessalonians, one of the apostle's earliest epistles:

> Finally, brethren, we beseech and exhort you in the Lord Jesus, that as you learned from us how you ought to live and to please God, just as you are doing, you do so more and more. For you know what instructions we gave you through the Lord Jesus. For this is the will of God, your sanctification: that you abstain from immorality; that each one of you know how to take a wife for himself in holiness and honor, not in the passion of lust like heathen who do not know God; that no man transgress, and wrong his brother in this matter, because the Lord is an avenger in all these things, as we solemnly forewarned you. For God has not called us for uncleanness, but in holiness.

Therefore whoever disregards this, disregards not man but God, who gives his
Holy Spirit to you. (4:1-8)

Another thing that we wish to say about Paul's
dispute with Judaism is, therefore, that this involved
only the basis of a sinner's righteousness in the
presence of God (this comes only by faith in Christ).
It does not concern the <u>standard</u> of morality, which
Paul agrees to be the law or Torah. "The law is holy
and just and good" (Rom. 7:12) -- but can help only
those who are in harmony with God.

In spite of much-touted differences, Paul would not
have rejected St. James' emphasis on operative morality
as the test of the Christian's "law of liberty."
Nothing could be more authentically Hebraic than James'
classic dictum (2:27): "Religion that is pure and un-
defiled before God and the Father is this: to visit
orphans and widows in their affliction, and to keep
oneself unstained from the world." This, in turn, sound
strikingly like the words of Jesus' parable, "Truly, I
say to you, as you did it to one of the least of these
my brethren, you did it to me" (Matt. 25:40)

In the Gospel narratives, Jesus is constantly
depicted as taking sides with the afflicted and despised,
upholding human values above all formal rules, traditions, and institutions. Whatever the early church may
have added to embellish the picture of Jesus' polemic
against the Pharisees,[115] we can be quite sure that
the historical picture is essentially right. He was
most certainly the kind of man who would never have
grown angry except at the oppression and exploitation
of the masses, and the hypocrisy and formalism of the
religious elite. His religious self-awareness went
back authentically to the greatest of the prophets.
His ideology was pure covenantal personalism.

This is why he was so conscious of his authority
in opposing a sterile and deadening tradition, as in
the great apothegms of Matthew 5: "You have heard it
said...but I say to you...." The most memorable of
these is in vv. 43ff."

You have heard it was said, "You shall love
your neighbor and hate your enemy." But I
say to you, Love your enemies and pray for
those who persecute you, so that you may
be sons of your Father who is in heaven; for

he makes his sun rise on the evil and on
the good, and sends rain on the just and
on the unjust. For if you love those who
love you, what reward have you? Do not
even the tax collectors do the same?
And if you salute only your brethren,
what more are you doing than others?
Do not even the Gentiles do the same?
You, therefore, must be perfect, as
your heavenly Father is perfect.

Is it altogether naive to think that a nasty
situation like the Near-Eastern impasse of today
might be somehow changed for the good, if only those
contending heirs of Abraham now living in Palestine --
the Jews and the Arabs -- could learn this lesson
from the greatest of Abraham's sons?

When Jesus said, "If any one strikes you on the
right cheek, turn to him the other also" (Matt. 5:30),
he was not promoting an apocalyptic dream -- as some
interpreters claim -- but was merely stating the
essential Hebraic covenantal ideal.[116]

Deuteronomy's series of blessings (28:1-6), noted
in our foregoing discussion, pronounced comprehensive
blessedness on those who keep the law. The Beatitudes
of Jesus, found in Matt. 5:3-10, show that this
blessedness is theirs who are at one with the God
who gave the Law:

Blessed are the poor in spirit, for theirs is
the kingdom of heaven.

Blessed are those who mourn, for they shall be
comforted.

Blessed are the meek, for they shall inherit the
earth.

Blessed are those who hunger and thirst for
righteousness, for they shall be satisfied.

Blessed are the merciful, for they shall obtain
mercy.

Blessed are the pure in heart, for they shall see
God.

Blessed are the peacemakers, for they shall be
   called sons of God.

Blessed are those who are persecuted for righteousness' sake, for theirs is the kingdom of
   heaven.

No man was persecuted more for righteousness' sake
than he who spoke these words. It is that we all might
be righteous like him that God at first committed
himself to a nation of people, calling them to be the
model of redeemed mankind.

Legalism is as sterile for Christians as it is
for Jews. When will we learn that we cannot coerce
anyone into being righteous or scare them into heaven?
The Bible is only about integrity and love: God's
jealousy for us, and our jealousy for him.

FOR FURTHER STUDY

On ḥesed:

N. Glueck, Ḥesed in the Bible, trans. A Gottschalk,
  Cincinnati: Hebrew Union College Press,
  1967

K. D. Sakenfield, The Meaning of Hesed in the Hebrew
  Bible: A New Inquiry (Harvard
  Semitic Monographs, 17), Missoula:
  Scholars' Press, 1978

On election:

J. Bergman, H. Ringgren, H. Seebass, TDOT, II, 73ff.,
                                      bāchar

  Choice of the king
  Choice of the priesthood
  "The place which Yahweh chooses"
  The election of the people
  Human choices as acts of religious confession

W. Zimmerli, OTTO, pp. 43ff.

  The election of Israel

On peoplehood; land:

J. Bergman, M. Ottosson, TDOT, I, 338, 'erets

  In ancient Near Eastern literature
  In the Old Testament

G. Bertram, TDNT, V, 596ff., paideuō, paideia, etc.

  God's discipline by law and wisdom
  God's discipline in the prophetic revelation
  The paideia concept in hellenistic and rabbinic
    Judaism
  The paideia concept in the New Testament

272

R. E. Clements, G. J. Botterweck, TDOT, II, 426ff., gôy

   Israel as a gôy
   Special religious development

V. Herntrich, G. Schrenk, TDNT, IV, 194ff., leimma, etc.

   The "remnant" in the Old Testament
   The thought of the remnant in Paul as compared
       with its occurrence in apocalyptic and the
       rabbis

J. G. Plöger, TDOT, I, 88ff., 'adhāmāh

   Specific theological considerations

       Cultic aspects
       Theological-anthropological significance
       The land of Israel

G. von Rad, K. G. Kuhn, W. Gutbrod, TDNT, III, 357ff.,
   Israel, etc.; Ioudaios, etc.

   Israel, Judah and Hebrews in the Old Testament
   Israēl, Ioudaios, Hebraios in Jewish literature
       after the Old Testament; in Greek hellenistic
       literature; in the New Testament

G. Stahlin, TDNT, V, 1ff., xenos, xenia, etc.

   Foreigner and foreign in the judgment of antiquity
   The custom of hospitality
   Foreign as a religious concept

H. Strathmann, R. Meyer, TDNT, IV, 29ff., Laos

   The people
   The peoples
   The election and privilege of the people
   Laos in the New Testament

On theocracy; church:

K. L. Schmidt et al., BKW, II/III, "Basileia"
   (= TDNT, I, 564ff.)

   Melek and malkûth in the Old Testament
   Malkûth shāmayim in rabbinic literature
   Basileia (tou Theou) in the early church

K. L. Schmidt, BKW, I/II, "The Church" (= TDNT, III, 487ff.)

W. Schrage, TDNT, VII, 798ff., sunagōgē, etc.

On covenant:

W. Eichrodt, TOT, I, 36ff.

>The covenant relationship: Meaning: History

A. Cazelles, TDOT, I, 445ff., 'ashrê

>The blessing in the development of biblical
>theology

G. Quell, J. Behm, TDNT, II, 104ff., diatithēmi, diathēkē

>The Old Testament term b^{e}rîth
>The transition from b^{e}rîth to diathēkē in the LXX
>and Jewish literature
>The New Testament term diathēkē

G. von Rad, W. Foerster, TDNT, II, 400ff., eirēnē, etc.

>The Greek concept of eirēnē
>Shālôm in the Old Testament; in rabbinic writings
>Eirēnē in the LXX; in the pseudepigrapha, Josephus
>and Philo; in the New Testament

J. Scharbert, TDOT, II, 279ff., brk, b^{e}rākāh

>brk in the sense of "bless," etc., in the Old
>Testament
>brk = "to bless," etc.
>The blessing in Old Testament theology

T. C. Vriezen, OOTT, pp. 377ff.

>The standards of the community (ethics)

M. Weinfeld, TDOT, II, 255ff., b^{e}rîth

>Semantic range
>Covenantal ceremony - function
>Covenant and law
>The covenants with Abraham and David: The royal
>grant

Covenant theology
The covenant in prophecy
The origin of the covenant concept

H. W. Wolff, <u>AOT</u>, pp. 166ff., 177ff., 185ff., 192ff., 214ff.

Man and woman
Parents and children
Brothers, friends and enemies
Masters and slaves
The individual and the community

W. Zimmerli, <u>OTTO</u>, pp. 48ff.

Yahweh, God of Sinai: Covenant and commandment

<u>On</u> <u>law</u> <u>and</u> <u>ethics</u>:

J. Bergman <u>et</u> <u>al</u>., <u>TDOT</u>, III, 270ff., <u>derekh</u>, etc.

W. Eichrodt, <u>TOT</u>, I, 70ff.

The covenant statutes: Secular law

Its distinctive character
Some crucial phases in the development of the law

<u>idem</u>, II, 316ff.

The effects of piety on conduct (Old Testament morality): norms; goods; motives

H. F. Fuhs, <u>TDOT</u>, III, 447ff., <u>hāragh</u>, etc.

Killing enemies in battle; political opponents; personal rivals
<u>hrg</u> as a crime; as a punishment
Yahweh as subject

V. Hamp, <u>TDOT</u>, III, 39ff., <u>gānabh</u>

J. Helfmeyer, <u>TDOT</u>, III, 388ff., <u>hālak</u>, h^alîkāh

Walking before Yahweh
Walking with God
Following after Yahweh or other gods
Going from Yahweh
Walking in the ways of Yahweh

K. Kleinknecht, W. Gutbrod, <u>BKW</u>, V/I, "Law"
(= <u>TDNT</u>, IV, 102ff.)

<u>Nomos</u> in the Greek and hellenistic world
Law in the Old Testament; in Judaism; in the
New Testament

W. Michaelis, <u>TDNT</u>, V, 42ff., <u>hodos</u>, etc.

The influence of Old Testament usage in the
pseudepigraphic and rabbinic writings
<u>Hodos</u> in the New Testament

G. von Rad, <u>OTT</u>, I, 190ff.

The significance of the commandments

<u>idem</u>, II, 388ff.

The law

W. Zimmerli, <u>OTTO</u>, pp. 109ff., 125ff., 133ff.

Yahweh's commandment

The location, terminology and nature of the
commandments
Liturgical and ritual commandments
Yahweh's commandments governing social
relationships and property

<u>On wisdom</u>:

G. von Rad, <u>Wisdom in Israel</u>, New York-Nashville:
Harper, 1972

U. Wilckens, G. Fohrer, <u>TDNT</u>, VII, 465ff., <u>sophia</u>, etc.

From the early Greek period to the philosophical
usage of the late antiquity
The Old Testament; Judaism; Gnosticism; The
New Testament

NOTES

1. See further art, "Jealousy" (O. Baab), _IDB_, II, 806f.; G. von Rad. "The First Commandment and Yahweh's Holy Zeal," _Old Testament Theology_, I, 203ff.

2. See art. "Love in the NT" (G. Johnston), _IDB_, III, 168ff.; ef. A. Nygren, _Agape and Eros_, rev. ed., 1953.

3. The majority of scholars, following N. Glueck, _Das Wort Hesed im alttestamentlichen Sprachgebrauch als menschliche und gottliche gemeinschaftgemässe Verhaltungsweise_, 2nd ed., Berlin 1961, interpret this word as referring basically to community obligation and loyalty; others (e.g. H. J. Stoebe in _THAT_, I, 600ff.) lay emphasis on the aspect of grace or goodness, coming to manifestation primarily in the area of social relationships. In any event, it is a deeply personalistic concept that governs its semantic range; what is basically at stake is divine and human integrity in mutual interaction.

4. Love that is based on morality and integrity unavoidably rejects ("hates") whatever is inimical to love's fulfillment.

5. YD⁽ is used in an elective sense in Hos. 5:3, 13:5, Amos 3:2, Nah. 1:7, and other passages (cf. Deut. 9:24). BḤR is used of Israel's election mainly in late texts, e.g., Deut. 4:37, 7:6-7, Isa. 41:8, Ps. 105:6.

6. I Sam. 10:24, II Sam. 6:21, Jer. 1:5, Hag. 2:23, Luke 9:35, I Pet. 2:4-6, etc.

7. See Chapter II, 1, b, (3), (b) "Mankind made from clay and Kingu's blood."

8. Gen. 2:15: hā'ādām is generic man; there is nothing specifically Israelite in this account to parallel the Babylonian / Sumerian focusing of "Enuma Elish."

9. E and P do not use the name "Yahweh" until their respective narratives of this god's self-revelation (Ex. 3:1ff., 6:2ff.). Following a pattern of radical assimilationism, J on the contrary speaks of "Yahweh" already in Genesis 2 (in the combined form, "Yahweh Elohim," borrowed from his source material). He goes so far as to state in Gen. 4:26b that "man began to call on the name "Yahweh" in the time of Seth, Adam's son -- thus making Yahwism a world religion from time primordial.

10. Gen. 17:7-8, 28:1-4, Ex. 6:4, Psa. 105:12-15, etc.

11. Chapter I, "Anthropomorphic personification as caricature."

12. G. E. Mendenhall, Law and Covenant in Israel and the Ancient Near East, Pittsburgh 1955; cf. V. Korošec, Hethitische Staatsvertrage, 1931. See also D. J. McCarthy, Old Testament Covenant, A Survey of Current Opinions, Richmond: John Knox, 1972.

13. A. Goetze, tr.

14. Cf. G. von Rad, Genesis, Philadelphia 1961, pp. 20ff., 153ff.

15. The most extensive treatment in English of the election of Israel is H. H. Rowley, The Biblical Doctrine of Election, London 1950; cf. art. "Election" (G. E. Mendenhall), IDB, II, 76ff.; W. Zimmerli, Old Testament Theology in Outline, D. E. Green tr., Atlanta: John Knox, 1978, pp. 43ff.

16. The niphal of BRK can mean "be blessed" (passive) or "bless themselves" (middle reciprocal); see the commentaries for and against each alternative. The word "land" in v. 1 translates Heb. 'areṣ (= geographic region or territory), whereas "earth" in v. 3 translates Heb. 'ᵃdāmâ, here meaning the tillable land, as in Gen. 4:14. The "families" (Heb. mišpᵉḥôt) are the clans who inhabit the tillable land, presumably within Palestine (not over the entire world), hence the

original reference was probably to the non-Israelite ethnic groups within the territory of David's realm. The rythmic poetic form reveals this passage as a solemn traditional recital, probably from the David cult-shrine at Jerusalem. The reference to the blessing appears also in Gen. 28:15 (J).

17. Cf. H. W. Wolff. "Das Kerygma des Yahwisten," Gesammelte Studien zum Alten Testament (Munich 1964), pp. 345ff.; P. F. Ellis, The Yahwist; the Bible's First Theologian, London 1969.

18. Cf. I Kings 12:28ff., 14:22ff., 16:31ff., etc.

19. I Kings 10:5-8

20. Major texts explicating this theme are II Samuel 7, II Sam. 23:1-7, Psalms 2, 110, 132, Isa. 9:1-6, 11:1-9. Cf. S. Mowinckel, He That Cometh, pp. 155ff.

21. On the Deuteronomic parenesis, see Chapter IV, 2, a, (2), (b) "Deuteronomy and the covenant confrontation." Although modern scholarship identifies at least the core of Deuteronomy as the lawbook used for Josiah's reform in 622 B.C. (see II Kings 22-23), major portions of it were probably in existence as much as a century earlier (after the fall of Samaria, 722 B.C., influencing Hezekiah's reform, ca. 700). Cf. G. von Rad, Studies in Deuteronomy, Chicago, 1953, pp. 60ff. This position is receiving increasing support in contemporary scholarship.

22. Relevant passages are too numerous to list; see the commentaries and books on prophecy. The basic form of oracular proclamation in the prophetic books is (1) denunciation (alt.: invective); (2) threat; cf. C. Westermann, The Basic Forms of Prophetic Speech, tr. H. C. White, Philadelphia 1967; also W. E. March in Hayes, ed., Old Testament Form Criticism, pp. 157ff.

23. See W. Zimmerli, Ezekiel (Hermeneia), pp. 322ff.

24. The "two families" of this passage are apparently Israel as an ideal whole, plus the Davidic house, both of which retain their elective standing in Yahweh's restorative purpose. See the commentaries.

25. Hag. 2:20; Zech. 6:9-14; cf. 3:8-9

26. The expiration of prophecy is forecast in the strongly negative language of Zech. 13:2ff. It is recorded as a historical fact in I Mac. 4:46, which indicates that no prophet was available to be consulted about the desecration of the temple ca. 167-164 B.C. But the revival of prophecy in the early church (see art. "Prophet in the NT" [B. D. Napier], IDB, III, 919f.) is a salient feature of its eschatological newness.

27. See art. "Ezra and Nehemiah, Books of" (R. H. Pfeiffer), IDB, II, 215ff.

28. Although the basic P narrative apparently arose during the Exile (see K. Elliger, Kleine Schriften zum Alten Testament, Munich 1966, pp. 174ff.), it received successive layers of priestly expansion (mostly cult legislation) during the postexilic period (see the works on biblical Introduction).

29. The most probable date of Chronicles is ca. 400 B.C. (see P. R. Ackroyd, IDBS, p. 157). It selectively cites Samuel-Kings in support of its ideal of a Davidic-Levitical theocracy (see the commentaries).

30. See M. Hengel, Judaism and Hellenism, I, 58-106.

31. See the books on postexilic Jewish history, e.g., E. Schürer, A History of the Jewish People in the Time of Jesus, pb., New York 1961, pp. 13ff. Primary sources for this history are the apocryphal books, I and II Maccabees.

32. Although the Roman papacy is the most ostensible (and successful) example of a Christian theocracy, Protestantism tends to reproduce it in such forms as New England Puritanism and in the radical sectarian experiments. The tendency of theocracy is to claim absolute divine authority for the institution or the power group served by the institution.

33. See art. "Shema, Reading of" (N. Shupak), EJ, XIV, 1370ff.

34. See arts. "Mezuzah" (L. I. Rabinowitz), EJ, XI, 1474ff.; "Tefillin" (L. I. Rabinowitz), EJ, XV, 898ff.

35. Cf. G. von Rad, _Deuteronomy_ (Philadelphia 1966), pp. 62ff.

36. Cf. K. Barth, _Church Dogmatics_, II, 2 (Edinburgh 1957), 3-506.

37. Cf. "The Divine-Human Encounter and the Courage to Be," P. Tillich, _The Courage to Be_ (New Haven 1952), pp. 160-73.

38. Cf. R. Gutteridge, _op. cit._, pp. 315ff. ("Luther and the Jews").

39. For a negative assessment of the role of Judaism in the New Testament period, see R. Bultmann, "The Church's Relation to Judaism and the Problem of the Old Testament, "_Theology of the New Testament_, I, 108ff. Compare the more positive views of W. D. Davies in _Christian Origins_ (London 1962) and other writings. The most elaborate analysis available is P. Richardson, _Israel in the Apostolic Church_, Cambridge 1969.

40. Cf. 1QS III, 17ff.: "God created man to rule the world, and appointed for him two spirits after whose direction he was to walk until the final Inquisition. They are the spirits of truth and of perversity. The origin of truth lies in the Fountain of Light, and that of perversity in the Wellspring of darkness. All who practice right-eousness are under the domination of the Prince of Light, and walk in the ways of light; whereas all who practice perversity are under the domina-tion of the Angel of Darkness and walk in ways of darkness...." (Gaster trans., pp. 43f.); cf. J. Gammie, "Spatial and Ethical Dualism in Jewish Wisdom and Apocalyptic Literature," _JBL_, 93 (1974), 356ff.

41. The Qumranian Essence, the Zealots, the Sicarii (cf. W. R. Farmer, _Maccabees, Zealots_ and _Josephus_, New York 1956).

42. Cf. K. Stendahl, ed., _The Scrolls and the New Testament_, New York 1957.

43. See Mark 8:27-31 par, where Jesus forbids his dis-ciples to proclaim his messiahship, while applying to his own ministry the tradition that the Son of

man must suffer and die. Cf. H. Raisanen, Das Messiasgeheimnis im Markusevangelium, Helsinki 1976.

44. Cf. R. Bultmann, Theology of the New Testament, I 3ff.; also idem, "The Eschatological Preaching of Jesus," Primitive Christianity in its Contemporary Setting, (p.b., New York o956), pp. 86ff.

45. K. Koch, The Rediscovery of Apocalyptic, tr. M. Kohl, Naperville: Allenson, 1972.

46. Cf. J. Beker, "Paul's Apocalyptic Theology: Apocalyptic and the Resurrection of Jesus," Paul the Apostle, The Triumph of God in Life and Thought (Philadelphia: Fortress, 1980).

47. See P. Richardson, op. cit., pp. 126ff. ("Romans: Paul's Interpretation of God's Purpose"), with special treatment of Rom. 11:28-32 and Eph. 2:11ff.

48. The provisions enacted by the Council of Jerusalem (Acts 15) represents a temporary compromise. Inevitably the emerging church would be compelled to make a definitive choice for Jewish ritual either as an essential and obligatory rule or as a hallowed but non-obligatory guide.

49. This came to clear manifestation in the "German Christian" movement allied with National Socialism. Under Hitler, a determined effort was underway to eliminate all that was distinctively Hebraic within the church.

50. An eager patriotism or community solidarity, taking precedence over loyalty to the gospel, is a familiar phenomenon in contemporary American church life; so too in other lands.

51. The German Evangelical Church made so many piddling compromises with the Nazi officials in a vain effort to protect its own formerly Jewish members that it retained little spirit for defending Jews outside its own fellowship; cf. Gutteridge, op. cit.

52. The Egyptians were among those who practiced circumcision, which became a distinctive Jewish rite only during the exile and over against the Babylonians, who did not practice it; see art. "Circumcision" (P. Hyatt), IDB, II, 629f.

53. See art. "Sabbath" (J. Morgenstern), _IDB_, IV, 135ff.; also A. J. Heschel, _The Sabbath: its Meaning for Modern Man_, New York 1952.

54. See the recent penetrating analysis of the Abraham traditions in Thomas L. Thompson, _The Historicity of the Patriarchal Narratives, The Quest for the Historical Abraham_ (BZAW, 133), Berlin-New York: Walter de Gruyter, 1974; also M. Noth, _History of Pentateuchal Traditions_, pp. 102ff.

55. A heated debate among contemporary scholars concerns the validity of M. Noth's theory of a ritually constituted "amphictyony" of Israelite tribes as the basis of Israel's primitive peoplehood (see especially C. H. J. de Geus, _The Tribes of Israel_, Assen 1976); all parties in the debate reject the traditional concept of a directly descended ethnic community.

56. See Joshua 9, I Sam. 21:1-9.

57. See art. "Priests and Levites" (R. Abba), _IDB_, III, 879-90; also A. H. J. Gunneweg, _Leviten and Priester_, FRLANT 89, Gottingen 1965.

58. See art. "Nethinim" (G. Henton Davies), _IDB_, III, 541.

59. Cf. Zech. 8:20-23; see art. "Proselyte" (M. H. Pope), _IDB_, III, 921ff.; G. F. Moore, _Judaism in the First Centuries of the Christian Era_, p.b., New York 1971, I, 323ff. ("The Conversion of the Gentiles").

60. E.g., Isa. 19:21-25, 49:8, Jer. 48:47, 49:6, Ezek. 29:13-14, Mal. 1:11; cf. the book of Jonah. In addition, there are a great number of passages contemplating Israel's victory over, or absorption of, the gentile nations.

61. Cf. C. Westermann, "The Way of Promise Through the Old Testament," B. W. Anderson, ed., _The Old Testament and Christian Faith_, pp. 200-24; see also W. Zimmerli's article, "Promise and Fulfillment" in the same volume, pp. 89-122.

62. See W. Brueggemann, _The Land: Place as Gift, Promise, and Challenge in Biblical Faith_, Philadelphia: Fortress, 1977.

63. The land of Canaan is repeatedly promised to the Israelites -- but as God's gracious gift, not as their right by purchase or conquest. Although certain late passages do identify this as an "eternal possession" ('ahuzzat ʿōlām, P in Gen. 17:8, 48:4; cf. Lev. 14:34), Israel held it always at Yahweh's terms; thus the law of the land's redemption, Lev. 25:24. As ancient Israel occupied Canaan by driving out or assimilating the original inhabitants, they were themselves forced to cede it to others. The God of history retains his prerogative of acting as final arbitor with respect to this land and every land.

64. For a survey of ethical options from the perspective of Christian theology, see H. Thielicke, Theological Ethics, ed. W. H. Lazareth, 2 vols., Philadelphia 1966.

65. Although Nazi ideology involves a positivistic assertion of the party will, its disregard of the rights of other interests characterizes it, like all positivistic ethical aims, as essentially amoralistic.

66. J. A. Wilson, tr.

67. S. N. Kramer, tr.

68. J. A. Wilson, tr.

69. Cf. S. Morenz's discussion of maat, and of Egyptian ethics in general, in Egyptian Religion, pp. 110-36.

70. The so-called "antimonarchical texts" in the Old Testament, such as Judg. 8:1ff. and I Sam. 8:1ff., survive as eloquent testimony to the resistance of Israel's free citizens against David's and Solomon's consolidation of power. Other texts, representing a more approving attitude toward the monarchy, reflect the altered political situation created by the threat of external aggression. On this problem see now F. Crüsemann, Der Widerstand gegen das Königtum, Die antiköniglichen Texte des Alten Testaments und der Kampf um den frühen israelitischen Staat, WMANT 49, Neukirchen-Vluyn 1978. On the opposition of the early prophets to certain kings, see S. J. De Vries, Prophet Against Prophet, Grand Rapids, Eerdmans, 1978.

71. On the religion-phenomenological meaning of holiness, see Chapter I, "Introduction."

72. On the formulaic function of "I am Yahweh (your god)," see K. Elliger, "Ich bin der Herr -- euer Gott," Kleine Schriften zum Alten Testament, Munich 1966, pp. 211ff.; W. Zimmerli, "Ich bin Jahwe," Gottes Offenbarung, Munich 1963, pp. 11ff.

73. Cf. H. W. Wolff, Amos' geistige Heimat, WMANT 18, Gottingen 1964.

74. Cf. Ex. 22:25, Lev. 25:36f., Deut. 23:19f. Isa. 24:2, Jer. 15:10, Ezek. 18:8, 13, 17, 22:12, Psa. 15:5, Prov. 28:8, Neh. 5:7, 10. See art. "Usury" (H. H. Cohn), EJ, XVI, 27ff.

75. On the history of tradition-development, see especially L. Perlitt, Bundestheologie im Alten Testament, WMANT 36 (Neukirchen-Vluyn 1969); cf. also art. "Covenant, Mosaic" (P. A. Riemann), IDBS, pp. 192ff.

76. On this pericope see E. W. Nicholson, Exodus and Sinai in History and Tradition (Richmond: John Knox, 1973), pp. 67ff.; also W. Beyerlin, Origins and History of the Oldest Sinaitic Traditions, tr. S. Rudman, Oxford 1965.

77. Cf. M. Noth, History of Pentateuchal Traditions, pp. 136ff.

78. See S. J. De Vries, YTT, pp. 73f.

79. Cf. K. Elliger, "Sinn und Ursprung der priesterlichen Geschichtserzahlung," Kleine Schriften zur Alten Testament, pp. 174ff.

80. Cf. Mal. 2:4-8.

81. See G. Schmitt, Der Landtag von Sichem, Stuttgart 1964, where it is argued that the basic element in this chapter dates from before Omri and reflects a unique historical occurrence from premonarchical Israel. This was not the establishment of an amphictyonic union (Noth) but the conclusion of a mutual oath of loyalty. The content of the agreement was a now-lost code of apodictic law, supplanted in the present text by the exhortations of vv. 14ff.

82. On the structure and ideology of this passage, see J. Muilenburg, "The Form and Structure of the Covenant Formulations," _VT_, 9 (1959), pp. 346ff.

83. See S. J. De Vries, "The Development of the Deuteronomic Promulgation Formula," _Biblica_, 55 (1974), 301-16.

84. See S. J. De Vries, _YTT_, pp. 141f.

85. Cf. the "covenant with Phinehas," Num. 25:10-13.

86. It has been extensively glossated in the spirit of the deuteronomistic school.

87. Deut. 5:1-5 is a specially designed narrative introduction; vv. 22-33 is a framework transition between the Decalogue and the beginning of the deuteronomic parenesis in chap. 6, identifying the deuteronomic lawbook (chaps. 12-26) as the full explication of the Decalogue. Cf. N. Lohfink, _Das Hauptgebot_ (Rome 1963), pp. 261ff.; also S. J. De Vries, _YTT_, pp. 173-75.

88. E.g., the reference to "houses" scarcely suits the situation of wilderness wandering.

89. Cf. M. Noth, "The Laws in the Pentateuch: Their Assumptions and Meaning," _The Laws in the Pentateuch and other Studies_, tr. D. R. Ap-Thomas (Edinburgh 1966), pp. 1-107.

90. See the pioneering work of A. Alt, "The Origins of Israelite Law," _Essays on Old Testament History and Religion_, tr. R. A. Wilson (Oxford 1966), pp. 79-132. In spite of various refinements, scholarship since Alt has not superseded the essential distinction between casuistic and apodictic law as distinct genres, each with its own specific _Sitz im Leben_ and function.

91. Cf. E. Nielson, _The Ten Commandments in New Perspective_, tr. D. J. Bourke (Naperville 1965), pp. 56ff.; and my review in _VT_, (1966), 530-34. See also J. J. Stamm and M. E. Andrew, _The Ten Commandments in Recent Research_, Naperville 1967.

92. See G. von Rad, _Old Testament Theology_, I, 190ff.; cf. W. Zimmerli, "The Theological Relevance of

the Law," The Law and the Prophets (New York 1963), pp. 46-60.

93. See Ex. 21:12, 15-17, 22:18-19, 21-22, 28, Lev. 18:8-16.

94. "Das Gesetz Leviticus 18," Kleine Schriften zum Alten Testament, pp. 232-59 (see also E. Gerstenberger, Wesen und Herkunft des apodiktischen Rechts, Neukirchen-Vluyn, 1965). Elliger identifies extensive redactional expansions throughout this chapter; cf, his commentary, Leviticus, HAT 4 (Tübingen 1966), pp. 230ff. See also S. F. Bigger, "The Family Laws of Leviticus 18 in their Setting," JBL, 98 (1979), 187-203.

95. See B. S. Childs, The Book of Exodus, pp. 417ff.

96. See idem, pp. 419ff.

97. See art. "War, Ideas of" (L. E. Toombs), IDB, IV, 796ff.

98. See art. "Crimes and Punishments," (J. Greenberg), IDS, I, 733ff.; cf. J. Boecker, Redeformen des Rechtslebens im Alten Testament (WMANT, 14), Neukirchen, 2nd ed. 1970.

99. See Childs, op. cit., pp. 422f.

100. See idem, pp. 423f., 425ff. The eighth commandment refers to movable goods, while the tenth refers to real property.

101. So E. Nielsen, op. cit., p. 91, following A. Alt, "Das Verbot des Diebstals im Dekalog," Kleine Schriften zur Geschichte des Volkes Israel (3rd ed., Munich 1963), I, 333-40.

102. I Kings 21

103. See Childs, op. cit., pp. 424f.

104. Cf. K. Baltzer, The Covenant Formulary, Philadelphia; Fortress 1971; also F. C. Fensham, "Maledictions and Benedictions in Ancient Near-Eastern Vassal-Treaties and the Old Testament," ZAW, 74 (1962), 1-9.

105. Cf. J. Muilenburg, The Way of Israel: Biblical Faith and Ethics, New York 1961.

106. See art. "Wisdom in the OT" (J. L. Crenshaw), IDBS, pp. 952ff.; also G. von Rad, Wisdom in Israel, New York-Nashville: Harper, 1972.

107. See M. Noth, "The Laws in the Pentateuch." Cf. also H. Gese, "Das Gesetz," Altestamentliche Vortrage zur biblischen Theologie (Munich): Chr. Kaiser 1977), pp. 55-84.

108. See art. "Law and Morality" (S. Berman) EJ, X, 1480-84.

109. Cf. H. L. Strack, Introduction to the Talmud and Midrash (Philadelphia 1945), pp. 3-64.

110. Cf. M. Hengel, Judaism and Hellenism, I, 107ff.

111. See J. Neusner, "The Written Tradition in the Pre-Rabbinic Period," JSJ, 4 (1973), 56-65; A. J. Salderini, "The End of the Rabbinic Chain of Tradition," JBL 93 (1974), 97-106.

112. See Chapter II, "Legalism."

113. For a concise statement of Jesus' relationship to his cultural and spiritual environment, see J. Barr, Old and New in Interpretation (New York 1966), pp. 149ff.

114. See art. "Ethics in the NT" (W. D. Davies), IDB, II, 167ff.; cf. A. N. Wilder, Eschatology and Ethics in the Teaching of Jesus, Rev. ed., New York 1950.

115. See especially Matthew 23, unparalleled in the other Gospels and reflecting the evangelist's special antagonism to this party. As an entree to the recent extensive discussion regarding the Pharisees, see art. "Pharisees" (E. Rivkin) in IDBS, pp. 657ff.

116. See R. Tannehill, The Sword of his Mouth (Philadelphia: Fortress, 1975), pp. 67-77.

Chapter IV

History as Responsible Dialogue with God

"THE LIVING GOD"

Greek philosophy can never be a congenial host to biblical religion because it insists on banishing God from history. The biblical God is not the "unknown knower" or the "unmoved mover." He is passionately involved in history -- a God who lives, committing himself and acting purposefully in the lives of human beings. The Bible, which records the revelation about him and from him, is no transcription of heavenly dictation, but the product of historical existence, calling upon human beings to respond, and responding to them in purposeful interaction, in which they become instruments to the realization of his (and their) eschatological goal.

Introduction: Notes on biblical epistemology[1]

a. Biblical existentialism

The term "epistemology" means the discipline and science of knowledge. It raises the question, "How do we know?" In address to the question of God it asks, "How do we know God?"

Greek philosophy speculated about being, essence, eternity. Ultimate reality was identified in static "being." Not so the Scriptures of Judaism and Christianity. The Bible, itself the product of history, is essentially concerned with God and man in history. Its concern is not with so-called secular history, but with history as a revelation of God. The way in which it approaches God is not with the question of his being or essence, but from the point of view of human existence in relationship with God -- that is, in historical confrontation with God.

It is very wrong to suggest that the Bible is a book of subjectivistic religion. Far from it: it actually offers sterile ground for private mysticism. Also, it does little to encourage the search for God from the point of view of inward self-consciousness, as in contemporary secular existentialism. What we may rightly call a biblical existentialism depends on three strongly marked characteristics: (1) theonomous ordering; (2) historical orientation; and (3) social structuring. Because God takes the initiative in revealing himself to man, the authentic religious experience can never be the achievement of our own effort.

Because the individual's confrontation with God involves man as a historical being, it takes account of all that past generations have contributed to his present state, and all that may happen to him and to those whom he may influence in the future. Because it addresses man as a social being, it demands that his response be considerate of others' well-being as well as one's own.

Biblical existentialism in the above definition is the enemy of an individualistic absorption with "feeling good," so prevalent in our day. The latter is what many people now come to church for. The church has become a grand spiritual massage parlor, coddling our egos and stroking our feelings. No more hymns in the grand theocentric tradition of the past, but sentimental songs of egotistic self-congratulation! No more sermons to worry our consciences and urge us to responsible action, but feeble diatribes for our amusement! A minimum of high liturgical praise to God and a maximum of informal chumminess! All this is far from the model of genuine biblical existentialism, calling us with the words (Ps. 95:7), "Today, if you shall hear my voice, harden not your hearts!" To the degree that this is an accurate description of what actually goes on in (not many, but most) present-day churches, it measures the extent to which contemporary religion has lost its grasp on "the achievements of biblical faith."

(1) Conventional dogmatics versus the Bible

The older style of Christian dogmatics was too strongly influenced by Greek models, hence was much concerned with the quest for the essence and being of God. Treatises on systematic theology tended to approach the subject of God with a discussion of who he is, what his attributes and qualities are, and what works he "performs" in the world.[2] Presupposed was the tendency to treat God as an object suitable for thorough investigation with the tools of philosophical inquiry. We ought to see that this method is altogether inappropriate, not only because God is no object but also because the Bible is no book of propositions concerning the being of God. If the latter were indeed true, there might be some justification for the proof-texting method by which theological propositions are supported, item by item, with unexamined passages from the Bible.[3] But it is not true. The Bible does not offer theoretical teaching about God. It never tries to state propositionally who or what God is. This is not to suggest that such questions may never be raised. They must be raised, and it is the responsibility of competent systematic theology to raise them. But systematic theology must begin with the datum of Scripture as it actually is -- not a concatenation of theological propositions, but a crystallization of spiritual witnesses concerning the experience of God's presence in individual, ever-variegated historical events.[4]

Some might be inclined to challenge the statement that the Bible does not define God. How about "God is a spirit" (John 4:24)? This is a description, not a definition. Then how about such a text as I John 4:8, "God is love?" Is this not the definition of God that it has often been taken to be -- as though wherever love is, there is God? The response is, again, that this is no definition, but a metonymy, a figure of speech substituting the part for the whole -- in this case love for God, because what we know about God comes to us in the experience of love. Or another passage, I John 1:5: "God is light." This again is no definition; it is a familiar biblical metaphor.

Passages like these do not in any way detract from the validity of the observation that the Bible does not tell us what God is in his essence. Philosophy can help us conceptualize and articulate some concept of what God is, but the Bible does not itself do this.

(2)   The name of God

It is no doubt very significant that the name by which the biblical God reveals himself is unique. To say that the name Yahweh is personal is to say that it is non-generic. It is not a definition-name, intended for identification and classification. Thus it is not like the word "God," which can be employed as a proper name, as it is here, but when spelled with a small "g" denotes simply a class or category of being. This device generally tends to reduce personalistic individuality, just as when we substitute titles such as "Mr.," "Rev.," "Sen.," "Pres." for the proper name of the person addressed. The "god" of Israel has a proper name, "Yahweh," which upon close scrutiny and detailed historical examination proves to be unparalleled. Even though some current lines of investigation claim to have found this name outside the Bible,[5] the Bible presents it as unique. There are many El's and many Baal's, but only one Yahweh. The gods of the polytheistic religions could be classified and categorized. They were all no more than separate aspects or manifestations of a single, monistic reality; thus they had generic names, or at most appellative names (honorific descriptions), representing their function within the cosmos. To know such names was to have a handle upon them, thus through ritual to control them. But these gods approached genuine personalism in no more than a tangential way; i.e., representatively and analogically, producing the inevitable caricature that we have previously described.6

The classical Old Testament passage introducing the unique name, Yahweh, is Ex. 3:14-15. In response to Moses' query about the identity of the deity addressing him, the text offers Yahweh's definitive self-revelation: "God said to Moses, 'I am who I am (ᵓehyeh ᵓašer ᵓehyeh).' And he said, 'Say this to the people of Israel, "I am (ᵓehyeh) has sent me".'" Following these mysterious affirmations, v 14 goes on with a less cryptic self-disclosure, "God also said to Moses, 'Say this to the people of Israel, "Yahweh, the god of your fathers, the god of Abraham, the god of Isaac, and the god of Jacob, has sent me to you"; this is my name forever, and thus am I to be remembered throughout all generations.'"

Many efforts have been made to explain the name Yahweh from the verb hāyāh, "to be," "to become" -- the basis of the elaborate punning in v. 14. Sophisticated and attractive explanations have been offered. They have to do with God's self-sufficient essence and his all-potential causality.7 Whatever validity they may have, they pertain only to the intent of the ancient glossator responsible for v. 14a, speculating on the symbolic meaning of the name Yahweh, which appears, as a grammatical form, to be the causal inflection of the verb "to be."

But careful literary analysis shows v. 14 to be the original continuation of v. 13. At the climax of this E narrative of epiphanic self-disclosure, the god of the fathers (v. 6) tells Moses that he is Yahweh. V. 14b entered the text either before or subsequently to v. 14a as an explanatory gloss on v. 12, misunderstanding kî ᵓehyeh ᵓimmak, "Surely I will be with you," as meaning "Surely Ehyeh (a symbolic proper name) will be with you."8

The upshot of this is to reinforce the affirmation of the uniqueness of the divine name, Yahweh. Israel, through Moses, received it as absolutely new.

(3) The pathway of intuitive experience

This line of argument is raised to accentuate the point that the God of the Bible is not someone who is to be understood in terms of essential being, but as someone who reveals himself to, and through, a people, within their historical experience.[9] This is, then, the prime mode of epistomology for the Bible, and ought to be the same for Biblical Theology and for Bible-oriented systematic theology in general. The way to God is not primarily through philosophy, however helpful it might be for understanding our prior apprehensions of God. Credo ut intelligam, " I believe on the way to understanding."[10] The God of the Bible must be known before he can be understood; and he is known intuitively, through spiritual apperception, as shared in a community of faith and attested by the witness of the people. Again we reassert that the Scriptures are essentially a testimony to God's presence in history. They record and reflect upon the spiritual apperception of the presence of God in his work. God's revelatory work comes to challenge us in the historical events in which we are involved and which concern us directly. These may be partially past -- but they continue into the present and future. God appears in and among men. His climactic appearance was in and through his Son, Jesus Christ.

We are justified in speaking, therefore, of biblical experientialism or existentialism. This is people-centered, covenant conditioned, and provides no support or basis for subjectivistic existentialism, pietism, or mysticism. The people of the Bible do experience God -- and they tell about it. "Let the redeemed of the Lord say so!"[11] That is what the Bible is all about; that is why we have the Bible. Its people told what they felt, had seen, had experienced -- not just in their inner being in a mystical way, but in their historical socially-oriented existence. In a number of Psalms passages we read of one who had been delivered going out to testify before "the great congregation."[12] Would that "testifying" today could continue on so soundly biblical a basis! The Psalmist's testimony was not to some inner emotion, but to Yahweh's great deed in public.

(4)   Scripture's witness to a living God

The thing that needs above all to be affirmed is
that the biblical God <u>lives</u>. This is why we cannot
dispense with the symbol of personhood; a thing or an
idea does not live. Yahweh lives: Jesus lives.

Very often we come upon passages in which Yahweh
swears by his own life, ḥay ɔa nî, "as I live!"[13] The
God of the Bible is no abstract being; he is living
transcendent power, alive and acting purposefully, con-
cernedly, in integrity and commitment.

That the Bible is historically oriented is a consequence of this fact. The other Scriptures in world
religions (and in modern sects like Mormonism) differ
radically at this point. The Bible is the product of
history because it has to do with the encounter of a
people with God in their history. The only way to
know God is through what he does -- what he does <u>for</u>
<u>us</u>. The scriptural witnesses spoke within their com-
munity of faith, and for all time, their interpretive
word about what God had done and would do. Gradually
a more complete and rounded-out knowledge of God began
to emerge, culminating (but not ending) in Christ.
Revelatory history continues to the present day, and
will continue until the end of time.[14] It is the ongoing task of the community of faith to stand open to
the reality of God's continuing elusive presence in
historical event, to be involved responsibly in dialogue with God in history's sturggles.

Excursus on canonization and the end of the era of
revelation

"Canon" means the Holy Scriptures of the Old and
New Testaments as a rule or standard for faith and
conduct. It also means the norm by which the particular writings which comprise these two parts of the
Bible gained acceptance.

The idea of the Canon has been much discussed in
recent biblical scholarship (e.g., J. Sanders, <u>Torah</u>
<u>and</u> <u>Canon</u>;[15] B.S. Childs, <u>Introduction to the Old</u>

<u>Testament as Scripture</u>).[16] It should be apparent that
this emerged as a historical process, and did not reach
completion until the Christian era, when both Judaism
and Christianity were forced to define the Scriptural
authority upon which they were henceforward to be prepared to base the defense of their respective beliefs.
Nothing has been so helpful in shedding light on this
often obscure problem as the discovery of the Dead Sea
Scrolls, presenting the scholarly world with actual
scriptural manuscripts from the last two centuries B.C.
and the first century A.D.[17]

A permanent legacy of the period of historical
criticism is a general awareness that every biblical
book reflects its own complex and often drawn-out
process of literary composition and redaction. Each
of these stages is important for the recovery of a
specific kerygmatic situation out of which, and to which,
the individual biblical passages direct a specific witness or message. In any event, we see this as a process of dynamic and ongoing revelation, presenting ever-
newer insights into the meaning of God's previous word
for a new day.[18]

But eventually this process of internal growth
came to an end. The literary expansion of the ancient
texts became no longer possible; what was laid down in
the text became sacrosanct. This is where the notion
of Canon begins to take hold. We cannot say precisely
when and how this occurred, but we do know that it
happened because further internal growth was now impossible. Henceforward the only pathway for the expansion of the biblical word was to be by the method of
exegesis -- commentary upon the sacred text.[19]

The evident ideology underlying this new state of
affairs was that revelation had terminated; this is
precisely the definition that the Jewish historian,
Josephus, offers in his famous statement about the
content of the Canon:

> There are not with us myriads of books
> disagreeing and contradicting one another,
> but only two and twenty books[20] containing
> the record of all time, and which rightly
> are believed in. Of these, five are those
> of Moses, which contain the laws and the
> tradition as to the origin of mankind till
> his death. This period falls little short
> of three thousand years. From the death of
> Moses till Artaxerxes, who was king of the

Persians after Xerxes, the prophets who
came after Moses wrote of the things that
came to pass in their times, in thirteen
books. The remaining four (books) contain
hymns to God and maxims for life for men.
From Artaxerxes to our own time all things
have been recorded, but not esteemed worthy
of like credit with those which preceded
them, because of there not being an exact
succession of prophets. There is practical
proof of how we treat these same writings,
for though so long a time has now elapsed,
no one has dared either to add to them or to
make any change. But it is natural to all
Jews straightway from the day of birth to
consider these as the teachings of God, and
to stand by them, and if needful gladly to
die on their behalf. (Contra Apion, i,8)

The era of revelation had been from Moses to Ezra.
Moses wrote the first, Ezra wrote the last. Scripture
is now finished and complete. This means that God had
once spoken, and now speaks no more. The only historical background that explains this ideology is the late
postexilic period and the first Christian century, when
Israel has long since lost its sense of historicality,
as well as the hope of nationalistic self-determination.
There was no longer any such thing as Heilsgeschichte --
except as ancient lore.[21] God had long since retreated
from the scene of History; the prophets were gone. Thus
the books of Moses, the writings of the prophets, and
the other pious books must be preserved intact and
revered, but could no longer be expanded through creative new additions.

Thus canonization actually came about through the
historical isolation of Judaism.[22] It did not occur all
at once, to be sure. Its earliest stage is probably reflected in the translation of the Old Testament into
Greek. This version, know as the Septuagint (abbr. LXX),
was carried out in Alexandria, Egypt, in the years
around, and immediately following, 250 B.C.[23] The very
fact that a large expatriate Jewish community needed an
enscripturated norm of divine truth, and could obtain
authoritative copies of the scriptural writings for
translation into their adopted language, is evidence
that the idea of a sacred Canon was already extant.[24]
A second stage in the canonization process was the
normalizing of the biblical text and a standardizing of
the contents. We can identify this in the mishnaic
traditions about a Jewish "synod" at Jamnia ca. A.D. 90;

but the most important evidence is the fact that biblical texts recovered from Qumran have been standardized by the first century A.D. A third and final stage was that of the official confessional declarations, particularly those of the early Christian synods, defining the precise contents of the Bible. Already at the first stage, further expansions within the biblical books had become impossible;[25] this was the essential move within the canonization process, for now it was only logical that deviations from one manuscript to another should be harmonized and that the respective religious bodies should eventually define the scriptural basis of their belief.

The significance of canonization for a dynamic concept of revelation is simply this: Scripture, finished and closed off, henceforth marks the confessional standard of new truth. It is the original flame by which the reflected light of future revelation is to be judged and interpreted. But canonization cannot in itself terminate revelation. The New Testament is the clearest evidence for this.[26] The God who once spoke can, and does, speak again.

b. Theological historicality

The question has to be asked next, "What is it that gives meaning and significance to historical event? What is it that makes an event historical, in distinction from non-historical?[27] To start with; only man has history. Inanimate being, or even the animal world, has no genuine history, for history requires self-awareness and conscious purpose. Historical events become meaningful to their interpreters when they come to recognize their teleological (i.e., purposeful) inner linkage. This is a perspective that can make a broad difference with respect to the humdrum details within a chain of daily events. For example, there is generally no historical significance to one's eating his breakfast. This is something one always does, and hopes he may never have to omit. Yet some particular person's missing his breakfast (Napoleon's at Waterloo?) may have far-reaching consequences, and could gain rich historical significance as a consequence. The Watergate guard regularly passed the door of the Democratic National Headquarters each night -- but one particular night he saw tape, grew suspicious, and

occasioned the eventual downfall of a president.
Potentially all simple ordinary things can lead to broad-
reaching consequences, leading to still others, eventually affecting the fortunes of a nation and world. John
Kennedy rode in his open automobile one day in November,
just as he often did. That day another factor was
present: an assassin. This driving through the streets
of Dallas at that time, under those circumstances, and
in the presence of that contrived threat, led to a historical disaster.

Both God and man are at work in revelatory historical event. What man does has significance, but only in
the perspective of the divine presence and control.

As history happens to us, we are confronted with
transcendence. That which is beyond us finitely manifests only a fragment (but a significant part nonetheless) of infinite Otherness. Ultimate incontingency
impinges on our existence amid, and by way of innumerable contingencies -- most of which may lack significance in themselves, yet all of which may gain significance beyond comprehension.

As we make history happen -- a potential for the
small as well as for the great -- our contingent freedom affects innumerable other contingencies, thus
partially, imperfectly, and contingently confronting
transcendent Being -- even that of the infinitely Other.

1. Divine sovereignty in historical event

     Our discussion addresses now the question of God's
role in history. This will also provide the indispensable context for an understanding of man's role in
response to God.

     a. The problem of history in ancient and modern
thought

     In order to appreciate the biblical achievement in
walking with God through history, we need to survey the
alternatives. We can divide our analysis into two
sections, distinguishing between mythological cultures
and demythologized cultures. In all of them, the
Bible's distinctive view is absent.

     (1) Its irrelevance in mythological cultures

     The mythological cultures of the ancient Near East,
as well as those of the distant Orient, were essentially
ahistorical.[28] They were unconcerned about history,
which had no significance for them because myth is timeless, celebrating a reality represented in primordial
prototypes, continually recovered, rehearsed, and re-
affirmed in cultic ritual. We see this pattern especially in ancient Egypt. Because the culture of
Egypt was timeless, it was drastically traditionalistic.
In Egypt nothing essentially new happened, or could
happen. To talk, then, about the "history" of Egypt
would have significance only to modern researchers. To
be sure, historical events did occur in ancient Egypt,
but the Egyptian mind was unprepared to see genuine significance in them. Certain grand achievements, such as
military victories, got written down, but this was solely for the glorification of the Pharaohs. In the end,
Egyptian culture was overwhelmed by history; because it
could not learn the lessons of history, Egypt succumbed
to an alien culture without comprehending the causes or
effects of its decline.

The ancient Babylonians, on their part, have left "historical" inscriptions in abundance. But again, these only catalogue triumphs in honor of the kings involved, and with the specific purpose of presenting these as thank-offerings to their patron gods. Historical events were also recorded -- but without organic interconnection -- for the purpose of prognosticating the future. Events from the early period, the time of Sargon I and Naram-Sin, are recorded in Omen-Texts and in the royal chronicles to help the diviners and astrologers determine the constellations. They were signs or symptoms of particular "times," providing useful tokens for determining similar favorable or unfavorable times, for the purpose of advising military expeditions in the future.[29]

We have nothing whatever from Canaanite or Phoenician culture that could be remotely described as having historiographic interest. It is somewhat different in the Hittite area of Asia Minor, where historiography with a primitive concept of organic connection began to emerge prior to the downfall of the Hittite empire.[30]

(2)   Its secularization in demythologized cultures

Greek historiography is essentially timeless, and at the same time radically secular.[31] The Golden Age historiographers, Herodotus, Thucydides, and Xenophon, produces masterpieces of literature which at the same time provide valuable historical information. These writers show little responsibility in vouching for their sources, but present fact and fiction on equal footing. Their purpose was to glorify the Greek achievement in fighting free from the Persians. Their radically secular historiography coincided with the radical retreat of mythological religion. Myth had to give way before historiographic writing, for it is the alternative to myth. Thus Greek culture found no way of integrating its "theology" with an awareness of historical interconnectedness.

The modern concept of history may also be characterized as basically secular. We often find this articulated in the discussions of the professional historians, and unfortunately it is assumed by many modern statesmen. Modern historians tend generally to deny the concept of teleology; that is, the notion that history is directed toward an ultimate goal. Thus current secular history interprets man's historical involvement as essentially meaningless, proceeding purely from opportunistic self-concern and the aggressive struggle of one group against another. In this view, history is essentially like the jostling of monkeys on a branch, or the scratching and pecking that goes on in a hen yard.

Inevitably, this view produces -- and implies -- a theological vacuum. It may acknowledge some proximate goal from the point of view of those immediately involved in the struggle, but only such as is arbitrarily given it by one group endeavoring to obtain mastery over other groups -- or of one individual over other individuals. The modern philosopher who has articulated this nihilistic view the most pointedly was Friedrich Nietzsche, affirming a radical individualism. Immanuel Kant, who taught the primacy of the will, had acknowledged its prime importance in giving meaning to reality.[32] Nietzsche's radical distortion of Kant's idea has influenced the development of positivistic amoralisms like Fascism and Nazism in the tragic era of the twentieth-century world. These movements were notoriously amoral in denying the rights of other groups, as well as of private individuals, in driving toward the realization of their arbitrarily chosen goals.

Secularistic existentialism, mentioned previously, likewise thrives in an atmosphere of radical Lutheran antinomianism and of kindred ideologies.[33] One historian who has recently revealed the theological destitution of this philosophy is Karl Löwith. In his book, Meaning in History,[34] Löwith makes the Christian meaning of history a matter of pure subjectivism, leaving the secular world to ruin and meaninglessness. There are many thinkers, sophisticated and naive, who adopt his philosophy and follow his example -- Sartre, for example. But is a world without God fit for man?

b. The theology of history in biblical thought[35]

(1) Biblical theology is orientated toward Heilsgeschichte rather than myth

The term Heilsgeschichte, literally "salvation history," is in common use among biblical theologians as the designation of divine and human interaction within the arena of history. Some scholars have gone too far, however, in dismissing the heathen gods from the historical scene.[36] It was not Israel along who believed that Deity was present in historical event. Israel's contemporaries believed this too. The actual difference was that Israel perceived the significance of its own involvement in history, as a confrontation and pilgrimage with God.

(a) A common cultural element: belief that the gods are at work in historical event

What was shared by ancient Israel with its contemporary cultures was the belief that the gods were operative in human history. Investigation into the literary and religious texts of the extrabiblical cultures, especially those of Mesopotamia and Asia Minor, reveal that the gods did march with the armies to determine victory or defeat. What we call historical event is something in which they were guiding, shaping, and determining. (We are indebted for this understanding particularly to the excellent recent study by Bertil Albrektson, History and the Gods.)[37] The shortcoming of the extrabiblical concept of historical involvement was that it lacked integration and coherence. The action of the gods had no purpose in terms of a greater design on their part, or of the destiny of their people.

It is important that we see clearly how very intensively the nonbiblical gods could become involved in historical events. Everything was, in fact, attributed to them -- almost to the point of ignoring the factor of human causality altogether. We should observe in the first example to be offered that this human factor is mentioned solely to account for the divine favor, rather than out of concern for an objective explanation of the historical event as such. We offer first a positive view of divine intervention, then a negative view.

A favorable view of divine intervention in history:
the Cyrus cylinder,

<u>ANET</u> 315-16[38]

Although the Achaemenid rulers of Persia[39] worshiped gods of their own (Ahura-Mazda eventually became their sole deity), Cyrus is represented in a
Babylonian clay document, prepared by the Babylonian
priests, as giving credit to the chief god of Babylon,
acknowledging him as a proper ruler in the place of
the native king, Nabonidus. This is a legitimation
recital, offering first a third-person description of
the event, and then Cyrus' first-person protocol of
divine designation:

> Marduk...scanned and looked (through all
> the countries, searching for a righteous
> ruler willing to lead him (in the annual
> procession). (Then) he pronounced the
> name of Cyrus, king of Anshan, declared
> him to be(come) ruler of all the world.
> And he did always endeavour to treat
> according to justice the black-headed whom
> he had made him conquer. Marduk, the great
> lord, a protector of his people/worshipers,
> beheld with pleasure his good deeds and his
> upright mind (and therefore) ordered him to
> march against his city Babylon. He made him
> set out on the road to Babylon, going by his
> side like a real friend....Without any battle,
> he made him enter his town Babylon, sparing
> Babylon any calamity. He delivered into his
> hands Nabonidus, the king who did not worship
> him. All the inhabitants of Babylon as well
> as of the entire country of Sumer and Akkad,
> princes and governors (included), bowed to
> him and kissed his feet....
>
> I am Cyrus, king of the world, great king,
> legitimate king, king of Babylon, king of
> Sumar and Akkad (etc.)...whose rule Bel
> and Nebo love, whom they want as king to
> please their hearts.
>
> When I entered Babylon as a friend and (when)
> I established the seat of the government in
> the palace of the ruler under jubilation and

rejoicing, Marduk, the great lord [induced]
the magnanimous inhabitants of Babylon [to]
love me], and I was daily endeavouring to worship him. My numerous troops walked around
Babylon in peace....I strove for peace in
Babylon....I [abolished] the corvee....I
brought relief to their dilapidated housing,
putting (thus) an end to their (main) complaints. Marduk, the great lord, was well
pleased with my deeds and sent friendly blessings to myself, Cyrus, the king who worshiped
him, to Cambyses, my son...as well as to all
my troops, and we all [praised] his great
[godhead] joyously, standing before him in
peace.

An unfavorable view of divine intervention in history:
Lament over Ur, <u>ANES</u> 617, 61940

In a remarkable Sumerian lamentation, the four
leading deities, An, Enlil, Enki, and Ninhursag, are
decreeing the destruction of the land of Sumer and its
chief city, Ur, before an invasion of Gutians:

That the day be overturned, that "law and order"
    cease to exist--
The storm is all devouring like the Flood--
That the <u>me</u> of Sumer be overturned,
That a favorable reign be withheld,
That cities be destroyed, that houses be destroyed,
That stalls be destroyed, that sheepfolds be wiped
    out,
That its oxen no longer stand in their stalls,
That its sheep no longer spread out in their
    sheepfold,
That its rivers flow with bitter water,
That its cultivated fields grow weeds,
That its steppes grow wailing plants,
That the mother care not for her children,
That the father says not "Oh my wife,"
That the young wife rejoice not in (his) lap,
That the young child grow not sturdy on (their)
    knee,
That the nursemaid chant not a lullaby,
That the home of kingship be changed,

That the seeking of oracles be suppressed,
That kingship be carried off from the land,
That its face be directed to inimical soil,
That in accord with the command of An (and)
      Enlil, "law and order" cease to exist--
(All this was) after An had frowned upon all
      the lands,
After Enlil had set his (friendly) face to
      inimical soil,
After Nintu had prostrated her (own) creatures,
After Enki had overturned (the course of) the
      Tigris (and) Euphrates,
After Utu had cursed the roads (and) highways--

The poet continues to elaborate the decree of destruction for another thirty lines, and then begins a narrative of its execution:

An, Enlil, Enki (and) Ninhursag decreed [this]
      (as) its fate--
The fate decreed by them can not be changed, who
      can overturn it!
The word commanded by An (and) Enlil, who can
      oppose it!
An has made the Sumerians tremble in their dwell-
      ing places, the people are terrified,
Enlil has made the day break bitter, has struck
      the city dumb,
Nintu, the mother of the Land, had brought...into
      it,
Enki has deprived the Tigris (and) the Euphrates
      of water,
Utu has banished justice (and) truth from the
      mouth (of men).
Inanna has given the battle (and) combat to the
      rebellious land,
Ningirsu has emptied out Sumer like milk,
On the land fell a calamity, one unknown to man,
One that had never been seen (before and) for
      which there were no words, one that could not
      be withstood,
On all the lands, the terrified, a disruptive
      hand was placed,
In their cities their city-gods stood aside,
The people, the terrified, could hardly breathe,
The storm fettered them, it returns not "the day"
      to them.

For the next three hundred lines the poet elaborates
what Enlil, the heavenly constable, did -- first to the
territorial cities and finally to Ur. The description
of ruin accords with the terms of the divine decree.
At the climax, we read of Ur's patron god, Sin, pleading to Enlil for mercy:

> Sin wept before his father Enlil,
> "Oh my father who begot me, what has my city done
>   to you, why have you turned against it!
> Oh Enlil, what has Ur done to you, why have you
>   turned against it!
> The offering-boats carried no offerings to the
>   father who begot him,
> Did not bring your bread (and) bread-offerings to
>   Enlil in Nippur,
> The en's (who lived) outisde the city, the en's
>   (who lived) inside the city have been carried
>   off by the wind (of desolation),
> Ur, like a city crushed by the pickaxe, was
>   counted among the ruins,
> The Kiur, the place where Enlil relaxes, has be-
>   come a desolate shrine.

Sin is here appealing to Enlil's self-interest; by
allowing the destruction of Ur, he is making it impossible for his cult to continue.

> Oh Enlil, gaze upon your city full of desolation,
> Gaze upon your city Nippur, full of desolation,
> Ur--(even) its dogs snuff not at the base of its
>   walls.
>
> . . . .
>
> Oh my father who begot me, turn my city from its
>   lonliness back to your arms,
> Oh Enlil, turn my city from its loneliness back
>   to your arms,
> Turn my Ekishnugal from its loneliness back to
>   your arms,
> Let Ur (once again) bring forth offspring, let the
>   people multiply for you.
>
> . . . .

Enlil answers his son Sin:

> "The desolate city--in its midst there was uttered
>   (nothing but) laments (and) dirges,
> In its midst there was uttered (nothing but)
>   laments (and) dirges,
> In its midst its people spend (their) days in
>   lament,
> Oh my son, you are its...noble son, what have you
>   to do with its tears!
> Oh Nanna, you are its...noble son, what have you
>   to do with its tears!
> The verdict of the assembly cannot be turned back,
> The word commanded by Enlil knows no overturning,
> Ur was granted kingship, it was not granted an
>   eternal reign,
> Since days of yore when the land was founded to
>   (now) when people have multiplied,
> Who has (ever) seen a reign of kingship that is
>   everlasting!
> Its kingship, its reign has been cut off, he is
>   aggrieved!
> Oh my Nanna, be not aggrieved, depart from your
>   city."

So Sin does depart from Ur, and in consequence the enemy hordes pour in to carry out their work of destruction. Perhaps Sin had not counted on this; in any event, he is so appalled when his own temple, Ekishnugal, is desecrated, that he goes back before Enlil to plead once again for mercy. This time Enlil is responsive, and promises a divine blessing on its restoration:

> May Ur be built in joy, may (its) people bow before
>   you,
> At its base may there be abundance, may Ashnan
>   dwell by its side,
> At its crown may there by joy, may Utu rejoice by
>   its side,
> Its dining table, may the abundance of Ashnan
>   embrace,
> May Ur, the city blessed by An, be restored for you.

The text ends with a statement of Sin's return, a prayer that divine wrath may now be directed against Ur's enemies, and a plea for continuing mercy on the city.

311

The reader of this pathetic lament is overwhelmed by Ur's sorrow. Jerusalem's exiles were not the only
ancient people who sang of bitter fate (Psalm 137;/cf.
Lamentations), for there must have been innumerable
poems like the one that we have just read, pouring out
grief for a beloved fallen city.

What is so remarkable absent from this poem is a
sense of moral responsibility. It mentions no reason
in the behavior of the inhabitants of Sumer or Ur that
requires their punishment, nor does it depict the god's
decree in terms of the city's blame. Their decree is
utterly irrational and arbitrary. Although the patron
god, Sin, pleads for his city, he departs from it in
the hour of crisis, precipitating the collapse of its
defenses, once he is convinced that his plea can have
no effect and he is no longer responsible for its fate.

(b) A biblical unicum: Israel is constituted
historically rather than mythically

On the plane of theology, biblical religion
recognized only one god. Quite apart from theoretical
speculation as to the possible existence of other
deities, which might have been acknowledged in a formal
way (the Israelites would not have understood the
abstraction, "existence"), the Israelites committed
themselves in operative loyalty to only one god, Yahweh.
(Here we leave aside apostates and compromizers, whose
religion fell below its potential.) In their covenantal religion, only one god could be tolerated. Only
one god was God; he alone was important because he
was in control of their lives.

More and more, their understanding of this only
god who alone was God expanded and grew, developing
eventually into a theoretical monotheism which denied
absolutely the existence of other gods. The Israelites
came to make him responsible for the history of other
nations as well as their own. He was Lord of the whole
world, absolute creator of all things and master of
human history. Nothing was outside his knowledge or
control -- not even the evil that he deplored.

Corresponding to its monotheistic conception of
God was Israel's radically historical conception of
themselves. They defined themselves not in terms of

mythic essentiality, but in terms of historical experience.[41] Throughout their history, Yahweh performed
many mighty acts, but it was the experience of deliverance from Egyptian bondage through Yahweh's mighty act
of salvation (Exodus 14) that constituted them to be
what, in patriarchal promise, they were destined to
be, i.e., his people in time and history. The Israelites remembered that previously they had been just a
wandering group of tribes, without place and land and
home.

Thus the remarkable confession of Deut. 25:5-8:

A wandering Aramean was my father; and he
went down to Egypt and sojourned there,
few in number; and there he became a nation,
great, mighty, and populous. And the Egyptians treated us harshly, and afflicted us,
and laid upon us hard bondage. Then we
cried to Yahweh the god of our fathers, and
Yahweh heard our voice, and saw our affliction, our toil, and our oppression; and
Yahweh brought us out of Egypt with a
mighty hand and an outstretched arm, with
great terror, with signs and wonders; and
he brought us into this place and gave us
this land, a land flowing with milk and
honey.

Before the event of the exodus, Canaan belonged to the
Canaanites; for Israel it was the land of promise, not
the land of possession. They were a slave people,
having no real existence in terms of historical self-
awareness prior to this founding event in their history. It was therefore God's act in historical time
that constituted them to be a people -- his people.
Inasmuch as they first became a people related to
this god, Yahweh, in terms of historical event, historical event continued to be significantly filled
with his will and presence as they moved from promise
toward fulfillment. In settling the land of Palestine,
they entered into a partial fulfillment of the promise --
and it is this that they celebrated in the "Credo"
of Deuteronomy. But the condition of the promise was
never finally satisfied, hence it was never completely
fulfilled. Because of their persistent backsliding,
the promise of land and abundant peoplehood was ever
held before them as an eschatological ideal, to which
they were called and by which they were attracted.[42]

Here we identify the origin and theoretical basis
of biblical eschatology. The people of Israel, historically constituted, continued to order their lives in
terms of a not-yet attained goal. Not only did they
strive after proximate goals -- those that could immediately come in covenantal living -- but after an ultimate, transcendental purpose. Thus their teleology was
eschatological. The ultimate perfection that they
sought was first of all qualitative, not quantitative.
That is, they looked for it in time, rather than at
the end of time. Biblical eschatology involves historical striving. It challenges a specific people in
a particular land, within the framework of a particular
historical situation. Yet its broadest perspective
includes all peoples in every land, within the framework of ever-changing historical contexts. This is
because "Israel" lives historically before God from
ʿôlām to ʿôlām. The meaning of this is not, "from
eternity to eternity," but "from time's remotest
beginnings to time's remotest continuation." The
radical historicality of biblical peoplehood reaches
out to fill all time and space.

In the final analysis, then, the correct way to
state the essential difference between nonbiblical
religion and biblical religion is this: Israel's
cultural neighbors were capable of making a place
for divine action in historical event, but only Israel
was capable of seeing a significant role for man.
Furthermore, it was Israel's unique understanding of
history as personalistic interaction between the one
God, Yahweh, and a special people, Israel, that gave
history the cohesion of purpose. History, for them,
is neither the meaningless convergency of chance nor
the irrational determinism of fate, but a meaningful
dialogue between God as the lord of history and man as
its responsible actor, ever reaching forward to perfection.

(2)   The biblical understanding of time

Time is the arena of history, along with space.
Chronological time is, in fact, another dimension of
space, as Einstein's relativity theory has taught us.
It is an abstraction by which we gauge movement. All
spatially limited beings are in constant motion, which
is comprehended in terms of chronological sequence;

314

i.e., quantitative time. As we human beings move from one event to another, we are in time, and to the extent that our movement is teleological (i.e., purposeful), it adds to time an element of eschatological significance. This temporal movement is set upon the background of space, so that every temporal event occurs in a particular place. But the place is the given, while time provides openness. Place defines contingency, limitedness, conditionedness, finiteness; time opens up a contingent freedom that reaches out to incontingency. The Bible is the only sacred book that takes the interaction of these two elements seriously.[43]

(a) Yahweh's sovereignty over time

It should not surprise us to find that the Bible affirms God's sovereignty over time. Genesis 1, the priestly creation story, does not claim that God made time. Since time is an abstration, it cannot be created. But it is an aspect of the order and structure of reality, ready to be put into the service of God in his creative work of ordering and structuring his universe. It should be noted that creation does not just occur all at once: it happens over six days, with the climax of divine rest on a seventh. The days of creation were surely no ordinary calendar days at the beginning of time -- as popular tradition supposes. Nor were they symbolic of extended geological periods -- an idea concocted by biblicistic apologists as a means of reconciling the Bible with science, but without exegetical warrant. "Day one," "day two," etc., provide a framework of meaning, showing that there is logical progression in God's perfect work of creation. In a sense, the world is always at "day one," at "day two," at "day three," etc., just as it is always moving toward fulfillment in "day seven."

As we look carefully at Genesis 1, we observe that God is doing three distinct things in order to produce order from primordial chaos:

(1) He separates distinct entities from the surrounding mass: light from darkness; waters above from waters below; dry land from sea; light-bearers from one another; each species of animal life "according to its kind"; the higher animals and man from other life;

315

(2) He classifies orders and species, providing identities and names;

(3) He assigns functions ("light-bearers" to rule day and night, man to rule the animals, etc.)

It is in an apocryphal book, Sirach, that we find one of the most reflective statements concerning God's sovereignty over time. In Ecclus. 39: 15-21, 33-34 we read:

> Let these be your words of thanksgiving:
> "All that the Lord has made is very good;
>   all that he commands will happen in due
>   time."
> No one should ask, "What is this?" or "Why
> is that?"
> At the proper time all such questions will
>   be answered.
> When he spoke the water stood up like a
>   heap, and his word created reservoirs
>   for it.
> When he commands, his purpose if fulfilled,
>   and no one can thwart his saving power.
> He sees the deeds of all mankind; there is
>   no hiding from his gaze.
> From the beginning to the end of time he
>   keeps watch, and nothing is too
>   marvellous for him.
> No one should ask, "What is this?" or "Why
>   is that?" Everything has been created
>   for its own purpose.
>
> . . . .
>
> All the works of the Lord are good, and
>   he supplies every need as it occurs.
> No one should say, "This is less good
>   than that," for all things prove good
>   at their proper time. (NEB)

Thus for Sirach, every created thing exists within a temporal pattern that is positively congenial to its salutory existence. The responsibility of man is (1) to recognize this and praise God for it; and (2) to adopt behavior suitable to the particular time and circumstance.

It is ironic that this authentically Hebraic statement got left outside the Hebrew canon while one that is riddled with non-Hebraic influence made it in. We are thinking of Qoheleth, who adopts a Greek attitude in denying that time has any significance for man, even while it remains under divine purpose and control. This is throughout his book, called Ecclesiastes, but comes to focus especially at the beginning of chapter 3. Here is a list of particular "times", each with a special purpose, but negating one another in a pattern of adversative parallelism:

> For everything there is a season, and a time
>   for every matter under heaven:
>
> a time to be born, and a time to die;
> a time to plant, and a time to pluck up
>   what is planted;
> a time to kill, and a time to heal;
> a time to break down, and a time to build
>   up;
> a time to weep, and a time to laugh;
> a time to mourn, and a time to dance;
> a time to cast away stones, and a time
>   to gather stones together;
> a time to embrace, and a time to refrain
>   from embracing;
> a time to seek, and a time to lose;
> a time to keep, and a time to cast away;
> a time to rend, and a time to sew;
> a time to keep silence, and a time to speak;
> a time to love, and a time to hate;
> a time for war, and a time for peace.
>
> What gain has the worker from his toil? I
> have seen the business that God has given to
> the sons of men to be busy with. He has
> made everything beautiful in its time; also
> he has put eternity in man's mind, yet so
> that he cannot find out what God has done
> from the beginning to the end. I know that
> there is nothing better for them than to be
> happy and enjoy themselves as long as they
> live; also that it is God's gift to man that
> every one should eat and drink and take
> pleasure in all his toil. I know that what-
> ever God does endures for ever; nothing can
> be added to it, nor anything taken from it;
> God has made it so, in order that men should
> fear before him. That which is, already has
> been; that which is to be, already has been;

and God seeks what has been driven away
(vv. 1-15).

Qoheleth is listing categories, not just of customary and habitual activities, but of teleologically directed actions. By balancing the one against the other
and by including trivial matters with weighty ones, he
seems deliberately to underscore a radical negation of
purpose. His recommendation is to be happy with what
one has, as the moment may give it. There is no use
striving; nothing that man may do can change the
purpose of God.[44]

Because this passage denies the significance of
human striving while affirming God's sovereignty over
time, it stands outside the mainstream of biblical
thought, challenging it rather than giving it a richer
dimension.

(b) Time sacramentalized in the Sabbath

Commandment IV: "Remember the sabbath day, to
keep it holy. Six days shalt thou labor, and do all
thy work; but the seventh day is a sabbath to Yahweh
thy god; in it thou shalt not do any work, thou, or
thy son, or thy daughter, thy manservant, or thy
maidservant, or thy cattle, or the sojourner who is
within thy gates; for in six days Yahweh made heaven
and earth, the sea, and all that is in them, and
rested the seventh day; therefore Yahweh blessed the
sabbath day and hallowed it." (Ex. 20:8-11)

Deut. 5:12-15 begins with "Observe" instead of
"remember, and concludes with a sharply different
movitation clause: "that your manservant and your
maidservant may rest as well as you." It continues
with the admonition, "You shall remember that you were
a servant in the land of Egypt, and that Yahweh your
god brought you out thence with a mighty hand and an
outstretched are; therefore Yahweh your god commanded
you to keep the sabbath day." This passage has often
been praised -- and deservedly so -- for its humanitarian grounding of religion. It provides a clear
basis for Jesus' dictum, "The sabbath was made for man,
not man for the sabbath." (Mark 2:27). But we must
not neglect to see that its real aim is to gear ritual
to Heilsgeschichte , God's saving deeds in history.

318

Israel is to keep the Sabbath not only out of sympathy for exhausted "servants" (= slaves), but out of remembrance that Yahweh has led them out of slavery.[45] Thus one day weekly is set aside in order to remember all the days of God's work in history, and specifically the great day that set them free (cf. Ex. 14:30).

The Exodus version of the sabbath commandment is directly related to the priestly story of creation, culminating in the statement of Gen. 2:1-3:

> Thus the heavens and the earth were finished, and all the host of them. And on the seventh day God finished his work which he had done, and he rested on the seventh day from all his work which he had done. So God blessed the seventh day and hallowed it, because on it God rested from all his work which he had done in creation.

Christians at first observed the Jewish sabbath, but eventually shifted to the first day of the week, "the Lord's day," to commemorate the resurrection.[46] No doubt the intensifying hostility between Jews and Christians hastened this development, particularly as Christians sought ways in which to dramatize their liberation from the acerbity of Torah rigorism. Without entering into the pro's and con's of this question, it can safely be said that the Christians were at least right in perceiving that no one day on the calendar is sacrosanct in itself, and that therefore, if sufficient cause arises, sabbath observance may rightly be shifted to another day. What present-day Christians -- alas -- do tend to forget is that the Sabbath is a precious and effective symbol of something very basic in biblical religion; viz., God's lordship over time.

As has been said above, the Sabbath is an eschatological symbol of perfection. By setting aside one day in seven, Israel was confessing that all days are God's, that all of time is potentially sacred.[47]

(c) Quantitative _versus_ qualitative time

Distinctions between an "outer" history and an "inner" history, between linear history and cyclical history, between "man's time" and "God's time," or between "secular time" and "sacred time" fall wide of the mark....The only ready-to-hand polarity that seems really applicable is a contrast between what we would call two different approaches to the identical temporal phenomena: the quantitative approach and the qualitative approach. The first sees time as a succession of essentially commensurate entities -- a given number of days or months or years. These temporal entities are susceptible to being spanned by the same measuring staff, hence can be tabulated mathematically. This is time as a quantum, comparable to space....The other approach sees time as a succession of essentially unique, incommensurate experiences. The day is an apprehensional unity, primitively conceived according to the event that gives it its character. Because such an event is revelatory of something more ultimate than the finite concerns of creaturely man, it points beyond itself to an eschatological fulfillment in an ultimately decisive day of divine action.

In ancient Israel...one God was Lord of history. History therefore was filled with positive potentiality. It had a goal and a meaning. Temporal event was seen as an ever-renewed opportunity and challenge for bringing this goal to realization. In the Old Testament the quantitative approach to time provided the framework of continuity, allowing for the interconnectedness of specific events. But it was the qualitative approach that gave historical event its revelatory significance, keeping Hebrew man continually alert to the possibility of the creatively new in his relationship to God and his fellow men. (Fron YTT, 343-45)

When a unique or unparalleled event occurs, there is by definition nothing whatever to which it can be compared, hence the event in question becomes revelatory of "the other" -- even of "the wholly other." But constantly the human mind strives to offset the dread of confronting something entirely unique by reducing it to categories of intellectual understanding, either by way of measurement or by way of comparison.... Quantifying measurement enters into use as an abstractive process by which one "time" is correlated with others purely on the basis of the passage of moving objects (the sun, moon, stars, timepieces, and the like) within a regular orbit or recurring routine. So also the qualifying approach that reduces temporal experience to analogies. Identifying a particular day for its special characteristics, the analytical mind makes intellectual and then linguistic comparisons with other days perceived to be somehow like it....The fact is that each unique historical experience, bordering on absoluteness and incontingency, nevertheless remains contingent and thus vulnerable to the leveling process involved in identification and categorization. (From S. J. De Vries, "Observations on Quantitative and Qualitative Time in Wisdom and Apocalyptic," John G. Gammie et al., edd., Israelite Wisdom, 1978, pp. 267f.)[48]

It seems very apparent that the priests were more prepared to think of time in a quantitative than in qualitative terms. It is they who theologized about history as a chronological quantum, but most of their concerns were quite practical. They had to administer a calendar...and regulate the cultic apparatus. It is they, therefore, who are found speaking of durations, of specific periods of time. When they define a particular day or time, it is with respect to its cultic character. Certainly the priests were very much aware of the distinctiveness of certain days, and expecially the great days of festival, for their greatest concern was to guard the sacred days, marking them off from all the other days on the calendar. But while they were ready to recognize -- rather, eager to emphasize -- the specialness of the holy days and seasons, they displayed little interest in unique historical event. It was mainly the bearers of Israel's charismatic tradition -- continuing from the time when the nation came into being, then passed on toward extinction, only to come to life again as Yahweh's new creation -- who recorded the significance of unique historical event. To them, time was not a phenomenon that levels every human experience, but something that lends it purpose and distinctiveness. Every day has its own special character. Every day is potentially revelatory. Every day presents a new choice, a new opportunity, a new responsibility. In each day man is at work, but God is at work too. (From YTT, 346)

In the Hebrew scriptures the quantitative measurement of time and the qualitative identification of time are joined in dynamic tension, helping man see his place in nature and in history. He belongs to the world of universality, but, in personalistic relation to his covenant God, he belongs more importantly to the world of unique events, the succession of opportunities ("days") that make him aware of an ever imminent responsibility to respond to the new crisis of God's address. It is this dialogue and interaction between

a transcendent but infinitely concerned Deity, and a
finite but eminently responsible humanity, that creates
the Bible's most special contribution to mankind's continuing effort to apprehend the meaning of historical
existence. (From YTT, 349-50)

(3)   The theological relevance of biblical historiography

What is the Christian theologian's concern with
Israel's history? From the perspective of both marcionizing liberalism and docetizing fundamentalism:
nothing.   Perchance a romantistic empathizing can find
some affinity in the prophets, in the psalmists, in the
great "heroes of the faith"; but otherwise Israel's
history is irrelevant.49 It is only the Christian
theology which acknowledges Israel's God to be the God
and Father of our Lord Jesus Christ that can also see
continuity from Israel's history to a Christian's
history with God. From this point of view, the history
of the church is just an extension of the history of
Israel. Both are rooted in faith in the same one God;
both are experienced by the same covenant people.50

What is the Christian's concern with Israel's
historiography, then? Surely, neither for antiquarian
curiosity nor for dogmatic substantiation. Since the
Old Testament records a historically-derived and a
historically-related revelation, its historiographic
writings require in a very special way to be seen as
theological witnesses to what God has done, both in
judging and in saving, on behalf of his covenant people.
The divine revelation that is known in historical
event has been received in the minds and hearts of an
experiencing, believing, and witnessing people. The
historiographic records that they have handed down to
us are an indispensable model of what revelatory
historical event can continue to be. They serve to prepare God's people to be receptive to analogous revelatory events in the ever-recurring present that is part
of their future with God.

(a)   Its antiquity and factual realism

Two special things need to be noted about the historiographic books of the Old Testament.[51] Each is
equally remarkable, when judged from the perspective
of contemporary accomplishments. One is their relative
antiquity; the other is their astounding factual realism.

When we speak of historiographic literature, we are
referring to such as makes perceptive, responsible use of
sources, traces an organic line of development from beginning to end, accounts for cause and effect in a
realistic way, and offers a believable, basically reliable image of the human persons who were involved in
the events described. Taking this in a strict sense,
it leaves out the mythological elements that are embedded in isolated biblical passages, as well as such an
epic account as the Pentateuchal narration, which only
peripherally records historical facts. Also margin-
ally related to historical factuality is the genre of
prophet legend, which is often schematic and offers a
large place to the element of wonder or miracle.[52]
But the Old Testament makes abundant use of two other
genres, the hero saga and the ethnological saga, which,
because of their dominant sociological interest, are
generally closely related to historical fact.[53]

When we turn our attention from isolated passages
to widely expansive narratives from the period of the
kingship, it is entirely different. Here we observe
the dominance of a genuinely historiographic interest.
This is true especially of (1) the history of David's
accession, extending from I Samuel 17 through II
Samuel 5; (2) the throne-succession narrative, extending from II Samuel 6 through I Kings 2; and (3) the
deuteronomistic history, a redactional arrangement of
sources extending from Joshua through II Kings. To
these we may add two notable postexilic historiographic
writings with a somewhat diminished sense of historical
factuality, viz., the Chronicler's adaptation of the
deuteronomistic history, and Ezra-Nehemiah.

When we look at the throne-succession narrative,
we are especially struck by its relative antiquity.
This was almost certainly composed by one man who lived
during the reign of Solomon (ca. 970-930 B.C.).[54] The
deuteronomistic history was prepared in stages, coming
to a culmination during the Babylonian exile, but its
earliest stage most likely dates from the time of
Hezekiah, ca. 700 B.C.[55] When we think that the famous
Greek historiographic compositions date from the fourth
and third centuries, B.C., the contrast is impressive.

As much as five or six centuries before the classical
Greek achievement, the Hebrews were writing real history.
All the essential elements of authentic historiography
are present in these two compositions. They make responsible use of source material. They maintain a uni-
fying theme of interpretation. They effectively identify
cause and effect in the historical events narrated.
They aim at a realistic image of the personages involved. Why could Israel achieve this? Because they
took history seriously. Man was, for them, no tool of
the gods, a puppet in a cosmic show. To be sure, God
was present as well as man, but not in such a way as to
reduce man's action to insignificance.

(b)   Its theological perspective

In spite of what has been said, this historiographic
literature retains the quality of theological testimony.[56]
Where imaginative, peripherally historical source-
materials are employed, God's action is naively recorded.
Otherwise the divine factor appears in numerous asides,
summations, and special programmatic interpretations
(e.g., II Kings 17).[57]

Everywhere, one single viewpoint holds the narration together: Man acts responsibly and purposefully
because God is simultaneously acting and holding him
accountable. This is what makes biblical historiography so different from, say, the Greek histories.
They were composed, frankly, to celebrate MAN. In
order that the heroism of Greece's saviors should not
be forgotten, they told their stories. The throne-
succession narrative is different, and so too is the
deuteronomistic history. We see that the first is not
written to glorify David, for it frankly states his
failings and weaknesses. Nor does it glorify Solomon,
though it does aim to legitimize his rule on the basis
of two factors: (1) the ineluctability of divine
punishment on David through his own blood-line, and
(2) the tenacity of the divine intent to install Solomon
in compensation for the wrong done to Uriah. In the
case of the deuteronomistic history, Israel is again
not glorified; rather, the deeds of the kings of both
its realms are told to explain why, first the northern
and then the southern, realm collapsed -- all with the
purpose of explaining and justifying Israel's judgment.
If the biblical histories celebrate anything, it is

GOD. Here lies an impressive element of transcendence. The biblical histories are precious theological testimonies to biblical religion brought
to reality in historical event.

(4)   Divine causation: natural and supernatural

In a previous section, we explained that classical
Hebraism did not allow room for a dualistic origin of
evil, including the notion of demonic temptation to
sin.[58] True to monotheistic personalism, the transcendental reality in every experiential event was
attributed to the presence and purposeful will of
Yahweh. Thus he grew in the minds of his devotees to
become more than the god of Israel. More and more
clearly, he became the God of all the world -- the God
of nature and the God of history. Although he was
not one with nature (pantheism), he was ever-present
in nature. Nothing that happens in man's world,
whether good or evil, occurs without his will. When
the biblical writers can offer no instrumental explanation for an astounding event, they are apt to say,
"the spirit of God came."[59] Understandably, the most
inexplicable and frightening occurrences reveal him
the more. In nature, this may come as a tempest, a
fire, a famine, a plague of locusts, or a sore sickness. In history, it may come as an army of plundering mauauders. Even when pitiably victimized, the
people of the Old Testament continue to interpret
locust plagues as "the day of Yahweh," and to see the
invading Assyrians as "the rod in Yahweh's hand"
(Joel 1-2; Isaiah 10).

Surely this will not satisfy the rational mind
of modern man, which has been taught by Aristotle and
Newton to look for non-mythical causes underlying every
phenomenon. (No one who has been trained according to
modern intellectual standards acts responsibly when he
takes refuge in the dualistic system that acknowledges
scientific causality for one set of phenomena while
seeking purely supernatural causes for another set of
phonomena.) Nevertheless, we need to keep in mind
that biblical theology does not operate from the monistic presuppositions of its starkly mythological
environment. It does not see God as part of the cosmic
process, and therefore the only effective factor of
causality. This is rightly rebuked by modern man,

wherever it comes to expression in superstititous
claims, but the Bible has transcended this mythic
concept -- not to the point of dismissing God, but
by recognizing both man and God as responsible, effective actors in the cosmic drama. This is why, for minds
that have been trained to look for scientific explanations, it is still right and proper to believe in God.
It is right to say that man caused something -- or
that certain natural factors caused something -- while
simultaneously affirming that God's will is effectively
present and operative. This is becuase he is the
necessary being that impinges on every finite contingency. Contingent beings operate within the finite
laws of their own inner essence, yet are constantly in
creaturely relationship with an ultimate incontingency impinging on them all. To say this in our philosophical language was, of course, far beyond the capa-
bility of the biblical writers; yet it provided the
actual, naive assumption of their world-view, nonetheless.

(5) Miracle and wonder in the Old Testament[60]

        Three preliminary remarks are in order to a serious
discussion of miracle and wonder in the Old Testament.
First, let it be understood that these elements are
rife in the contemporary culture. This means that a
heightened supernaturalism is far from distinctive
of the Bible, but manifests itself as a prolific
growth within the popular piety of the entire ancient
world. In other words, it was a widespread linguistic
and ideological convention of the time to attribute
natural and historical events directly to supernatural
causation.

        This observation leads to our second remark, to
the effect that the Bible, and especially the Old
Testament, is remarkable for its restraint in developing the elements of miracle and wonder for symbolizing
the presence and purpose of God. This restraint was,
however, due more to the Bible's highly developed sense
of historicality than to any want of imagination concerning the reality of the supernatural world.

        Our third preliminary remark is that the Bible
understands everything that happens as involving a level
of divine causation. Everything that happens is filled

with God's power and is effected by his will. This means
that what we call "miracle" is in no way essentially
different from ordinary events, except in its unusual-
ness. Whenever the unusual happens -- even Saul's
military enthusiasm (I Samuel 11) or David's musical
inspiration (I Samuel 16) -- this is attributed to
God's "spirit," or to some other symbolical manifestation of his power.

Before we proceed further, a rather serious popular
misunderstanding needs to be cleared up. A willingness
to acknowledge that specific biblical passages may be
introducing imaginative, non-literal elements is in no
way inimical to either the historical rootedness of the
Bible or the predominance of solidly historical factuality. This all depends on the precise nature and
intent of the individual passage. As has been empha-
sized, the writing of realistic historiography, with all
its theological perspective, represents one of the Old
Testament's early and notable achievements. Even though
such material does not have the direct aim of presenting
so-called "objective" history, as defined by modern
academic standards, it does provide a reliable account
of historical events in their organic interconnectedness, for this is directly instrumental to its theological function of witnessing to Israel's historical
interaction with God. At the same time it is clear
that the Bible (the New Testament as well as the Old)
feels free to incorporate highly imaginative materials
whenever this suits its need and purpose. Although it
eschews raw anthropomorphic myth, it does go so far,
in special circumstances, as to incorporate fragments
of prebiblical myth. It also makes frequent use of rebaptized mythic symbolism and analogy. Most generally,
it interprets the divine action within a given event
with the simple statement that Yahweh did or said
something -- perhaps even that he "thought" something
(as if a human writer could actually know what the Deity
was thinking!).[61] To incorporate at certain points
the element of explicit wonder or miracle is simply
an extension of this same creative and imaginative freedom. That is to say, it is entirely a matter of the
writer's choice of the most appropriate and evocative
imagery and symbolism, which of course needed to be
commensurate with the particular literary genre that
was being used.

With these points in mind, we need to look directly
at the materials that feature wonder and miracle, observing an often forgotten distinction, viz., that in
some passages it is God who is performing a wondrous

327

act, while in other passages it is a God-filled man who is performing it. We shall see that the largest proportion of the passages in question speak only of God's act, not man's. It is misleading to speak of God's action as miracle. It is simply an anthropomorphizing liberty, not essentially different from the direct description of the Deity in terms of anthropomorphic attributes. What may be stated as a qualitative description of Yahweh is here presented in a narrative of divine action.[62]

Old Testament narrative materials describing the action of God fall into two distinct groups. The first is subbiblical; the second represents normative biblical personalism. Both are designed to convey a sense of mysterium tremendum, a response to the awesome presence of God in human life.

A. The first group, which we have described as subbiblical, consists of a very limited number of special passages. Here prebiblical myth has been incorporated within an orthodox interpretive framework, with little or no modification. These are virtually all in the J prehistory, at Genesis 2-3, Gen. 6: 1-4, and Gen. 11:1-11. They feature the forming of man from clay, the primordial garden with its four rivers, the mystical trees, the taking of woman from man's rib, the fertility-providing serpent, the "sons of God" begetting monsters, a jealous Yahweh destroying the tower of Babel. A number of less lapidary elements drawn from prebiblical myth have been introduced into the J flood story in Genesis 6-8.[63] In addition, we encounter undigested prebiblical myth incorporated into lyrical poetry at Josh. 10:12-14 (the standing still of the sun and moon).[64] These explicitly mythological elements have been rendered quite innocuous in the presence of developing Yahwism, which dares to present them as they are because there is apparently no longer any serious danger of their being taken literally. Throughout the Old Testament, mythological allusions continue to be presented in a purely metaphorical way. This enriches the pictorial power of the language of praise. Yahweh, having conquered all the heathen gods, has commandeered their language of myth, which henceforth serves as an evocative expression of his own holiness and power.

B. Thus we come to the second group of passages in which God is depicted as acting in a wondrous way. Although myth has been reduced to allusion, daring anthropomorphic and theophanous images continue to convey the effective power of the divine presence.

It is essential to our purpose to list these passages according to their specific genres, for this reveals their life-setting, function, and purpose. They may be identified as follows:

1. Theophanies (see Chapter I):[65]

    Abram's covenant ritual, Genesis 15
    The destruction of Sodom, Genesis 19
    The ladder to heaven, E in Genesis 28
    The burning bush, J in Exodus 3
    The deliverance at the sea, J and P
        in Exodus 14
    The Sinai theophany, J, E, and P in
        Exodus 19-40
    The cloud of glory, Numbers 10
    The gift of quails, Numbers 11
    The commander of Yahweh's army,
        Josh. 5:13-15
    Appearances to Gideon, Judg. 6:11-27,
        36-40
    Appearance to Samson's mother, Judg.
        13:2ff
    Song of Deborah, Judges 5

2. Epiphanies (see Chapter I):

    Appearances to Abram, J and E in
        Genesis 15, P in Genesis 17
    Appearance to Hagar, J in Genesis
        16, E in Genesis 21
    The Mamre visitors, Genesis 18
    Isaac's sacrifice, Genesis 22
    Appearance at Bethel, J in Genesis 28
    Appearance at Mahanaim, Gen. 32:1-2
    Appearance at Peniel, Gen. 32:22ff
    Appearance at Bethel, P in Gen. 35:9-15
    Appearance to Jacob, Gen. 46:1-7
    Appearance to Moses, E in Ex. 3:1-15
    Call of Moses, J in Exodus 4, P in Ex.
        6:1-13
    Water at Marah, Ex. 15:22-25
    The gift of Manna, Exodus 16
    Water at Meribah, Ex. 17:1-7 (JE),
        Num. 20:1-13 (P)
    Appearances to Joshua, Josh. 1:1-9,
        7:10-15, 8:1-2, 18
    The angel of Bochim, Judg. 2:1-5
    Appearances to Gideon, Judges 7

329

3. Holy-war stories (rising to a level of exaggerated supernaturalism in late examples)

   Joshua 10, 11
   Judges 4, 7, 20
   I Sam. 7: 2ff, 11:1ff., 14:16ff.
   II Sam. 23:9-12
   II Kings 19:25 (= Isa. 37:36)
   II Chronicles 22

4. Divine punishment stories

   Yahweh rejects Israel, Numbers 14
   Yahweh punishes Korah, Dathan, and Abiram,
      Numbers 16
   The fiery serpent, Num. 21:4-9
   Pestilence on David, II Sam. 24:1-17
   Sickness on Uzziah, II Chron. 26:16-21

5. Cultic legends

   Fire from the altar, Lev. 10:1-3
   Israel's sin and the zeal of Phinehas,
      Num. 25:1-13
   Ark legends: Joshua 3, 6, I Samuel 5-6,
      II Sam. 6:6-9

6. Ethnological saga

   The Rizpah saga, II Sam. 21:1-14

7. Prophet legends

   Charismatic designation story, I Samuel 9-10
   Prophet-authorization story, I Kings 19:1-18
   Instrumental fulfillment story, II Kings 3

8. The Jonah _mashal_

9. Apocalyptic

     All these narratives feature the irruptive, often
menacing, presence of God. In the isolated Rizpah saga,
historical factuality is probably present in the famine
which sets the scene; but this is peripheral to the
structure of the story, and in any case its attribution
to Yahweh does not exceed the normal bounds of Hebraic
ideology, which identifies God's presence and will in
every natural calamity (see II Sam. 24:1ff.). It may
not be beside the point to look for a historical kernel

in some of the other types of narrative, expecially in theophanies such as the J version of the crossing of the sea (Exodus 14), where the wind and the sea reflect a decisive and clearly remembered historical setting. Nevertheless, an exaggerated curiosity about the historicality of a narrative like this is entirely out of keeping with its kerygmatic intent, which is simply to articulate the awesomeness of Yahweh's numinous presence in the foundational experience of Israel's deliverance. Thus we ought to avoid the method of supernaturalistic rationalism, which probes for a scientific "fact" in these accounts, often setting aside as idle fancy the text's own obvious concern for the centrality of God's decisive action.[66]

In late Old Testament literature, we encounter a genre that has no ostensible historical basis whatever. Actually, we have but one example of it -- the <u>mashal</u> (extended parable) of Jonah.[67] Jonah is no more factually real than the Good Samaritan of Jesus' parable (the hero is fictionally identified with a historical prophet mentioned in II Kings 14:25). Besides the fish that swallows Jonah and spits him up, the story is full of marvelous features: a prophet of Yahweh who runs away when told to deliver a message; pagan sailors who fear Yahweh; a storm that seeks only Jonah as a victim; a wicked city that repents in a single day; the cucumber vine and the worm. A literalistic interpretation sacrifices the powerful message of this book, which is full of precious irony, and is told for the sole purpose of holding up the mirror to late-Jewish smugness.[68]

Finally we mention the note of sustained wonder in the events that occur within the prophetic visions and in apocalyptic. These are patently ecstatic and imaginative. They are futuristic, hence have no direct relationship to narrated historical event.[69]

II

What we have said thus far is intended for clearing the ground for the second main group of Old Testament narratives in which wonder or miracle is an essential element. In this group, a human being -- some charismatic person -- performs a wondrous act. It is only here that we are warranted in speaking about "miracles." Yet it is essential to realize that to the Hebrew narrators these particular acts would in no wise be understood as "abrogations of natural law," as we

generally define miracles. Each of these stories is
told to convey an impression of God's power to work
in and through God-filled men. These persons perform
these wondrous acts in order to reveal God's presence
and power within them. They are themselves symbols of
God's ideal presence in every man and in every human
event, so that we can make an appropriate comparison
with the symbolization of Yahweh's sovereignty over all
of time in the Sabbath, of his ownership over the whole
world in the promise of the Holy Land, and of his
elective love toward the entire human race in his election of Israel. In other words, whatever element of
historical factuality may underlie each individual
narrative belonging to this group, their intent is symbolic. They witness to divine power in general, but
they also teach and admonish. Didactic and admonitory,
they provide edifying examples of how God's power is
ideally present in human life. They are theologically
potent, whether or not they draw directly upon historical event.

It is important to see that all the stories belonging to this category can be assigned to the broad
genre of "legend," which is defined as any imaginative account of exemplary action.[70] As the men of
these legends were filled with God, so all men are
called to be filled with God's power. There are three
main sub-types, reflecting a meaningful development
from earlier to later forms:

    1. Hero legends

        The Samson cycle, Judges 13-16[71]
        The Davidic hero-legend, I Samuel 17
          (interwoven with a hero-saga)[72]
        Joseph as an interpreter of dreams,
          Genesis 40-41

    2. Prophet legends

        a. Within the Pentateuch:

            The plagues of Egypt cycle (featuring
              Moses as prophet), Exodus 7-11[73]
            A prophetic controversy story, Numbers 12
            Prophet legitimation stories,
               Num. 11:24-30
            A power-demonstration story (Balaam),
               Numbers 22-24

        b. Within the deuteronomistic history:

Power-demonstration stories: I Sam.
19:18-24; II Kings 2:19-22, 23-24;
4:1-7, 8-37, 38-41, 42-44; 5:1-27;
6:1-7; 13:20-21
Prophet-legitimation stories, I Kings
13:1-32; I Kings 17:1-16, 18:1-18,
41-46; 18:21-39; II Kings 1:2-17;
6:8-23; 6:24--7:17[74]

3.   Apocalyptic legend

Daniel 1-6

What must be observed in considering this list as
a whole is that whatever charismatic persons may do is
wondrous, whether or not human and natural factors are
involved. It is especially instructive to observe
that the more highly supernaturalistic accounts show
their derivation from early, more naturalistic accounts.[75] We would have to say that Samson's marvelous exploits, such as killing a thousand Philistines with the jawbone of an ass (Judg. 15.15), is
not strictly speaking a miracle. Here a definition of
miracle as something that is impossible for a human
being would indeed apply to his exploit, even though
"natural" factors would have been operative, for it
has to be just as impossible for one man -- even a
Samson -- to kill a thousand Philistines in one great
fight as for an Elijah to bring fire from heaven or
for Elisha to make an axehead float. On the other
hand, if we define miracle as something that is contrary to the laws of nature, very few of the events
recorded in the preceding list would qualify as
miracles. The design of all of them is to symbolize
the power of divine presence. From the biblical
point of view, there is no essential difference between Moses calling down the plagues on Pharaoh and
Samson's walking off with the gates of Gaza.   Both
are "spirit-filled" events.[76] Both speak the language
of reverential response to a numinous reality. What
marks these "miracle stories" of the Old Testament
as distinct from their widespread parallels in the
nonbiblical world is the monotheistic personalism
which they presuppose.

In the case of the apocalyptic legends of Daniel
it is the human qualities of unparalleled discretion,
fidelity, and wisdom that symbolize a special divine
presence in the book's heroes. This is a more rationalized form of charismatic power than that which

appears in the brawny exploits of a Samson and in the "magical" tricks of the prophets -- but all alike speak the language of numinous presence.

The final dictum for interpreting the Old Testament's tales of wonder and miracle is, then, that these are not important for what they <u>tell</u> but for what they <u>say</u>. They are not historiographical, but ideological. They are testimonies not to what God has done, but to what God can do.

The Old Testament language of God's symbolic presence in the wondrous is a heritage that the writers of the New Testament knew and understood.[77]

(6) Prayer and divine responsiveness

An important symbol of personalistic interaction in historical event is that of prayer and divine responsiveness. It is not only that God chooses, calls and demands. Man in his ever-present need appeals to him for deliverance, the satisfaction of basic wants, and protection from further harm. To be sure, every religion that has at least a meagre personalistic basis assumes the possibility of appeal to Deity. It is a measure of relative ideological purity if the supplicant has direct access to God's attention, rather than having to feel completely dependent on priestly ministrations and rituals. In the Old Testament, and especially New Testament religion, this notion of intense responsiveness has received rich development, reaching a climax in the image of Christ's intimacy with God as his Father.[78]

In the light of the persistence of the shallow and one-sided biblicism that insists that "prayer changes things," and especially in view of the current mania for faith-healing, it is important to guard the biblical concept of personalistic interaction from the distortions and misappropriations to which it is susceptible. These modern misconceptions are not new; they have been in the world ever since religion began. Man has always attempted to manipulate God. As personalism developed, personhood was caricatured. Because it is often possible to manipulate human persons -- which is to an extent to depersonalize them -- it was imagined that Deity could also be manipulated. Modern piety has abondoned ritual and magic, but professes to accomplish the same result with prayer.

Two things are made clear in the Bible about God's responsiveness to prayer: (1) He is ever attentive to his people's need, responding to them even before they cry to him (cf. Ex. 3:7-9); (2) He will always respond to them by giving them what they need. This awareness goes with Israel's serious appropriation of the symbol of fatherhood. Of course, divine fatherhood is balanced off by the image of divine lordship; therefore it remains clear that Yahweh will respond in his sovereign wisdom, in ways perhaps beyond man's ken. "As the heavens are higher than the earth, so are my ways higher than your ways, and my thoughts than your thoughts." (Isa. 55:9)

The Old Testament shows little development of the concept of individual prayer. Israel sees itself essentially as a social entity, hence generally depends on specially God-filled mediators to voice its requests to God. The passages that speak of mediators making intercession for the people are those that are filled with crisis; the people have covered themselves with sin and guilt, and now have nowhere else to turn. Thus Moses prays when Israel worships the golden calf (Ex. 33:12-17), or wants to return to Egypt (Num.14:13-20). Amos appeals to God because of Israel's backsliding and imminent destruction (Amos 7:1-6). In Daniel 9, Ezra 9, and Nehemiah 9, appeal to God is made because of widespread, often unnamed, apostacies. Always the expectation is that God will respond favorably; thus when even his chosen prophets fail to move him, as in Jer. 11:14-17, 14:11-12, 14:17-15:4, Ezek. 9:8-10, it is evident that Israel's wickedness has driven him to utter exasperation.

In the face of a calamity like the destruction of Jerusalem, it was easy to think that Yahweh was finished with his people forever. Yet the book called Lamentations is testimony to the fact that the survivors did not cease to believe that their prayers for relief could, and would, be heard.

The psalter is filled with public and individual laments, which are motivated entirely by the belief that Yahweh cares, Yahweh hears, Yahweh helps. The question is not if, but only when.

An especially instructive psalm-form is that which recent scholars have called the "psalm of declarative praise" (Westermann).[79] This involves an unusual degree of dynamic interaction. First the suppliant complains of his miseries, next he appeals for relief. Suddenly his pleas change to praise and thanksgiving, and these in turn to testimony. One can see this in Psalm 22, Jonah 2, and similar passages. Somewhat different is the great theophany prayer of Habakkuk 3, where the suppliant at last draws strength from remembrance of the past evidences of Yahweh's power.[80]

In polemic against foreign cults, such as Baalism, special emphasis was placed on divine responsiveness. This is the ringing theme of the prophet-authorization legend in I Kings 18:21-39 (Elijah on Mount Carmel), where the word ʿānāh, "answer," appears at several crucial places in the story's structure:

> The people did not answer him a word. (v. 21)
> "The god who answers by fire, let him be God!"
>   And all the people answered, "It is well
>   spoken!" (v. 24)
> They...called on the name of Baal,,,"O Baal, answer
>   us!" But there was no voice, and no one
>   answered. (v.26)
> They raved on...but there was no voice; no one
>   answered, no one heeded. (v. 29)
> Elijah said, "O Yahweh...let it be known this day
>   that thou art God in Israel, and that I am
>   thy servant....Answer me, O Yahweh, answer me!"
> So Yahweh answered, and the people said, "Yahweh, he is
> God, Yahweh he is God." (v. 39)[81]

Sometimes God takes a long, long time to answer -- or so it seems to those who wait. The prophet Habakkuk cries to Yahweh of violence and injustice (1:1-4), asking why, with eyes too pure to look on evil (v.12), he tolerates the wicked for a single moment. (v.13) He takes his stand in his place of watching to see what the answer will be concerning his complaint (2:1), and Yahweh answers with the admonition, "If it seem slow, wait for it; it will surely come, it will not delay." (v. 3). It is by his own righteousness that one shall live in faithfulness to God. (v. 4).

But what if God does not answer at all? Is this not the mark of one whom he has forsaken -- of one who deserves to be forsaken? Do we not read of God's enemies in II Sam. 22:42 (= Ps. 18:41), that "they looked, but there was none to save, they cried to Yahweh, but he did not answer them?" The "friends" of Job preach

336

that his boils demonstrate this to be true of him. The triumph of Job's faith is that, despite his boils, and despite the seeming unresponsiveness of God, he continued to believe that God does see, he does care, he will answer![82] He may not answer by fire; he will answer in his own way and in his own time. But he will answer. He is Israel's Lord, but also Israel's Father. Though he may seem lofty and far away, he is elusively, comfortingly near:

> Our Father who art in heaven,
> Hallowed by thy name,
> Thy kingdom come.
> Thy will be done,
>   On earth as it is in heaven.
> Give us this day our daily bread;
> And forgive us out debts,
>   As we also have forgiven our debtors;
> And lead us not into temptation,
>   But deliver us from evil.   (Matt. 6:9-13)

(7)   The end of history

(7)   The end of history
(a)   In normative biblical eschatology

Classical Hebraic thought speaks of a goal, but not of an end, to history. Within the framework of time, divine and human interaction reaches forward to an ever more perfect fulfillment. The prophets, beginning with Amos (5:18-20), announce an awesome "day of Yahweh" -- the day when history will reach its climax. I restate the following from my book, Yesterday, Today and Tomorrow:

> Since tradition clearly provides the pattern for eschatology, there is no sense in trying to assess the meaning of "the day" past and "this day" present. The future "day of Yahweh" is like any prior day in which God has confronted man. It is simply the coming day...when Yahweh will act decisively once again. At least one prophetic passage, Isa. 2:11-17, makes this explicit, beginning with the announcement, "For Yahweh Sebaoth has a day...," and concluding with the interpretive epitome, "So Yahweh alone will be exalted on that day." In the early passages, at any rate, "the day of Yahweh" is not to be understood as the termination of

337

history....The interpretive framework is
not chronological, placing this day within
or at the end of a sequence of days, but
qualifying, characterizing it as a day of
Yahweh's decisive action, in which all the
complexities and ambiguities of the present
situation are brought to a complete -- and
in this sense final -- resolution. But,
as Yahweh has often acted decisively in the
past, so there may need to be recurring days
of Yahweh in the future. In fact, "today" --
this very day -- may be a "day of Yahweh.".....
There are an intriguing variety of ways in
which the future day of Yahweh's acting...
may come to manifestation. In some passages
it is described adjectivally, in others it is
characterized by an action or event. One way
or another, it finds its essential identity
in that it is Yahweh's special day....Only
those days become actively his day on which
he manifests himself decisively and revealingly, in judgment or in salvation. (p. 341)

(b)   In the apocalyptic view of time

Continuing to quote from Yesterday, Today, and
Tomorrow, we observe a radical difference in apocalyptic:

Something different...is the method of
apocalyptic. Apocalyptic follows in the
train of the late expansions to the prophetic oracles...in which the day of Yahweh's
action often becomes so full and complex that
it loses any proximate resemblance to the
original situation of crisis. The future has
become increasingly abstracted from the present.
It is no longer an extension of the present but
an epoch of its own, detached from the present
and irrelevant to it. Chronological interests
intervene to define a duration of time lying
ahead ere Yahweh will come to act. Zech. 14:21
reflects this mentality by epitomizing the
future day as a state of being rather than
as the bearer of a decisive event....Inevitably,
the reference to a single day becomes unsuit-
able. Isa. 61:2 makes šānâ, "year," parallel
to yôm, "day." A number of eschatological
passages speak vaguely of yāmîm bāɔîm, "coming
days," or of ɔaḥᵃrît hayyāmîm, "in days after-

ward." Or they exchange "on that day"
for "in that time." Within the canonical
literature, Daniel takes the ultimate
step in equating the "time" of God's
coming with the absolute end (qēṣ). Only
by ending history can God act in it....
Taking its clue perhaps from Ps. 90:4,
fully developed apocalyptic solves the
problem of the indefinite extension of
God's yôm by declaring that "one thousand
years are as one day in the testimony of
the heavens" (Jub. 4:30; cf. Ep. Barn.
15, 2 En. 33, II Pet. 3:8). In other
words, God's time is not measured like
man's time. But this procedure emphatically divorces God from human history.
(pp. 342-43)

Although apocalyptic and apocalypticism have previously been described,[83] it is essential to clarify
the time-concept which this movement presupposes.

In its fully developed form, apocalyptic shows
three basic features: (1) bizarre symbolism borrowed
from myth; (2) strange supernatural happenings, also
borrowed from myth; and (3) an overriding concern for
the divine plan for the end time (or the end of time).
Its essential concern is not, Why is Israel so sinful? --
the question of classical prophetism. Even though a
profound sense of sinfulness does remain, the problem
of apocalyptic is, Why does Israel suffer? Here the
monotheistic election/covenant concept changes its
focus from man's integrity within the elective fellowship (man's responsibility) to God's integrity in protecting his chosen people within a hostile, apparently
unmanageable world. Accordingly, the outlook of
apocalyptic is pessimistic, speculative, and separatistic. It is occasioned by stress and despair. Its
parenetic function is simply to encourage the faithful to persevere.

As has been suggested, apocalyptic makes a radical
choice for the quantitative concept of time. It thereby hardens the divine purpose into a plan, while denying the teleology of human striving. History thereby
becomes irrelevant. Time is abstracted, history is
segregated (dualism) and periodized (futurism).

Students of the Bible can make no headway in applying biblical theology to modern concepts of time and
history unless they fully recognize how drastically
apocalyptic has altered the classical biblical model.

Excursus on the reversal of saving history in Daniel 9

Modern-day apocalypticists have a field-day with
this chapter, using it as the basis for ingenious cal-
culations for the end of the world.[84] Like everything
else in the Bible, it requires a diligent historical
exegesis if it is to yield its true meaning to us.[85]
One should be aware of the fact that it draws heavily
on two special passages from the Old Testament. The
first of these is Jer. 25:11-12, predicting a seventy-
year exile in Babylon (cf. 29:10); the second is the
Jubilee pattern of Leviticus 25 (7 years times 7 = 49
years). We should also note a very rare phenomenon,
the fact that here alone the book of Daniel refers to
Israel's prophets. Ordinarily, the apocalyptic writings do not mention them, but they are mentioned in vv.
2, 10 and 24. The purpose is the same as in Zech.
1:2-6, which is to recall the prophets' message of doom
as a lesson that has not yet been learnt.

We must study the relationship between Daniel 9 and
Zechariah 1 very closely. Daniel is correcting the
normative eschatological tradition, as presented in
Zechariah, concerning the coming era of salvation.
Zechariah is a book that is precisely dated from the
second to the fourth years of Darius' reign, 520 to
518 B.C. In 1:12, the "angel of Yahweh" makes explicit
reference to Jeremiah's seventy years: "O Yahweh of
hosts, how long wilt thou have no mercy on Jerusalem
and the cities of Judah, against which thou hast had
indignation these seventy years?" The answer is that
Yahweh is about to act. The temple is soon to be re-
built, and Jerusalem is to be restored. Thus the
seventy years of judgment are finished, and the era of
salvation is about to begin.

Although the book of Daniel was actually written
ca. 165 B.C., at the worst moment of the persecution
under Antiochus Epiphanes, the writer poses as an
ancient author living at the very same period as
Zechariah, which is the end of the exile and the beginning of the time of restoration. He too refers to

Jeremiah's seventy-year prophecy, but places an entirely different interpretation on it:

> "In the first year of Darius...I, Daniel,
> perceived in the books the number of years
> which, according to the word of Yahweh to
> Jeremiah the prophet, must pass before the
> end of the desolations of Jerusalem, namely,
> seventy years." (9:1-2)

Unlike Zechariah, Daniel does not see the seventy years as terminating the time of wrath. They only symbolize a longer period of wrath, seven times seventy years. In vv. 24-27, Gabriel answers Daniel's prayer by telling him that the fulfillment of Jeremiah's prophesy is to be divided into two separate periods, first the seventy-year exile ending with Darius, and then a seventy-times-seven-year period beginning with Darius. This makes another 490 years, seven times longer than the original exile, and far longer than the 381 years of the pre-exilic temple (967-586 B.C.)! Now, it is true that the restoration period was not all that the prophets expected it to be. The Jews never did regain political independence. Under the Persians, and now under the Greeks, their position in the world had grown more and more difficult, culminating in the desperate times of Antiochus Epiphanes. In any event, Daniel sees the entire Restoration period as an era of continuing wrath, rather than as an era of eschatological bliss. To him, it is sevenfold worse than the exile in Babylon.

We are provided here with a unique insight into the nature of apocalyptic revelation. Daniel is no prophet; never does he claim to be one. Rather, he is a "wise man," an interpreter of dreams and visions (thus 1:20 passim), and he writes this book specifically for the "wise" who are mentioned in 12:3. Thus his book is not for open publication, like the writings of the prophets, but is intended as secret understanding for the end-time. It is a true apocryph (something hidden and recently discovered):

> But you, Daniel, shut up the words, and seal
> the book until the time of the end. Many
> shall run to and fro, and knowledge shall
> increase. (12:4; cf. 9)

341

Daniel has a quite special notion of salvation.
His book contains absolutely no word of parenesis,
for the time of repentance is past. Thus the absolute
dualism of 12:10, "Many shall purify themselves, and
make themselves white, and be refined; but the wicked
shall do wickedly; and none of the wicked shall understand; but those who are wise shall understand." For
Daniel, salvation is gnosis -- not the metaphysical
oneness of the Christian Gnostics, but a knowledge of
where one is in history. Daniel's concept of divine
activity has become radically deistic. Time itself
has become autonomous and unalterable, so that, although
prepares it, he is restrained from acting in it until
it is completed.

Here is a radical denial of Heilsgeschichte, saving
history. In classical prophecy, history is filled
with divine purpose. It is revelatory because it involves responsible human action within the inescapable
context of a relationship with a judging and saving
God. Hence prophetism's urgent call to repentance,
faith, and hope, something that Daniel himself responds
to in his long prayer of 9:3-19, where he seeks to move
God to mercy through confession. Nevertheless, the
dominating apocalyptic motif of this chapter regards
what the prophets expected to be an era of salvation
as an era of wrath. Dan. 9:25 refers to it as "troubled
times." This in effect interprets the postexilic era
as a time of God's absence (what Job was complaining
about!). This radically secularizes the concept of
history, which has now become purely demonic because
nothing since Darius has happened except an intensifying, and now uncontrollable, proliferation of evil.
How very modern Daniel sounds!

We note also that Dan. 9:24-27 symbolizes the postexilic period as the very reversal of the time of saving history before the exile. His three periods mock
their counterparts, (1) the settlement in Canaan, (2)
the time of the kingdom, and (3) the exile, all of which
are rendered meaningless to Israel in the present circumstances:

> Seventy weeks of years are decreed con-
> cerning your people and your holy city, to
> finish the transgression, to put an end to
> sin, and to atone for iniquity, to bring in
> everlasting righteousness, to seal both
> vision and prophet, and to anoint a most
> holy place. Know therefore and understand
> that from the going forth of the word to

restore and build Jerusalem to the coming
of an anointed one, a prince, there shall
be seven weeks. Then for sixty-two weeks
it shall be built again with squares and
moat, but in a troubled time. And after
the sixty-two weeks, an anointed one
shall be cut off, and shall have nothing;
and the people of the prince who is to
come shall destroy the city and the sanctuary. Its end shall come with a flood,
and to the end there shall be war; desol-
ations are decreed. And he shall make a
strong covenant with many for one week;
and for half of the week he shall cause
sacrifice and offering to cease; and upon
the wing of abominations shall come one
who makes desolate, until the decreed end
is poured out on the desolator.

Here are the sixty-two weeks of the Restoration
period nullify the pre-exilic period of the kingdom.
A "troubled time" has rendered meaningless Israel's
ancient time of peace, power, and greatness. Heilsgeschichte has been supplanted by "Unheilsgeschichte."

From this analysis of Daniel 9, apocalypticism's
drastic revision of Hebraic prophecy can be put into
its true perspective. We have called apocalyptic a
subbiblical mechanism, and such it truly is. Apocalyptic gives up on time and history. For it, there is no
salvation except at the end of time and history.

(8) Biblical historicality in the New Testament

New Testament eschatology requires its own separate
treatise, hence we once more restrict our remarks to
absolute essentials.[86] There are two dominant impulses
in New Testament eschatology, each diametrically
opposite to the other. The first is reflected in the
authentic thought of Jesus himself, while the second
predominates in the thinking of Paul.

As the Gospels depict Jesus' forerunner, John,
proclaiming the "kingdom of God" -- that is, the imminent fulfillment of eschatological perfection --,
they depict Jesus as self-consciously working for that

fulfillment in his own ministry. Luke has him reading from Isaiah in the Nazareth synagogue, and then announcing, "Today this scripture has been fulfilled in your hearing." (4:21) Nevertheless, Jesus rejected the highly ideological symbolism of apocalyptic, devoting himself to working as the prophets did for the improvement of covenantal living. His notion that God was performing his saving work through his own efforts accords closely with the classical conception of prophetic eschatology.[87]

Although Paul did not in any way neglect biblical morality, he was much more strongly influenced than Jesus was by the apocalyptic concept of time and history. For him, the gospel era was not just fulfilled time, as it was for Jesus, but definitely the end of time. He took this so seriously that he advocated some drastic departures from normal social behavior in order to suit the emergency character of what he conceived to be the world's last hour. Thus his advice to refrain from marriage in I Cor. 7:25ff. This also accounts for his unbounded zeal in missionizing. He talked freely of two distinct epochs, the one past and the other now dawning. He chided the Jews for their inability to see the glory of God's new and final day (cf. II Cor. 3:7-15). His urgent aim was to reconcile the world to God before it was too late (II Cor. 5:18-21): "Behold, now is the acceptable time; behold, now is the day of salvation!" (II Cor. 6:2). The Lord would soon return; he only waits until wickedness has reached its absolute fulness, in order that his glory might be magnified in his victory (II Thess. 2:1-12).

Without suggesting that apocalyptic has nothing useful to contribute to the biblical concept of history, we would insist on making one point clear: it has imposed an incongenial quantifying element in its notion of periods and epochs. In the final analysis, this can be traced to the Babylonian notion of distinct "times," which have pre-ordained characteristics of their own.[88] It is only when they subtract this erroneous, subbiblical element that the heirs of the biblical tradition will be able to authenticate for themselves the enduring spiritual accomplishments of the apocalyptic ideal.

2. The scope of human freedom

We have gone into detail to explain the Hebraic notion of history as divine-human interaction. We have discussed Israel's apprehension of God's presence and purpose in history. Now we need to direct our attention to its conception of man's part. Just what is the scope of human freedom and responsibility? How is it that man stands in partnership with God as history's creator? To answer this, we must see first the centrality of the parenetic appeal throughout Scripture, defining the responsibilities and capabilities of man, for this is the basis of his freedom and limitations.

a. The centrality of the parenetic appeal

One grand generalization that would express the heart of the Bible's intent and function would be to say that it is one long parenesis. Parenesis (alt.: paraenesis) is exhortation or admonition. Its aim is to urge those who are tempted to shift from their present course not to shift, or to urge those who need to change to do so. It has to do with human decision-making. It cares deeply that those who are doing right shall continue to do so, and that those who are doing wrong shall turn to the right while they still can. Thus it is entirely in the nature of biblical religion that it applies itself readily to missionary appeal, pastoral consolation, and the pragmatic effort to change what is wrong in the world and turn men away from evil. The Bible is no book of theological abstractions, but a practical guide for the improvement of human life.

This aim comes out, of course, in the designedly parenetic sections; i.e., those that are specially constructed as appeals for conscious, immediate choice. What we need to see is that all of Scripture is functionally parenetic -- even those sections that record the past and that predict the future.

(1) Historiography and prophetic eschatology are functionally parenetic

345

The Hebrews were so intensely interested in the future because they knew they had a share in shaping it; also because they believed their God was waiting on their action. Actually, it was not until the prophets had made them aware of God's will and purpose in the ominous historical movements threatening their late nationhood that they began to think very much about what the future would bring, and then it was in terms of what God was about to do in response to man's doing -- never in terms of bare "historical" occurrence. Always the future day that awaited them was predicted in terms that were calculated to influence their present behavior. If it was to be a day of woe, it was designed to move them to repentance and conversion; it it was to be a day of bliss, it was designed to move them out of despair. Thus Israel's concern with the future was, if anything, eminently practical and personalistic. It involved the personhood of God and the personhood of man in free interaction, both of which were guaranteed because the future was not predetermined but open to the loving, trusting partnership of God as history's purposeful shaper and man as history's responsible actor. We can say, then, that Israel's concern for the future was related to its momentary existential responsibility in a way analogous to its concern for the past. Israel's historiography was not simply antiquarian. The past was important because it informed the present. "That day" (in the past) was the illuminating image of "this day," helping the nation see how it should act now. So too the "that day" of the future, which we so often find deriving its model from an ideal in the past that no longer is, but which one hopes may be recovered through responsible action in the here and now. Thus, in an ultimate meaning, both historiography and eschatology are forms of parenesis, holding the covenant people to an ever present choice between "life and good, death and evil" (Deut. 30:15). (From YTT, 282)

The preceding statement was developed from a painstaking, empirical study of the entire range of biblical statements concerning the quality of time. This appeared in my book, Yesterday, Today and Tomorrow. What it means, in short, is that biblical discourse about both past and future is actually concerned with the present. What has gone by and what is still to come illuminate what is happening now.

The Hebrew vocabulary of time itself reflects this attitude. To the Hebrew, time is not on the move, progressing from past to present to future. Rather, time is now; what is eminently real is the present moment,

in opposite directions as its faint, yet revealing shadows. Thus the Hebrews use the same expressions for the past and the future, as follows:

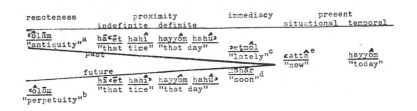

a Usual translation: "eternity"
b Usual translation: "eternity"
c Usual translation: "yesterday"
d Usual translation: "tomorrow"
e From root of cēt, "situation," hence "time"

Excursus: Critique of secular existentialism

Karl Löwith says in _Meaning in History_,[89] pp. 185f., "The theoretical observation of natural space-time and the distinction of an indifferent 'now'-point from its 'before' and 'after' do not explain the experience of a qualitative historical time. A historical now is not an indifferent instant but a _kairos_, which opens the horizon for past as well as for future." So far, so good; but then Löwith seriously errs in adding, "The significant now of the _kairos_ qualified the retrospect on the past and the prospect upon the future, uniting the past as preparation with the future as consummation." This is just the wrong way to say it. It is not the present that illumines the past and future, as Löwith says, but the past and future that illumine the present. His argument is speculative and not based on empirical data; ours is based on what Scripture itself offers.

(2)   Direct exponents of the parenetic appeal

When we speak of historiography and eschatology
as having a parenetic function or impact, we do not
intend to obscure the fact that special genres are
direct exponents of the parenetic appeal; i.c., they
are specially sturctured to this purpose. There are
three prominent elements in Scripture having this
structure: prophetic admonition, deuteronomic confrontation, and New Testament epistolography. Each
requires a word of description.

(a)   Prophetic admonition

Direct appeal to moral decision is not prominent
in the prophetic writings. Much more in the foreground
in the judgment oracle, structured as invective against
the wrongdoer, and as threat or announcement of punishment. Here the prophet appears directly as Yahweh's
herald, proclaiming for God what the addressee does
not wish to hear. This is especially prominent in the
earliest written book of prophecy, Amos (ca. 750 B.C.),
where the only happy notes are found in additions from
redactors living long after the time of Amos.[90]

Nevertheless, even so stern a prophet as Amos
could not refrain from interjecting an element of hope
in occasional, but prominent, words of appeal and admonition. The prophet reveals his own personal concern in
his remodeled word of priestly torah (5:14f.):

Seek good, and not evil
    that you may live;
and so Yahweh, the God of hosts,
    will be with you, as you have said.
Hate evil, and love good,
    and establish justice in the gate;
it may be that Yahweh, the God of hosts,
    will be gracious to the remnant of Jacob.

In the same chapter Amos expresses the pathos of
Yahweh himself, urging an abrupt change of behavior
that will turn Israel from ruin to righteousness (5:23f.):

Take away from me the noise of your songs;
        to the melody of your harps I will not listen.
But let justice roll down like waters,
        and righteousness like an ever-flowing stream.

Similar warnings and admonitions are found in all
the prophets of judgment. Grim as their picture of the
future may be, they continue to make clear that the
choice is Israel's own to make. No ineluctable fate is
theirs; doom is certain only if they harden their hearts
and continue on in their ruinous course. We recall
expecially the powerful words of Ezek. 18:30-32:

Therefore I will judge you, O house of Israel,
every one according to his ways, says Yahweh
God. Repent and turn away from your transgressions which you have committed against me,
and get yourselves a new heart and a new spirit!
Why will you die, O house of Israel? For
I have no pleasure in the death of any one,
says Yahweh God; so turn, and live.

(b)   Deuteronomy and the covenant confrontation

One biblical book that deserves a far higher
esteem on the part of Christians is Deuteronomy, the
fifth book of the Pentateuch. This is because the
parenetical concern of the entire Bible is more sharply
focused here than anywhere else.[91] Many are misled by
thinking that Deuteronomy is a book of law, and it does
present law. In fact, the core of the book, chapters
12-26, is a codification of covenant law; yet its
massive parenetical framework makes clear that the
obligation it imposes is more in the hortatory than
in the imperative mood.[92] This is not legislation so
much as admonition. Everything comes to an impressive
climax in 30:15ff.: "See, I have set before you this
day life and good, death and evil. If you obey the
commandments of Yahweh your god which I command you
this day, by loving Yahweh your god...then you shall live
and multiply, and Yahweh your god will bless you....But
if your heart turns away, and you will not hear...I
declare you this day that you shall perish."

The reader will note that in the just-cited passage, the expression "this day" appears three times. This is typical of Deuteronomy, which has the word hayyôm almost sixty times, not counting its occurrences in set prepositional combinations like "until this day" (ʿad hayyôm hazzeh).[93]

Israel's heilsgeschichtliche traditions are rehearsed not as hallowed memories, but to be given relevance in the new situation of confrontation and decision in which [Israel finds itself.] The specific requirements of covenant living are now drawn together in simplified form as a clear guide for a perplexing present and a perilous future. The choice is Israel's -- irrevocable, immediate and inescapable: "I call heaven and earth to witness against you hayyôm that I have set before you life and death, blessing and curse; therefore choose life, that you and your descendants may live." (30:19)...A recurrent sense of crisis and a continuing awareness of the opportunities and responsibilities of each new day provided the dynamic force for the creation of this literary accretion [Deuteronomy]. The commandments may be referred to as having been issued in the past -- yes; but the... commandments that demand to be obeyed are in fact being issued now, "today." Thus the authoritative rule by which Israel must choose to govern its life is no ancient set of sacred tablets, dug up as it were from the hallowed past. Through the mediator, the new "Moses," God speaks today. His revelation is now. He is very alive and present; therefore his demand is urgent. Israel must respond, one way or another, because the voice of God is near. The word that they must obey is not far off in the heavens or belonging to remote antiquity; it is "in their hearts and in their minds," pressing upon them and demanding their decision.[94] Also, the very frequency and repetitiveness of this Deuteronomic formulation suggests to the attentive observer that Israel was in spite of it all, much too prone to go on deferring its choice to still another "today," wearing out, at last, the patience of a continually pleading God. (From S. J. De Vries, "The Development of the Deuteronomic Promulgation Formula," Biblica 55 [1974], pp. 301, 315-16)

(c)   New Testament epistolography

350

The two most prominent New Testament genres are Gospel and Epistle. The Gospel story is not told, we observe, to provide historical information, but to create belief; and the belief it seeks to inculcate is not theoretical or intellectual, but experiential and spiritual. Thus a programmatic passage near the end of the Fourth Gospel (20:30-31):

> Now Jesus did many other signs in the
> presence of the disciples, which are
> not written in this book; but these
> are written that you may believe that
> Jesus is the Christ, the Son of God,
> and that believing you may have life
> in his name.

This sounds more than a little like Deuteronomy, "Therefore choose life!" (30:19)

Similarly the epistles, especially those of Paul and James. It is not only in the sharply hortatory sections (parenesis in a narrow sense)[95] that Paul urges a life-bringing faith (= trusting commitment), but throughout his writings. Let us not be misled by the didactic and controversial sections; all is in the service of creating a new believing community -- one, as we have seen, that did not disregard moral obligation. The epistles are no reflective treatises, but urgent and pragmatic instructions in the service of this community. The goal of Paul's entire ministry is to create the "new man in Christ" (see Romans 6).

Thus the entire Bible, from beginning to end, expects man to respond. The reader who fails to hear God's address is deaf. If he hears it but refuses to obey, he consigns himself to death.

b. Man's freedom and limitations

How then ought man to act? Obviously according to the measure of his freedom and limitations. Because he is contingent in his being, his freedom is not unbounded, even though it is real. Because he bears the image of his Creator, his limitations do not excuse him from exercizing his freedom and his own creative power.

351

(1)   The dimensions of human boundness

Let us make a list of those things that impose
limits on man's freedom. They are of two sorts, internal
and external. Man is limited by virtue of his own
finite creatureliness, and he is limited by the structures of the world and society in which he lives, moves,
and has his being.

His personal restraints are the following:

Hereditary limitations: his congenital physical
    and mental capabilities;
Educational opportunities and accomplishments:
    one can do only what one knows;
Family heritage and nurture: the help and hind-
    rance provided by parents, sibling rivals,
    relatives and friends;
The effects of sin and error: one's own and those
    of others close to oneself.

His external restraints are the following:

One's present health and physical circumstances;
The attitudes and responsibilities of one's
    present family relationships;
The laws, mores, institutions of the society in
    which one must work;
The political situation, affecting one's social
    and economic opportunities.

Even such a person as may have "perfect" health,
vast riches, and unparalleled opportunities is not
without internal and external restraints on which he
can do. An Adolf Hitler and a Howard Hughes only
deceive themselves in their solipsistic titanism.

Everyone who lives in this world impinges on
each one of us -- one way or another. Even when we
try to ignore those whom we wish to ignore, they affect
us nonetheless. Our very disregard affects us.

Everything that we have done, and that other
persons have done, affects us now. What an illusion it
is for the radical individualist of our myopic generation to claim to act out of absolute freedom from
the restraints that tradition and history have brought!
We are influenced by these things, even so.

Nothing goes back to what it was. The life and the history of everyone is like a cosmic billiard game. Beginning when the triangle is broken, each ball assumes a new position, determining the player's next stroke and the new positions of each ball, until the game is over. Only, the game of life is never over. It goes on and on and on. Each play is predetermined by what has gone on before.

Thus it does no good to pretend that we can be or do anything we wish. If one is married, one cannot simply be unmarried. True, one can get a divorce -- or become widowed. But then he or she is not really unmarried again; he or she is a divorced or widowed formerly married person.

We cannot simply disregard the effect of our (or others') sin and folly. True, they, and we, may repent. Ruined relationships may be mended, but the damage of sin remains. It is said that Nature forgives but never forgets. This is true of all creaturely, historically conditioned reality. No one really remains unaffected, even when a transgression is forgiven and atonement has been made.

A realization of this truth should not make us sad, but glad. It is precisely this boundness, including what we and others have been in the past, that defines and dignifies our freedom. That is to say, what makes a sinner's repentance so glorious is relief within boundness. Grace is never precious except to those who need it!

(2)   The dimensions of human freedom

Despite his finiteness, man has a freedom that is akin to God's freedom. The essential meaning of the imago dei is that man shares in three divine works: creation, judgment, and redemption.[96]

(a)   The power to create

God created and creates the world. It constantly
exists through the conscious exercise of his will.
Creaturely man likewise creates. Everything that he
does makes a difference in the world around him. His
life is more than the dropping of a pebble in a pool,
causing a temporary swirl before plunging to the bottom.
Because he makes his fellow human beings conscious of
his being and will, they cannot avoid being affected
by him, resist him as they may. In a positive sense,
there are no limits on what human beings may create
along the lines of potentiality that are consistent
with their limitations. To be sure, there is a re-
striction on the number of books or plays or symphonies
that one may write before one drops dead; but massively
and comprehensively, the totality of human production,
over the whole range of history, past, present, and
future, is limited only by the outer bounds of the
universe itself. Sometimes man creates things that are
bad and harmful -- whether by his design or in spite
of it. Here creator man encounters the seemingly infinite dimensions of demonic possibility, for all that
can go right may also go wrong. Nevertheless, the
divine Creator is accessible to his appeals, and will
guide him in his errors as well as in his triumphs.
In the final analysis, nothing that man creates has
positive goodness, except as it reflects the presence
and purpose of the divine Creator who has created him.

(b) The power to judge

God judges and will judge the world. At every
moment, all that God has created passes in inspection
before him. So too man, created with the divine image,
constantly judges. He has been given the power to
discern good and evil. This does not really make him
"as God" -- as the serpent promised in the Garden
(Gen. 3:5) -- it only makes him like God. He may not
have divine knowledge, but he may know and judge all
that God has made. He is being held morally responsible to govern in God's place, exercising control for
God over his good world, for the greatest development
of its potential for good. Where evil arises in the
place of good, he must act as God for its suppression,
correction, and eradication. In the biblical view,
the evils that impinge on finite existence can have no
other purpose than the greater good that comes from
overcoming them.[97] It is the duty of man, the judge,

to further good and eradicate evil.

(c)   The power to redeem

God redeems and will redeem the world; so too must man. What has gone astray is set right through God's intervention in human history. He appeared in his Son, to suffer a God-forsaken death, in order to redeem the world. If man would share in this redemptive work, he too must suffer, and triumph in suffering.

(3)   Human responsibility

(a)   The possibility of the creatively new

What God taught the nation of Israel, we can apply individually to ourselves. Although Israel's sin and apostasy had condemned them to bitter exile, God was not finished with them. His purpose was to make a new beginning, announced in such glowing words as those of Isa. 43:18-19:

> Remember not the former things,
>   nor consider the things of old,
> Behold, I am doing a new thing;
>   now it springs forth, do you not perceive it?
> I will make a way in the wilderness
>   and rivers in the desert.[98]

Man's freedom to make a new beginning, after falling, is grounded in God's freedom to make something creatively new. He does not tolerate an impasse; things either get worse and worse, or better and better, but the decisive moment will come when man must choose which way to go. In any event, man is constantly called to repentance because God repents himself of the evil. To punish man for the wrong that he has done is God's strange work.[99] It is not his purpose to destroy but only to chasten; hence if things do go from worse to worse, it has to be man's fault. He refuses to choose when he is free to choose.

Even when sinful man has done much to ruin his own life and the lives of others around him, the possibility still exists that he may begin to act once again according to God's design. Though now a marred and blemished image of God, his imperfect work of creation, judgment, and redemption will have some positive value in the broad perspective of God's design.

(b) Man is responsible to act freely in the context of his limitations

When man chooses, he must choose from the position where he now is. If he has wandered far from God -- like the prodigal son in the parable -- he has a long, long way to come back. What one has been, and now is, provides the context of his present freedom.

There are two opposite forms of idolatry confronting man in this moment of responsible choice: to deify his own ego by acting as though he were not bound by the parameters of his creaturely existence, or to deify the parameters, giving the finite elements in his environment an absolute status. Thus, for instance, a black person who has been disadvantaged and now seeks liberation cannot act in responsible freedom by ignoring who he is and where he has come from. He acts in creative freedom only as a liberated black person who is now struggling to overcome the handicaps of his heritage and environment. On the other hand, if he simply succumbs to his handicaps, using these as an excuse for giving up the struggle for dignity and opportunity, he will be absolutizing the arbitrary strictures of his social environment, seeking to excuse himself of responsibility and putting all the blame on "God."

We are never locked in by our previous choices (and those of other people), yet we fail to exercise responsible freedom when we try to ignore the choices we have made. We may regret them we may seek to reverse them, but we can never ignore them. Creative choice is made only in the context of choices that we have previously made, or of choices that have been thrust upon us by others.

It is in this interaction with our previous choices, and the totality of our contingent existence, that we are in conversation with God. He is the absolutely Incontingent amid all our contingence. We are not free if we try to act in incontingency, for this is self-deification; we are not excused from acting freely when we succumb to our contingency. We are truly free only when we make something new out of the old, and make something free out of that which is bound. This is purposeful history-making -- man's conversation with God!

Why do some people choose to die when they may live? Because dying is easier than living. Because not choosing is easier than choosing. Because remaining a slave to evil habit is easier then struggling free from it. Because it is more satisfying to blame God than to blame oneself.

This is the unforgiveable sin, the "sin against the Holy Spirit."[100] When we refuse to respond to God, demonic possibilities open up. We have entered on the pathway of death, and if we continue on this perilous pathway, it will bring us to the hell of everlasting estrangment from God. Yet we hear his voice; and though we have chosen evil, we may still choose good. Our historical existence will have to continue from where we now are -- not from some primordial Eden of perfect innocence -- but God begins the conversation anew.

FOR FURTHER STUDY

On the divine name:

W. Eichrodt, TOT, I, 178ff.

    The name of the covenant God

G. von Rad, OTT, I, 179ff.

    The revelation of the name Jahweh

On history:

B. Albrektson, History and the Gods (Coniectana Biblica, OT Series I),

    Lund: Gleerup, 1967

R. J. Blaikie, 'Secular Christianity' and God Who Acts, London: Hodder and Stoughton, 1970

G. von Rad, OTT, II, 99ff.

    Israel's ideas about time and history, and the prophetic eschatology

T. C. Vriezen, OOTT, pp. 188ff.

    Revelation in history

On time

J. Barr, Biblical Words for Time (Studies in Biblical
    Theology), Naperville, 1962

G. Delling TDNT, IX, 581ff., chronos

    Chronos in the Greek world
    Time in Judaism
    Chronos in the New Testament

E. Fuchs, TDNT, VII 269ff., sēmeron

    Presuppositions in the Old Testament and Judaism
    The usage of the New Testament

G. von Rad, G. Delling, TDNT, VII, 943ff., hēmera

    "Day" in the Old Testament
    New Testament usage

G. Stählin, TDNT, IV, 1106ff., nun

    The presuppositions of the New Testament concept
        of nun
    The New Testament Now

H. W. Wolff, AOT, 83ff.

    The Old Testament concept of time

On the sabbath:

N. E. A. Andreasen, The Old Testament Sabbath (Society

of Biblical Literature Dissertation Series, 7),
   Missoula: Scholars' Press, 1972

E. Lohse, <u>TDNT</u>, VII, 1ff., <u>sabbaton</u>, etc.

   The sabbath in the Old Testament; in Judaism; in
   the New Testament; in the early church

S. Terrien, <u>EP</u>, pp. 390ff., 401ff.

   The day of the Sabbath
   The day of the Lord

H. W. Wolff, <u>AOT</u>, pp. 135ff.

   The Sabbath

On <u>wonder</u>:

G. Bertram, <u>TDNT</u>, III, 27ff., <u>thauma</u>, etc.

W. Eichrodt, <u>TOT</u>, II, 151ff.

   The maintenance of the world

      Law in the natural process
      Miracles
      Providence

A. Oepke, <u>TDNT</u>, III, 194ff., <u>iaomai</u>, etc.

   Sickness and healing outside the Bible; in the
      Old Testament and Judaism; in the New Test-
      ament

K. H. Rengstorf, _TDNT_, VII, 200ff., sēmeion

    Sēmeion in the Greek world; on Jewish soil
    ʾôt, ʾātāʾ mûtāʾ in post-biblical Judaism
    Sēmeion in the New Testament

K. H. Rengstorf, _TDNT_, VIII, 113ff., teras

    Non-biblical Greek usage
    The Old Testament and Greek Judaism
    Post-biblical Judaism
    The New Testament

On eschatology and apocalyptic:

G. Bornkamm, _TDNT_, IV, 802ff., mustērion, etc.

G. Delling, _TDNT_, VIII, 49ff., telos, etc.

    The end in Jewish apocalyptic
    Telos in the New Testament

A. Oepke, _TDNT_, V, 858ff., parousia, pareimi

    Old Testament presuppositions for the technical
        use of terms in the New Testament

    Progress and regress in Judaism
    The technical use of pareimi and parousia in the
        New Testament
    Theological summary

H. D. Preuss, _TDOT_, II, 20ff., bôʾ, ʾāthāh

    Coming (qal) and bringing (hiphil) into the land
    bôʾ as fulfilling
    bôʾ (hiphil) as a term for God's guidance in
        history

The coming judgment
The coming and fulfilled salvation
Yahweh as the coming one

G. von Rad, <u>OTT</u>, II, 301ff.

Daniel and apocalyptic

H. Seebass, <u>TDOT</u>, I, 207ff., ʼach^{a}rît

H. W. Wolff, <u>AOT</u>, pp. 149ff.

The hope of man

W. Zimmerli, <u>Man and Hope in the Old Testament</u> (Studies in Biblical Theology), Naperville, 1968

W. Zimmerli, <u>OTTO</u>, pp. 227ff.

Old Testament apocalypticism

NOTES

1. The reader should compare the following sections with this book's Foreword, in which David Mellick phrases many of our propositions in the language of philosophical discourse.

2. E.g., C. Hodge, <u>Systematic Theology</u>, I (New York 1871), 366-441; K. Barth, <u>Church Dogmatics</u>, 5 vols., New York 1955-1977; cf. P. Tillich, <u>Systematic Theology</u>, I (Chicago 1961), 163-289.

3. E.g., The Vatican II declaration, Constitutio dogmatica de divina revelatione. where Scriptural support is constantly adduced without critical exegesis.

4. See Introduction, "The only normative theology is situational and experiential."

5. It is reported to have been found in the third millenium, B.C., Ebla texts (by oral communication from D. N. Freedman; cf. his article, "The Real Story of the Ebla Tablets, " BA, 41/4 [Dec., 1978], pp. 143ff.); for the theory that "Yahweh" is a cult-name for the god El, see F. M. Cross, "Yahweh and El," Canaanite Myth and Hebrew Epic (Cambridge, Mass.: Harvard University Press, 1973), pp. 60-75.

6. Chapter I, "Anthropomorphic personification as caricature"

7. For the extensive literature on this subject, see the commentaries and art. "God, Names of" (B. W. Anderson), IDB, II, 407ff.

8. The majority of scholars assume that v. 14 is original (E), while v. 15 is a secondary expansion. This assessment is based on the assumption that ʿôd ("also," "again") in v. 15 has been supplied by the supplementer responsible for v. 15. However, it could have been added as a gloss if v. 14a or v. 14b was interpolated first; the main indication that this was the case is the overall structure and genre of the E material, vv. 4b, 6, 9-13, 15. This is a narrative of epiphanic self-disclosure concluded by a definitive revelation of the name by which this god was to be worshiped in Israel: Yahweh. The poetic parallelism of v. 15b (zeh šemî leʿôlām, wezeh zikrî ledōr dōr) reflects the purpose of solemn liturgical recital. V. 14a represents a secondary effort to a explicate the meaning of the name Yahweh on the basis of etymological punning from the causative form of the verb "to be" (HYH).

9. Thus the biblical God is first worshiped under names, later with the name Yahweh; under altered historical circumstances, biblical worshipers gave up the use of this name for surrogate titles diminishing the level of epiphanic personalism.

10. St. Anselm; cf. K. Barth, Anselm: Fides Quaerens Intellectum, trans. I. W. Robertson, Richmond 1958.

11. Ps. 107:2

12. Ps. 22:25, 35:18, 40:9, etc.

13. Num. 14:21, 28, Jer. 22:24, Ezek. 5:11, etc. Very often the oath formula refers to Yahweh's life in the third person: "As Yahweh lives....!"

14. This is stated deliberately and advisedly over against the traditional notion that revelation came to an end with the completion of the scriptural Canon; cf. the Excursus.

15. Philadelphia: Fortress, 1972

16. Philadelphia: Fortress, 1979. See also P. R. Ackroyd, Continuity: A Contribution to the Study of the Old Testament Religious Tradition, Oxford 1962; G. W. Coats and B. O. Long, edd., Canon and Authority, Essays in Old Testament Religion and Theology, Philadelphia: Fortress, 1977.

17. See F. M. Cross, The Ancient Library of Qumran and Modern Biblical Studies, Garden City, 1958; also F. M. Cross and S. Talmon, edd., Qumran and the History of the Biblical Text, Cambridge, Mass.: Harvard University Press, 1975.

18. See on G. von Rad in Introduction.

19. First appearing in the Qumran pesharim as well as in primitive midrash; cf. M. Martin, The Scribal Character of the Dead Sea Scrolls, 2 vols., Louvain 1958.

20. Gen., Ex., Lev., Num., Deut. (5); Josh., Judg.- Ruth, Sam, Kings, Chron., Ezra-Neh., Esth., Job, Dan., Isa., Jer.-Lam., Exek., The Twelve (13); Ps., Prov., Eccl., Song (4)

21. The shift can be clearly seen as early as Ecclus. 44-50, where the "Praise of Famous Men" raises up a series of pious paradigms from Israel's past, isolated from any organic historical interconnection between them; so also the apocalypses, Philo, the Mishna.

22. When Israel's consciousness of participation in history failed, revelatory experience was all but ended. The bat-kol of later rabbinic tradition was little more than a private mystical experience.

23. See art. "Septuagint" (E. Tov, R. A. Kraft), IDBS, pp. 807ff.

24. Childs's otherwise impressive reconstruction of the canonization process is deficient in appreciation of the significance of this earliest stage; see op. cit., pp. 84ff.

25. The so-called "post-Septuagintal" textual glosses derive from rival recensions, which had received these additions in the process of their independent development; cf. F. M. Cross, "The Evolution of a Theory of Local Texts," Cross and Talmon, edd., Qumran and the History of the Biblical Text, pp. 306ff.

26. Although it does not directly claim revelatory status for itself, the early church soon moved to accord it this status on the basis of its inspiration and apostolic derivation (cf. art. "Canon of the NT" (F. W. Beare), IDB, I, 520ff.; also R. M. Grant, "The New Testament Canon," Ackroyd and Evans, edd., Cambridge History of the Bible, I, 284ff.).

27. With the following, cf. R. G. Collingwood, The Idea of History, New York 1946; H. Butterfield, Christianity and History, New York 1949; P. Tillich, Systematic Theology, III, 300ff.

28. On the following, see S. J. De Vries, YTT, pp. 343-45.

29. See W. W. Hallo and W. K. Simpson, The Ancient Near East, A History (New York: Harcourt Brace Jovanovich, 1971), pp. 158-63 ("for: The Prediction and Control of Events").

30. CF. H. Cançik, Grundzüge der hethitischen und alttestamentlichen Geschichtsschreibung, Wiesbaden: Otto Harrassowitz, 1976.

31. See C. B. Welles, "The Hellenistic Orient," R. C. Dentan, ed., The Idea of History in the Ancient

Near East (New Haven: Yale University Press, 1955), pp. 133ff.

32. On Kant, see W. Windelband, A History of Philosophy (New York 1893), pp. 551ff. On Nietzsche, see K. Löwith, "Nietzche's Revival of the Doctrine of Eternal Recurrence, "Meaning in History (p.b., Chicago 1949), pp. 214ff.

33. See the writings of Martin Heidegger, mediated to theologians through the writings of F. Gogarten and others.

34. Op. cit., pp. 182ff.

35. See H. W. Wolff, "The Understanding of History in the Old Testament Prophets," C. Westermann, ed., Essays on Old Testament Hermeneutics (Richmond 1963), pp. 336-55.

36. So S. Mowinckel and N. H. Ridderbos apud B. Albrektson, History and the Gods, (Lund: Gleerup, 1967) p. 11.

37. See the preceding footnote. Cf. H. W. F. Saggs, "The Divine in History," The Encounter with the Divine in Mesopotamia and Israel, pp. 64-92.

38. A. L. Oppenheim, tr.

39. See art. "Persia" (M. J. Dresden), IDB, III, 739ff. This dynasty reigned from 539-332 B.C.

40. S. N. Kramer, tr.

41. See Chapter III, "The election of a peculiar people."

42. See Chapter III, "Election as an eschatological symbol."

43. See S. J. De Vries, YTT, pp. 348f., n. 11.

44. See idem, "Observations on Quantitative and Qualitative Time in Wisdom and Apocalyptic," pp. 27-72.

45. Thus Yahweh's interaction with Israel in historic event becomes integrally connected to the humanitarian concern of Hebraic religion.

46. See art. "Lord's Day" (C. C. Richardson), IDB,
    III, 151ff.

47. See n. 42.

48. This volume was dedicated to Samuel L. Terrien and
    was published by Scholars' Press and Fortress
    Press. The article cited is on pp. 263-76.

49. See H. J. Kraus, "Das Verständnis der Prophetie
    (J. G. Eichhorn)," Geschichte der historisch-
    kritischen Erforschung des Alten Testaments, 2nd
    ed., Neukirchen, 1969, pp. 144-47; idem, "Ewalds
    verständnis der Prophetie," ibid., pp. 205-8;
    idem, "Bernhard Duhms 'Theologie der Propheten,'
    ibid., pp. 275-83. For a hundred years, exegesis
    under the influence of historicistic-romanticis-
    tic criticism has praised "the great prophets"
    while relegating the substance of Israelite
    religion to the status of naive primitivity. As
    one consequence from this, the "revolt" of the
    prophets was distorted out of all proportion.
    Contemporary scholarship sees them as radically
    theonomous rather than autonomous (see S. J. De
    Vries, Prophet Against Prophet, pp. viii, 148ff.).

50. This insight has not yet borne its proper fruits,
    whether in Biblical Theology or in Systematic
    Theology. Cf. J. Barr, Old and New in Inter-
    pretation.

51. Although the Pentateuch reflects historical event,
    it is essentially epic in structure and concep-
    tion, both within its major literary sources
    (J, E, and P) and as a redactional whole. The
    Old Testament contains didactic narrative such
    as Jonah and Esther, which are neither structur-
    ed nor intended as historiographic. The historio-
    graphic books directly aim to interpret history;
    the list includes Joshua, Judges, Samuel, Kings,
    Chronicles, Ezra-Nehemiah, even though much
    imaginative, nonhistorical materials appear with-
    in them. Our term "historiographic literature,"
    refers specifically to those materials in this
    list that conform to some degree to the criteria
    set out in the following paragraph.

52. See S. J. De Vries, Prophet Against Prophet,
    pp. 52ff.

53. See idem, "David's Victory Over the Philistine as Saga and as Legend," JBL, 92 (1973), 23-36; also idem, "Temporal Terms as Structural Elements in the Holy-War Tradition," VT, 25 (1975), 80-105.

54. Cf. G. von Rad, "The Beginnings of Historical Writing in Ancient Israel,: The Problem of the Hexateuch and Other Essays, tr. E. W. T. Dicken, New York 1966, pp. 166-204. The definitive analysis of this document appears in L. Rost, Die Ueberlieferung von der Thronnachfolge Davids, BWANT, III/6, Stuttgart 1926, reprinted in Rost, Das kleine Credo (etc.), Heidelberg 1965, pp. 119ff.

55. Contemporary discussion of this document is based on the definitive work of M. Noth in Ueberlieferungsgeschichtliche Studien, Halle/Salle 1943; cf. G. von Rad, "The Deuteronomic Theology of History in I and II Kings," Problem of the Hexateuch, pp. 205-21.

56. See S. J. De Vries, Prophet Against Prophet, pp. ix-x.

57. Cf. von Rad, "The Beginnings of Historical Writing in the Old Testament," The Problem of the Hexateuch and other Essays, tr. E. W. Trueman Dicken (New York 1966), pp. 166-204.

58. See Chapter II, "The theory of demonic seduction."

59. I Sam. 11:6, 18:10, etc; this becomes the well-known "revelatory event formula" introducing prophetic oracles, as at Jer. 11:1, Ezek. 12:1, 13:1, etc.

60. Cf. the recent study by J. Rogerson, The Supernatural in the Old Testament, Guildford and London: Lutterworth, 1976. This is written as a semipopular study book, giving an intelligent theological treatment of a troubling subject, with specific discussion of relevant passages.

61. E.g., "But the thing that David had done displeased Yahweh," II Sam. 11:27; "Therefore Yahweh was very angry with Israel, and removed them out of his sight," II Kings 17:18. Always God's inner emotions are inferred from the historical expression of these emotions, an anthropopathic metaphor.

62. Ideologically it is the same to state directly that God is wonderful in his mighty deeds and to narrate a sequence of events in which God is depicted as doing something wondrous. The narrative is equivalent in the imagery of theophany to the descriptive praise.

63. E.g., "Yahweh shut him in," Gen. 7:16b; "God made a wind blow," Gen. 8:1.

64. See J. R. Halladay, Jr., "The Day(s) the Moon Stood Still," JBL, 87 (1968), 166-78.

65. For the epiphanies and theophanies, see Terrien, The Elusive Presence, pp. 63ff., 106ff. See also J. K. Kuntz, The Self-Revelation of God, Philadelphia, 1967, J. Jeremias, Theophanie: Die Geschichte einer alttestamentliche Gattung, Neukirchen-Vluyn 1965.

66. This method occasionally reaches out to absurd possibilities; e.g., the suggestion that Elijah poured naphtha instead of water on the Carmel altar, setting it alight with sun-rays focused through a burning glass (Montgomery-Gehman, Kings (ICC), in loco). The biblical wonder-workers end up as magicians and charlatans.

67. See G. Landes, "Jonah: A Mašal?," Gammie, ed., Israelite Wisdom, pp. 137-58.

68. The clue to the book's meaning is found in 4:2, "I pray thee, Yahweh, is not this what I said when I was yet in my country? That is why I made haste to flee to Tarshish; for I knew that thou art a gracious god, and merciful, slow to anger, and abounding in steadfast love, and repentest of evil"; also in Yahweh's twice-repeated challenge to Jonah, "Do you well to be angry?" (4:4,9). Jonah, representing a narrow view of Israel's elective privilege, is fearful that the traditional covenantal words will also be applied to Nineveh, achieving their proper universalistic potential.

69. See further on apocalyptic below.

70. See J. A. Wilcoxen's remarks on pp. 78f. in J. H. Hayes, Old Testament Form Criticism. Cf. A. Jolles, Einfache Formen, 4th ed., Tübingen 1968, pp. 23-61; also S. J. De Vries, Prophet Against

Prophet, pp. 52ff., K. Koch, The Growth of the Biblical Tradition, New York 1969, p. 186.

71. See J. Crenshaw, Samson: A Secret Betrayed, A Vow Ignored, Atlanta: John Knox, 1978.

72. See De Vries, "David's Victory Over the Philistine as Saga and as Legend," JBL, 92 (1973), 23ff. The hero-saga is from David's early days and comprises I Sam. 17:12a, 14, 17-23a, 24-25, 41,48b, 50, 55-58, 18:2. The hero-legend is from the middle of the ninth century B.C. and comprises I Sam. 17:1-11, 32-40, 42-48a, 49, 51-54.

73. See S. J. De Vries, "The Time Word maḥar as a Key to Tradition Development," ZAW, 87 (1975), 65-80.

74. For a structural analysis of these narratives, see idem, Prophet Against Prophet, pp. 53-92. The types listed feature an element of wonder, while certain other types do not. All the prophet legends aim to show the source of a prophet's spiritual power and to exemplify how an ideal prophet ought to act. For criteria of the level of historicality, see idem, pp. 100-3.

75. Cf. I. Seeligmann, "Menschliches Heldentum und göttliche Hilfe," TZ, 19 (1963), 386-411.

76. So also in the New Testament. In the Lukan prologue, Elisabeth's pregnancy after the years of natural child-bearing have passed (cf. Sarah, Hannah in the Old Testament) is just as marvelous as Mary's pregnancy without the aid of man; the pronouncements of Simeon and Anna in the temple are as marvelous as the singing of the angels to the shepherds.

77. See further Chapter V, "Theophanous reflexes of the resurrection tradition."

78. John 1:14, 18, "And the Word became flesh and dwelt among us, full of grace and truth; we have beheld his glory, glory as of the only Son from the Father....No one has ever seen God; the only Son, who is in the bosom of the Father, he has made him known."

79. C. Westermann, The Praise of God in the Psalms, tr. K. R. Crim, Richmond 1965, pp. 81ff., 102ff.

80. Vss. 17-18, "Though the fig tree do not blossom, nor fruit be on the vines, the produce of the olive fail and the fields yield no food, the flock be cut off from the fold and there be no herd in the stalls, yet I will rejoice in Yahweh, I will joy in the God of my salvation." See the commentaries.

81. See S. J. De Vries and E. C. Meyer, Journal of the Methodist Theological School, 9/2 (1971), 9ff. See also above, Chapter II, "The sinner's action."

82. See Chapter V, Introduction, "Job's groping for a caring God."

83. See Chapter II, "Apocalyptic dualism and futurism."

84. The Russelite (Jehovah's Witnesses) and Adventist movements continue to propose ingenious schemes for directly applying this chapter to contemporary events, calculating an imminent end to history. See also the Hal Lindsay books. Although refraining from such fancies, traditionalistic exegetes such as E. J. Young fall into serious error in striving for a literalistic interpretation.

85. What follows is especially indebted to J. C. H. Lebram, "Apokalyptiek als keerpunt in het joodse denken," NTT, 30 (1976), pp. 271-81, scheduled to appear as "Daniel und die Propheten" in OTS.

86. See R. Bultmann, The Presence of Eternity: History and Eschatology (New York 1957); also Theology of the New Testament, I 3ff., 37ff., 329ff., II, 75ff., 95ff. Cf. W. D. Davies and D. Daube, edd., The Background of the New Testament and its Eschatology (Cambridge 1956); art. "Eschatology of the New Testament" (E. S. Fiorenza), IDBS, pp. 271ff.

87. See W. Marxsen's analysis of "the Jesus kerygma," art. "Christology of the NT," IDBS, pp. 146-48.

88. See S. J. De Vries, YTT, pp. 344f.

89. See n. 34.

90. 9:11-12, 13-15

91. See S. J. De Vries, "Deuteronomy: Exemplar of a Non-Sacerdotal Appropriation of Saving History,"

J. I. Cook, ed., <u>Grace Upon Grace</u> (Grand Rapids: Eerdmans, 1975), pp. 90-105.

92. See the comprehensive analysis of N. Lohfink, <u>Das Hauptgebot</u>, Rome 1963.

93. See S. J. De Vries, <u>YTT</u>, pp. 164f.

94. Deut. 30:11-14

95. See D. Bradley, "The Topos as a Form in the Pauline Paraenesis," <u>JBL</u>, 72 (1953), 238-46; also art. "Parenesis" (D. Schroeder), <u>IDBS</u>, p. 643, where further literature is cited.

96. See Chapter "The <u>imago dei</u>: Man as created creator."

97. See Chapter V, "Man's pathway through suffering."

98. See B. W. Anderson, "Exodus Typology in Second Isaiah," Anderson and W. Harrelson, edd., <u>Israel's Prophetic Heritage</u> (Muilenburg Festchrift, New York 1962), pp. 177-95.

99. Isa. 28:21

100. Mark 3:29 par. To choose death in the place of life quenches the Holy Spirit and nullifies the offer of divine forgiveness.

Chapter V

A Meaning and Purpose in Finite Existence

THE CARING GOD"

In the four preceding chapters, we have learned to know the God of the Bible as "the holy God," "the righteous God," "the jealous God," and "the living God." One more insight is needed to round off a personalistic apprehension of God's being. He is also a caring God. It is this that can give man assurance in the face of death, and in all the strains and cares of finite existence. The biblical God does not guarantee that his people will not suffer, and they are not excused from death. But they are able to face these "evils" because they know he cares.

When we use the word, "care," we are using it in both its accepted meanings: (1) to be vitally concerned and sympathetic; (2) to nurture effectively and purposefully. Is there a special biblical word to express God's caring? The Hebrew words rāham, rāhamā (verb and noun, respectively) come very close: this is the stronge urge and compassion of the womb. A New Testament word, usually translated "love" (verb and noun), is also very close to the mark. This is agapaō, agapē, as used distinctively in the New Testament, particularly in the classic text, John 3:16, "For God so loved (i.e., cared for) the world, that he gave his only Son, that whosoever believes in him should not perish but have everlasting life." Agapē is not emotion or affection; it is God's caring self-giving! God cares enough for our suffering to suffer himself; he cares enough about our dying to die in our place.

Introduction: Man's loneliness in a hostile universe

a. "Are you there, God?"

In this age of advanced technology, we human beings
still have much to be frightened about. It is not so
much the floods and the fires and the earthquakes; we
know how to avoid them or minimize their potential
damage. If we live on a San Andreas fault, we have
the option of moving away. The wild beasts no longer
scare us -- unless we deliberately put ourselves where
they still run loose. Famine, pestilence, and disease
still terrify the undeveloped nations, but we see
little of them in our affluent society. Yet there
are evil forces preying upon us that seem to be beyond
human knowledge -- or beyond man's will to cope with
them. If it is cancer -- it is either that new cancer-
causing agents seem to appear faster than possible
strategies for coping with this dread sickness. Or
else it is that we just cannot get enough self-control
to break the cigarette habit.

The human race has always had the most to fear
from its own kind. This is still so in the most primitive societies, such as in New Guinea, where all the
tribes are continually stalking down susceptible individuals belonging to rival groups. Shockingly, this
is also true in the sophisticated modern societies,
such as those of the United States and the Soviet
Union. Both have put men in earth orbit; both have a
rich culture and vast wealth; both have laws to ensure
the stability and security of the social system. Yet
they both scare the other countries to death -- as they
scare themselves. It is stated frankly that the security of the modern world depends entirely on the balance of terror between these two giant powers! What
irony that the world is safe only because America and
Russia could devastate each other with a half hour!

But international politics is only the macrocosm
of terror that contains a welter of local and private
hells. In our best neighborhoods, a woman is afraid
to walk the streets for fear of rape and murder. The
dope pushers prowl our schools. Drunks threaten to
demolish us on the highway. If we manage to stay
alive, we may be robbed and cheated. If we seek security in love, our lover may turn away from us, our
children scorn and abuse us!

Yes, civilization and technology have not eliminated evil. Rational control of our universe has not brought happiness and peace. In spite of the fact that we all eat better, work less, play more, and move around far more freely than in the ancient world, fear is still with us. The greatest fear is to be forsaken, to feel emptiness and meaninglessness, to believe that no one cares.

If we know that someone cares, we can face up to life's hazards. On whose love, then, can we depend? Father's, mother's? Husband's, wife's? Hopefully so, but even when our mother forsakes us, God cares. This is the final reality that gives us courage to face life and death.

In a British film about the sinking of the _Titanic_, a Red Cross worker offers coffee and sandwiches to a group of women survivors. The survivors are dejected and apathetic. They all refuse to eat, but one woman is more vehement than the others, and to her the Red Cross worker says, "Come, dear, you simply have to try to take care of yourself. You have to keep on living. Nothing that you do can bring back the dead." The answer was, "I don't want to eat, do you hear? When my husband went down with that ship, God sank with him!"

This woman's God was dead because he did not seem to care about her husband. We can well understand her attitude, for it is how many people would think in similar circumstances. If God cannot -- or will not -- prevent the loss of everything that is near and dear to me, I refuse to believe in him!

How unfortunate that so many who lose dear ones, or health, or property, lose God too! Loss is compounded by an even greater loss; and if you don't even have God to hold on to anymore, only grim death is attractive.

How important it is, then, to nourish ourselves in an authentically biblical faith. The peoples of the Bible came to know all the hells that exist -- yet they held on to their faith in a caring God. If we are nurtured in their heritage, when tragedy strikes us and we cry out in the dark, "Are you there, God?" he will be there.

    b.   Job's groping for a caring God (Job 19:23-27)

Job 19:25 has become firmly fixed in Christian lyrical and liturgical tradition as a witness to the resurrection:

> For I know that my Redeemer lives,
>   and at last he will stand upon the earth,
> and after my skin has been thus destroyed,
>   then from (King James: in) my flesh shall I
>   see God.

The Hebrew preposition min means "from" or "out of"; hence this text certainly does not affirm the notion of bodily resurrection.[2] Nor does it directly predict Christ. Job is looking for a gō'ēl. a near kinsman like the Boaz of Ruth, who will stand by him and take his part.[3] The gō'ēl that Job affirms is one who will appear between him and God, enabling him to confront God with his problem. In a deeper sense this text does point to Christ, who in his time fulfilled the role of gō'ēl, bringing God to us in his own person (John 14:9). In the deepest meaning, Job and the gospel stand together in affirming that God cares. Neither Job nor the gospel explains why human beings must suffer -- or why they must often suffer unjustly. They only affirm that they do not suffer meaninglessly.

Using this great passage from Job as an introduction to this entire chapter, it is important to get a clear focus on its message through careful exegesis. First, we offer a judicious translation, free from the influence of church tradition:

> Oh if it could only be
>   that my words might be written in a book,
> inscribed with an iron stylus and lead
>   forever in the rock engraved!

> But as for me, I know my redeemer lives,
>   and one having the last word[4] stands on the
>   dust.
> And after they thus strip off my skin,
>   even outside my flesh I shall behold[5] God --
>   whom I shall behold at my side!
> And when my eyes -- not those of a stranger[6] --
> see him
>   my kidneys shall collapse inside me!
>   (vv. 23-27)

These particular words cannot be understood except in the context of the whole chapter -- indeed, of the entire book![7] At the beginning of chapter 19, Job is replying to Bildad and complaining about his companions' torments. "How long will you torment me and break me in pieces with words?! (v. 1) "Even if it be true that I have erred, my error remains with myself. If indeed you magnify yourselves against me, and make my humiliation an argument against me, know then that God has put me in the wrong....Behold, I cry out 'Violence!', but I am not answered." (vv. 4-7) Job is saying that the reason why he seems guilty -- that is, remains in his disease and humiliation -- is that God keeps him walled in, not allowing any breakthrough for understanding. Going on in this same vein, Job describes in passionate terms the estrangement and distress that have been brought upon him because he seems to be cut off from God. "My brethren are far away from me, my kinfolk, my close friends, my guest, my maid-servants, my own personal valet, even my wife and my young children -- all these intimate companions despise me because I seem to be marked by God's curse. God has put me into complete darkness. I know that I am right, but he does not allow me to understand or be understood. There is no comprehension or resolution."

Thus Job pleads with his friends to sympathize with the special nature of his predicament. But they refuse to help or offer understanding. They pursue him as God pursues him, without relenting, making his torment worse (vv. 21-22). It is precisely here that Job erupts with his tremendous affirmation about knowing his redeemer or go'el -- about somehow, someday "seeing" God. His go'el will have the last word; Job will appear in God's presence.

Throughout the book, Job continually returns to the same theme of seeking vindication for himself. An outline of the dialogue between him and his three so-called "friends" will show the structural place of this persistent theme:

Job: I curse the day of my birth! 3

Cycle I

Eliphaz: You have sinned; repent and God will
restore you. 4-5
Job: You are false friends; God is a tormentor.
6-7

Bildad: God is just; he will regard one who is
righteous! 8
Job: I <u>am</u> righteous -- but I haven't a chance
against his accusations. 9-10

Zophar: God is mightier than you think; you are
guiltier than you will admit. 11
Job: I would argue my case with God. But I have
no chance for this, even in death.
12-14

Cycle II

Eliphaz: You are proud and deceitful; but remember that the wicked shall not escape!
15
Job: It is God's affliction that marks me as
wicked, but this is misleading. I
cry to heaven for a witness! But there
is no hope. 16-17

Bildad: Make no mistake: God punishes the wicked.
18
Job: Have pity on me, for God has unjustly
afflicted me -- yet I know that my
redeemer lives! 19

Zophar: Repent, repent! The wicked cannot
escape! 20
Job: But only consider how often the wicked do
excape! 21

Cycle III

Eliphaz: Your self-righteousness cannot please
God; humble yourself and be saved! 22
Job: If only I could appear before God, he would
vindicate me (or would he?). Here
on earth he seems indifferent. 23-24

Bildad: Puny men ought to be silent before God!
25, 26:5ff.
Job: But I am innocent! 26:1-4, 27:1-12

(Expansions in 24:18ff., 27:13ff. -- parts of
Zophar's speech?)

Job's final peroration

(1) I remember happier times. 29
(2) But how wretched I am now! 30
(3) I swear that I am innocent! 31

In this entire structure of dialogue,[8] Job never
rises to greater confidence than in chapter 19. It
is very important to be aware of the fact that the
gō'ēl of 19:25 has parallels in similar affirmations
at other places within the various cycles. In
chapter 9 Job complains bitterly that he cannot contend with God. There is no chance for a fair trial,
with him as accuser. He mentions a possibility which
he immediately withdraws:

There is no umpire (mōkîaḥ) between us,
who might lay his hand upon us both.
Let him take his rod away from me,
and let not dread of him terrify me.
Then I would speak without fear of him,
for I am not so in myself. (vv. 33-35)

This is in his speech to Bildad, and he says much
the same thing in his first reply to Zophar (13:1ff.)
In chapter 16, in his second reply to Elihu, there is
a specially passionate outburst:

O earth, cover not by blood,
and let my cry find no resting place.
Even now, behold, my witness (ʿēdî) is in heaven,
and he that vouches for me (śāhadî) is on high.
(v. 18-19)

Unfortunately, such a one does not exist here on
earth -- a witness to come between Job and his "friends"
in order to adjudicate their dispute here and now. He
emphatically rejects the counsel of his "friends,"
who think that they can offer the valid and authentic
reason for Job's suffering -- which is that he is
suffering for his own guilt. No, he says, God has

382

another reason; if only I could find out what that reason is! Thus Job constantly hopes for a confrontation with God. The underlying problem of the book of Job is not actually the question of why a man must suffer, or even why a man must suffer unjustly. The basic problem is the hiddenness of the divine purpose, the fact that God does not reveal why man must suffer.

Israel's antique conception of Yahweh's saviorhood had become somewhat obscured by the time of Job, which was composed during or after the Babylonian exile,[9] a time when the wisdom literature was becoming a predominant form for the expression of Jewish piety. After the return from exile, the concept of Yahweh at work in the life of his people, bringing salvation in historical event, was gradually being pushed into the background. It was believed and confessed, but no longer operative. The Jews continued to accept it as a dogma, but they no longer experiened it as a nation. More and more they found themselves struggling with the problem of why righteous people suffer while wicked people prosper. Nothing seemed to have any meaning for the Jews except the universal Near-Eastern equation, voiced by the three "friends" of Job, that virtue brings blessings while sin brings punishment; hence if one suffers, he must be sinful in spite of his claim to righteousness. A growing transcendentalizing of the concept of God's sovereignty also took place in the postexilic period; it only accentuated the problem.

This is the background of Job's complaint. It is the remoteness of God, his apparent unconcern for Israel's present history -- not to speak of the life of individual Jews -- that comes to poignant expression in Job's anguish. Thus this book represents a highly individualistic protest against a retreat from classical Hebraic faith. In one sense, the book of Job -- and especially the poems of Job -- borders upon blasphemous titanism. Job is a sort of Prometheus who would grasp hold on God, thereby seeming to transgress upon the divine prerogative. This is inevitably what must tempt man whenever God remains hidden. For Job, God is too aloof; he cannot be approached. The people of the biblical covenant still believe that their God is responsible for the operation of moral law within the universe, but somehow things have got out of kilter.

Job's apparent titanism is one reason why this book has been so liked in modern times. It seems to dare to say things about God that are neither orthodox nor traditional. True, the book is not traditional in the way it approaches this momentous problem, but it is traditional in the sense that it confronts traditional problems and struggles with traditional concepts. In the deepest sense, this book represents covenant personalism in an ultimately intensive form. It is simply developing the deepest implications of this notion, wrestling with the meaning of human freedom within the context of the divine responsibility and the divine commitment. According to Israel's highest tradition, Yahweh is answerable. He is answerable not because man demands it, but because he makes himself answerable. Any God who commits himself to a people, retaining control over the operation of the moral laws of the universe for the benefit of this people, must remain answerable when these laws no longer seem to work. Job is, in this light, no Titan; he is rather a symbol of Israel itself. Job is not transgressing when he calls God to account. He maintains throughout the book a proper sense of reverence for God, and never actually blasphemes. He knows that at the deepest level of his being, God will be just and will act justly -- only, Job cannot find out the basis of that justice. Therefore he cries out for a come-between, someone who will break through this curtain of darkness and allow the sufferer to come into the presence of God; for at the moment when that occurs, everything will surely be set right.

Thus Job definitely does believe in covenant personalism. His problem is that he takes his faith too seriously. The only thing he does not make sufficient allowance for is the distance between himself as finite creature and God as infinite Creator.

On the basis of these observations, we may stake the conclusion that the book of Job is concerned not with theodicy but with epistemology. It is not a book that aims to justify the ways of God, or to work out some kind of philosophical answer to man's most perplexing questions. Rather, it is a striving for the assurance that God cares. Its aim is a more direct, more personal revelation -- one that leads beyond dogma to individual appropriation.

Many misinterpretations of this book have been
occasioned simply by the failure to recognize that
epistemology is its real question. Its concern is
not the existence of evil, nor is it the problem of
injustice. It is the problem of hiddenness and meaninglessness. If the problems of theodicy and suffering actually were central, then the book's final
answer would be altogether inappropriate and ineffective.
In matter of fact, modern philosophers are generally
unsatisfied with its answer to the problem of evil
and injustice in the world. It is interesting that
McLeish's play, J.B., rejects the book's own conclusion in favor of another. What is not understood
here is that Job's answer is theological rather than
philosophical. Furthermore, it answers the book's real
question of epistemology, "Why does God remain hidden?"

In chapters 38-42, God seems to be bullying Job,
putting him down, setting him in his place. "Who is
this that darkens counsel with words without knowledge?
Gird up your loins like a man, I will question you,
and you shall declare to me." (38:1-2) God goes on
to ask Job whether he participated in creation and can
explain all the mysteries of the cosmos. Of course,
the answer to these rhetorical questions has to be an
emphatic no! God presents himself in a whirlwind, but
this is to reassure Job rather than to cow him. God is
elusive -- but he is present and real, even if elusive?
This leads Job at least to the confession, "I know
that thou canst do all things, and that no purpose of
thine can be thwarted....I had heard of thee by the
hearing of the ear, but now my eye sees thee; therefore I despise myself, and repent in dust and ashes."[10]
(42:1-6) Job's fault lay not in his desire for confrontation, but only in his failure to make due allow-
ances for his creaturely limitations. Finitude can
never probe the infinite; it can only touch the fringe
of its borders. We creatures can never intrude into
the deepest mysteries of divine purpose; if we can at
least glimpse God in the whirlwind, this is enough to
tell us that he cares and that he is in control.

Thus the conclusion of Job does present a very
meaningful answer to its most central question. The
question is, "Are you there, God?" The answer is,
"Yes, be still!"

Job assures us that God is present in our suffering, that he cares. He is not absent, as it may seem.

There may be little justice in the world, but from God's perspective, there is purpose and meaning even in the world's wrong and injustice. The world will probably never see any completely satisfying, ideally just situation -- that we know.[11] We as responsible human beings, made in the image of God, are called upon to do whatever we can to establish greater justice and well-being; and unless we do our best, we are in no position to complain that God is unjust. But even when our efforts fail and when we go astray, God knows and God cares.

1. Living and dying before God

While we are young, and as long as we still have
our parents and grandparents, we feel insulated from
death as a personal problem. Most young people prefer
not to think about it at all -- to push it out of
their thoughts. But as one grows older, one comes to
realize that there will be an eventual end to one's
individual existence. It is well, then, for the young
to make full use of life, heeding the wise words of
Qoheleth:

> Remember also your Creator in the days of
> your youth, before the evil days come, and
> the years draw nigh, when you will say, "I
> have no pleasure in them"; before the sun
> and the light and the moon and the stars
> are darkened and the clouds return after
> the rain...before the silver cord is snapped,
> or the golden bowl is broken at the cistern,
> and the dust returns to the earth as it was,
> and the spirit returns to God who gave it.
> Vanity of vanities, says Qoheleth; all is
> vanity. (Eccl. 12:1-8)

The way a person lives prepares him for a meaningful dying. A person's attitude toward death determines
the quality of his life. That we must die is no surprise; what is surprising is that we have a chance to
live! From eternity to eternity, amid all the hurtling
galaxies, two specks of human life came together and
created the new life that is me! I'll be here, alive,
until I am dead -- until the natural vital force that
formed me has been spent. But it makes all the
difference to me whether I believe that when life is
over, I go out into Nothing, or go out into Everything
-- whether utter emptiness awaits me, or the arms of
God.

a. The problem of death[12]

(1) The acceptance of death

One thing that distinguishes man from the animals is that he is capable of anticipating his own death as the termination to the years of life allotted to him. Although we human beings feel death as a very deep and poignant tragedy when early sickness, accident, or warfare strikes down a person full of life and young of years, to welcome it is normal for those who have grown weary of life -- the aged, the weak, and the suffering. To them it comes as a kind of sweet solace, or at least surcease from suffering, and oblivion from weariness. Henry W. Longfellow expresses it well in his poem, "Nature":

> So nature deals with us, and takes away
>> Our playthings one by one, and by the hand
> Leads us to rest so gently, that we go
>> Scarce knowing if we wish to go or stay....

We are also familiar with the attitude of those who wish to die when it is not their time to die. This is a pathological condition, a delusion of those who are spiritually or psychologically disturbed. Such persons may become suicidal, requiring treatment as sick persons, administered to on an emergency basis. But apart from the performance of self-murder, which is entirely within the realm of human capabilities, there is also a psychological disturbance which aims at harming oneself, a kind of unreasoning masochism that finds perverse delight in inflicting injury upon oneself. This may take the form of alcoholism or addiction to a harmful drug, or of other injurious behavior. Sometimes it takes the form of severe neurotic distrubance, in which we embrace those things that make happiness ever less obtainable. Here one is steadily strangling oneself to death by cutting off the vital air of social fellowship.

We have been well taught that there is nothing heroic or noble about suicide except in the most extreme circumstances -- when our very life has less value than something else. This behavior actually falls within the area of martyrdom, where one accepts a death inflicted by others (even if it be carried out at one's own hand!) for the sake of country or religion. This, society has universally acclaimed as a high virtue. Sometimes it happens in political resistance to oppression, sometimes in spying, sometimes in armed combat. Modern-day Israel finds high inspiration in recalling the self-murder of the Jewish garrison at Masada in the face of the final

Roman attack, A.D. 73. For Christians, nothing can
surpass Christ's willingness to accept death on the
cross in perfect loyalty to his vision of obedience
to the divine will. Thus the grasping of death when
it might be avoided is praiseworthy only when some
higher good may be obtained; it is universally condemned when it is merely an escape from life and an
abandonment of responsibility.

(2)   The rejection of death

The tendency of the human spirit is to reject
death and choose life. We instinctively know that we
have been born to live, not to die. Thus every normal
and healthy-minded human being rejects death, even
toward the end, until it becomes clear that life has
little more to offer. One of the peculiar powers of
the human mind, with its dimensions of memory and
imagination, is to anticipate the moment of death.
We can anticipate our own death in a way that the non-
rational animal world cannot. Every living creature
must die, and in a sense every living being has been
born to die. This is the way of nature. A dog or a
cat dies without reflecting upon it or anticipating it.
Reflecting upon it and anticipating it, we tend to
mythologize and caricature it as in itself a tremendous and bitter tragedy, a contradiction of our higher
being. Though as animals we are inescapably mortal,
this higher element within us encourages us to toy
with the illusion of immortality.

This tendency is intensified by special problems
arising from the very peculiarity of human existence,
all of them being caught up and comprehended within
our rationality and power of imagination. Death may
be repudiated by many, at least in their longings and
desires, because of the disappointments of their dreary
life; one life-span may seem insufficient to right the
many wrongs which confront them along the pathway of
their existence. Who of us ever comes to complete
fulfillment of what we consider to be our proper rights,
our ideal destiny? How many wrongs have been done to
us that require to be set right? Furthermore, one
lifetime can scarcely suffice to vindicate the truth
to which we may have committed ourselves. We may think
that we are right, and we may long for a future day

when we will be proven right, but death is likely to come first. Again, one lifetime is too short to impart value and perspective upon one's individual accomplishments. Who of us know, while we are still alive, the range of influence and significance which our own life may bring?

Thus we all long for exemption from death. Humankind has sought all sorts of substitutes as consolation, but wealth and property prove to be vanity in the end, as Qoheleth continually reminds us:

> There is an evil which I have seen under the sun, and it lies heavy upon men: a man to whom God gives wealth, possessions, and honor, so that he lacks nothing of all that he desires, yet God does not give him power to enjoy them, but a stranger enjoys them; this is vanity; it is a sore affliction. (Eccl. 6:1-2)

Many seek name and fame; though these may continue for a while, what meagre consolation can they ultimately provide for a life that is, in itself, not fulfilling? All that men may achieve, individually and collectively, in this world will soon be forgotten. Our name may become famous, so that we may even be recorded in the history books -- yet for those who must die this is mainly an idle abstraction, bringing little solace in the end.

The ancient Israelites thought highly of the value of posterity. To be bereft of children, or worse still, to have no children -- especially males to carry on the family name -- was felt to be a great calamity. It was one's children and grandchildren who could give the illusion of an ongoing life. For us moderns this is also true, and we can perhaps take some consolation in it. Each of us may perhaps reproduce himself, so that our children and grandchildren carry on something of our own life. This is the design that nature intended, for from nature's point of view, it is the perpetuation of the human species that has more significance than the survival of the individual. But again, for the individual person this is an abstract delight, one that must vanish as a shadow at his own death. As Qoheleth says:

> If a man begets a hundred children, and
> lives many years, so that the days of his
> years are many, but he does not enjoy
> life's good things, and also has no burial
> (= possibly may be deprived of proper
> burial), I say that an untimely birth is
> better off than he. (Eccl. 6:3)

We cannot conclude this section without mentioning still another delusion with which many attempt
to mitigate the sting of death. There is a great deal
of confusion in Christian attitudes toward death.
This happens to be one subject on which Christian
thought remains very disturbed and perplexed, largely
because the Christian tradition has accepted incon-
gruous elements from competing concepts of death.
This has become the stock of many funeral materials,
offered the bereaved in the typical memorial service.
But it is largely based on a literalistic appropriation of highly symbolic apocalyptic motifs, dis-
tracting many Christians facing death from the Bible's
essential achievement with respect to the problem of
death. The sublime naivete of expecting to walk about
in heaven in golden slippers is another delusional
abstraction, one that does many persons more harm than
good. On this we will have more to say later.

b. Ancient Near-Eastern interpretations of death

A correct perspective on the main achievements of
biblical thought with respect to death can be provided
only against the background of a fairly complete description of ancient Near-Eastern attitudes toward death.
When we clearly see these alternatives, we may be able
to savor with greater appreciation the peculiar attitude of the ancient Hebraic tradition. Three main blocks
of religious culture impinged directly upon ancient
Hebraic thought. They were Egyptian, Canaanite-
Phoenician (the nearest), and Mesopotamian. Perhaps
with some danger of overschematization, we may signal-
ize the alternatives as follows:

Egypt: embracing life, masking death as life;
Ugarit: embracing death as the most meaningful
        part of life;

391

Mesopotamia: embracing life as a temporary
            respite from death;
Israel: embracing life as the foil of death.

(1) Egypt

Ancient Egypt lay so near to Palestine that its
attitudes toward life and death might be expected to
have had considerable impact on Hebraic attitudes,
yet there is little evidence of such influence. This
is a fact that in itself has significance. The Israelites must have deliberately rejected the Egyptian view,
seeing in it something radically inconsistent with their
own understanding of human existence.

The Egyptians made a great deal of the mortuary
cult,[13] which was the sacralizing of death. We know
that they developed to a high art the practice of
mortuary science, the technique of embalming, the
preparation of the coffin, the preservation of corpses.
Who is not fascinated with the mummies of Egypt? How
remarkable it is that Ramesses II is still sufficiently
intact to be examined by the specialists at the Louvre
and treated by medical techniques! (It appears that
Ramesses has contracted fungus disease at his advanced age!) Everyone is impressed, furthermore, by
Egypt's massive tombs, the pyramids built for early-
dynasty Pharaohs. Alongside them are a vast array of
imposing funeral monuments throughout Egypt, serving
the same function. Here we have an astonishing exhibi-
tion of aristocratic optimism respecting the meaning
of death; for the man who had the financial means, death
could be rendered sweet and pleasant. But at what a
price! When we think of the economic resources that
had to be provided, and the untold social wrongs that
had to be endured by the unfortunate in order to erect
these gigantic mausoleums, each of which served only
a relatively small number of highly privileged individuals, we understand how little it actually meant
for the uplift of mankind. Death could be made sweet
only for the very few, while the mass of the people
were left with little hope or illusion to cling to.
For them, death had small consolation except in providing cessation from the dreariness and weariness of
life.

Death in the primeval establishment of order:
<u>ANET</u> 914

An Egyptian mythological text used as a magical spell for the preservation of a deceased person depicts him as Osiris, the god of death and resurrection, addressing Atum, the god of creation:

> Words spoken by the Osiris Ani: "O Atum, what is it? I am departing to the desert [the land of the dead], the silent land!"

Atum answers:

> "It has no water, it has no air -- deep, deep, dark, dark, boundless, boundless -- in which thou livest in the peace of heart of the silent land. Sexual pleasures are not enjoyed in it, (but) a blessed state is given to (thee) in recompense for water, air, and sexual pleasure, and peace of heart in recompense for bread and beer."
> Thus spoke Atum.

The deceased protests:

> "In the sight of thy face? Indeed, I cannot bear the lack of thee! Every (other) god has assumed his place in the forefront of (the sun barque) Millions-of Years.!"

Atum replies:

> "Thy place belongs to thy son Horus" -- thus spoke Atum -- "Indeed, it shall be that he sends forth the great, while he also shall rule thy place, and he shall inherit the throne which is in the Island of Flame. It is further decreed that a man shall see his fellow, (so that) my face shall see thy face."

The deceased questions still further as Osiris:

> "O Atum, what is (my) duration of life?" -- thus he spoke.

Atum's answer:

> "Thou art (destined) for millions of millions
> (of years), a lifetime of millions....Further,
> I shall destroy all that I have made, and this
> land will return into Nun, into the flood-
> waters, as (in) its first state. I (alone)
> am a survivor, together with Osiris, when I
> have made my form into another state,
> serpents which men do not know and gods
> do not see."

Thus death is disguised life. Its duration is
for millions of millions of years, until Atum shall
change everything that he has created back into the
chaotic shapelessness from which it was originally
drawn. Death does not shatter the order and meaning-
fulness of creation, but represents the ultimate
state of restfulness toward which the present rest-
less world is moving. Each man is his own Osiris,
containing within his own self the meaning of death
and life. Ultimately, the Egyptian mind allows no
distinction between death and life, which are inseparable aspects of the same reality. Atum has created
death as another form of life.

Sinuhe's image of blissful death, ANET 22[15]

The story of Sinuhe became very popular in Middle-
Kingdom Egypt. It is preserved in numerous papyri,
but some specialists have surmised from its conclusion
that it was originally inscribed on the tomb-walls of
its hero, explaining how he achieved an ideal Egyptian
burial after a life of perils. Although the historian
is interested in this story mainly for its realistic
account of the political and cultural situation inside
and outside Egypt during this particular period, we
offer its concluding paragraph to illustrate its
ideology of death:

> There was constructed for me a pyramid-tomb
> of stone in the midst of the pyramid-tombs.
> The stone-masons who hew a pyramid-tomb took
> over its ground-area. The outline-draftsmen

designed in it; the chief sculptors carved
in it; and the overseers of works who are in
the necropolis made it their concern. Its
necessary materials were made from all the
outfittings which are placed at a tomb-shaft.
Mortuary priests were given to me. There
was made for me a necropolis garden, with
fields in it formerly (extending) as far as
the town, like that which is done for a chief
courtier. My statue was overlaid with gold,
and its skirt was of fine gold. It was his
majesty who had it made. There is no poor
man for whom the like has been done. (So) I
was under the favor of the king's presence
until the day of mooring had come....

To be buried in a pyramidal tomb was, in essence,
to be merged with the primeval hillock of creation,
so that death symbolizes the beginning of continuing
life. Compatible with this notion is the idea that
Osiris, the god of death, is also the god of life
and fertility, reborn like Baal at the spring of each
year.

Dispute over suicide, ANET 405-7[16]

    This text comes from a time of political upheaval,
the interval of relative instability between the Old
and Middle Kingdoms of Egypt, ca. 2000 B.C. So perilous
have times become that life no longer seems worth living. The speaker has a dialogue with his own soul or
ka, with whom he has to have an agreement lest it forsake him when he takes his own life. The speaker wants
to burn himself to death, but his soul has objections.
The first part of the dialogue is a prose repartee
between them, in which the soul argues that the
speaker has not prepared a proper burial place, and
then recommends the course of hedonistic abandonment
to pleasure: "Pursue the happy day and forget care!"
This leads to the second part of the dialogue, which
is all in eloquent, moving poetry. Falling into four
distinct strophes, it finally produces the soul's
consent. We shall cite this entire section in full:

Strophe I: My reputation will be offensive if I heed
            your advice.

    Behold, my name will reek through thee
        More than the stench of bird-droppings
        On summer days, when the sky is hot.
    Behold, my name will reek through thee
        (More than) a fish-handler
        On the day of the catch, when the sky is hot.
    Behold, my name will reek through thee
        More than the stench of bird-droppings,
        More than a covert of reeds with waterfowl.
    Behold, my name will reek through thee
        More than the stench of fishermen,
        More than the stagnant pools which they have
            fished.
    Behold, my name will reek through thee
        More than the stench of crocodiles,
        More than sitting in the assembly among the
            crocodiles.
    Behold, my name will reek through thee
        More than a (married) woman
        Against whom a lie has been told because of a
            man.
    Behold my name will reek through thee
        More than a sturdy boy of whom it is said:
        "He belongs to his [father's] rival!"
    Behold, my name will reek through thee
        (More than) a treacherous town, which plots
            rebellion,
        Of which (only) the outside can be seen.

Strophe II: Everybody is hateful and treacherous.

    To whom can I speak today?
        (One's) fellows are evil;
        The friends of today do not love.
    To whom can I speak today?
        Hearts are rapacious:
        Every man seizes his fellow's goods.
    (To whom can I speak today?)
        The gentle man has perished,
        (But) the violent man has access to everybody.
    To whom can I speak today?
        (Even) the calm of face is wicked;
        Goodness is rejected everywhere.
    To whom can I speak today?
        (Though) a man should arouse wrath by his evil
            character,
        He (only) stirs everyone to laughter, (so)
            wicked is his sin.

To whom can I speak today?
  Men are plundering;
  Every man seizes his fellows (goods).
To whom can I speak today?
  The foul fiend is an intimate,
  (But) a brother, with whom one has worked, has
    become an enemy.
To whom can I speak today?
  No one thinks of yesterday;
  No one at this time acts for him who has acted.
To whom can I speak today?
  (One's) fellows are evil;
  One has recourse to strangers for uprightness
    of heart.
To whom can I speak today?
  Faces have disappeared:
  Every man has a downcast face toward his fellows.
To whom can I speak today?
  Hearts are rapacious;
  No one has a heart upon which one may rely.
To whom can I speak today?
  There are no righteous;
  The land is left to those who do wrong.
To whom can I speak today?
  There is lack of an intimate (friend);
  One has recourse to an unknown to complain to
    him.
To whom can I speak today?
  There is no one contented of heart;
  That man with whom one went, he no (longer)
    exists.
To whom can I speak today?
  I am laden with wretchedness
  For lack of an intimate (friend).
To whom can I speak today?
  The sin which treads the earth,
  It has no end.

Strophe III: Death is beautiful.

  Death is in my sight today
    (Like) the recovery of a sick man,
    Like going out into the open after a con-
      finement.
  Death is in my sight today
    Like the odor of myrrh
    Like sitting under an awning on a breezy day.

397

Death is in my sight today
    Like the odor of lotus blossoms,
    Like sitting on the bank of drunkenness.
Death is in my sight today
    Like the passing away of rain,
    Like the return of men to their houses after
        an expedition.
Death is in my sight today
    Like the clearing of the sky,
    Like a man fowling thereby for what he knew not.
Death is in my sight today
    Like the longing of a man to see his house
        (again),
    After he has spent many years held in captivity.

Strophe IV: The dead will be in the company of the gods.

Why surely, he who is yonder
    Will be a living god,
    Punishing a sin of him who commits it.
Why surely, he who is yonder
    Will stand in the barque of the sun,
    Causing that the choicest (offerings) therein
        be given to the temples.
Why surely, he who is yonder
    Will be a man of wisdom,   .
    Not hindered from appealing to Re when he speaks.

Conclusion: The soul's reply

What my soul said to me: "Set mourning aside,
thou who belongest to me, my brother! (Although)
thou be offered up on the brazier, (still) thou
shalt cling to life, as thou sayest. Whether it
be desirable that I (remain) here (because) thou
hast rejected the West, or whether it be desirable
that thou reach the West and thy body join the
earth, I shall come to rest after thou hast
relaxed (in death). Thus we shall make a home
together."

COMMENT: Since this literary gem speaks for itself,
little need be added except an observation of the programmatic nature of the soul's last repartee. Even in
self-inflicted death, the suicide will still be cling-
ing to life. Death only disguises a life that continues in the world beyond.

Cynicism and hedonism: <u>ANET</u> 467, The Song of the Harper[17]

Even the satisfaction of being buried in a magnificent tomb could turn to ashes because of the prevalence of grave-robbing. Thus the illusions of a continuing life with which especially the prosperous endeavored to console themselves could not always assure the ancient Egyptian that the life after death was better than the fleeting pleasures of the present world. Depicted on the walls of tombs is the common motif of a harper, entertaining guests at a festal banquet. He seems to be mocking the presumptions of a glorious death in this Middle Kingdom text inscribed in such a tomb:

> The song which is in the House of King Intef, the triumphant, and which is before the singer with the harp.
>
> Prosperous is he, this good prince,
> Even though good fortune may suffer harm!
> Generations pass away, and others remain
> Since the time of the ancestors.
> The gods who lived formerly rest in their pyramids,
> The beatified dead also, buried in their pyramids.
> And they who built houses -- their places are not.
> See what has been made of them!
> I have heard the words of Ii-em-hotep and Hor-
>   dedef,
> With those discourses men speak so much.
> What are their places (now)?
> Their walls are broken apart, and their places
>   are not --
> As though they had never been!
> There is none who comes back from (over) there,
> That they may tell their state,
> That they may tell their needs,
> That they may still our hearts,
> Until we (too) may travel to the place where they
>   have gone.
> Let thy desire flourish,
> In order to let thy heart forget the beatifica-
>   tions for thee.
> Follow thy desire, as long as thou shalt live.
> Put myrrh upon thy head and clothing of fine
>   linen upon thee,

Being anointed with genuine marvels of the god's
   property.
Set an increase to thy good things;
Let not they heart flag.
Follow thy desire and thy good.
Fulfill thy needs upon earth, after the command
   of thy heart,
Until there come for thee that day of mourning.
The Weary [of Heart][18] hears not their [mourn]ing,
And wailing saves not the heart of a man from the
   underworld.

REFRAIN: Make holiday, and weary not therein!
Behold, it is not given to a man to take his
   property with him.
Behold, there is not one who departs who comes
   back again!

(2) Ugarit

It was natural for the Egyptian, blessed by
nature and surrounded by comparative abundance, to
embrace life while making death as life's continuance.
Along the less fertile coasts of the Levant, farming
was much more difficult. Grains were scarcer than in
Egypt; so too was food taken from slaughtered animals;
since these were likely to be lean grazing stock or
animals from the hunt. For liquid nourishment there
was wine pressed from grapes grown on rugged hill-
sides, rather than cheap beer brewed from mash. Storms
were more violent in this region. Men had to work pre-
cariously in the forests or on the sea. Thus death
seemed as real to the people of this region as did
life -- perhaps more so. Their chief god, Baal,
who was the god of fertility, was also the god of
storm, signifying that death and violence are the
paradoxical concomitants of life, peace, and fruitfulness.

Although the Canaanites have long been known from
the Bible, and their near neighbors, the Phoenicians,
from classical literature, it is the excavations at
Ras Shamra in northern Syria, ancient Ugarit, which
have provided us with a sufficient abundance of texts
to allow us a substantial access into the mythic

thought-world of this peculiar region. Biblical scholars have recognized their great importance because they provide the immediate background of the biblical polemic.[19]

In the Ugaritic myths, Baal and the other storm-gods are depicted in a primordial struggle against Yamm, god of the sea and of watery chaos, which must be restrained from encroaching on the dry land and made submissive to the intrusion of men.

Another dominant mythological motif is Baal's struggle with Mot, the god of death, who slays him but is unable to keep him from rising again. Yet, paradoxically, still another motif depicts Baal as Rapu', the god of the underworld. These are aetiologies of the life-death paradox, seen also in Anath-Astarte, who is depicted as the deity of love and war[20] similarly to the Akkadian Ishtar and the Hindu Kali. Here death seems to be more real than life: death is life, as life is death.

We shall illustrate the paradox of Ugaritic mythology with examples of myth from the cult of fertility and from the cult of the dead, each of which appear to have been a prominent element in ancient shrine ritual.

From the fertility cult: ANET 139-41, Baal versus Mot[21]

The Baal cycle, celebrating the fertility god's victory over various rivals, is too extensive to be cited except in brief extracts. Baal has subdued Yamm and pacified Anath, the goddess of war. Now he has to face the grim menace of Mot. It is Anath, now appearing as goddess of love or fertility, who will aid him. Toward the end of the Baal myth, Mot sends a message to Baal, demanding his submission. Baal is terrified. He resigns himself to Mot's order to descend into the depths of the earth. Apparently the story tells of how Mot actually kills him in a long lacuna in the text, which commences once again with a messenger's report to El, the god of heaven:

We [ca]me to the pleasance of Dabr-land,
    To the beauty of Shihlmemat-field.
We came upon Baal
    Fallen on the ground:
Puissant Baal is dead,
    The Prince, Lord of Earth, is perished.

The text follows with a description of El's ritual of mourning -- apparently an accurate reflection of northwest Semitic funeral practices:

[He] sits on the ground,
    Pours dust of mouring on his head,
    Earth of mortification on his pate;
    And puts on sackcloth and loincloth.
He cuts a gash with a stone,
    Incisions with...
He gashes his cheeks and his chin,
    He harrows the roll of his arm.
He plows his chest like a garden,
    Harrows his back like a plain.
He lifts up his voice and cries:
"Baal's dead! -- What becomes of the people?
    Dagon's Son! -- What of the masses?
    After Baal I'll descend into earth."

Anath, learning of Baal's death, does the same things, then buries Baal with an elaborate sacrificial ritual, aided by Shapsh, Torch of the gods. El installs Ashtar the Tyrant in Baal's place. Meanwhile bloody Anath takes her revenge on Mot:

A day, days go by,
    [and Anath the Lass] draws nigh him.
Like the heart of a c[ow] for her calf,
    Like the heart of a ew[e] for her lamb,
    So's the heart of Ana[th] for Baal.
She grabs Mot by the fold of his garment,
    Seizes [him] by the hem of his robe.
She lifts up her voice and [cries]:
    "Now, Mot! Deliver my brother."
Responds the Godly Mot:
    "What wouldst thou, O Maiden Anath?
I indeed have gone have wonder'd
    Every mount to the heart of the earth,
    Every hill to the earth's very bowels.
Lifebreath was wanting 'mong men,
    Lifebreath among earth's masses.
I came to the pleasance of Dabr-land,
    The beauty of Shihlmemat-field.

I did masticate Puissant Baal.
I made him like a lamb in my mouth;
    Like a kid in my gullet he's crushed.
Even the God's Torch Shapsh
    Who wings over heaven's expanse,
    Is in Mot the Godly's hand."
A day, even days pass by,
    From days unto months.
    Then Anath the Lass draws nigh him.
Like the heart of a cow for her calf,
    Like the heart of a ewe for her lamb,
    So's the heart of Anath for Baal.
She seizes the Godly Mot --
    With sword she doth cleave him.
With fan she doth winnow him --
    With fire she doth burn him.
With hand-mill she grinds him --
    In the field she doth sow him.
Birds eat his remnants,
Consuming his portions,
Flitting from remnant to remnant.

The reference to days and months passing before
Anath answers Mot's taunt by slaying him is a clear
clue to the aetiological meaning of this episode.
Baal dies in the fall of the year, when earth's vegetation dies. Mot reigns supreme while the earth lies
dormant. In the spring Anath kills Mot, winnowing and
grinding him as the peasants grind their old grain in
order to prepare for the planting of the new.

But the narrative continues with an account of
Baal's own revival, leading in the sequel to an in-
decisive battle between him and Mot. The remarkable
fact that Mot revives as well as Baal, and that in the
end neither of them achieves permanent mastery over
the other, points beyond the motif of spring rejuvena-
tion to the ongoing reality of an eternal struggle
between life and death. Here are the concluding lines,
telling of Baal's fight with Mot:

They... like camels:
    Mot's firm, Baal's firm.
They gore like buffaloes:
    Mot's firm. Baal's firm.
They bite like snakes:
    Mot's firm. Baal's firm.
They kick like chargers:
    Mot falls. Baal falls.
Above Shapsh cries to Mot:

403

"Hearken, now, Godly Mot!
Why striv'st thou with Puissant Baal? Why?
Should Bull El thy father hear thee,
He'll pull out they dwelling's pillars.
Overturn thy throne of kingship,
Break thy staff of dominion!"
Sore afraid was Godly Mot,
Filled with dread El's Beloved Ghazir....

Here the text becomes so broken that the reader can gather little from it except that Mot desists from his effort to destroy Baal. Having already driven his rival Ashtar from the throne that he had usurped, Baal is once again installed in lordly glory. The myth is, to be sure, a liturgy for the worship of Baal. Hence it affirms a very tentative primacy of life over death, but the ascendancy of life which the myth celebrates is occasioned by the persistent presence of death. This is as ontologically real as life itself. In the final analysis, death seems more powerful than life, because its rule is forever.

From the cult of the dead

In a rival mythological tradition appearing in the Ugaritic tablets, death seems to be directly worshiped as a variant form of life. This tradition has to do with the shades or ghosts or deified dead, called RPIM, plural of RPU. There can be no question but that these are ideologically identifiable with the enigmatic "Rephaim" of the Old Testament, mentioned mainly in late, mythically sanitized texts like Ps. 88:10, Job 26:5, Prov. 9:18, 21:16, Isa. 14:9, 26:14, 19. What interests the student of Ugaritic literature is the fact that other heroes and deities, specifically Danel, Baal, and perhaps El himself, are equated in certain passages with RPU. The intent of this is to provide a special role for the RPIM, as chthonic deities, in the fertility process.

There are three tablets containing the so-called "the Rephaim texts" usually given a place within the legend of Aqhat. They tell of El summoning the RPIM to a feast at his farm. We take the liberty of citing G. R. Driver's summary of these tablets:

El relates how he has summoned the shades
and the ghosts to his palace....He then tells
how they have come there with all haste and
how one Repu-baal, described as champion of
Baal and Anat, is there honoured; and re-
peating the account of their coming there,
he adds that one Hyly, described as a prince
and a king, is also honoured there....El
now instructs the shades and the ghosts to
listen to him; and he announces that the
victor Baal is to be anointed with oil
and become king and occupy his throne....
He then tells again of his summons to them,
their coming with all haste and their
arrival on the third day at his farm....
The speaker... tells his son that his shrine
is built and that Anat will take him by the
hand and kiss his lips. There he will find
his brother waiting on El, there mortal men
and heroes pour forth the praises of El's
name, and there too Repu-baal and Hyly are
honourably treated....In the meantime,
while Anat goes off hunting or visiting
heaven, others (presumably the servitors
of El) have slaughtered cattle, gathered
olives which are as refreshing as silver
and gold are useful to travellers, and made
ready tables fragrant with vine-blossom;
various wines are decanted and special
cakes are baked. Then the shades and the
ghosts spend six days feasting at the
banquet.[22]

Ugaritic specialists have seen the feast described
here as a disguised funeral, understood as a sacrifice to the RPIM by which to guarantee the life and
fertility of the living.[23] The mention of Baal as a
hero, here likewise designated as "Repu," from the
same verbal root, may indicate that the above episode
belongs in ideological sequence after the narrative
of his death and revival.

The description of the RPIM as engaged in riotous
feasting explains why the verbal root RP' in the
cognate language, Hebrew, which means "heal," appears
to be the basis of the biblical "Rephaim," rather
than the root RPH, "be weak."[24] The gods of the
underworld, the shades or dead ancestors, had the
power in Ugaritic mythology to "heal" or restore the

earth's fertility and to bring life. But herein lies
also the paradox that dying may be a way to life, or
that life is actually a form of dying. Further biblical references to rop^{e}'im (active participle of RP'),
usually translated "physicians,"[25] may be illumined
by this paradox. In Gen. 50:2 those so designated
are morticians who prepare the body of Jacob. In II
Chron. 16:12, where Asa is blamed for having consulted
such personages about his lame feet, rather than Yahweh,
it is at least possible that the reference is to his
making contact with mediums or necromancers, as in
I Samuel 28.

We need to penetrate through the outward form of
the mythological story to the ritual Sitz im Leben if
we are to discern the practical impact of the RPIM
motif on ancient Ugarit's attitude toward death and
the dead. According to ancient authors, the Syrian-
Phoenician funerary cult was more orgiastic than any
Irish wake.[26] Naturally, it was carried out with
great fervor upon the burial of the deceased; but
apparently it brought with it a recurrent, frenzied
worship of the dead, occupying much of the time, and
many of the material and physical resources, of its
devotees. It apparently had a large element of the
apotropaic, that is, the intent to ward off the power
and frightfulness of death, thus it was a device for
insuring the life and continuing fertility of those
who were still alive. This cult featured gross
gluttony, and sometimes even cannabalism; naturally,
also sexual excess. But its most prominent feature
was alcoholic revelry. If we are to judge from the
RPIM texts and others similar to them, this banquet-
ing and reveling occupied days on end, recurring
whenever the "worshipers" were up to beginning it
all over again. This can be seen as a direct way of
expressing life as death, for to surfeit oneself
repeatedly, and to riotous excess, with the good things
that fertile nature has provided could only precipi-
tate the early onset of illness and wasting disease --
or at the very least, of poverty and ruin.

We cite two recently published texts depicting
RPU as El indulging with his guests in the gluttonous
banquet of life and death:

    [Th]en drinks RPU, king of eternity,
        Then drinks [El] strong and majestic.
    He takes his place alongside Astarte,
        Even Godly Judge alongside Had,

A shepherd who sings and plays
    The zither, the flute, the tambourine, and the
    cymbals;
Alongside the dancers DŠN,
    Alongside the good companion KTR.
And they drink to Anat the might.... (RS 24.252;
my trans., after Virolleaud)[27]

El offers in his house a mṣd,
    A ṣd within his palace.
He cries out to summon the gods, saying to them,
    "You shall eat, O gods, also you shall drink!
You shall drink wine to inebriancy,
    fermented wine unto drunkenness."

. . . .

Astrate and Anat arrive;
    Astrate prepares the nšb for herself,
    And Anat the shoulder.
The porter of El's house (addresses) the feasters:
    "Please observe the rule --
Prepare for yourselves the nšb,
    For the dog prepare the shoulder."
El takes his seat alongside Aš[erah],
    El seats himself in his banquet hall.
He drinks, [does El, of] wine to inebriancy,
    And of fermented wine to drunkenness.
He walks toward home,
    Directs himself to his bedroom.
He...
    And he meets Baal's ḫby with two horns and a
    tail.
He wallows in his excrement and urine;
    The voice of El, [even the voice] of El
    Becomes the voice of those who go down into
            the ground. (RS 24.258; my trans.,
            after Virolleaud)[28]

The drunkenness and the vomiting are typical. As
El's roisterous voice fades into the stupor of silence,
he becomes the very embodiment of the gods of the
underground, the gods of death.

    (3) Mesopotamia

The land between the Tigris and the Euphrates was
subject to storm and drought. Here human prosperity was

less precarious than on the Levant, yet more un-
predictable than in Egypt. It depended as much on
organization, diligence, and hard work as on nature's
own bountifulness. People who were not out on the
steppelands tending herds and flocks, or in the
fields tilling the soil, were likely to be at work
dredging and mending the canals that led water to
the verdant acreage. All was carefully regulated
from the towns and cities, where gods ruled as well
as kings.[29]

The struggle between life and death seems understandably less violent in Mesopotamia than in Ugarit.
For one thing, death is, in itself, not mythified,
like Mot of Ugarit. For another thing, Mesopotamian
mythology displays a greater curiosity than that of
Ugarit in the state of life after death, i.e., the
underworld. As excavations at Ur have revealed, at
least the first great Mesopotamian civilization,
that of Sumer, made extravagant preparations for the
world beyond death, paralleled only by those of the
Egyptian Pharaohs.[30] It was evidently believed that,
for the rich and might, the grim underworld could be
turned into a place of tolerable comfort.

Mesopotamian mythology, quite understandably,
has the theme of a seasonal struggle between the
forces of life and fertility on the one hand, and
those of death on the other hand. This is an aetiology for nature's atumnal dormancy and spring reju-
venation. Certainly this alternation is not depicted
as death's own paradoxical gift of healing, as in
Ugarit (the RPIM); nor is it seen as a battle between
rival gods or goddesses, as in Baal's and Anath's
combat with Mot. There was a popular cult of Dumuzi,
the shepherd god and male deity of fertility (= Tammuz
in the Bible; cf. Ezek. 8:14); the women, ever yearning for the power of fertility in their own bodies,
wept as Inanna, the goddess of love. This motif
assumed its standard form in the famous myth of
Inanna's descent to the Nether World.[31] This bold
lass, Enlil's daughter and also goddess of war,
determines to destroy the power of Ereshkigal, the
goddess of death residing in the underworld. She
is admitted through the portals, protected with seven
apotropaic ornaments or garments, but each of these
is confiscated until she is bereft of them all. She
becomes sick and dies, then is hung up naked like a
hunk of meat. As a result, fertility disappears on

earth, and all the world mourns. Inanna's messenger
goes from one god to another for help, and finally
obtains from Enki, the god of wisdom, the food and
the water of life. When he sprinkles this sixty times
on the decaying meat of Inanna's corpse, she revives.
Once back on earth, she searches for the substitute
that Ereshkigal requires. It turns out to be her
lover Dumuzi, who has been completely unmoved by her
death and now becomes the victim of her revenge.[32]

As can be seen, this is essentially a replica-
tion of the Osiris myth of Egypt and of the Baal-
Anath myth of Ugarit. The dying and rising god motif
is standard in monistic religious myth. Something
distinctive of Mesopotamian culture is its persistent
concern for the possibility of human immortality,
and it is this which we do well to illustrate in the
following pages.

Gilgamesh and the land of the living, ANET 48[33]

The vast popularity of the Gilgamesh literature
throughout ancient Mesopotamia indicates that the
various peoples living in this region were less devoted to speculation about a semi-deified existence
in the world beyond death, and more interested in the
prospects of achieving some kind of immortality,
which would function as a substitute for the life of
the present world -- or as a foil to death itself.
As we saw in a previous example, Atrahasis or Utnapishtim achieved immortality because he proved to be
in possession of a god-like wisdom, something
unattainable by ordinary man.

Remembered as a hero from the hoary past, Gilgamesh gradually assumed mythic proportions. In an
early, Sumerian, form of his epic, it is his heroic
exploits that offer him a hold upon immortality. It
begins with the following lines:

The lord toward the Land of the Living set his
    mind,
The lord, Gilgamesh, toward the Land of the
    Living set his mind;
He says to his servant Enkidu:

"O Enkidu, not (yet) have brick and stamp brought
   forth the fated end,
I would enter the 'land,' I would set up my name,
In its places where the names have been raised up,
   I would raise up my name,
In its places where the names have not been raised
   up, I would raise up the names of the gods."

Upon Enkidu's advice, Gilgamesh appeals for Utu's
permission and assistance in a project to enter the
Land of the Living by cutting down the cedar trees of
ferocious Huwawa:

"O Utu, I would enter the land, be thou my ally,
I would enter the land of the cut-down cedar,
   be thou my ally."
Utu of heaven answers him:
"...verily thou art, but what art thou to the
   'land?'"
"O Utu, a word I would speak to thee, to my word
   thy ear,
I would have it reach thee, give ear to it.
In my city man dies, oppressed is the heart,
Man perishes, heavy is the heart,
I peered over the wall,
Saw the dead bodies...floating on the river;
As for me, I too will be served thus; verily 'tis so
Man, the tallest, cannot stretch to heaven,
Man, the widest, cannot cover the earth.
Not (yet) have brick and stamp brought forth the
   fated end,
I would enter the 'land,' I would set up my name,
In its places where the names have been raised up,
   I would raise up my name,
In its places where the names have not been
   raised up, I would raise up the names of the
   gods."

This moving appeal accomplishes its purpose.
Utu grants Gilgamesh the help of seven demon-like
heroes. Enlisting fifty heroes from Erech, the party
makes its way over seven mountains and comes at last
to the forest of Huwawa. Frightful as he is, Huwawa
fless at the first show of force. Eventually his
head is cut off. Gilgamesh has apparently achieved the
immortality he has been seeking through this heroic
exploit.

410

Within original Sumerian documents, the motif of
Gilgamesh' search for immortality seems to attain
little development beyond the example that has just
been offered. There is a Sumerian poem predicting
and lamenting his death, then describing his pres-
tigious march through the underworld, his final place
of destiny. This is no more than an affirmation of
death as another form of life.[35]

The Semitic civilizations that succeeded the
Sumerian developed the Gilgamesh traditions into a
wide-reaching epic. Here the contest with Huwawa is
put in a position of subordination to the broader
theme of personal immortality beyond the fame and
name attainable by heroes. We have seen that Enkidu
is depicted as Gilgamesh' alter-ego, created to be
half beast and half man.[36] When he and Gilgamesh
offend Ishtar, the gods decree that Enkidu must die.
Gilgamesh understandably sees his buddy's death as
the foretoken of his own. From the Assyrian version
we cite the following words of his bitter lamentation:

> "Hear me, O elders [and give ear] unto me!
> It is for Enkidu my [friend], that I weep,
> Mourning bitterly like a wailing woman.
> The axe at my side, my hand's trust,
> The dirk in my belt, [the shield] in front of me,
> My festal robe, my richest trimming --
> An evil [demon] rose up and robbed me!
> [O my younger friend], thou chasedst
>   The wild ass of the hills, the panther of
>   the steppe!
> We who [have conquered] all things, scaled [the
>   mountains],
> Who seized the Bull [and slew him],
> Brought affliction on Hubbaba,[37] who [dwelled in
>   the Cedar Forest]!
> What, now, is this sleep that has laid hold [on
>   thee]?
> Thou art benighted and canst not hear [me]!"
> But he lifts not up [his eyes];
> He touched his heart, but it does not beat.
> Then he veiled (his) friend like a bride...
> Storming over him like a lion,
> Like a lioness deprived of [her] whelps.
> He paces back and forth before [the couch],

Pulling out (his hair) and strewing [it...],
Tearing off and flinging down (his) finery,
  [As though] unc[lean]!

. . . .

For Enkidu, his friend, Gilgamesh
Weeps bitterly, as he ranges over the steppe:
"When I die, shall I not be like Enkidu?
Woe has entered my belly.
Fearing death, I roam over the steppe...."

Advice of the ale-wife: ANET 89-90, Gilgamesh
epic[38]

    Gilgamesh resolves to search out Utnapishtim
(= Atrahasis), the only man to have achieved immortality.
For this he has to undertake an incredibly long journey.
Everyone along the way attempts to dissuade him. As
he waits at an inn to be ferried across a wide sea at
the edge of the world, he pours out his heart to an
ale-wife. The advice she offers in reply epitomizes
the hedonistic wisdom of the popular mind. Gilgamesh
is speaking in this extract drawn from the old-Baby-
lonian recension:

    "He who with me underwent all hard[ships] --
    Enkidu, whom I loved dearly,
    Who with me underwent all hardships --
    has now gone to the fate of mankind!
    Day and night I have wept over him.
    I would not give him up for burial --
    In case my friend should rise at my plaint --
    Seven days and seven nights,
    Until a worm fell out of his nose.
    Since his passing I have not found life,
    I have roamed like a hunter in the midst of the
        steppe.
    O ale-wife, now that I have seen thy face,
    Let me not see the death which I ever dread."
    The ale-wife said to him, to Gilgamesh:
    "Gilgamesh, whither rovest thou?
    The life thou pursuest thou shalt not find.
    When the gods created mankind,
    Death for mankind they set aside,
    Life in their own hands retaining.
    Thou, Gilgamesh, let full be thy belly,

412

Make thou merry by day and by night.
Of each day make thou a feast of rejoicing,
Day and night dance thou and play!
Let thy garments be sparkling fresh,
Thy head be washed; bathe thou in water.
Pay heed to the little one that holds on to thy
    hand,
Let thy spouse delight in thy bosom!
For this is the task of [mankind]!"

One cannot help wondering whether the ale-wife
has any connection with the RPIM of Ugarit. Is it
merely that wisdom comes in drink? Or is the ale-
wife a symbol of the alcoholic excess that disguises
death as life?

Gilgamesh fails to seize immortality: ANET 92-93,
95-96, Gilgamesh epic[39]

Torn and worn, Gilgamesh at last arrives at the
far shore of the sea and comes into the presence of
Utnapishtim. After telling him of his purpose, he
hears the following sage words from Utnapishtim's lips:

Do we build a house for ever?
    Do we seal (contracts) for ever?
Do brothers divide shares for ever?
Does hatred persist for ever in [the land]?
Does the river for ever raise up (and) bring on
    floods?
The dragon-fly [leaves] (its) shell
That its face might (but) glance at the face of
    the sun.
Since the days of yore there has been no
    [permanance];
The resting and the dead, how alike [they are]!
Do they not compose a picture of death,
The commoner and the noble,
    Once they are near to [their fate]?
The Anunnaki, the great gods, foregather;
Mammetum, maker of fate, with them the fate
    decrees:
Death and life they determine.
(But) of death, its days are not revealed.

413

This is the occasion for Utnapishtim to tell Gilgamesh the story of the flood, which is strikingly similar to the biblical account, featuring a boat that Utnapishtim builds beforehand and the sending out of birds to find dry land. Once the flood had subsided, Enlil came to bestow immortality on Utnapishtim and his wife in recognition that they indeed possessed a godlike wiseness.[40]

It is for the gods, not for Utnapishtim, to bestow immortality on Gilgamesh. The former may be willing to introduce him to the divine assembly for their consideration, but sets a prior test to determine whether Gilgamesh indeed has the makings of an immortal. The test is simply to stay awake for seven nights:

> "But now, who will for thy sake call the gods to
>   Assembly
> That the life which thou seekest thou mayest find?
> Up, lie not down to sleep
>   For six days and seven nights."

Gilgamesh tries, but inevitably fails; Utnapishtim and his wife prepare proof to show him when he awakes:

> As he sits there on his haunches,
> Sleep fans him like the whirlwind.
> Utnapishtim says to her, to his spouse:
> "Behold this hero who seeks life!
> Sleep fans him like a mist."
> His spouse says to him, to Utnapishtim the Faraway:
> "Touch him that the man may awake,
> That he may return safe on the way whence he came,
> That through the gate by which he left he may
>   return to his land."
> Utnapishtim says to her, to his spouse:
> "Since to deceive is human, he will seek to
>   deceive thee.
> Up, bake for him wafers, put (them) at his head,
> And mark on the wall the days he sleeps."
> She baked for him wafers, put (them) at his head,
> And marked on the wall the days he slept.

So each day she places a new wafer before him. Awakening on the seventh day, Gilgamesh tries to pretend that he has fallen asleep for only an instant:

"Scarcely had sleep surged over me,
When straightway thou dost touch and arouse me!"
Utnapishtim [says to him], to Gilgamesh:
["Go], Gilgamesh, count thy wafers,
[That the days thou hast slept] may become known
    to thee:
Thy [first] wafer is dried out,
[The second is gone] bad, the third is soggy;
    The crust of the fourth has turned white;
[The fifth] has a moldy cast,
    The sixth (still) is fresh-colored.
[The seventh] -- at this instant thou has
    awakened."
Gilgamesh says to him, to Utnapishtim the Faraway:
["What then] shall I do, Utnapishtim,
    Whither shall I go,
[Now] that the Bereaver has laid hold on my
    [members]?
In my bedchamber lurks death,
And wherever I se[t my foot], there is death!"

Gilgamesh and the boatman go to the water to wash
themselves and to prepare for their journey homeward.
Once Utnapishtim's wife sees how good Gilgamesh looks
when washed of his grime and clad in new garments, she
is moved to plead for the bestowal of a final favor.
He is called back and Utnapishtim tells him of a
lifegiving plant that grows on the sea bottom:

"Gilgamesh, thou hast come hither, toiling and
    straining.
What shall I give thee that thou mayest return
    to thy land?
I will disclose, O Gilgamesh, a hidden thing,
And [a secret of the gods I will] tell thee:
This plant, like the buckthorn is [its...].
Its thorns will p[rick thy hands] just as does
    the rose.
If thy hands obtain the plant, [thou wilt find
    new life]."

Gilgamesh responds instantly, only to be disappointed in the end:

No sooner had Gilgamesh heard this,
    Than he opened the wa[ter-pipe],
He tied heavy stones [to his feet],
They pulled him down into the deep [and he saw
    the plant].

He took the plant, though it pr[icked his hands].
He cut the heavy stones [from his feet].
The [s]ea cast him up on its shore.
Gilgamesh says to him, to Urshanabi, the boatman:
"Urshanabi, this plant is a plant apart,
Whereby a man may regain his life's breath.
I will take it to   ramparted Uruk,
    Will cause [...] to eat the p[lant....!]
Its name shall be 'Man Becomes Young in Old Age.'
I myself shall eat (it)
    And thus return to the state of my youth."
After twenty leagues they broke off a morsel,
After thirty (further) leagues they prepared for
    the night.
Gilgamesh saw a well whose water was cool.
He went down into it to bathe in the water.
A serpent snuffed the fragrance of the plant;
It came up [from the water] and carried off
    the plant.
Going back it shed [its] slough.
Thereupon Gilgamesh sits down and weeps,
His tears running down over his face.
[He took the hand] of Urshanabi, the boatman:
"[For] whom, Urshanabi, have my hands toiled?
For whom is being spent the blood of my heart?
I have not obtained a boon for myself,
For the earth-lion have I effected a boon!
And now the tide will bear (it) twenty leagues
    away!"

Gilgamesh now gives up his quest. He has just
one more claim to immortality. As he approaches his
city Uruk, he invites Urshanabi to inspect its ram-
parts and its brickwork, for this must suffice as his
claim to fame.

(e) Adapa's failure: ANET 101-2[41]

Another well-loved myth suggests that mankind is
denied immortality out of envy on the part of the gods,
a motif found also in Gen. 3:22 (cf. 11:6-7). Adapa,
the primeval wise man, should have been given immortality, like Atrahasis or Utnapishtim, but is
denied it; the myth tells how this came about. It
begins by stating the situation:

Wide understanding [Anu] had perfected for him to
    disclose the designs of the land.
To him he had given wisdom; eternal life he had
    not given him.

All is in the hands of Ea, Akkadian equivalent of
Enki, the god of wisdom, who devises a trick to keep
Adapa in his place. Adapa breaks the wing of the south
wind because it had sunk his fishing boat, for which
he is summoned to account in the court of Anu. Ea gets
him ready by offering him two sage words of advice,
the first helpful, the second deceitful and disastrous.
First he helps Adapa gain favor with the heavenly
doorkeepers by dressing as in mourning, and then having
him tell the doorkeeper-gods that he is grieving for
them.[42] Adapa is ushered into Anu's presence, who is
disposed to grant him his request. But here is Ea's
second piece of advice:

> ...As thou standest before Anu
> When they offer thee bread of death,
> Thou shalt not eat (it). When they offer thee
>   water of death,
> Thou shalt not drink (it). When they offer thee
>   a garment
> Put (it) on. When they offer thee oil, anoint
>   thyself (therewith).

Thus Ea makes Adapa believe that the gods will
try to poison him; the truth is that they will offer
him the bread of eternal life. But Ea's plan works.
After hearing Adapa's explanation of why he broke the
south wind's wing, Anu admits that he has divine
wisdom, and should be given immortality as well. Anu
says:

> "Why did Ea to a worthless human of the heaven
> And of the earth the plan disclose,
> Rendering him distinguished and making a name
>   for him?
> As for us, what shall we do about him? Bread
>   of life
> Fetch for him and he shall eat (it)." When
>   the bread of life
> They brought him, he did not eat; when the water
>   of life
> They brought him, he did not drink. When a
>   garment
> They brought him, he put (it) on; when oil
> They brought him, he anointed himself (therewith).

The ending seems very abrupt, but its meaning is clear:

> As Anu looked at him, he laughed at him:
> "Come now, Adapa! Why didst thou neither eat
>   nor drink?
> Thou shalt not have (eternal) life! Ah, per[ver]se
>   mankind!"
> "Ea, my master,
> Commanded me: 'Thou shalt not eat, thou shalt
>   not drink'."
> "Take him away and return him to his earth."

Thus in the end mortal man is the sport and mockery of the Mesopotamian gods.

      c.   Israel's acceptance of death and affirmation
         of life

Considerable space has been devoted to exhibiting examples of the literary treatment of the subject of death in the various ancient Near-Eastern cultures. This has not been done simply because of the inherent interest of these materials. It has been done in order to dramatize the distinctiveness of the Israelite attitude toward death, as seen in the sobriety and restraint with which it approaches this subject. What is so remarkable in the Israelite attitude is its rejection of the vast and varied mythological speculation of its neighbors! It has no mortuary cult; it has no feast of the dead and no dying and rising god; it has no myth of the search for immortality. No sign of an impoverished imagination, this very lack is, rather, an eloquent testimony of faith! For Israel, Yahweh was the God of life and the God of death, and that was enough. Bitter as death might be, it could never sever a mortal man's connection with the God who had brought him to existence. Death is simply the road-sign at the end of life's highway. Man in the boundness of his life, coming from out of boundlessness, goes out once again into the boundlessness of his Creator's power. Nothingness was the point from which he had begun; the nothingness of death is the point to which he will return; what counts is the precious life that has been given him before his days shall end. It is not the quantity of days or years that give life its meaning, but their quality. Even if the quantity be unreasonably short, it is more quality that counts to make life worth living.

The Old Testament attitude toward death is one of the Bible's great achievements. It is in every way consistent with a biblical understanding of divine transcendence in the midst of immanence and expresses the authentic meaning of divine and human personhood. As such, it has much to offer modern man in search for the meaning of his existence.

(1) The rejection of monistic mythologies

It is important to observe specific passages in which the Old Testament, along with postbiblical Jewish literature, wrestles with mythological motifs inimical to its essential stance of personalistic monotheism. As a whole, Israelite religion and theology remained remarkably consistent in adhering to its own distinctive attitude toward death.

(a) Death as punishment

As in the case of Enkidu's death, death could readily be construed in ancient Near-Eastern culture as the god's designed and purposeful punishment for human sin, particularly when it came too soon, or in some specially painful or gruesome manner. This idea barely surfaces in the Old Testament. In spite of the fact that the infliction of the death sentence was as common in ancient Israel as among its neighbors (but the Old Testament does have strict controls over it!",[43] the Old Testament offers virtually no support for the idea that human death is in itself a penalty for sin.

There is, to be sure, the threat of death set as a penalty for transgression in Genesis 2-3. But before we examine this passage directly, we should make appropriate adjustments for certain New Testament formulations which are likely to bias the Christian interpreter in his approach to this passage.

As is well known, Paul expresses himself very pointedly in his identification of death as a penalty for Adam's sin. One passage is I Cor. 15:21-26, from which we extract the following:

> For as by one man came death, by a man has come also the resurrection of the dead. For as in Adam all die, so also in Christ shall all be made alive....For he must reign until he has put all his enemies under his feet. The last enemy to be destroyed is death.

Here Paul's rhetorical technique is to set Christ the life-giver in impressive contrast to the death he has come to conquer. In a very similar passage, Rom. 5:12-26, Paul also contrasts Christ with Adam, identifying Christ as the bringer of grace and justi-fication over against Adam as the bringer of death. The reader can scarcely misunderstand his intent, for Paul repeatedly identifies death as sin's consequence:

> Therefore as sin came into the world through one man and death through sin, and so death spread to all men because all men sinned.... Death reigned from Adam to Moses....Many died through one man's transgression....The judgment following one trespass brought condemnation.... Because of one man's trespass, death reigned through that one man....One man's trespass led to condemnation for all men....By one man's dis-obedience many were made sinners....Sin reigned in death....

Even while Paul's doctrine can be seen as in itself a logical and unforced interpretation of the Genesis account, the following two considerations must govern our evaluation of it: (1) This is distinctive Pharisaical doctrine, a heritage of Paul's first-century Jewish schooling; (2) Paul is thinking of spiritual death as much as of physical death, par-ticularly in the Romans passage.

Although a detailed exegesis of these passages would be out of place here,[44] some brief explanation of the preceding statements is required. With regard to the first point, we observe that among the wide array of Jewish literature available to us, a direct connection between sin and physical death is not made except here in Paul and in two late first-century Pharisaic documents, II Esdras and II Baruch. This appears quite explicitly in II Esdr. 3:7, 7:48, 118-120, II Bar. 23:4, 48:42-43, 51:15, 54:15. What appears in these passages is enough to convince us that they directly draw from the same ideological source as Paul. II Esdras and II Baruch were composed a decade or two after Paul's own writings, and are each apocalypses employing Daniel as a structural model.[45] They are, in fact, very close in time to the New Testament book of Revelation. In short: here is evidence that the Pauline passages in question reflect the apostle's elsewhere-observed dependence on apocalyptic ideology, and that the Pharisaical school of Gamaliel was the specific source of this line of speculation.[46]

With respect to our second point, we briefly mention the following: (1) in Romans 5 Paul has been set to writing as he does by a mention of Christ's death (vv. 6-10); he continues in chapter 6 by drawing consequences from his teaching in terms of release from spiritual -- not physical -- death. (2) throughout Rom. 5:12-26 Paul writes of Christ's act as a liberation from sin, not from physical death itself. Taken together, these clues suggest that it is mainly mankind's spiritual death, its estrangement from God, that he has in mind as the consequence of Adam's transgression.

The summary of the preceding observations is that Paul's interpretation of the fall story in Genesis is isolated and late; further, that it is primarily (though probably not exclusively) spiritual death, rather than physical death, that he sees as sin's penalty. In any case, we are bound to approach Genesis in its own right. What does it actually say on this question?

First, let us recall an earlier observation concerning the remarkable isolation of this tradition. Neither the Old Testament nor mainline Judaism draws any direct consequences from the story of Adam's fall.[47] Next we must look at the text of Genesis itself, seeking to understand it on its own terms. Death is directly referred to in 2:17 ("In the day that you eat of it you shall die") and in 3:3 ("God said, 'You shall not eat of the fruit of the tree which is in the midst of the garden, neither shall you touch it, lest you die'"). A long line of inter-preters have been confounded by the fact that the primeval pair did not actually die immediately, as the threat very clearly implies. True, Yahweh's word to the man in 3:19 speaks of death -- but only as the ultimate and inevitable termination of a wearisome and unrewarding life of toil. In another connection, we have argued that vv. 17-19 is drawn from folk-wisdom as an aetiology of mankind's struggle with the earth (hā'ādām versus hā'adāmah).[48] The J writer undoubtedly means these verses to serve as a fulfillment of the threat of death in 2:17, despite the incongruity that we have observed. It is not too difficult to perceive that the threat and the reference to it in the dialogue between the woman and the serpent were drawn by J from his source material. In its original Canaanite form, this material in-tended the divine threat to be taken literally; God or the gods were scaring man into obedience by the severity of the consequence of transgression; the serpent, symbol of vegetative fertility, planted in the woman's mind the suspicion that the threat was intended only for effect, and that she and the man would actually experience "life" rather than death if they took the bold course of seizing the forbidden fruit.

The summary of this analysis is that the notion of death as sin's penalty appears barely on the fringe of normative biblical thought. Where it is indeed normative is in the sin/punishment syndrome of extra-biblical monistic fatalism. This notion is not dis-tinctively or normatively biblical, nor is it in any way an achievement of monotheistic personalism. That a human being may die an untimely or painful death as the direct result of his own sin and folly is the observation of human wisdom in general.

(b)   The search for immortality

Mesopotamian mythology appears to be deliberately set aside in three isolated extrapolations of myth taken up as part of J's Genesis prehistory.[49] The Yahwist does not deem it necessary to rewrite the

crudely anthropomorphic representations in his
material, for this is thoroughly sanitized in his
effectively monotheistic contexting. We cite these
fragments of submerged myth, as follows:

> Then Yahweh God said, "Behold, the man has
> become like one of us, knowing good and
> evil; and now, lest he put forth his hand
> and take also of the tree of life, and eat,
> and live for ever....He drove out the man;
> and at the east of the garden of Eden he
> placed the cherubim, and a flaming sword
> which turned every way, to guard the way
> to the tree of life. (3:22, 24)

> When men began to multiply on the face of
> the ground, and daughters were born to them,
> the sons of God saw that the daughters of
> men were fair; and they took to wife such
> of them as they chose. Then Yahweh said,
> "My spirit shall not abide in man for ever,
> for he is flesh, but his days shall be a
> hundred and twenty years." The Nephilim
> were on the earth in those days, and also
> afterward, when the sons of God came in to
> the daughters of men, and they bore children
> to them. These were the mighty men that
> were of old, the men of renown. (6:1-4)

> As men migrated from the east....they said,
> "Come, let us build ourselves a city, and
> a tower with its top in the heavens, and
> let us make a name for ourselves, lest we
> be scattered abroad upon the face of the
> whole earth." And Yahweh said, "Behold,
> they are one people, and they have all one
> language; and this is only the beginning of
> what they will do; and nothing that they
> propose to do will now be impossible for
> them. Come, let us go down, and there con-
> fuse their language, that they may not
> understand one another's speech." So
> Yahweh scattered them abroad from there
> over the face of all the earth, and they
> left off building the city. (11:2-8)

The tree of life, mentioned first at Gen. 2:9,
may be a redactional addition; in any case it is
not identical with the tree from which the forbidden

fruit was taken. Like the garden itself, it symbolizes the possibility of an unending, perfect life.
Sinful man is driven away from both of them because
his transgression has made the possession of unending life dangerous and demonic. Deity alone can
be entrusted with unending life because, if man
should have it, he would become a perfect devil.

The power to create new life has been given
humankind. This is, in itself, a godlike potency
(see Gen. 1:27ff.). Genesis 6 reproduces the crude
myth in which human females bear monsters with the
aid of supernatural beings called "the sons of god."
To counteract the titanic grasping for immortality
that may come to manifestation in unrestrained
gigantism or heroism, J presents Yahweh's own decree
in v. 3, to the effect that setting a term to human
longevity must control this reaching for immortality.
After all, man is "flesh" (baśar), and it is only
Yahweh's spirit (rûaḥ) that gives him life. Life is
God's own possession, hence he determines to exercise his prerogative in rationing it to this, his
most volatile creation.

Finally, the ability to communicate linguistically
and the ability to build abiding edifices represent
godlike creative gifts to mankind. Together, these
make civilization, man's great achievement, possible.
When done in defiance of God, they may represent still
another attempt to snatch the immortality that God
has retained for himself alone. This is the spiritual
meaning of the strange, mythic story of Genesis 11.
The Yahwist, finding it eloquently effective for con-
veying the normative biblical notion of the denial
of immortality to man, incorporated it in its present
context in order to prepare for his introduction to
the patriarchal narration appearing in the next
following chapter.

In sum: far from embracing the notion of human
immortality, the Bible early and decisively dispenses
with it. Human life is God's gift, and as such it can
be, and will be, withdrawn at God's pleasure.

(c)   Sheol and the underworld

In the Old Testament, there are no chthonic
deities, no mythological depictions of life in an
underworld. To be sure, the Israelites did not
restrict themselves simply to speaking of the grave
(qeber) as the resting place of the dead. They
allowed themselves a choice of allusional terms that
had been more or less sanitized from their mythic
associations in extrabiblical and subbiblical ideology. Such are šaḥat, "shaft," bôr, "pit," and
ʾbaddôn, "perdition"; here are sent, in Ezekiel's
bold metaphor, the nations that are hostile to
God's people (Ezek. 32:17ff.). By far the most
frequent expression is šᵉʾōl (the equivalent of LXX,
NT hadēs), which is difficult to translate but, to
judge from its verbal root, Š'L, "ask (an oracle)",
apparently refers to the place from which oracles
come (cf. Akkadian ša'ilu, "one who consults spirits").
In the vast majority of passages, sheol is simply a
synonym for death or the grave. The Old Testament
scarcely ventures to attribute any kind of life to
those who are there. Job is as daring as any, yet
in the following citation it is clear that the
existence of those who have died is nothing else than
sweet oblivion, a surcease from toil and injustice:

Why did I not die at birth...?
For then I should have lain down and been quiet;
    I should have slept; then I should have been
    at rest,
with kings and counselors of the earth
    who rebuilt ruins for themselves,
or with princes who had gold,
    who filled their houses with silver.
Or why was I not as a hidden untimely birth,
    as infants that never see the light?
There the wicked cease from troubling;
    they hear not the voice of the taskmaster.
The small and the great are there,
    and the slave is free from his master. (3:11-19)

This is the Old Testament's normative, canonical
position. Deut. 18:11 (cf. Lev. 19:31) specifically
designates the consultation of mediums, wizards, and
necromancers as an "abomination," along with divi-
nation, soothsaying, augury, and sorcery. I Chr. 10:13
condemns king Saul for this sin, and this is likewise
the clear intent of I Samuel 28, a narrative that prepares for the account of Saul's death at Gilboa by
depicting him as guilty of this same sin. "The "witch"

whom he seeks out is, in fact, a medium. Whether or
not the narrative actually intends to present the
rising of Samuel's ghost as a factual event, it very
clearly does intend to condemn Saul for it. Its
unmistakable irony lies in the fact that the very
ghost of Samuel speaks Saul's doom.

It is in this connection that we furthermore take
note of Israelite fear of contact with the dead
(Num. 5:2, 19:11-22; cf. Lev. 21:1-4, 10-12). This
also explains the forbidding of certain practices
associated with the Canaanite funerary cult (Lev.
19:28, Deut. 14:1). The fact that v. 10, immediately
preceding Deut. 18:11, prohibits the burning of sons
and daughters suggest that the frequently condemned
Molech cult (cf. II Kings 21:6) was ideologically akin
to the cult of the RPIM in Ugarit.[50]

Mythological speculation about the underworld is
almost certainly the source of inspiration for the
notion of a hades or hell in the apocalyptical
literature. The most notable passage is I Enoch 17-23
(cf. 108). Within other streams of Jewish apocalyptic
speculation, this idea hardly surfaces; we note
especially the restraint of II Esdras -- perhaps three
centuries later than I Enoch -- even with its pressing
concern for the state of the dead until the time of
final judgment.[51]

Although this is scarcely the place to enter into
an extended discussion of the hades-hell idea in the
New Testament, we do take special note of Jesus'
parable about Lazarus and the rich man in hades, Luke
16:19-31. In light of the fact that the New Testament
has indeed adopted a variety of apocalyptic concepts,
as well as the genre of apocalyptic itself, it would
be hazardous to suggest that the evangelist (or his
tradition) is not employing this in a fully realistic
sense, yet the probability remains that it is little
more than literary license. Let us remember, in any
event, that it is a parable. Lazarus in Abraham's
bosom is no less, and no more, real than the Good
Samaritan and the Prodigal Son.

(d)   Immortality of the soul

Finally we observe that neither the Old Testament nor the New Testament offers the typical Greek notion that the human soul survives apart from the body after death. This is based on a metaphysical dualism which, as we have seen, identifies the body as unreal and ephemeral, while cherishing the soul as real and eternally immortal. To be sure, at least one apocryphal writing, the Wisdom of Solomon, appears to make important concessions to this notion; cf. 3:1ff. This is by no means the only Greek concept accepted by this book.[52] All the same, we need to remember that it definitely represents a sharply isolated cultural situation, that of the Jewish diaspora in Hellenistic Egypt. It in no way represents the general attitude of Palestinian Judaism, whether in the pre-Christian or immediate post-Christian period.

In those passages where St. Paul adverts to the coming glory of being with Christ (II Cor. 4:14-5:8, Phil. 1:20-24; cf. I Cor. 13:10-12), there is never a suggestion on his part that physical dying is a precondition to union with Christ, as though one needed to escape from the body in order to ascend to the clear light of the heavenly vision. This is, indeed, what Christian Gnosticism made of such Pauline deliverances. Paul is still Jew enough to go no further than the outer bounds of apocalyptic ideology. His meaning is that the present age obscures God; when he dies, he will pass beyond it into the eschaton that God is preparing in Christ. Even though this goes significantly beyond the classical Hebraic view, it falls short of the dualistic separation of body and soul characteristic of the Greek mentality.

(2) Embracing life as a foil to death

Hebraic thought does not deny the reality of death or disguise it as life. On the other hand, it refuses to give death equal status with life. Death is no more -- but also no less -- than the termination of vital creaturely existence. It represents the outer boundary of creaturely finitude, the border point dividing man from God. Thus it is to be regretted because it represents the loss of life, but this does not mean that death robs human life of significance. If the infinite Being who has brought each of us into this momentary vital existence has also given us the capacity of becoming at least fleetingly aware of his presence, the life he has created does indeed have lasting significance. The infinite Subject has created myriad finite subjects like ourselves to glimpse his own being and reflect his own glory.

But, as has been stated, death is to be regretted. This is not to say that it is a colossal tragedy. The Hebrews understood that life is the only meaningful answer to death. If death must come to everyone at last, concluding the quantitative extent of life's duration, it can be counterbalanced only by investing life with a transcendant quality guaranteeing its enduring significance beyond death. Life _coram deo_ ("in God's presence") is life everlasting, something that death itself cannot destroy.

Thus the Hebrews knew that death was the time to weep. They also knew that, until death, it is time to affirm and celebrate life.

(a) The sorrow and tragedy of death

Death is painful because it robs us of life. The Old Testament knows how to express what we all know: that life itself is dying. We increase in strength and vitality through childhood and puberty to young adulthood, and then gradually begin to decline into the debilitude of old age. Shakespeare's child on the stage of life becomes a child again, now as a doddering old man.[53] At last death arrives, quietly closing the door of life.

In our culture, for a hospital patient to exclaim, "I'm dying!", when not actually in a critical condition would likely identify that patient as a melodramatic hypochondriac. In ancient Israelite culture, it was normal for one healed of serious illness to declare:

> The snares of death encompassed me;
>> the pangs of Sheol laid hold on me;
>> I suffered distress and anguish. (Ps. 116:3)

Anything that deprives one of God's people of full life in his presence -- and that would include exile and imprisonment (cf. Psalms 42-43) as well as sickness or severe injury (cf. Ps. 88:3ff.) -- is described as a tentative and partial dying. An especially gripping description is that of I Sam. 25:37-38:

> When the wine had gone out of Nabal, his wife told him these things, and his heart died within him, and he became as a stone. And about ten days later Yahweh smote Nabal, and he died.

Nabal's heart dies when he is stricken with a paralyzing stroke; at last Yahweh intervenes to terminate his life.

If even life itself is a dying, death is surely inevitable for all who are alive on earth. This is often cast into proverbial sayings:

> We must all die, we are like water split on the ground, which cannot be gathered up again. (II Sam. 14:14)

> As for man, his days are like grass;
>   he flourishes like a flower of the field;
> for the wind passes over it, and is gone,
>   and its place knows it no more (Ps. 103:16)

> All flesh is grass,
>   and all its beauty is like the flower of the field.
> The grass withers, the flower fades,
>   when the breath of Yahweh blows upon it;
>   surely the people is grass. (Isa. 40:6-7)

Death is inevitable, and it is also final. When death comes, the game of life is over:

> As the cloud fades and vanishes,
>   so he who goes down to Sheol does not come up;
> he returns no more to his house,
>   nor does his place know him any more (Job 7:9-10)

> Are not the days of my life few?
>   Let me alone, that I may find a little comfort
> before I go whence I shall not return,

>   to the land of gloom and deep darkness,
>   the land of gloom and chaos,
>   where light is as darkness. (Job 10:20-22)

> Dost thou work wonders for the dead?
>   Do the shades rise up to praise thee?
> Is thy steadfast love declared in the grave,
>   or thy faithfulness in Abaddon?
> Are thy wonders known in the darkness,
>   or thy saving help in the land of forget-
>   fulness? (Ps. 88:10-12)

> The fate of the sons of men and the fate of
> beasts is the same; as one dies, so dies
> the other. They all have the same breath,
> and man has no advantage over the beasts;
> for all is vanity. All go to one place;
> all are from the dust, and all turn to dust
> again. Who knows whether the spirit of man
> goes upward and the spirit of the beast goes
> down to the earth? (Eccl. 3:19-21)

All the same, the Hebrews saw death as natural, and as part of God's design for creaturely existence. There were four special situations in which it would be viewed as positively tragic:

(1) When it is untimely, robbing a man of a long and full life;
(2) When it leaves a man without children to honor and remember him;
(3) When it comes violently;
(4) When it deprives him of a decent and honorable burial.

The apocryphal book, Tobit, is a major exponent of the Jewish horror for dying unburied. The old man Tobit is himself an examplar of courage and piety as he hastens out to snatch up the unburied dead before their pitiable corpses can be desecrated.[54] His own major personal concern is that his son Tobias shall be on hand to bury him when he dies.[55] This book gives us good reason to believe that the Jews in diaspora were often put in peril of remaining unburied -- a calamity that has recurred countless times even in our own "enlightened" age!

The Jews have always known how to behave when it is time to weep. In the biblical era, their mourning

practices were markedly demonstrative. Weeping was
so prevalent at funerals that certain persons,
especially women, offered themselves as professionals
(Jer. 9:17ff., Eccl. 12:5, II Chr. 35:25; cf. Matt.
9:24). There was nothing distinctively biblical
about this; it was customary in the entire ancient
Near East.[56] We may rightly inquire whether the
Canaanite-Ugaritic cult of the dead had an influence.
Even if this were present, the question is not one
of phenomenological similarities, but of theological
distinctiveness; and in this respect there can be no
question but that normative Hebraic ideology firmly
rejected both the mythology and the explicit ritual
of this inimical cult.

(b)   The affirmation of life

1)   The counsel of a wise man (Qoheleth)

Gerhard von Rad found great difficulty in justifying a place for Qoheleth within the same Scriptural
Canon that contains the writings that witness to
Heilsgeschichte because this unique book explicitly
denies its ongoing relevance.[57] His assessment that
Qoheleth does deny teleology in human striving is
correct; nevertheless, a blindness to this book's
contribution to the over-all biblical achievement
offers evidence of an inadequacy in von Rad's definition of the biblical norm.

The writer of Ecclesiastes was probably a Palestinian Jew living during the second half of the third
century, B.C.[58] This was the heyday of the Ptolemaic
rule. It was not a good time for Judaism, nor was
it a particularly bad time. It was simply an indifferent time, a meaningless time. Judaism appeared
to be going nowhere, to have no destiny in the world.
Qoheleth, the fictional speaker of this book (otherwise identified as Solomon, 1:1ff.), confesses that
he can make nothing out of Israel's traditional
affirmation to the effect that the God of the world
is guiding the peculiar destiny of this people.
Furthermore, he makes bold to question many of its

traditional pious dogmas, particularly that the
righteous prosper while the wicked suffer. Thus
Qoheleth does get very low marks indeed for his
inability to affirm the concept of history as meaningful interaction between man and God. Nevertheless,
Judaism has done well in preserving this book for
its sacred Canon. Above all else, it informs us that
life has a positive meaning even when a sense of
historical destiny has been lost.

It is not so much the inevitability of death
that Qoheleth fears, as the meaninglessness of life.
In his view, it is definitely better to be alive than
to be dead:

> He who is joined with all the living has hope,
> for a living dog is better than a dead lion.
> For the living know that they will die, but
> the dead know nothing, and they have no more
> reward, but the memory of them is lost.
> (9:4-5)

It is this pasage that corrects a possible wrong
impression created by snatching the following out of
context:

> ...Better is...the day of death, than the day
> of birth. It is better to go to the house of
> mourning than to go to the house of feasting.
> (7:1-2)

In the context Qoheleth says: "A good name is
better than precious ointment....[Death].....is the
end of all men, and the living will lay it to heart....
The heart of the wise is in the house of mourning....
Better is the end of a thing than its beginning."
(vv. 1, 2, 4, 8) Qoheleth simply means that death
alone puts the entire life of a person in perspective;
it is only when one is grieving over the loss of that
person that one fully values his worth.

Thus Qoheleth does not exalt death, nor does he
wish for it. We must also resist the popular verdict
to the effect that he is unduly sceptical, even to
the point of cynicism. It is not, in fact, clear
that he has been strongly influenced by Hellenistic [59]
thinking, in spite of recent studies to that effect.
Qoheleth stands firmly within orthodox Hebraic tradition, and functions entirely as a worthy representative of classical Hebraic wisdom.[60] The truth is that

he is impatient with the many cheap answers that he
has been hearing concerning what gives value to human
life. Some say it is riches, others say it is power,
others say it is fame, still others say it is wisdom
itself. In one passage after another, he scathingly
demolishes each of these in turn. Because there are
some Jews who are offering still another alternative,
a formalistic "righteousness," he even goes so far as
to advise: "Be not righteous overmuch, and do not make
yourself otherwise; why should you destroy yourself?"
(7:16)[61] Far from this being offensive to authentic
Hebraic piety, it only affirms what we read in the
classical wisdom saying found in Jer. 9:23-24:

> Let not the wise man glory in his wisdom, let
> not the mighty man glory in his might, let not
> the rich man glory in his riches; but let him
> who glories glory in this; that he understands
> and knows me, that I am Yahweh who practice
> steadfast love, justice, and righteousness in
> the earth; for in these things I delight, says
> Yahweh.

This is actually what is intended in the conclusion of Qoheleth's book, which literary critics
have often seen as a corrective addition:

> The end of the matter: all has been heard.
> Fear God, and keep his commandments; for
> this is the whole duty of man. For God will
> bring every deed into judgment, with every
> secret thing, whether good or evil.
> (12:13-14)

This provides the perspective from which the
reader should evaluate Qoheleth's positive recommendation. He does have a positive, up-beat attitude,
despite the constant negativity of his running critique upon the false values that he surveys. One
can hear this positive note coming through as a
recurrent refrain:

> There is nothing better for a man than that
> he should eat and drink, and find enjoyment
> in his toil. This also, I say, is from the
> hand of God. (2:24)

> It is God's gift to man that every one should
> eat and drink and take pleasure in his toil.
> (3:13)

433

Behold, what I have seen to be good and to be fitting is to eat and drink and find enjoyment in all the toil with which one toils under the sun the few days of his life which God has given him, for this is his lot. Every man also to whom God has given wealth and possessions and power to enjoy then, and to accept his lot and find enjoyment in his toil -- this is the gift of God. For he will not much remember the days of his life because God keeps him occupied with joy in his heart. (5:18-20)

I commend enjoyment, for man has no good thing under the sun but to eat and drink, and enjoy himself, for this will go with him in his toil through the days of life which God gives him under the sun. (8:15)

Go, eat your bread with enjoyment, and drink your wine with a merry heart; for God has already approved what you do. Let your garments be always white; let not oil be lacking on your head. Enjoy life with the wife whom you love, all the days of your vain life which he has given you under the sun, because that is your portion in life and in your toil at which you toil under the sun. Whatever your hand finds to do, do it with all your might; for there is no work or thought or knowledge or wisdom in Sheol, to which you are going (9:9-10)

Light is sweet, and it is pleasant for the eyes to behold the sun. For if a man lives many years, let him rejoice in them all; but let him remember that the days of darkness will be many. All that comes is vanity. (11:7-8)

Rejoice, O young man, in your youth, and let your heart cheer you in the days of your youth; walk in the ways of your heart and the sight of your eyes. But know that for all these things God will bring you into judgment. Remove vexation from your mind, and put away pain from your body; for

youth and the dawn of life are vanity.
Remember also your Creator in the days
of your youth, before the evil days
come.... (11:9-12:1)

It is most certainly wrong to accuse Qoheleth of
hedonism, for in 2:1ff. he offers a direct and scathing
critique of the pursuit of pleasure for its own sake.
His counsel lies on two distinct levels: pragmatic
and theoretical. On the pragmatic level he is advising making the most of what God provides: "This
is your portion (heleq) in life." To grasp for more,
and to cherish the symbols of success in place of the
reality, is idolatry.[62] On the theoretical level he
advises a reverent humility -- knowing the proper
place of creaturely man in the face of the world's
impenetrable mysteries. Asking for more is trying to
play God. Along with doing righteousness and loving
hesed, the duty of man is to "walk humbly with your
God"! (Mic. 6:8)

2) A praise-filled life overcomes death

It is a mistake to take Qoheleth's recommendation
as implying a secular worldliness, for it is "the
fear of God" that must provide the perspective for
enjoying God's gift of life. The life that overcomes
death is lived on the vertical level as well as on
the horizontal level. We turn to certain outstanding wisdom sayings in the Psalms for the most impressive statements of this perception. In a psalm
of complaint, Psalm 17, the pious writer describes
the wicked who are accusing and threatening him,
requesting Yahweh to protect him. In the light of
Qohleth's reference to cherishing one's proper heleq
(portion), his assessment of his enemies' lifestyle
is especially revealing:

Arise, Yahweh, confront them, overthrow them!
    Deliver my life from the wicked by thy sword,
from men by thy hand, O Yahweh,
    from men whose portion (heleq) in life is
    of the world.
May their belly be filled with what thou hast
stored up for them;

may their children have more than enough;
may they leave something over to their babes.
(13-14)

The psalmist seems to be saying that the fulness of
earthly goods which his adversaries are enjoying may
be all that they have, hence they will fall ultimately
under God's condemnation. Perhaps the psalmist himself has been deprived of these things; if so, he
consoles himself with the assurance that he has something better, something that is more important than
earthly goods. It is the awareness that God is
caringly and revealingly present:

As for me, I shall behold thy face in righteousness;
when I awake, I shall be satisfied with be-
holding thy form. (v. 15)

Traditionally, this has been interpreted as a
reference to resurrection. This is very doubtful in
the light of the late emergence of that idea. It is
not at all certain that the imperfect verbs in this
verse are futuristic, or that the "awaking" is experienced by the psalmist himself.[63] Thus, as a
minimum, the psalmist may be saying that he receives
a vision of divine righteousness, revealed in God's
own comforting presence -- that he is fully consoled
by the "awakening" of God's "form." With or without
the eschatological reference, this is a remarkable
confession that the vertical dimension fully com-
pensates for any blurring of the horizontal dimension
of life.

Very similar is Ps. 73:23ff. This too is a wisdom psalm. The writer has been reflecting on the
disturbing fact that wicked men seem to get along in
life better than the righteous. He had been at the
point of denying God's existence until he began to
meditate on the prospect of the wicked's eventual
destiny, which is certain to be evil. Their prosperity is ephemeral and illusory (vv. 18-20).
Thus the psalmist reassures himself with the cer-
tainty that God is always near and real:

I am continually with thee;
    thou dost guide me with thy counsel,
    and afterward thou wilt receive me to glory.
Whom have I in heaven but thee?
    And there is nothing upon earth that I desire
    beside thee.

My flesh and my heart may fail,
   but God is the strength of my heart and my
   portion (ḥēleq) for ever.
For lo, those who are far from thee shall perish;
   thou dost put an end to those who are false
   to thee,
But for me it is good to be near God;
   I have made the Lord God my refuge,
   that I may tell of all thy works.   (vv. 23-28)

The life that is the foil of death is, then, a
life in the nearness of God. This means that life's
most vital part is enjoying God's presence, praying
to him and praising him. It is the task of the living
to praise God.

Many psalms say this, but we turn now to one
that says it better than most others. It is not
actually in the Psalter, but in Isa. 38:10-20.[64] We
shall quote the entire psalm, a song of praise to
Yahweh for life in the face of death:

I said, In the noontide of my days I must depart;
   I am consigned to the gates of Sheol for the
   rest of my years.
I said, I shall not see Yahweh in the land of the
living;
   I shall look upon man no more among the inhabitants of the world.
My dwelling is plucked up and removed from me like
a shepherd's tent;
   like a weaver I have rolled up my life;
he cuts me off from the loom;
   from day to night thou dost bring me to an end;
I cry for help until morning;
   like a lion he breaks all my bones;
   from day to night thou dost bring me to an end.
Like a swallow or a crane I clamor, I moan like a
dove.
   My eyes are weary with looking upward.
   O Lord, I am oppressed; be thou my security!
But what can I say? For he has spoken to me,
   and he himself has done it.
All my sleep has fled
   because of the bitterness of my soul.
O Lord, by these things men live,
   and in all these is the life of my spirit.
O restore me to health and make me live!

At this point the psalmist experiences relief; Yahweh has intervened, and he is brought back from death:

> Lo, it was for my welfare that I had great
> bitterness;
>> but thou hast held back my life from the pit
>> of destruction,
>> for thou has cast all my sins behind thy back.
> For Sheol cannot thank thee,
>> death cannot praise thee;
>> those who go down to the pit cannot hope for
>> thy faithfulness.
> The living, the living, he thanks thee, as I do
> this day;
>> the father makes known to the children thy
>> faithfulness.

If Yahweh is to be praised, it must be through the living who have been saved from death. It is they who can tell their children of his faithfulness. Now that his life has been threatened, the psalmist dedicates the remainder of his days on earth to praise:

> Yahweh will save me,
>> and we will sing to stringed instruments
> all the days of our life
>> at the house of Yahweh.

(3)   Resurrectionism

There are a number of late prophetic passages in which the idea of a resurrection or restoration from death comes to expression. These are Ezek. 37:1-14, Isa. 25:6-8, 26:19, 65:17-20. In the light of two essential considerations, it will not be useful to review these passages in detail. These are: (1) in each of these passages, it is Israel as a people that is in view, not individual dead persons, so that the image of revival from death is actually a promise of national restoration; (2) the image itself lay ready to hand in the thought-world of the Canaanites, Egyptians, and Mesopotamians, each of whom had a mythology of a dying and rising god. As with various other mythological motifs, the Israelites were adept at employing such an image in metaphor and allusion, without the literal acceptance of the image. All the same, these passages may witness to a tendency toward speculation that the individual dead may actually rise. Although the Ezekiel passage is certainly not apocalyptical,[65] the three Isaiah passages do tend in this direction, coming not from the pen of the original prophet but from early apocalypticists of the postexilic period.

As has been observed, Jewish apocalyptic came more and more to rely on the drastic periodization of time in its forecast of the future. The present age is an age of sin and spiritual death; the age to come will be a time of judgment and salvation. It is no doubt an entirely logical development that this ideology should eventually produce the notion of resurrection, yet it is not always clear whether this meant the revival of the body, or simply the survival or restoration of life apart from the body. This ambiguity can be seen in I Enoch, which envisages the first in chapters 83-90, but the second in chapters 91-94. That particular apocalypse belonged to the Hasidic sect, and probably dates from the early years of the second century, B.C. Speculation about resurrection is found sporadically throughout the literature of the intertestamental period.[66] Within the canonical Old Testament, it comes to clear expression only once, and that is in Dan. 12:1-3, a passage that closely reflects the time and the ideology of I Enoch.

Some interpreters believe that this passage has been strongly influenced by Iranian Zoroastrianism.[67] The Michael mentioned in Dan. 12:1 certainly does have the role of Saoshyant, who comes to judge the world and revive the dead. In any event, this passage depends for its understanding on a knowledge of the period that produced this apocalyptic book. Elsewhere, the visions of Daniel have been referring to the persecution of the Hasidic Jews by the Seleucid ruler, Antiochus Epiphanes. We must turn to I Maccabees and II Maccabees for a detailed description of this trying period; especially to II Maccabees 6-7, containing certain elements of legend, but based upon essential factuality. This was the "time of trouble" referred to in Dan. 12:1. The promise is that "your people" shall be delivered, i.e., "everyone whose name shall be found in the book." The reference is to the "God-fearers" (cf. Mal. 3:16) -- the Hasidic faithful of Daniel's own group. The text goes on in v. 2 to make the remarkable prognosis of resurrection:

> And many of those who sleep in the dust of
> the earth shall awake, some to everlasting
> life, and some to shame and everlasting
> contempt.

Inasmuch as the text speaks of "many," not of all, the
best explanation of its meaning is that it refers to
the Jews who have been slain by Antiochus, such as
the pitiable Eleasar of II Maccabees 6, or the mother's
seven sons in II Maccabees 7. But not all who died have
died for the true faith of Israel. Accordingly, some
will awaken to everlasting life but others to shame
and everlasting contempt.

The text goes on in v. 3 to say: "And those who
are wise shall shine like the brightness of the firma-
ment; and those who turn many to righteousness, like
the stars for ever and ever." This should not be
taken as a further allusion to those who awaken from
the dead, for it refers to all the Hasidic Jews,
the truly "wise," those who work to turn many to the
righteousness of the Torah.

This passage does not yet preach individual
resurrection -- certainly not the resurrection of
all men. Furthermore, it does not directly imply
bodily resuscitation. This is a notion found in II
Maccabees 7's narrative of the martyr sons, who fling
away the organs of their body with the declaration
that they expect to see them come back together again! [68]
Dan. 12:2 actually lies much closer to the ideology of
Isa. 25:6-8, etc., predicting the resurrection of
Israel as a people.

Most assuredly this unique passage represents an
authentically Hebraic and essentially biblical belief:
that death cannot conquer God or his saints. Even
at the far edge of finite existence, as God's faithful are in peril of being pushed into the dark chaos
of nothingness, he holds them in a life that is eternal.

d. Death and life in the New Testament

(1) Christ's resurrection and the Christian's
resurrection

The subject of Christ's resurrection again deserves a treatise of its own. Our purpose, in concluding this section, is a very modest one: from the perspective of the normative biblical achievement to sketch the essential outlines of the New Testament affirmation. Like Christ's victory over sin, his victory over death virtually leaps from the pages of the New Testament. It is a prominent theme especially in the writings of Paul, who, by his own testimony, was converted from the most zealous persecutor of Christianity to its most ardent propagandizer through the conviction that Christ is alive.[69] The resurrection provides the thematic structure of Acts, commencing the story of Christianity's expansion with an account of Peter proclaiming, "This Jesus...God raised...up, having loosed the pangs of death, because it was not possible for him to be held by it." (Acts 2:23-24) The fact of Christ's resurrection inspires the hope that keeps Christianity alive; so I Pet. 1:3-4:

> Blessed be the God and Father of our Lord
> Jesus Christ! By his great mercy we have
> been born anew to a living hope through the
> resurrection of Jesus Christ from the dead,
> and to an inheritance which is imperishable,
> undefiled, and unfading, kept in heaven
> for you.

We shall briefly survey the major exponents of this theme. Sound historical methodology dictates that we pay particular attention to Paul, whose epistles represent the earliest literary materials within the New Testament.[70]

(a) Paul

Although Paul is continually referring to Christ's resurrection (cf. Acts 17:31-32), it is significant that it is in I Corinthians that he addresses himself to it in a formal way. This letter was written for the specific purpose of counteracting the docetizing, gnosticizing tendencies of the Corinthian congregation, or of its cultural environment;[71] hence Paul's purpose must be seen as an effort to reaffirm the bodily and historical reality of Christ, who is now alive because he arose from death, and not because he has set aside the vestige of an illusional fleshliness.

Nevertheless, this same Paul refrains from speculating whether the crucified body of Jesus has been rescuscitated. Even in I Corinthians 15, where he so enthusiastically rejoices in the reality of Christ's resurrection, he resists this line of speculation. It is well to note that he puts his own vision of Christ, as received at the time of his conversion (v. 8) alongside the appearances of Christ to others (vv. 4-7). We interpret him rightly, therefore, when we hear him saying that Christ is alive, without trying to describe precisely how he is alive. This particular question is addressed in vv. 35ff., where the apostle responds to the question, "How are the dead raised? With what kind of body do they come?" Arguing that that which "is sown a physical body is raised a spiritual body" (v. 44), Paul concludes that "flesh and blood cannot inherit the kingdom of God" (v. 50). A logical consequence is that the resurrection of Christians will also be spiritual: "Just as we have borne the image of the man of dust, we shall also bear the image of the man of heaven." (v. 49)

Further light can be shed on Paul's doctrine by careful attention to his statement in Rom. 6:4-5, 9-11, where he tells what it is like to be alive with Christ:

> We were buried therefore with him by baptism into death, so that as Christ was raised from the dead by the glory of the Father, we too might walk in newness of life. For if we have been united with him in a death like his, we shall certainly be united with him in a resurrection like his....For we know that Christ being raised from the dead will never die again; death no longer has dominion over him. The death he died he died to sin, once for all, but the life he lives he lives to God. So you also must consider yourselves dead to sin and alive to God in Christ Jesus.

We can scarcely go astray in acknowledging this as normative New Testament teaching. It refelcts a relatively primitive, yet enthusiastically vital, level of early Christian thinking about Christ's victory over death.[72] The various other New Testament statements on this subject should be weighed from its perspective.

442

(b)   The post-resurrection appearances

    The earliest Gospel, Mark, originally had a
remarkably brief account of Jesus' resurrection.[73]
The remaining Synoptics follow its example by providing their own expansive and distinctly different
narratives of this same event.   So too John.   Each
testifies that the Jesus who died so cruel a death
was not conquered by that death, but arose from the
grave.   Various lists of witnesses are provided
among them in support of the narrator's testimony.

    A feature that ought not to be overlooked is the
strange mysticality of the risen Jesus.   This feature
appears in Luke's account of his journey to Emmaus
(24:13ff.), where he mysteriously vanishes as he
breaks bread with his companions (v. 31).   Luke has
it also in his accounts of the ascension: Jesus
just vanishes into heaven (Luke 24:50, Acts 1:9).
John has this too in his story of Jesus' appearance
to Mary Magdalene: suddenly he is there; he refuses
to let her take hold of him (20:11ff.).   So also in
the story of his sudden materialization within the
closed doors (20:19ff.), in which the references to
Thomas's viewing of his torn hands and side are
designed as an antidote against docetic speculation.
John has it also in chapter 21, where Jesus gives
fish and bread to his disciples, but does not eat
them himself (vv. 9-13).

    The actual rescuscitation of Jesus' physical body
is barely suggested in these accounts, thus this
appears to be an element of speculation venturing
beyond the norm of primitive Christian belief.   It
seems to be implied by Matthew's account of the
bribing of the guards (28:11ff.), and perhaps also
by John's reference to the grave-cloths in the tomb
(20:5-6, 11-12).[74]

    (c)   Theophanic reflexes of the resurrection
          tradition

In a foregoing section[75], it was observed that theophany and legend are two specific genres employing this special imagery. The first uses it as a vehicle for symbolizing the divine presence; the second for expressing the divine power in God-filled men. These same two genres quite naturally came to expand the original proclamation about the risen Christ.[76]

Although the miracle stories in the Gospels may reflect a historical background, they are designed, like the Old Testament hero-legends and prophet-legends, to exemplify the divine presence in Jesus.[77] In the light of the vitality of the resurrection tradition, it seems natural that stories of the raising of the dead (the widow's son, Luke 7:11-16; Jairus' daughter, Mark 5:35-43 par; Lazarus, John 11) should be included among them. The reference to the graves being opened and the dead arising at the moment of Jesus's death, appearing in Matt. 27:32f., shows the influence of apocalyptic ideology on the thinking of this particular Evangelist, who in various other ways reveals a heavier reliance than the other Gospel writers on first-century Jewish patterns of belief.[78]

(2) Apocalyptic and non-apocalyptic images of personal destiny

We conclude by noting that the New Testament clearly presents the hope and expectation of a life beyond death -- though this need not necessarily be understood in terms of the quantitative extension of time. This was already the trend within first-century Judaism, and Judaism continues to share with Christianity a belief that those who are in harmony and oneness with God cannot be cut off from him in death. Both Jews and Christians must guard this precious belief from the crude mythologies which their Hebraic forebears repudiated in a long-ago past. It is especially important for them to be aware of the meaning of religious language, not distorting or trivializing its symbolism through naive literalistic interpretations. For the benefit of Christian inquirers, we present briefly the following examples from two different kinds of religious language found within the New Testament.

(a) Apocalyptic: Rev. 20:4-6, 12-14

Even this designedly apocalyptic book refrains
from asserting a bodily rescuscitation for those who
reign with Christ in eternity:

> Then I saw thrones, and seated on them were
> those to whom judgment was committed. Also
> I saw the souls (psuchas, not pneumata)[79] of
> those who had been beheaded for their testi-
> mony to Jesus and for the word of God, and
> who had not worshiped the beast or its image
> and had not received its mark on their fore-
> heads or their hands. They came to life, and
> reigned with Christ a thousand years. The
> rest of the dead did not come to life until
> the thousand years were ended. This is the
> first resurrection. Blessed and holy is he
> who shares in the first resurrection! Over
> such the second death has no power, but they
> shall be priests of God and of Christ, and
> they shall reign with him a thousand years....
> I saw the dead, great and small, standing
> before the throne, and books were opened.
> Also another book was opened, which is the
> book of life. And the dead were judged by
> what was written in the books, by what they
> had done. And the sea gave up the dead in it,
> Death and Hades gave up the dead in them, and
> all were judged by what they had done. Then
> Death and Hades were thrown into the lake of
> fire. This is the second death, the lake of
> fire.

(b) Non-apocalyptic: I John 2:28-3:3

In those passages where he writes of wanting to
be with Christ, Paul falls short of describing how
a life beyond death will be (II Cor. 4:14-5:8, Phil.
1:20-24). In any event, his expectation seems to be
more mystical than apocalyptic. As he so clearly
says in Romans 6, the resurrection life is now.
Death can only remove the last barrier to a perfect
union with Christ.

Very similar in its use of religious imagery is John's statement in I John 2:28-3:3.[80] For this apostle, to live in perfect love within the Christian community marks us as "children of God," and this is all that we shall ever be, in this world or in the world to come. Contemporary Christians might do well to emulate this example in refraining from idle speculation, while devoting themselves with greater energy to following the guidelines that he has offered in this passage:

> And now, little children, abide in him, so that he appears we may have confidence and not shrink from him in shame at his coming. If you know that he is righteous, you may be sure that every one who does right is born of him. See what love the Father has given us, that we should be called children of God; and so we are. The reason why the world does not know us that it does not know him. Beloved, we are God's children now; it does not yet appear what we shall be, but we know that when he appears we shall be like him, for we shall see him as he is. And every one who thus hopes in him purifies himself as he is pure.

2. Man's pathway through suffering

a. The dimensions of evil

Like other vital beings, we humans have been created to live. Even as we subside into dying while still alive, it is the living rather than the dying that has significance. To live is good, yet as finite beings we require the parameters imposed by our eventual and inevitable death to accentuate the goodness of life. It is because we can die, and must die, that our ephemeral life has value and meaning. Death is the boundary of our vital existence, beyond which is (choose one):

(1) nothingness;
(2) the infinite life that is God!

This is the precise model upon which we must also evalute happiness _versus_ suffering, good _versus_ evil Like other vital beings, we humans have been created to be happy, to enjoy life. Pain and suffering arise as threats to, and depredations upon, our vital life. If something is askew in our physical or spiritual equilibrium, we suffer pain. Disease may cause this; or the want of food and drink; or exposure to the elements; or violence from nature, animals, or our fellow men. Inasmuch as this is a dynamic universe, it is inevitable that an infinite collision of atoms must produce some conflict and disharmony, inflicting injury along the way. It is the law of nature, indeed, that organisms in competition with one another should draw nourishment from the tissues of other vital species, so that some must die that others may live. As the monistic mythologies have affirmed, death is part of the life-process, so that suffering and death are a necessary part of life and happiness. This is even true of our own individual existence. Without the birth-pangs that accompany our first entrance into life, and the death-rattle that ushers it out, our life could not be. Suffering is the framework that paradoxically renders positive significance to happiness and pleasure.

The challenge of suffering is like the challenge of death. We may conquer it by reacting against it.

The various kinds of evil that confront us provide
a stimulus for effective response. We learn how to
build earthquake-proof buildings; we learn how to
control forest-fires; we learn how to protect ourselves against ravening beasts (including poisonous
microbes!); we learn how to grow better crops; we
learn how to design safer highways. Evil too is
clever -- that we know. It often seems to be a
step or two ahead of the good that reacts to it.
This is especially true of societal evil, which
threatens to frustrate our every effort toward
ameliorating the conditions of civilized existence.
There is now the death-ray and the H-bomb, which seem
perilously close to shattering everything that ages
of rising civilization have painstakingly produced.
The devil is almost infinitely powerful -- yet he
too is restrained by a good God infinitely greater
than himself.

What matters above all is to know that God cares
-- and that man himself will care enough to struggle
ever onward to overcome evil. It is only in this
way that the design of creation can be fulfilled.

It is important for us to reflect upon the fact
that not all evil is of the same dimension and of
the same quality. First, there is the kind that
comes as inborn creaturely limitations or defects,
whether by themselves or in combination with other
forms of evil. This may be defined as a handicap
to an individual's constitutional potentialities.
One thinks, for instance, of a child born with a
crippling or even life-threatening defect, whether
derived from genetic disorder, or from an accident
at birth or at the fetal stage. Similar defects
may arise early or late in life: blindness, deaf-
ness, the loss of limbs, and the like. The evil
of such lamentable conditions is compounded, we
know, in the midst of poverty and ignorance, where
parents are incompetent or do not care, where society
itself has inadequate means for helping the unfortunate
individual to cope with his or her handicap. With
or without the element of contributing human liability,
the handicapped individual is entirely victimized
by this particular form of evil. What is the answer
to it? It can be nothing else than a strenuous effort
on the individual's part, assisted by parents,
friends, and agencies, to carve out as meaningful and
satisfying an existence as possible. The God who
created a universe capable of producing such inequities

448

created also the possibility of coping with them --
perhaps even of overcoming them. Surely, the good
that such a handicapped person achieves has infinitely greater lustre than the casual successes of
ordinary people. We look at a Helen Keller, for
instance, and marvel at her heroism and that of
her teachers!

Another form of evil consists of what we may call
natural calamities external to the personal self:
earthquakes, fires, tornados and hurricanes, pestilence and disease. God has also created his universe
capable of producing these evils, and they may fall
on anybody and everybody. The effects of this kind
of evil may be vastly increased wherever people crowd
together in vulnerable terrain, knowing or not knowing
their susceptibility. The people themselves may
unknowingly (or again, knowingly) increase their own
susceptibility. Thus the throngs inhabiting the
monsoon-flooded mudflats of India, or the hungry
villagers whose goats devour vegetation faster than
it can replenish itself. Some anthropologists and
demographers have seen this as nature's self-limiting
process, keeping the human species, like all other
species, from eating a swath across the green earth.
In this sense, even war can do some good. The
observation that is pertinent here is that also this
kind of evil tends to produce a positive response.
Certainly our race's impressive technological achievement has been mainly stimulated by the desire to
alleviate the effects of this kind of evil. As we
compare most of the people who are alive today --
even those in undeveloped countries -- with those who
lived a thousand, two thousand, or five thousand
years ago, the comparison is almost embarrassing.
If that kind of historical retrospect is too much
for some of us, we have only to look back at how our
own parents and grandparents lived, or at how people
lived on the American frontier. Food is now far more
abundant, more nutritious, more delicious, more varied,
than what they had. Housing is incomparably better.
Clothing is abundant, stylish, variegated, pleasing
to wear. Transportation is far easier and safer.
We can predict hurricanes, avoid earthquake areas,
and vaccinate ourselves against disease. So here
again, evil can be a stimulus to ever-increasing good.
If it did not exist in this form, little of the
greater good that we enjoy would have come to exist.

A third form of evil is that which man himself
produces, whether wittingly or unwittingly, purposely
or inadvertently. Individuals do it, society does it.
They do it, sad to say, with the good means that have
been placed in their hands. Those born with intelligence and strength, those born with wealth and in the
midst of culture, those with freedom and opportunity,
those with high intelligence and polished skills --
all commit evil. We inflict it upon ourselves, on
our spouses and children, on our fellow workers and
fellow citizens. We do it alone and in groups. We
commit evil as nations and as civilizations. We are
the victims and we make others our victims. Most
generally, one evil counter-balances and limits
another evil, so that the effect of each is held in
check, but at times all hell breaks loose and the
jaws of Abaddon yawn before us. Thus Viet-Nam with
its continuing horrors. Thus the Nazi holocaust.
Here God's design is not the sole causal factor, for
man, made in God's image, frustrates God's design.
Yet even here evil tends to stimulate good -- the
good of learning how to cope, of learning how to
prevent a repetition of disaster.

Evil has very generally been interpreted as a
punishment for sin. It is certainly true that sin
contributes to each of the kinds of evil that we have
described, and in a meaningful sense the evil that
results can be described as its punishment. Thus if
a drunken driver goes to jail, the evil of his con-
finement is but the consequence, and the just desert,
of his own sinful behavior. But a precise equation
is perilous because the drunken driver may not get
caught and pay the penalty, whereas he may run down
a pedestrian and lame him for life, inflicting untold
evil on an innocent victim. In the sense that a moral
God has made a universe capable of producing violence,
conflict, and injustice, evil may be a punishment, but
on the other hand, it may not be punishment at all. We
all can, and must, learn from evil, whether we suffer
it or others suffer it, but it is folly to speak of it
as the token of divine wrath in direct reprisal for a
specific sin.

Like all of human culture, the Hebraic faith
recorded in the Bible struggles with the problem of
evil, together with the problem of injustice that
arises from the incongruity between the performance of
an evil act and the application of its effects or
consequences. As a cultural substratum, Israelite

orthodoxy tended to cherish the pious dogma that righteousness begets reward, while wickedness begets punishment.[81] But this was simply the naive heritage of a common cultural stance within the entirety of ancient Near-Eastern society. What the Old Testament achieves as its distinctive insight is the assurance that God knows and cares. This came ever to greater clarity as biblical religion moved toward a greater awareness of the implications of the monotheistic personalism which it had embraced.

God cares; God saves; God heals; God feeds; God comforts. He does not wait to make sure that the sinner deserves his lavish goodness. He simply gives to all who are willing to accept his generous gift. "Your Father who is in heaven...makes his sun rise on the evil and on the good, and sends rain on the just and the unjust." (Matt. 5:45)

Goodness is in the universe, ready to counterbalance every evil. It is up to man to care enough to cherish the good and overcome the evil.

b. The meaning of suffering in nonbiblical thought

Most of what is relevant here has already been covered under the subject of sin. We shall therefore do no more than summarize the main options.

(1) Contemporary interpretations of evil

In Eastern pessimism, nature and sense are interpreted as ineradicably evil, and the passions lead unavoidably to increased suffering. Hence the Hindu doctrine of <u>karma</u> (fate and rebirth). The world is a prison. We quote these lines from a south Indian folk-song:

> How many births are past, I cannot tell,
>   How many yet to come, no man can say;
> But this alone I know, and know full well,
>   That pain and grief embitter all the way.

451

Here the only hope and salvation are extinction of consciousness, Nirvana. This belief can only encourage passivity with respect to every effort toward cultural amelioration.

In classical thought, fate and chance were held as the main dynamic forces. The major options for coping with evil were Stoicism, which encouraged its adherents to ignore pain, along with pleasure; and Epicureanism, which encouraged its adherents to avoid pain and pursue pleasure.

These philosophies have their followers today. In modern western culture we identify an optimistic amelioration in every form of moralistic idealism, as well as in every form of materialistic evolutionism. Both assume that natural evil is simply a defect that can be overcome with sufficient effort. Somehow, man can lift himself up by his bootstraps. Unfortunately, those who follow these philosophies seldom take sufficient account of sin -- the human propensity to choose evil instead of good.[82] There is also the irrationalism of the nihilistic revolt. We see this in all forms of sadism and masochism. Engendered by disillusionment with the possibilities of technology and every cultural impulse, its tendency is to surrender to sin, masking as good the inevitable evil that results.

(2)   Evil in ancient Near-Eastern thought

In the cultural world of the Hebrews, a groping uncertainty held the day. The dominant belief was that suffering and injustice are punishments for human wrongdoing, but since so much suffering seemed to be undeserved, the sufferer was tempted to succumb to anxiety and bewilderment, concluding that his protector god was either fickle or weak. A few examples from its religious literature will illustrate this sad dilemma.

(a)   On the hiddenness of god

Prayer to every god, <u>ANET</u> 391-92[83]

As has been said, suffering betokened transgression. Here is a Sumerian ritual provided with
an interlinear Assyrian translation, showing how
useful it was to have a prayer that could be used
for supplication to any god that might have been
offended (cf. the Athenian "Unknown god," Acts 17):

> May the fury of my lord's heart be quieted toward
>   me.
> May the god who is not known be quieted toward me;
> May the goddess who is not known be quieted
>   toward me.
> May the god whom I know or do not know be quieted
>   toward me;
> May the goddess whom I know or do not know be
>   quieted toward me.
> May the heart of my god be quieted toward me;
> May the heart of my goddess be quieted toward me.
> May my god and goddess be quieted toward me.
> May the god [who has become angry with me] be
>   quieted toward me;
> May the goddess [who has become angry with me] be
>   quieted toward me.

. . . .

> In ignorance I have eaten that forbidden of my god;
> In ignorance I have set foot on that prohibited by
>   my goddess.

The suppliant goes on to say that he knows that his
transgressions are many, but he is unaware which of
them has been offensive in this particular case, or
which particular god or goddess it may be who is
punishing him:

> The lord in the anger of his heart looked at me;
> The god in the rage of his heart confronted me;
> When the goddess was angry with me, she made me
>   become ill.
> The god whom I know or do not know has oppressed
>   me;
> The goddess whom I know or do not know has placed
>   suffering upon me.
> Although I am constantly looking for help, no one
>   takes me by the hand;

When I weep they do not come to my side.
I utter laments, but no one hears me;
I am troubled; I am overwhelmed; I can not see.
O my god, merciful one, I address to thee the
   prayer, "Ever incline to me";
I kiss the feet of my goddess; I crawl before thee.

. . . .

How long, O my goddess, whom I know or do not
   know, ere thy hostile heart will be quieted?
Man is dumb; he knows nothing;
Mankind, everyone that exists, -- what does he
   know?
Whether he is committing sin or doing good, he
   does not even know.
O my lord, do not cast thy servant down;
He is plunged into the waters of a swamp; take
   him by the hand.
The sin which I have done, turn into goodness;
The transgression which I have committed, let
   the wind carry away;
My many misdeeds strip off like a garment.

This continues in intensified form for a few more
lines, and ends with the plea that the deity in
question may now behave like a true parent:

   May thy heart, like the heart of a real mother,
      be quieted toward me;
   Like a real mother (and) a real father may it be
      quieted toward me.

Hittite prayers, ANET 394-96, 400[84]

   The two factors of uncertainty that merge in the
just-quoted Mesopotamian prayer are kept somewhat
separate in each of the following Hittite prayers.
In the first, the main problem is uncertainty regarding the identity of the god or gods who are responsible for sending a plague:

   Hattian Storm-god, my lord, and ye, Hattian gods,
   my lords! Mursilis, the great king, your servant,
   has sent me (with the order)...Speak as follows:

454

What is this that ye have done? A plague ye
have let into the land. The Hatti land has been
afflicted by the plague. For twenty years now
men have been dying in my father's days, in my
brother's days, and in mine own since I became
the priest of the gods. When men are dying in
the Hatti land like this, the plague is in no
wise over. As for me, the agony of my heart
and the anguish of my soul I cannot endure any
more. When I celebrated festivals, I worshiped
all the gods, I never preferred one temple to
another. The matter of the plague I have laid
in prayer before all the gods making vows to
them (and saying): "Hearken to me, ye gods,
my lords. Drive ye forth the plague from the
Hatti land! The reason for which people are
dying in the Hatti land -- either let it be
established by an omen, or let me see it in a
dream, or let a prophet declare it!" But the
gods did not hearken to me and the plague got
no better in the Hatti land. The Hatti land
was cruelly afflicted.

The text goes on at great lengths to detail the
measures that have been taken to establish the occasion
of this persistent plague. For a while, the suppliant
addresses the Storm-god alone, since it seems most
likely that he is at cause. But the suppliant comes
back to address all the gods once more. Toward the
end he raises the suggestion that it may be specifically the Sun-goddess of Arinna who is offended.
The suppliant concludes with a final plea, designed
to attract the attention of whichever god it may be:

Whatever rage (or) anger the gods may feel, and
whosover may not have been reverent toward
the gods, -- let not the good perish with the
wicked! If it is one town, or one [house], or
one man, O gods, let that one perish alone!
Look ye upon the Hatti land with favorable eyes,
but the evil plague give to [those other]
countries!

In the second example, Kantuzillis addresses
the Sun-god alone and accepts the blame for himself,
but still confesses ignorance as to his specific
transgression:

Would that my god might now freely open his hear
(and) soul to me and [tell] me my fault so that
I might learn about it! Either let my god speak
to me in a dream! Would that my god would open
his heart to me and tell [me] my [fau]lt so
that I might learn about it! Or let the sibyl
tell me, [or] let the Sun-god's seer tell [me]
from the liver (of a sheep). Would that my
god might freely open [his heart (and) soul] to me
and tell me my fault so that I might learn about
it! Let me know how to improve on your worship!

Dialogue about Human Misery, <u>ANET</u> 440[85]

Often compared with the book of Job, this composition features repartee between a troubled man and
his "friend." The trouble of which the man complains
is not his own suffering alone, but the widespread
suffering and injustice that he sees throughout
society. Various possible explanations are advanced
and refuted. In the following lines, the man complains about topsy-turvy conditions in the present
situation of social upheaval:

Among men I have made observations, (but) the
    signs were variable.
The god does not stop the advance of the Šarrabu-
    demon.
In the canals the begetter draws the ship,
(While) his first-born lies in bed;
The oldest brother moves about on his way like a
    lion,
(While) the second son delights in driving a mule.
In the street the senior son hunts disgracefully
    (for plunder).
(While) the second son distributes food to the
    needy.
In the presence of a leader I, who humble myself,
    what do I gain?
I must submit (even) to my slave:
The wealthy and thriving man despises me -- the
    last (of all).

The "friend" replies that this incongruity may actually
be the gods' plan; he addresses the man with sarcasm:

456

(O) wise (and) strong one, endowed with insight,
Your heart is eating itself (when) you treat God
   unjustly.
The mind of the god, like the center of the
   heavens, is remote;
His knowledge is difficult, men cannot understand
   it.
The product of the hand of the goddess Aruru is
   life in general.
The premature offspring is always thin:
A cow's first heifer is inferior,
Her second offspring is twice as large.
The fool gives birth to an outstanding son,
The mighty hero   to one whose designation is
   quite different.
Let him know (that) people cannot understand
   what the counsel of a god is.

The sufferer then replies that most of the evil he
complains of has been caused by the falseness and
venality of human beings towards one another:

Give heed, my friend! Understand my meaning,
Guard the choice expression of my speech.
(People) extol the word of a prominent man, expert
   in murder,
(But) they abase the humble, who has committed
   no violence.
They justify the evildoer, whose iniquity is...,
(But) they drive away the righteous, who gives
   [heed] to the god's counsel.
They fill with precious metal the...of the bandit,
(But) they empty of food the larder of the helpless
   man.
They strengthen the mighty man, whose retinue is
   [wicked],
(But) they ruin the weakling, they cast down the
   feeble.
Even me, helpless (as I am), the upstart
   persecutes.

The "friend" answers that it is the gods themselves
who have bestowed on humankind ingenious speech,
conferring falsehood and untruth forever. The inevitable result is the victimization of those who
lack "protection." This brings the dialogue to an
end; the man has no further recourse than to protest
his own humility and truthfulness, and to cast himself on the mercy of the gods:

Be merciful, my friend; listen to my woe!
Help me! See (my) misery, and you will truly
   understand.
A wise and imploring slave am I.
Help and encouragement I have not experienced
   for an instant.
I walked quietly through the squares of my city,
My voice was never loud, my speech was low;
I did not raise my head, I looked (down) at the
   ground.
Like a slave I was not glorified in the assembly
   of [my peers].
May the god Ninurta, who..., supply help!
May the goddess Ishtar, who..., have mercy upon me!
May the shepherd, the sun of my people,[86] [have
   mercy].

(b) On the meaningless of human activity: ANET
     437-38, "The Pessimistic Dialogue between
     Master and Servant"[87]

   This remarkable document, the epitome of utter
cynicism, offers itself as our final selection because it illustrates a profound feeling of meaninglessness and despair. Nothing can be done to determine
whether good or evil will result from a specific
course of action. In a series of stylized responses,
an imperious master and a fawning slave entertain and
dismiss every purposeful activity. These are: (1)
riding to the palace for an interview with the king;
(2) dining at table; (3) going hunting in the wilderness; (4) attacking an enemy; (5) building a house;
(6) seeking reconciliation with an enemy; (7) start-
ing a rebellion; (8) making love to a woman; (9)
offering a sacrifice to one's god; (10) giving food
to one's country; (11) doing something helpful for
one's country. There is a twelfth which will be
cited below, but first we quote the ninth to demonstrate how this attitude of cynicism had effected
even religious behavior:

   "Servant, obey me." Yes, my lord, yes. "Bring
   me at once water for my hands, and give it to
   me; I will offer a sacrifice to my god." Offer,
   my lord, offer. A man offering sacrifice to
   his god is happy, loan upon loan he makes.

"No, servant, a sacrifice to my god will I
not offer." Do not offer (it), my lord, do
not offer (it). You may teach a god to trot
after you like a dog when he requires of
you, (saying), "(Celebrate) my ritual" or
"do not inquire (by requesting an oracle)"
or anything else.

The twelfth is the conclusion:

"Servant, obey me." Yes, my lord, Yes.
"Now, what is good? To break my neck,
your neck, throw (both) into the river --
(that) is good." Who is tall enough to
ascend to heaven? Who is broad enough
to embrace the earth? "No, servant, I
shall kill you and send you ahead of me"
(Then) would my lord (wish to) live even
three days after me?

   c. The meaning of suffering in biblical thought

     As has been stated, it is monotheistic per-
sonalism -- not always perceived in all its implications -- that provides the Bible's distinctive answer
to the problem of evil, suffering, and injustice. The
people of the Old Testament were no less concerned
with this problem than other peoples of the ancient
world. They suffered a lot, individually and collectively. Judaism has continued to suffer throughout
the course of history. Here and there, Christianity
has suffered too. There is no reason for modern-day
representatives of the biblical heritage to be timid
or confused in ministering pastorally to people in
suffering and need, for the biblical stance has been
tested and proven in many crucibles.

   (1) The suffering of the righteous individual

   (a) The prevalence of evil in the Old Testament

The book of Job draws our attention as the prime exemplar of Israel's struggle with the problem of the suffering of the righteous individual. However, we need to be aware that this phenomenon was neither rare nor isolated; according to biblical evidence, it not only occurred often, but generally. This is why the Psalter is replete with examples of individual and collective laments;[88] this is why much of the wisdom literature is so gloomy, and why apocalyptic was able to take such vigorous root.[89] Especially in the exilic and postexilic times, things got difficult for many Jews, inside and outside Palestine. There were few resources to lift the majority of those who resided in this relatively hilly country above the level of bare subsistence, and often even this was withheld from them. Meanwhile, the means of relieving this condition through their own efforts was sharply limited because they had been deprived of political and economic self-determination. Foreigners came to exploit them. They had no say in setting their own taxes. And one day they found that even their sacrosanct religious practices had been banned.[90] In the diaspora, meanwhile, Jews often lived without rights or protection, subsisting only through the grudging tolerance of foreign officials.[91]

The measure of biblical Israel's experience of pain has been strikingly called to the writer's attention through his own recent analysis of the language of time. It was found that most of the terms used to qualify the noun cēt, meaning "time" or "occasion," have to do with evil and suffering. A few of these terms are quite specific, but the most familar are rāc, racâ, "evil," and sārâ, "distress." Even more interestingly, the word which the Hebrew writers so often use for qualifying historical events, yôm ("day") is used even more widely with reference to evil, and with an even greater range of expressive qualifiers. I share the following extract from my book, Yesterday, Today, and Tomorrow:[92]

> The present day is sometimes described by
> characterizations, particularly in laments,
> complaints, and salvation oracles. Laments
> speak of a yôm sārātî or yôm sar lî, "day of
> my distress" (Ps. 86:7, 102:3); also of a yôm
> 'eqrā' or yôm qār'ēnû, "day when I/we call(ed)"
> (Ps. 102:3, 20:10). All these refer to the
> suppliant's present day of suffering. So

likewise the complaint in Jer. 17:16-18, which
speaks of the present yôm 'anûš, "day of desperation," and yôm ra‹â, "day of evil." The
parallel passages, II Kings 19:3 and Isa. 37:3,
speak of "this day" as a yôm ṣarâ wᵉtôkēhâ
ûnᵉ'aṣâ, "day of distress, rebuke, and dis-
grace.".... Lam. 1:7 speaks of Jerusalem's present "days of affliction and bitterness"
(yᵉmê ‹onyāh ûmᵉrûdêhā); Hos. 9:7 refers to
present "days of reckoning and recompense"
(yᵉmê happᵉquddâ...yᵉmê haššillum); Ps. 49:6
has the prepositional phrase, "in evil days"
bîme ra‹); Ps. 102:4 has a simple yamay,
"my days."

As we analyze the use of present yôm, we soon
see that a basic distinction needs to be made
between the day that is historically present
in existential distinctiveness and the day
that is present only in gnomic discourse....
The latter refers to a "today" that is continually repeated and hence continuously
present. The gnomic present, using a form of
yôm or of ‹et, is the present of various
kinds of gnomic discourse: exhortations,
proverbs, aphorisms. It is the present to
which the wisdom sayings pertain, hence it
is repeated and repeatable as long as the
sayings are true....The substantive yôm
occurs a few times in combined forms with
reference to the gnomic present. Many of
the passages involved are wisdom sayings,
and, not surprisingly, the combinations in
question borrow heavily from similar terminology with ‹et. What is very intense and
particular in the historical present is
here generalized as a dogma. Wisdom sayings
speak of yômô, "his day," i.e., the wicked
man day of judgment (Ps. 37:13, Job 18:20);
more specifically, of a yôm 'appô, "day of
his (God's) anger" (Job 20:28), a yôm ‹ebrâ,
"day of wrath" (Job 21:30, Prov. 11:4), a yôm
'ed, "day of distress" (Job 21:30), a yôm
qᵉrāb ûmilḥāmâ, "Day of battle and war" (Job
38:23), and a yôm hᵉrēgâ, "day of slaughter"
(Jer. 12:3). Following in the wisdom pattern,
an individual lament turns the historical
present into the gnomic present ("day when I
call," Ps. 56:10; cf. Ps. 20:10, 103:3, above).

The expression, yôm ṣārâ, "day of distress,"
becomes the gnomic present in Nah. 1:7
(hymn of theophany) and Jer. 16:10 (individual lament). The gnomic yôm rāʿâ, "day of
evil," is mentioned in Ps. 27:5 (individual
thanksgiving), 41:2, 50:15 (wisdom hymns).

The gnomic present is also referred to in
many passages where the plural of yôm is used.
There are days of youth, bᵉḥûrôt (Eccl. 11:19,
12:1), days of vanity, hebel (Eccl. 7:15; cf.
9:9), days of darkness, haḥošek (Eccl. 11:8),
days of vigor, ʿalûmîm (Job 33:25), days of
affliction, ʿonî (Job 14:14), days of evil,
rāʿ, rāʿâ (Ps. 94:13; Eccl. 12:1), days of
famine, rᵉʿābôn (Ps. 37:19), and days of
hired service, śākîr (Lev. 25:50). When one
reads this list, he is deeply impressed by
the sorrowful realization on Israel's part
of the tragic and mournful side of life.
The list may be extended by noting the
gnomic passages in which the qualifiers of yôm,
plural, occur in the predicate position; one
hears almost as a platitude that (all) one's
days are "few and evil" (Gen. 47:9), "empty
breath" (Job 7:16), "pain" (Eccl. 2:23), "like
an evening shadow" (Ps. 102:11), "Like a passing
shadow" (Ps. 144:4), or "like a hireling"
(Job 7:1).

This impressive list in itself sheds light on
the reason why the Old Testament -- and the New
Testament too -- so regularly comes to the defense
of the "poor," "humble," "afflicted," "downcast,"
"oppressed," and the like. Apparently there were not
a great many of the other kind around. To suffer and
be poor was no virtue, but for most it certainly
was unavoidable.

(b)   Job's acceptance of evil.

It is in this connection that we turn once more
to the book of Job, which we found in the introduction
to this chapter to be concerned not directly with the
problem of suffering and injustice, but with the
problem of God's hiddenness. This time we pay close

462

attention to the prologue to the book, narrating
the origin of Job's predicament. In all likelihood,
those interpreters are correct who speak of an ancient
folk-tale as the basis of this narrative, which concludes in the epilogue of chapter 42.[93] It is also
relevant to take note of the fact that the Job of
the dialogue cycles is not entirely congruous with
the Job of the folk-tale. Nevertheless, there is
little justification in consigning the latter to
extra-Israelite culture, or to a prebiblical or
subbiblical level of theological sophistication.
What Job says and does here is authentically Hebraic.
With respect to the biblical attitude toward evil,
it is right on target.

The structure of this narrative prologue is
important. It is carefully designed to accentuate
two distinct levels in Job's acceptance of evil:

Introduction, 1:1-5

    a. His character, 1
    b. His possessions, 2-3
    c. His protective piety, 4-5

1. Job's first trial, 1:6-22

    a. The interview between Yahweh and the satan
        The situation of Day One: a conference
          in heaven, 6

        (1) The satan's report, 7
        (2) The challenge

            (a) Job's reputation, 8
            (b) Insinuation of special privileges,
                 9-10
            (c) A prediction, 11

        (3) Permission granted, 12

    b. The calamity (day Two)

        The situation, 13

        (1) Four reports of disaster, 14a

            (a) Oxen and asses plundered, 14b-15
            (b) Sheep burnt, 16
            (c) Camels stolen, 17
            (d) Sons and daughters killed, 18-19

(2) Job's reaction

    (a) His behavior, 20
    (b) His declaration, 21

c. The verdict, 22

2. Job's second trial, 2:1-10

  a. The interview between Yahweh and the satan
    The situation (day Three): conference in
    heaven, 1

    (1) The report, 2
    (2) The challenge

      (a) Job's reputation confirmed, 3
      (b) An insinuation of self-interest, 4
      (c) A prediction, 5

    (3) Permission granted, 6

  b. The calamity

    (1) The affliction, 7-8
    (2) The suggestion of Job's wife, 9
    (3) Job's response

      (a) Reprimand to his wife, 10a
      (b) His declaration, 10b

  c. The verdict, 10c

The pattern of repetition and variation within this narrative indicates the points of stress and climax. First there is the definition of Job's character: He is blameless and upright, one who fears God, and turns away from evil (1:1, 8, 2:3). The element of tension is effectively introduced in 1:10, where the satan (literally, prosecutor or public accuser)[94] insinuates that the blessings and possessions which God has given Job fence him off from calamity, so that there is no real test of his righteousness and piety. "Does Job fear God for nought?" Is he pious because it pays? The first test, then, is to take away his blessings and possessions. Job passes the test; though he grieves his loss, he worships God: "Naked I came from my mother's womb, and naked shall I return; Yahweh gave, and Yahweh has taken away; blessed be the name of Yahweh." (1:21) In other words, if God takes away what he has freely given, what right have we to complain?

But this is preliminary to the real trial.[95] The test will now be whether Job will remain God-fearing when positive evil comes upon him. It is one thing to be stripped of one's possessions, becoming naked before God as on the day of one's birth. Here one no longer has a plus; he is back at point zero. But what will happen when calamity reduces him to a negative level of existence, below the point of simple destitution, pushed into conscious and constant agony? When life itself becomes a burden, what then? "Skin for skin," says the satan. Perhaps Job pretends piety just to stay even with God: "All that a man has he will give for his life." (2:4) To this test too Yahweh agrees, and Job is reduced to loathsome sores in the ashheap. His wife comes to counsel that he curse God and get it over with. And this is Job's reply: "Shall we receive good at the hand of God, and shall we not receive evil?" (2:10)

Job has been the paradigmatic happy man. He was also the paradigmatic pious man. When Job refuses to respond in the expected way to his wife's advice, as he had refused to respond in the expected way to the messages of his servants, he proves that he does indeed fear God for nought. Job is here teaching us two essential things about our existence: (1) In creaturely life, evil comes with good, and to deny the evil is an act of idolatrous self-deification; (2) The evil of life can lead to good when we treat it as part of a benignant and purposeful design. Job shows that the truly pious man accepts pain and sorrow along with pleasure and prosperity. Even the evil that now overwhelms him is from the hand of God. God is as free to give evil as he is free to give good. If one accepts good from God, one must also be ready to accept evil. The joys of the past did not come because God had been obligated to give them, but in sovereignty and wisdom. So also, the evils of the present day have come only through divine sovereignty and wisdom.

At the end of the book, we learn that the God who had taken away could also give again.

(2) The problem of theodicy

As the individual suffers, the nation suffers. We
have discussed the problems of hamartiology and the
concept of apocalyptic. Here let us take note of
three special problems that arise in Old Testament
literature to complicate the problem of Israel's
suffering.[96]

One question -- noted previously -- is why Yahweh's
covenant people must suffer invasion and exile. The
answer is their apostacy from his covenant.[97] The
Israelite kingdoms collapse, as predicted by the prophets. Tragic events give credence to the extremely
unpopular interpretation of God's intent that they
had offered. Refusing to behave as the singer of
love songs, the calamaties that had come proved that
the prophets had verily spoken from God (Ezek. 33:30-33).

A second question -- also previously noted -- is,
Why do the innocent have to suffer along with the guilty,
the children with their fathers?[99] The Bible does not
attempt to answer this head-on, but suggests that good
will come out of the evil as the innocent shun the
pathway of the guilty and as the children refuse to
sin with their parents (Ezekiel 18). Furthermore, a
new branch will sprout from the stump; a holy remnant
shall live on to bear the fulfillment of God's
promises.[100]

A third question is, How about the wickedness of
those whom God has sent to punish Israel? This is
what Habakkuk complains about in 1:13; cf. 2:1-4.[101]
Later, the gospel of the return from exile was
supported by the doctrine that the nations were indeed
too severe in carrying out Yahweh's intended punishment on his people. Israel had suffered <u>double</u> for
all her sins (Isa. 40:2; cf. Zech. 1:12ff.)

A fourth question was the one raised mainly by
the apocalypticists: Why does God wait so long?[102] This
is a question to which their answer, seen in dualistic and futuristic dimensions, proved wrong. God
is still waiting. What about the Polish ghettos? What
about the concentration-camps? But from another angle,
God has never been waiting at all. He has always been
present with his people, even in their extremest
anguish.

(3) The ultimate revelation: God cares by
suffering with us.

It would be tempting to start a new chapter to this book by elaborating our belief that God's ulti-¹⁰³ mate answer to human suffering is his own suffering. It is better to end where we are, noting the Moses who intercedes for his people, but fails to enter the promised land himself; a prophet like Jeremiah who bears in his own flesh the sorrows of his people's sins; the suffering servant of Isaiah 52-53, who bears the iniquities of many.[104] These are types of one who was to come in a later age, who was destined to demonstrate this truth for the entire race of mankind.

God cares by suffering himself. This is the meaning of the cross -- and this is why the cross brings more offense, but at the same time reveals greater power, than the wisdom of the Greeks or the signs demanded by the Jews (I Cor. 1:18, 22-25). This is why those who feed the hungry, minister to the sick, and visit the prisoner, really are doing it for Christ (Matt. 25:31-46). Christ is in those who suffer, as God is in Christ as he suffers.

According to Mark 15:33 (cf. Matt. 27:46), Jesus never felt so far from God as in the hour of his crucifixion. That is why he cried out, "My God, my God, why hast thou forsaken me?" He was quoting a precious psalm, the twenty-second. It certainly echoed all the anguish that Jesus must have felt. Yet surely he would have known it well enough also to remember that as the psalm descends to the very depths of grief and despair, it suddenly breaks out in a cry of joy:

He has not despised or abhorred the affliction of the afflicted; and he has not hid his face from him, but has heard, when he cried to him! (v. 24)

For the psalmist, God proved to be even nearer in the hour of agony and death than he ever had been. This very hour was an hour of life and deliverance. God is there in our suffering and dying! This Jesus also knew. He demonstrated it in his own life and death -- and that is why he lives forever, for death cannot destroy the divine power that is caringly present in the suffering and death of God's own people.

It is to proclaim this joyous good news in all its fulness that the Bible came to have a New Testament in addition to an Old.

(4) A psalm for those who must suffer and die (Psalm 90)

Styled as a collective psalm of complaint, but reflecting the wisdom traditions of the postexilic period,[105] Psalm 90 serves beautifully to epitomize the biblical search for meaning and purpose in finite existence. Various guesses have been offered as to why it has been ascribed to Moses, since this is literally beyond the range of historical possibilities. Yet the ascription to Moses is astoundingly apt, for he is the mediator of revelation par excellence, the exemplary "man of God."[106] In the light of our foregoing display of the use of time-words, particularly yôm, "day," as linguistic signals for the experience of sorrow and suffering, one should note a feature of this psalm's language that is generally overlooked even by the most detailed commentaries; the recurring use of time-words. The problem of the psalm is not human mortality in itself; it is the apparent unconcern of an eternal God for the temporally conditioned trials of mankind. Thus we take note of the reference to God's eternity in vv. 1-2, accentuated by the startling contrast offered in v. 4 between mankind's thousand years and God's single night. So also "all our days," "our years," v. 9; "the years of our life," v. 10; "number our days," v. 12; "in the morning" and "all our days," v. 14: "many days" and "many years" in v. 15.

The problem of Psalm 90 is that man cannot live long enough to perceive the reason why he must suffer. He must die long before he will learn whether God is actually punishing him for his own fault, or for some other purpose. He turns at the end to pray for good and blessing to balance evil and sorrow, so that the value and significance of human effort may at least be secured.

1   A prayer of Moses, the man of God:

PROEM

O Lord, an abiding place Thou art,
    Thou hast been ours from generation to
    generation;
2   before mountains were born
    or Thou didst conceive earth and world.
    (3:3; 3:3:4)

I

3   Thou dost reduce humankind to dust
    and sayest, "Go back, mankind!",
4   for a thousand years in Thy eyes
    are like the day of yesterday when it trans-
    pires,
    or like a watch in the night. (3:3; 3:3:2)

5   Thou wipest them out as though they were but a
    dream,
    as, in the morning, grass that sprouts up;
6   in the morning it flourishes and sprouts,
    but by evening it has faded and withered.
    (3:3; 3:3)

II

7   Assuredly, we are consumed in Thy anger,
    and in Thy wrath we are overwhelmed;
8   Thou placedst our iniquities before Thee,
    our unknown sins in the light of Thy presence
    (2:2, 3:3)

9   Assuredly, all our days pass by in Thy wrath,
    completed are our years with a sigh:
10   the days of our years in these (circumstances)
    may be seventy years,
    or even eighty years if we have strength,
    yet their greatest reach is only toil and trouble
    as they quickly pass and we fly away!
    (3:3; 3:3; 3:3)

469

11 Who knows the force of Thy anger
        or, according to Thy proper fear, Thy wrath?
12 To number our days, teach us that,
        and we shall acquire a wise heart!
        (3:2; 3:3)

                        III

13 Repent, O Yahweh! -- how long yet?
        Oh have pity on Thy servants!
14 Satisfy us each morning with Thy steadfastness,
        that we may shout and rejoice
        throughout all our days! (3:2; 3:2:2)

15 Give us (time) to rejoice equal to the days when
    Thou didst afflict us,
        even the years when we looked on disaster;
16 let there appear to Thy servants Thy mighty deed,
        even Thy majestic power on behalf of their
        posterity! (3:3; 3:2)

                        CODA

17 Thus may the favor of Yahweh our god be on us,
        and the work of our hands, establish on our
        behalf;
        indeed, the work of our hands, establish it!
        (5:4:4)

COMMENT. The proem sets the theme not only for Strophe
I but for the entire psalm. Although it anticipates
v. 3 in articulating God's agelessness, it has the
intent of affirming the changelessness of the covenantal relationship with Israel, which is said to have
existed not only throughout all human generations,
but before the creation of the world. The Lord
('adōnāi, a name often used in late literature to
feature Yahweh's sovereignty) is identified as his
people's māᶜôn, as in Ps. 71:3 and 91:9. This is to
say that, no matter what comes, they cleave fast to
him and appeal to him to keep them secure in his
power.

                        470

Human ephemerality is the theme of the first strophe, but one must understand that this has been expressly designed to prepare for the second, and eventually the third, strophe. The real problem is not that man must die, but that he may die experiencing God's seeming wrath and anger. This is precisely what Strophe II is saying: the members of the covenant community complain that, individually and collectively, their allotted span of life does not give them sufficient perspective to perceive what lies beyond the present, continuing experience of divine wrath. In vv. 11-12, which is the dramatic center of the psalm, the speaker articulates the community's inability to calculate the full measure of time that will be required before God's "fear" will be adequately reflected in the hearts of men. Turning away from that, he prays instead for the "heart of wisdom" that each individual may acquire by "numbering" -- i.e., treasuring -- each day on earth that has been allotted to him. Meanwhile he turns to Strophe III to God, now addressed by his covenantal name, Yahweh, in an appeal to balance off the days of wrath with a commensurate number of good days. He does not venture, like the apocalypticists, to calculate the coming days of evil and of good upon a cosmic abacus; leaving it all in Yahweh's hands, he ventures only to ask that good may somehow compensate for evil -- and if not in his own days, then in the days of his children (v. 16). For many, many days, the community has experienced wrath (ḥemâ), anger ('ap), disaster (rāʿâ), toil (ʿamal) and trouble ('awen). What it prays for now is to witness Yahweh's mighty deed (pāʿal), his majestic power (hadār). With the favor (noʿam) of Yahweh, their earthly striving ("the works of our hands") will not finally be in vain, for he shall establish it.

FOR FURTHER STUDY

On <u>divine</u> <u>caring</u>:

Q. Quell, E. Stauffer, <u>BKW</u>, I/I, "Love" (= <u>TDNT</u>, I, 21ff.)

    Love in the Old Testament
    The word for love in pre-biblical Greek
    Love in Judaism
    Jesus
    The apostolic age
    The sub-apostolic age

H. Ringgren, <u>TDOT</u>, II, 350ff., <u>gā'āl</u>, <u>gō'ēl</u>, <u>g^e'ullāh</u>

On <u>life</u> <u>and</u> <u>death</u>:

R. Bultmann, G. von Rad, G. Bertram, <u>BKW</u>, II/II, "Life and death" (= <u>TDNT</u>, II, 832ff.)

    Life and death in the Old Testament
    The Greek background
    Evidence from the Septuagint and Judaism
    Life in the New Testament
    Death in the New Testament

R. Bultmann, <u>TDNT</u>, III, 7ff., <u>thanatos</u>, etc.

    <u>Thanatos</u> in Greek usage
    The concept of death in the New Testament

W. Eichrodt, <u>TOT</u>, II, 210ff.

    Sheol
    The grave and survival in the grave
    The problem of ancestor worship
    The importance of Israelite religion of Israel's beliefs about the dead
    The demons

<u>idem</u>, II, 496ff.

    The indestructibility of the individual's
            relationship with God (immortality)

F. F. Hvidberg, <u>Weeping and Laughter</u>: A <u>Study of
             Canaanite-Israelite Religion,</u>
             Copenhagen-Leiden 1962

H. Ringgren, <u>TDOT</u>, III, 404ff., <u>hll</u>, hillûlîm, t^{e}hillāh

H. W. Wolff, <u>AOT</u>, pp. 99ff., 119ff.

    Life and death
    To be young and to grow old

W. Zimmerli, <u>OTTO</u>, pp. 155ff.

    Mastery of everyday life and its concrete secrets
        (wisdom)

<u>On evil and suffering</u>:

J. Botterweck, <u>TDOT</u>, I, 27ff., 'ebhyôn

    The ›ebhyôn in expectation of divine help

        The enemies of the 'ebhyôn
        Affliction, illness, loneliness, nearness to
           death
        Religious classification of the 'ebhyôn
        Yahweh deliverer of the 'ebhyonîm
        'ebhyôn in late prophetic proclamations of
           salvation

H. Bultmann, <u>TDNT</u>, IV, 313ff., <u>lupē</u>, etc.

    The Greek understanding of <u>lupē</u>
    The understanding of sorrow in the Old Testament
           and Judaism
    <u>Lupē</u> in primitive Christian writings

W. Eichrodt, <u>TOT</u>, II, 483ff.

    Sin and evil

H. J. Fabry, <u>TDOT</u>, III, 208ff., <u>dal</u>, etc.

F. Hauck, E. Bammel, TDNT, VI, 885ff., ptōchos, etc.

    Ptōchos in the Greek world
The poor in the Old Testament; later Judaism;
        the New Testament

W. Michaelis, TDNT, V, 904ff., paschō, etc.

    The LXX and Judaism
The suffering of Christ
The suffering of Christians

A. Oepke, TDNT, IV, 1084ff., nosos, etc.

    Sickness and sin
Sickness as vicarious suffering

NOTES

1. See art. "Love in the NT" (G. Johnston), IDB, III, 168ff. Our interpretation is directly based on textual usage, for it is semantic function within a specific linguistic tradition (that of the New Testament church) that counts more than general Greek usage or etymology. (See the caveat of J. Barr in The Semantics of Biblical Language, Oxford 1961, pp. 211, 216ff.).

2. Old Testament usage is consistently partitive, causative, or comparative. Speculation about a wider range of usage from cognate prepositions in other Semitic languages is precarious.

3. Cf. A. R. Johnson, "The Primary Meaning of [the Root G'L]," SVT, I (1953), 67-77; also R. de Vaux, Ancient Israel, pp. 21f.

4. The word 'aḥărôn, a relational adjective from the preposition 'aḥēr ("after," "afterward"), functions as a substantive in poetic parallelism with gōʾēl. In this context it must mean, "the last speaker"; cf. Isa. 44:6.

5. Twice-repeated in vv. 26-27a is a form of ḤZH, a more mystical kind of seeing than in the synonym R'H, translated "see" in v. 27b.

6. Translating w^elô$\cdot$-zar as in genetival parallelism with the pronominal suffix of "my eyes"; this is preferable to taking this phrase as the direct object of "see."

7. See the influential treatment of Job by S. L. Terrien in IB, III, 873ff.; also by the same author, Job: Poet of Existence (Indianapolis-New York, 1957).

8. The peroration on Wisdom, chap. 28, and the speeches of Elihu, chaps. 32-37, are generally recognized as secondary additions to the book.

9. The strong tendency of recent scholarship to date the poem of Job during the Babylonian exile has been strongly influenced by S. L. Terrien's article, "Quelques remarqes sur le affinités de Job avec le Deutéro-Esaie," SVT, 15 (1966), 295ff. The major argument for a postexilic date has been, and remains, recognition of this period as the time when Israel's wisdom literature -- of which Job is the highest exponent -- came to prominence. As with Psalm 90 (see my interpretation below, pp. 468-71), one should observe that the exile was only the model for Israel's time of destitution; it was duplicated in exaggerated intensity in the deprivations experience by many Jews in the Greek period, especially under Antiochus IV Epiphanes (see Chapter IV, Excursus on Daniel 9).

10. Admiration for the apparent titanism of Job has led to disappointment, and even a feeling of disgust and betrayal, when superficial readers have come to this -- to them -- utterly unsatisfying conclusion. The problem has not been resolved by those biblical critics who have sought to give another reading than "I repent" for Heb. wenibamti in v. 6. As I interpret the book, Job did offend in failing to take due account of creaturely finitude in the presence of the divine transcendence in the evils of creaturely existence; he "repented" when corrected by the theophanous revelation.

11. We need constantly to keep in mind the warnings
    made by Reinhold Niebuhr in "False Absolutes in
    Christian Interpretations of History," Faith and
    History, A Comparison of Christian and Modern
    Views of History (New York 1949), pp. 196-213.

12. See Lloyd R. Bailey, Sr., Biblical Perspectives
    on Death, Philadelphia: Fortress 1979; also
    "Life and Death," in H. W. Wolff, Anthropology
    of the Old Testament (Philadelphia: Fortress
    1974), pp. 99ff.

13. See S. Morenz, "Death and the Dead," Egyptian
    Religion, pp. 183ff.; also H. Frankfort, Ancient
    Egyptian Religion: An Interpretation (New York
    1961), pp. 88-123.

14. J. A. Wilson, tr.

15. J. A. Wilson, tr.

16. J. A. Wilson, tr.

17. J. A. Wilson, tr.

18. Osiris

19. Among a number of recent works popularizing the
    affinities between the Bible and Ugarit, the
    most influential is J. Gray, The Legacy of
    Canaan (2nd ed., Leiden 1965); see also L. R.
    Fisher, ed., Ras Shamra Parallels, I (1972),
    for a systematic listing of parallels. The
    dangers of "pan-Ugaritism" are pointed out by
    J. C. de Moor in the concluding paragraph of
    his article, "Ugarit," IDBS, p. 930; see also
    his article (with P. van der Lugt, "The Spectre
    of Pan-Ugaritism," BO, 31 (1974), 3-26.

20. As pointed out by M. H. Pope in his paper, "Anat
    and Kali, some Parallels?," presented at the
    Annual Meeting of the American Oriental Society,
    April 22-24, 1975.

21. H. L. Ginsberg, tr.

22. G. R. Driver, Canaanite Myths and Legends From
    Ugarit (Edinburgh 1956), p. 9.

23. This connection was elucidated by M. H. Pope in his paper, "The Cult of the Dead at Ugarit," at The Ugarit Symposium sponsored by the Middle West Branch of the American Oriental Society, Feb. 25-27, 1979.

24. So Koehler-Baumgartner, Lexicon in Veteris Testamenti Libros (Leiden 1953), p. 903, contra Brown-Driver-Briggs, A Hebrew and English Lexicon of the Old Testament, (Oxford 1906), in loco. However, RPH may be merely a dialectical variant of RP', carrying a specialized semantic level of meaning derived from a common biradical root.

25. Sing.: Jer. 8:22; pl.: Gen. 50:2, Job 13:4, II Chron. 16:12; cf. Ecclus. 10:10, 38:1

26. Cf. H. Gese, "Die Religionen Altsyriens," C. M. Schroder, ed., Die Religionen der Menschheit, 10/2 (Stuttgart 1970), pp. 90-92. Compare the Bacchic and Saturnalian rites of Graeco-Roman civilization.

27. Ch. Virolleaud, "Les nouveaux textes mythologiques et liturgiques de Ras Shamra (XXIVe campagne, 1961)," Ugaritica, V (1968), 551ff.

28. Ibid., pp. 546ff. See B. Margalit, "The Ugaritic Tale of the Drunken Gods," Maarav, 2 (1979-80), 65-120.

29. See T. Jacobsen, "Mesopotamia: The Cosmos as a State," "Mesopotamia: The Function of the State," H. Frankfort, ed., The Intellectual Adventure of Ancient Man, pp. 125ff., 185ff.; also M. Beek, "The Land and Climate of Mesopotamia," Atlas of Mesopotamia (London and Edinburgh, 1962), pp. 9ff.

30. See art. "Ur" (T. Jacobsen), IDB, IV, 735ff., reporting on the work of L. Woolley. "The findings left little doubt that the kings and queens of Ur were followed in death by their courtiers and personal attendants, who, dressed in their best, the soldiers with their spears, the musicians with costly harps, the grooms leading the royal ox cart, entered the grave chamber or the sloping ramp that led into the burial pit in order to follow their master into the world beyond." (736)

31. <u>ANET</u> 52ff. (S.N. Kramer, trans.); cf. the Akkadian parallel, "Descent of Ishtar to the Nether World (E. A. Speiser, trans.), "<u>ibid</u>., 106ff.

32. See also the Dumuzi myths, as in <u>ANET</u> 41 ff., T. Jacobsen, <u>The Treasures of Darkness</u>, pp. 47-71.

33. S. N. Kramer, tr.

34. E. A. Speiser, tr.

35. See "The Death of Gilgamesh," S. N. Kramer, trans., <u>ANET</u> 50f.

36. See Chapter II, 1, b, (3), (c) "The creation of Enkidu."

37. = Sum. Huwawa

38. E. A. Speiser, tr.

39. E. A. Speiser, tr.

40. Chapter II, 1, b, (3), (d) "Utnapishtim becomes a god."

41. E. A. Speiser, tr.

42. They are Tammuz (Sum. Dumuzi) and Gizzida.

43. See art. "Crimes and Punishments" (J. Greenberg), <u>IDB</u>, 733ff.

44. See further the commentaries.

45. See the introductions to these respective books by G. H. Box and R. H. Charles in R. H. Charles, ed., <u>The Apocrypha and Pseudepigrapha of the Old Testament</u>, II (Oxford 1913), pp. 542ff., 470ff.

46. See W. D. Davies, <u>Paul and Rabbinic Judaism</u>: <u>Some Rabbinic Elements in Pauline Theology</u> (London 1948), pp. 285ff.

47. See Chapter Two, "The Fall of Mankind"

48. See n. 47.

49. These three passages belong to a special category of submerged myth described in Chapter IV, "Miracle and wonder in the Old Testament,"

50. See art. "Molech, Moloch" (J. Gray), IDB, III, 422f. It is not generally recognized that the identification of this mysterious god (originally Molk or Malk = Heb. melek, "king") must be influenced by the fact that his ritual was located at the Vale of Hinnom (= Ge-henna, later a name for the underworld) according to II Chron. 28:3 and Jer. 32:35. The geographical extension of the latter is the Valley of Rephaim, a name cognate with RPU, RPIM; cf. arts "Rephaim" (R. F. Schnell), "Rephaim, Valley of" (G. A. Barrois), IDB, IV, 35f.

51. 5:41f., 5:56-6:10, 7:75-115

52. The writer knows Homer, the tragedians, perhaps also Plato, the Stoics, the Pythagoras. Plato's doctrine of creation from pre-existent matter appears in 11:17, the Stoic doctrine of the cardinal virtues in 8:7, the logos idea in 7:24f. Other Greek ideas are that wisdom emanates from God, that it initiates its devotees into its secrets, that God loves humanity, that God is omniscient and omnipresent. Cf. J. M. Reese, Hellenistic Influences on the Book of Wisdom and its Consequences, AnBib 41, Rome 1970.

53. "As You Like It," Act II, Scene 7.

54. 2:2-8, 12:12f.

55. 14:10-13

56. Along with numerous literary references in ancient Near-Eastern literature, one should study pictorial representations such as those in ANEP, 634, 638 (p0. 208ff.).

57. Old Testament Theology, I, 454ff., Wisdom in Israel, pp. 226ff.

58. See the commentaries; also Hengel, Judaism and Hellenism, I, 115-30.

59. See R. Braun, Kohelet und frühhellenistische Popularphilosophie, BZAW 130, Berlin: Topelmann, 1973,; cf. Hengel, op. cit., pp. 210-37.

60. See R. N. Whybray, "Conservatisme et radicalisme dans Qohelet," Sagesse et Religion, Colloque de Strasbourg (Octobre 1976), Strasbourg: Presses Universitaire de France, 1976, pp. 65ff.

61. See R. N. Whybray, "Qoheleth the Immoralist? (Qoh 6:16-17)," Gammie, ed., Israelite Wisdom, pp. 191ff.

62. Cf. J. G. Williams, "What Does it Profit a Man? The Wisdom of Qoheleth," J. Crenshaw, ed., Studies in Ancient Israelite Wisdom (New York: KTAV, 1976), pp. 375ff.

63. Heb. behaqîṣ is vocalized as an infinitival phrase in the causative stem requiring temunatĕkā, "thy form," as direct object of the verb; but the LXX reads the Heb. consonants with the vowels for the causative passive, allowing "thy form" to function as subject. For the linguistic arguments, see the commentaries.

64. The so-called "Song of Hezekiah." That it is a very late addition to the Isaianic text can be seen from the fact that it is missing in the section borrowed for Isaiah from II Kings 18:13-20:19. See the commentaries and S. J. De Vries, Yesterday, Today and Tomorrow, pp. 238f.

65. Ezek. 37:1-14 is a salvation oracle from the early exilic period, employing the striking vision of the restored corpses as an illustrative image (mashal) for Ezekiel's refutation of the people's offensive saying, "Our bones are dried up, and our hope is lost; we are clean cut off" (11).

66. For the passages and their interpretation, see the section on "Resurrection in the Apocrypha and the Pseudepigrapha" in T. H. Gaster, "Resurrection," IDB, 39ff. See also the discussion in "The Origin and Development of the Resurrection Belief," D. S. Russell, The Method and Message of Jewish Apocalyptic (Philadelphia 1964), pp. 366ff.

67. See A. Lacoque, The Book of Daniel (Atlanta: John Knox Press, 1979), pp. 234f.

68. The date of II Maccabees is in the middle of the first century B.C., and it uses source material no earlier than ca. 110. This is approximately 50-60 years later than Daniel (ca. 164) and allows for a significant passage of time to allow for this radically individualistic line of speculation to develop.

69. I Cor. 15:8-10, Gal. 1:12-16; cf. Acts 9

70. Paul's authentic writings date from ca. A.D. 48-50 (Galatians) to after A.D. 60 (the captivity epistles). The earliest Gospel, Mark, was composed ca. A.D. 70. See the commentaries and New Testament Introductions.

71. See W. Schmithals, Die Gnosis in Korinth.

72. See further J. C. Beker, Paul the Apostle: The Triumph of God in Life and Thought (Philadelphia: Fortress, 1980), Chap. 8, "Paul's Apocalyptic Theology: Apocalyptic and the Resurrection of Christ."

73. The Gospel ends, as printed in the RSV, with 16:8. For possible explanations of this seemingly abrupt ending, see the commentaries and books of Introduction. Even with vv. 9-20, which are not attested in the best manuscript witnesses, Mark's resurrection account is remarkably sparser than those of the other Gospels.

74. Cf. R. H. Fuller, The Formation of the Resurrection Narratives, Philadelphia: Fortress, 1980.

75. Chapter Four, "Miracle and Wonder in the Old Testament"

76. See L. J. McGinley, Form-Criticism of the Synoptic Healing Stories (Woodstock, Mass., 1944), pp. 72-95.

77. See art. "Miracle" (S. V. McCasland), IDB, III, 392ff.; R. H. Fuller, Interpreting the Miracles, Philadelphia 1963.

78. Cf. G. Strecker, Der Weg der Gerechtigkeit --
    Untersuchung zur Theologie des Mattaus, FRLANT
    82, Gottingen 1962; W. Trilling, Das Wahre
    Israel; Studien zur Theologie des Matthäus-
    Evangeliums, STUNT 10; Munich 1964; K. Stendahl,
    The School of St. Matthew and its Use of the
    Old Testament Philadelphia 1968.

79. The latter might imply a hellenizing separation
    of soul from body; as it is, it is the "life"
    or vital self that survives death, as in
    classical Jewish apocalyptic.

80. On the ideology and theological programme of
    the Johannine letters, see R. Bultmann, Theology
    of the New Testament, II, 3ff.; also art.
    "John, Letters of" (D. M. Smith), IDBS, pp. 486f.

81. Explicating the Deuteronomic principle (cf.
    Deut. 30:10ff.) that righteousness produces
    life, wickedness produces evil, numerous aphorisms
    in Proverbs and other Jewish wisdom books (in-
    cluding the Psalms) articulate the good or evil
    consequences of moral behavior. Nowhere is the
    dogma of evil from evil more explicitly expressed
    than in the tirades of Job's friends (cf. Job
    15:17-35; 18:5-21).

82. Cf. Paul Tillich's description of the "demonic"
    throughout vol. III of his Systematic Theology;
    see also Reinhold Niebuhr, The Nature and Destiny
    of Man (New York 1947), pp. 178-300; E. Brunner,
    Man in Revolt (Philadelphia 1947), pp. 114-67;
    M. de Unamuno, The Tragic Sense of Life in Men
    and in Peoples, trans. J. E. C. Flitch, London
    1931.

83. F. J. Stephens, tr.

84. A. Goetze, tr.

85. R. H. Pfeiffer, tr.

86. The king

87. R. H. Pfeiffer, tr.

88. See the classic study by S. Mowinckel, The Psalms
    in Israel's Worship (Nashville-Oxford, 1962),
    I, 193ff., II, 1ff.

89. In spite of undue influence from the sociological theories of Max Weber, there is substantial truth in P. D. Hanson's identification of the apocalypticists with the deprived (The Dawn of Apocalyptic, Philadelphia: Fortress, 1975); but see my stricture in Gammie, ed., Israelite Wisdom, p. 275, n. 40.

90. See M. Hengel, Judaism and Hellenism, I, 303ff.

91. See C. Guignebert, The Jewish World in the Time of Jesus, trans. S. H. Hooke (London 1939), pp. 211f.; R. H. Pfeiffer, History of New Testament Times (New York 1949), pp. 166-96.

92. pp. 44-46

93. So most modern commentaries, cf. S. L. Terrien in TB. In all probability the folktale circulated in oral tradition, but has been adapted by the poet of Job as the narrative basis for his composition.

94. The Heb. noun śatān is used as a generic word for a human adversary, whether against men (Num. 22:22, 32, I Sam. 29:4, II Sam. 19:23 [E 22]) or against God (I Kings 11:14, 23, Ps. 109:6); it produces a denominative verb, inflected also as a participle, meaning "to be or act as an adversary" (Zech. 3:1, Ps. 38:21, 71:13, 104:4, 20, 29). In Zech. 3:1f. haśśatān opposing Joshua acts as a public prosecutor. So also in Job 1-2, where he functions as a veritable "devil's advocate" to ferret out incriminating evidence against Job. All the same, he is performing a useful task in terms of assuring the integrity of Yahweh's universe. In both passages he is no more than a mythical or even metaphorical figure. In I Chron. 21:1 on the other hand (cf. the parallel in II Sam. 24:1) the determinative is dropped, producing a probable proper name, and accordingly a realistically intended demonic personage, the so-called Satan who appears regularly in the New Testament.

95. At this point Yahweh passes no final judgment; this comes only at 2:10.

96. See art. "Suffering and Evil" (O. A. Piper), IDB, IV, 450ff.

97. See Chapter III, "The prophets of Judgment."

98. Cf. also Zech. 1:2-6, 7:9-14.

99. See Chapter II, "The Old Testament and Jewish concept of sin."

100. Isa. 4:2ff., 7:3, 10:20-22, 11:10-16, etc.; see art. "Remnant" (E. Jenni), IDB, IV, 32f.

101. See Chapter IV, "Prayer and the divine responsiveness."

102. See Chapter IV, "The apocalyptic view of time."

103. Cf. A. Heschel, "The Theology of Pathos," The Prophets (New York 1962), pp. 221-31.

104. Cf. G. von Rad, Old Testament Theology, II, 238-77.

105. See the commentaries, many of which opt for the exile period as the time of composition (cf. Lamentations for a similar emphasis on present suffering). But it is this psalm's emphasis on the experience of continuing wrath-filled time, approaching that of Daniel 9, that marks it as a probable product of the late postexilic period. Specific affinities with Job and Qoheleth underscore this assessment.

106. Modern scholarship is in general agreement about the fictitious character of the psalms-superscriptions. On affinities with the tradent-circle responsible for Chronicles, see H. J. Kraus, Psalmen, II (erd ed., Neukirchen-Vluyn, 1966), p. xxx. The intent of this particular superscription is to give this psalm a status analogous to Torah.

Conclusion

What has been laid out in this book offers a firm basis for coming to grips with the perennial question of what is normative in the Bible. We are now in a position to establish from witing the Bible itself a firm principle of hermeneutics. In this we are endeavoring to confirm with greater clarity the insight of the Reformers that the Bible must be its own interpreter: _Scriptura interpretes Scripturae_. The strength of our claim is that it is able to take seriously the content of the entire Canon. It is not, however, as though each idea and every individual ideal within the scriptural Canon are of equal normativity. This is the conceit that encourages each person to choose his own favorite text: "Elke ketter heeft zijn letter" (Every heretic has his prooftext") -- as a Dutch proverb expresses it. Eliminated are such cul-de-sac"s as Ebeling's "canon within the Canon" -- the doctrine of justification by faith.[1] So also Luther"s "wass Christum treibet," and even von Rad"s _Heilsgeschichte_.

What then is normative in the Bible? As we have tried to show: that which accounts for biblical continuity amidst all its discontinuity; and at the same time, that which accounts for those truly distinctive elements of biblical faith that emerge from the midst of the commonality shared with its ancient cultural environment. Biblical faith has many facets, but its heart and soul are monotheistic personalism. This is the scarlet thread that runs through the entire biblical heritage while marking it off from ancient and modern rivals.

Another way to put this is to say that what is normative in Scripture is (1) what made and makes biblical religion distinctive; (2) what gave it, and may give it, the vigor to survive every trial and vicissitude; and (3) what makes it relevant for all ages of history and for all conditions of human existence. Ultimately, these three tests are the same, for only those elements that were distinctive contributed to the survival of biblical faith, and only those same elements retain relevance for contemporary human life (see the Introduction).

1. Elements shared by biblical religion with other ancient religions

     What has been stated is not to be taken as a dene-
gration of non-distinctive elements in biblical relition,
or of non-authentic modifications within the biblical
tradition. Each of these has expressed an essential
concern in the ongoing struggle of human culture to cope
with the problems of human existence. In the face of
contemporary problems, some or even many of them might
turn out to retain some usefulness, even though within
their ancient setting they generally represented a
blurred and one-sided apprehension of the truth. We
moderns need to realize, for instance, that the ancient
myths were after all holy words, so that, if we can
only put ourselves into a humble and receptive mood, we
too may hear some profound and perhaps worthy truth
coming to expression within them. All the same, it
is important for us to know where we must dig our trench-
es in defending the citadel of biblical faith. When
modern understanding comes to discard certain modes
of thought that can no longer aid toward authentic human
self-understanding, it will be essential that we learn
to distinguish between what the Bible stands for and
what it does not stand for, between what it has borrowed
from the culture of its time and what it has added in
terms of distinctive creative growth to the common
cultural heritage. Contemporary western civilization
is in a very real sense biblical civilization -- but
how much of this is ephemeral, incidental, and non-
distinctive, and how much is essential?

     Let us review briefly the main elements shared by
ancient biblical religion with the religious culture
of its time, identifying the various points at which
it has made a significant modification.

     a. An awareness of the Holy

     It is not just in the Bible that one may encounter
the Holy, but in each of its rival contemporary faiths.
It is found in the Egyptian religion, in the Canaanite

religion, in the Mesopotamian religion; also among the Hittites, the Greeks, and so forth. All the faiths and religions of the world are based on an awareness of the Holy. In man's confrontation with the supernatural, there are the two separate elements of revulsion -- a fleeing away and dread-filled terror -- and of attraction or fascination. It is the tension between these two, the revulsion and the attraction together, that determines the dynamic of vital religion. Yahwism definitely had that quality. It was not just an abstract, intellectual, theoretical system of dogma, but testimony to a deep, vital experience of the presence of God. What makes a difference within the biblical heritage is the element of covenantal integrity, banishing the irrational from numinous dread. The God who reveals himself to his people does indeed confront them with his awesome majesty and power, sometimes in wrath rather than with reassuring words of salvation. Yet this God is a God who reveals himself as Father, as one who cares, as one who has committed himself irrevocably to his people -- ultimately as one who suffers with his people to the point of dying. Thus even while Israel experienced wrath, they continued to receive the assurance that God was there, suffering in their suffering, for their ultimate good. It is at this point that we see a clear demarcation between biblical religion and nonbiblical religion. Most remarkably in Mesopotamian religion, there was a very high level of anxiety throughout ancient Near-Eastern culture. It never succeeded in attaining to a concept of one God who is in control of everything, an authentically personal Deity infinitely committed to the wellbeing of his people, acting without any ulterior motivation. The God of the Bible is essentially different from the other gods in that he does not seek anything from his people except their responding loyalty and spiritual devotion. He is not there to be flattered; he is not there in order that they might carry on an elaborate cultic institution in his honor. Even though the people of the Bible do adopt cultic and institutional forms as vehicles for their piety, these are, at least in theory, subordinated to the understanding that Yahweh had called and chosen them, graciously accepting their worship as an expression of gratitude and devotion. The experience of his numinous presence, though it might stun and shock and astound, nonetheless is accompanied by the revelation of his beneficent intent.[2]

b. Anthropomorphic supernaturalism

Anthropomorphic analogues applied to Yahweh are
those exclusively that are compatible with the image
of transcendental personalism. These are, specifically,
the image of lordship -- implying a proprietorship of
accepting and belonging -- and of parenthood. The
fatherhood of God is an especially potent image. Yahweh
is a Father who is involved in the very life of his
people, not in a generative way, but as an infinitely
parenting Person. He nurtures, disciplines, and above
all loves. Although these are themselves anthropomorphic or anthropopathic images -- symbols borrowed from
an observation of human life -- they avoid the attribution to Deity of every human passion and craving, as
in the case of the polytheistic religions. Biblical
anthropomorphism selects only those qualities that
accentuate the worth and distinctiveness of personhood,
that imply integrity and genuine spiritual concern.
These are the very elements that also lend dignity to
human personhood -- which explains consequently why
biblical piety remains so deeply concerned with spiritual
and intersocial development within human relationships.

c. A sin-guilt-punishment mechanism

Many interpretations of the Bible go astray in
attributing to it the doctrine of a sin-guilt-punishment mechanism, as though this were distinctive of the
Bible in comparison with other religions. Not so!
All the religions of the ancient Near East believed in
this mechanism. The difference in the biblical view
is that it breaks an automatic or dynamistic connection
between them. The divine superintendency over cosmic
morality is guarded in such a way as to preserve God's
sovereign freedom, and at the same time man's freedom,
to turn away from entrapment in this mechanism. It
is this that directly makes possible an authentic
responsibleness in human persons before God, even while
they are in their sin and transgression. In other words,
for the Bible neither God nor man is locked into a fatalistic pattern. Surely, there is a direct connection
between sin, punishment, and suffering; but this does
not indelibly label God as Judge or man as criminal.
Even though biblical man is never excused of responsi-

bility to make good use of the opportunity. Even while the sinner is experiencing the consequences of his sin, the opportunity of repentance and restoration is continually being held out to him. This authentically biblical belief is exactly what guilty people need to know and hear. Pastors must be cautious not to tell their parishioners that their suffering is unconnected with some fault or transgression of their own, for this may well be the case. It does no good to obscure the personal element of responsibility as people suffer the effects of their own or some other person's folly. It is mentally healthful to deal honestly with these realities. Nevertheless, the biblical message is that, while we are in our sin, God's grace is ever being held out to us -- not just once but continually. Every day is a new day of salvation if we are willing to receive it and use it as such. Although God does not accept our sin, he does accept sinners. This is something that the Bible alone has learned to say clearly, adding the dramatic emphasis of God's own special gift of himself in his Son, showing that he even takes human sin upon himself. The Bible knows precisely what forgiving involves; when it talks about God forgiving sinners, we may be sure that these are no hollow words.

d.   Cultic institutionalism

Another element that biblical religion shares with other religions is cultic institutionalism, involving a professional priesthood or ministry, a pattern of ritual and administration, and structures and properties set aside for its interests. True, the people of the Bible had these as well as the other peoples of their environment. They even had bloody sacrifices. It is interesting to read von Rad's explanation of the historical process by which the ancient Israelites, penetrating into the land of Canaan, occupied various shrine-sites in the land, took them over and rebaptized them, turning them into Yahweh shrines. They adopted much of the ritual and perhaps also the actual priestly personnel from these ancient shrines.[3] Thus the development of an elaborate cultic apparatus among the ancient Israelites represented an element of significant compromise with a completely different order of religions practice. This became especially prominent with the rise of David's monarchy and the building of Solomon's temple. However, ancient Yahwism remained

virile enough to make this adaptation without committing apostacy from its essential principles. True,
there was a struggle, but Judahite Yahwism gradually
eliminated inimical elements. The exile turned the
tide permanently. It became possible to enrich biblical worship by sanitizing pagan myth and ritual.
Traditional cultic patterns and structures became
entirely ancillary to the celebration of covenant
personalism. The people of the Bible did not reject
formal worship, nor did they repudiate a professional
priesthood; quite on the contrary, these gradually
became rigidly fixed in theory and practice, so that
only traumatic historical forces could uproot the old,
and allow entrance for the new. Eventually biblical
faith did find the means to survive without the traditional cult and priesthood. We who are heirs of the
biblical tradition see in this an important lesson
concerning the proper place for churchly structures,
policies, and personnel. To be authentically biblical,
we need to keep these elements in a place of subordination and instrumentality, never allowing them to become an end in themselves. We need to learn especially
from the prebiblical and nonbiblical religions how
remorselessly an institutionalized religious apparatus
can quench out the spark of an authentically personalistic faith.

e. A theological basis for morality

Theological ideal undergirding moral sanctions are
not something that we find only in the Bible. As we
study the documents of faith outside Israel, we find
that there, too, moral behavior has a theory to support
it. The Bible on its part places ethics on the firm
ground of its distinctive theology, vastly different
from that of Israel's ancient neighbors. The latter
were driven to morality out of fear. The people of the
Bible were drawn to morality out of love. This is the
vast difference between them. It is especially important for contemporary Christians to understand that
biblical ethics cannot therefore be something arbitrary
or autonomous; it must be based rather upon biblical
theology, with its unique understanding both of God and
man. The essential element in biblical theology is its
earnest attempt to grapple with the meaning of divine
and human personhood, explicated especially in the

traditions of covenant and election. Theologically
rooted and socially orientated, biblical morality
becomes at last the expression of honor to God and of
respect for human kind. The Bible is ever committed
to the uplifting of mankind created in God's image,
committed to the redemption of mankind in the solidarity
of covenantal oneness. Although the successors of the
ancient Israelites themselves became particularistic
and separatistic, the Bible cherishes a vision of
broad universalism, so that in classical Old Testament
ideology, the concerns that the Israelites expressed
for their fellow Israelites were extended to human
beings outside their fellowship.[4] There are explicit
provisions in biblical law on behalf of the sojourner
and the foreigner.[5] When later generations forgot the
true meaning of Abram's call, God raised up still other
Jews, such as Jesus and Paul, to reaffirm that this is
indeed the true intent of biblical ethics.

f. Divine causation in historical event

Those who have read this book carefully are aware
that it is definitely wrong to characterize extrabiblical religion as unconcerned about divine action in
historical event. To the extent that they took history
seriously at all, the contemporaries of the ancient
Hebrews believed that their gods were in fact involved
in history. Nothing happened without the will of the
gods; they were present and active in everything that
occurred. What is truly distinctive about biblical
faith is this: that divine action in history involves
responsible human causation, leading purposefully to
the realization of God's higher glory and man's greater
good. This is above all the surprising achievement of
Old Testament historiography, appearing many centuries
prior to the writing of the Greek classics. It is
important theologically that the biblical writings have
taken seriously and handled realistically the element
of human participation in historical event. These
writings do not see the divine will as something imposed
upon man from the supernatural world, as in the conceptions of the extrabiblical religions. True, God was
at work, but man was also at work as the responsible
actor in history's drama. God effectuates his will
among mankind through interaction, response, and dialogue. God and man together interact for (and in some

493

situations against) God's glory and man's good -- eschatological goals that remain as a constant challenge to
greater striving. They can never be regarded as secure
accomplishments within the structures of finite existence, but define a purpose to human striving, encouraging responsible human interaction with God. When
these eschatological goals are grasped and held, they
become like a bird squeezed to death in the hand of a
careless child. Preserved for their own sake, they
become idols and drive God away.

2. Nondistinctive and distinctive elements in biblical religion

a. Nondistinctive elements

If we can keep firmly in mind what has been said, we may be able now to confront our contemporary options more effectively. Let us make a summation of religious elements, presented in the Bible, which contemporary Christian piety seems to regard more highly than it should. This varies, of course, from one group and denomination to another. As we list these, we shall see that each has been borrowed from the culture of the biblical world -- and hence should be evaluated as part of the common heritage -- or has arisen within the biblical tradition as something incidental, temporary, or even erratic.

First of all we mention supernaturalism. True, the Bible is a supernaturalistic book. Today people tend to take sides for or against supernaturalism. and everything stands or falls on this issue. Those who have been strongly influenced by modern science are inclined to dispense with the supernatural, along with miracle, and are tempted to reject the Bible because it contains so much of these elements. Others are anxiously and nervously committed to guarding it at all costs. What we may now say, having analyzed biblical supernaturalism on its own terms, is that this is neither unique to the Bible nor distinctive of biblical religion. The element of supernaturalism has been purified and refined within the biblical tradition so as to present the most worthy possible image of God's resplendent holiness. Neither the Old Testament nor the New Testament proliferates unrestrainedly the element of the supernatural or the miraculous. This is what is truly marvelous about the Bible! These elements are restricted to specific genres, those of theophany and sacred legend, which develop their own special language of spirituality so as to convey a worthy and effective image of God's most awesome presence in the midst of men. We would say that the Bible reverently presents a modest element of wonder in order to make it serve the pure vision of God's unique personhood, daring to employ it as an ideological and linguistic vehicle specially designed to express its most unique apprehension of the mysterium tremendum. Then let the gawkers stand aside! The biblical God is no grand performer in a cosmic circus. "An evil and adulterous generation seeks for a sign; but no sign shall be given to it except the sign of the prophet Jonah." (Matt. 12:39) This is a word that Jesus spoke, one who himself performed many mighty signs; he wanted men to see that God's presence in human personhood -- expecially his own most perfect human personhood -- is the grandest miracle of all.

Surely another nondistinctive element of biblical piety -- but one given great prominence in contemporary religiosity -- is a dependence on cultic mechanisms. By this we mean the entire apparatus of formal and official religion. This is not to suggest that Christianity should discard its forms, liturgies, rituals, and ministries. Far from it: There is an important place for the organized church, an institutionalized worship experience, and an ordained leadership. There is really little good to say about religious amateurism. Yet at the same time we emphasize that these do present in themselves a constant hazard and temptation, for unless used rightly they tend to stifle initiative, freedom, and creative spontaneity in the expression of religious feeling. To the extent that they can be kept instrumental to the expression of a vital and authentic biblical faith, they are useful and necessary. But they are neither essential, nor unique, nor distinctive, so far as biblical faith itself is concerned, and must never be allowed to be handled as such.

A final element of nonessentiality in contemporary Christian piety is it residue of apocalyptic ideology. As has been said, apocalyptic arose in a time when everything was out of joint. Historically conditioned, it spoke a language that was useful in its special situation but that has now lost all relevance except for those who know how to interpret -- and retranslate -- its language. When appropriated literalistically, it becomes dangerous. Those who do not understand this are sure to err. Let us ponder the fact that apocalyptic was a mode of religious expression that New Testament Christianity made only very cautious use of; it was quickly discarded after the apostolic era, and has always been regarded with suspicion within the European church. Judaism, on its part, has all but discarded it. Once the era of high eschatological fervor was past, it came to be regarded as presenting far more

496

problems for biblical piety than answers.

   b.   Distinctive elements

All the embellishments, diversions, and bypaths have now been set aside so that we can look directly on those elements which make biblical piety distinctive, which account for its astounding survivability, and which make its message relevant for this age and every age. These are worth defending to the last ditch. They are:

(1)   The Bible's unique view of divine transcendence and immanence;
(2)   Its insight into human dignity, responsibility, and salvability;
(3)   Its lifelong celebration of covenant people hood;
(4)   Its view of man's partnership with God in shaping history;
(5)   Its grasp of a life that transcends evil and conquers death.

With respect ot (1) God, (2) man, (3) society, (4) history, and (5) human existence, the Bible has worked out a distinctive and essentially consistent stance. Elements of discontinuity and of continuity within its variegated elements have proven to be equally significant in defining this stance. At the same time, its distinctive affirmation on each of these questions comes to maximum clarity at precisely those points where it has shared much with the common culture out of which it emerged. The Bible has been engaged in a historical dialogue with its environment and with itself; and the answers which it has held out to posterity, dearly won through agonizing probing and struggle, are those that have not only stood the test of time but proven to be of enduring helpfulness in coming to grips with the world's most pressing and persistent problems. While it cannot be said that the Bible offers final answers -- thus making the theological task henceforward unnecessary -- it does uncover the ultimate questions, and it does respond to them in a distinctive, consistent, and uniquely satisfying way.

497

Those who hope for progress in the future cannot go forward without a deep sympathy and appreciation for the past. In the area of common human culture, we value especially those great breakthroughs that have come in the field of technology: first, the use of tools; later, the arts of agriculture and the techniques of animal husbandry; still later, the invention of writing -- especially the alphabetic script, which democratized learning -- ; since the Middle Ages, a vast display of mechanical, chemical, and electronic marvels. But all these would be useless, or worse than useless, without the great achievements of the spirit, and here the heritage of Hebraic faith must receive its due recognition for its unparalleled success in illuminating the meaning of divine and human personhood. The devils have not yet been banished from our universe; indeed, the devils that technology has created are far more frightening than any that were known to primitive man! We shall treasure, then, the hope that the biblical heritage, promising to bring God and man to an ever more effective partnership, may eventually drive back every demon that exists, until the ideal good that the Creator has intended will become a reality.

> When all things are subjected to him, then the
> Son himself will also be subjected to him who
> put all things under him, that God may be
> everything to every one. (I Cor. 15:28)

NOTES

1. See especially "Word of God and Hermeneutics," _Word and Faith_ (Philadelphia 1963), pp. 305ff.; cf. H. Diem, _Dogmatics_ (trans. H. Knight; Edinburgh and London, 1959), pp. 252ff.

2. A regular element in the biblical theophany narratives is the word of reassurance, "Fear not," followed by a promise (Ex. 20:20, Judg. 6:23, II Kings 6:16, Matt. 28:5, Luke 2:10, etc.).

3. See "The Crisis Due to the Conquest," _Old Testament Theology_, I, 15-35.

4. A monotheistic personalism inevitably comes to an assertion of the universality of God's lordship and fatherhood. If there is only one true God, the elect must themselves expand to contain, at least in potential, the entirety of humankind.

5. Ex. 22:21, 23:9, Lev. 23:22, etc. See art. "Sojourner" (T. M. Mauch), IDB, IV, 397ff.

INDEXES

1. Scripture

505

507

2. Ancient Near-Eastern texts

3. Subjects

516

ABOUT THE AUTHOR

Simon John De Vries is a scholar, educator, and minister.
He was born in Denver, Colorado, in 1921, but received
his higher education in Grand Rapids, Mich. (Calvin
College, A.B., 1943; Calvin Theological Seminary, Th.B.,
1949) and in New York City (Union Theological Seminary,
S.T.M., 1950; Th.D., 1958). He has also done graduate
study in Leiden (Holland) and Tübingen (Germany). Prior
to entering a career of teaching, he served in the U.S.
Marine Corps for three years (1st Lt.) and for eleven
years as pastor in three parishes. His ordination is
in the United Presbyterian Church. He taught as
instructor in Old Testament at Drew Theological School
(1957-58), as Associate Professor of Religion in Hope
College and Instructor in Hebrew at Western Theological
Seminary (1961-62), as Associate Professor of Old Testament at the Methodist Theological School in Ohio (1962-
68), and as Professor of Old Testament at the same
institution since 1968. Professor De Vries has been a
Fulbright scholar in Holland and a Lilly Foundation
fellow in Germany; also a fellow at The Ecumenical
Institute for Theological Studies in Jerusalem (1973)
and a visiting professor at King's College in London,
England (1978). He has published three books:
Bible and Theology in The Netherlands (1968), Yesterday,
Today, and Tomorrow (1975), and Prophet Against Prophet
(1978). His commentary on I Kings will be published as
part of the Word Biblical Commentary. Professor De
Vries has written over 130 scholarly articles on biblical and theological subjects for a variety of journals
and encyclopaedias. He makes his residence, along with
his wife Betty, in the city of Delaware, Ohio.